MW00643738

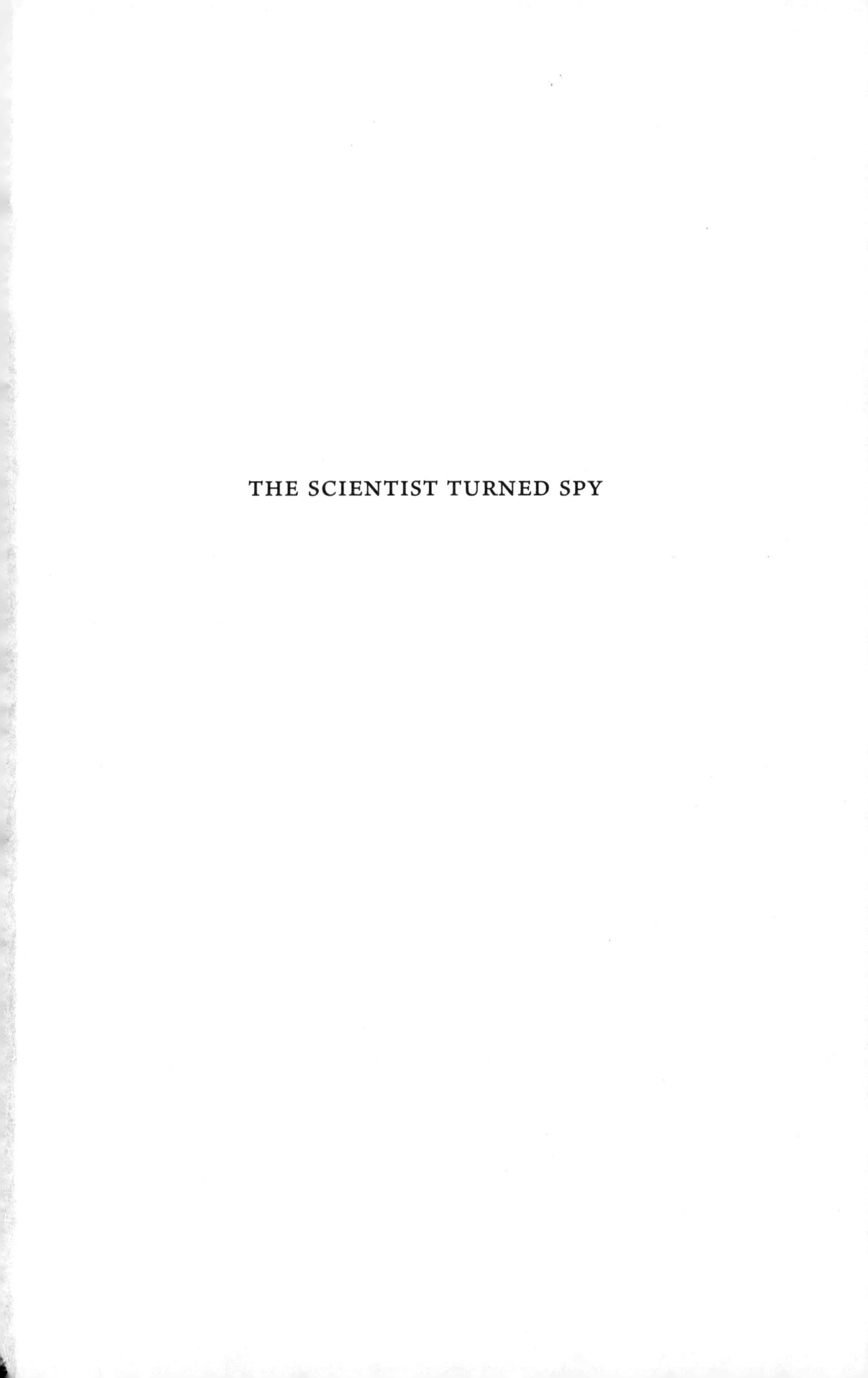

THE SCIENTIST TURNED SPY

JEFFERSONIAN AMERICA

Charlene M. Boyer Lewis, Annette Gordon-Reed, Peter S. Onuf, Andrew J. O'Shaughnessy, and Robert G. Parkinson, Editors

The Scientist Turned Spy

André Michaux, Thomas Jefferson, and the Conspiracy of 1793

Patrick Spero

UNIVERSITY OF VIRGINIA PRESS
Charlottesville and London

The University of Virginia Press is situated on the traditional lands of the Monacan Nation, and the Commonwealth of Virginia was and is home to many other Indigenous people. We pay our respect to all of them, past and present. We also honor the enslaved African and African American people who built the University of Virginia, and we recognize their descendants. We commit to fostering voices from these communities through our publications and to deepening our collective understanding of their histories and contributions.

University of Virginia Press

Printed in the United States of America on acid-free paper

First published 2024

9 8 7 6 5 4 3 2 1

LIBRARY OF CONGRESS CATALOGING-IN-PUBLICATION DATA

Names: Spero, Patrick, author.
Title: The scientist turned spy : André Michaux, Thomas Jefferson, and the Conspiracy of 1793 / Patrick Spero.
Other titles: André Michaux, Thomas Jefferson, and the Conspiracy of 1793
Description: Charlottesville; London : University of Virginia Press, 2024. | Series: Jeffersonian America | Includes bibliographical references and index.
Identifiers: LCCN 2024005180 (print) | LCCN 2024005181 (ebook) | ISBN 9780813952185 (hardcover) | ISBN 9780813952192 (ebook)
Subjects: LCSH: Michaux, André, 1746–1802. | Genêt Affair, 1793. | United States—Foreign relations—1789–1797. | United States—Foreign relations—France. | France—Foreign relations—United States. | Espionage—United States—History—19th century. | Michaux, André, 1746–1802—Travel. | Botanists—France—Biography. | American Philosophical Society.
Classification: LCC E313 .M537 2024 (print) | LCC E313 (ebook) | DDC 973.4/3092 [B]—dc23/eng/20240202
LC record available at https://lccn.loc.gov/2024005180
LC ebook record available at https://lccn.loc.gov/2024005181

Cover art: *Bust,* F. Andrew Michaux, 1880 engraving by Henry Bryan Hall, after Rembrandt Peale (The Miriam and Ira D. Wallach Division of Art, Prints and Photographs: Print Collection, New York Public Library); *portrait,* Thomas Jefferson, stipple engraving by H. B. Hall, after G. Stuart (rawpixel.com); *landscape,* detail of *A View of the Mountain Pass Called the Notch of the White Mountains (Crawford Notch),* Thomas Cole, 1839 (Andrew W. Mellon Fund, National Gallery of Art); *map,* detail of *The United States of North America, with the British territories and those of Spain: according to the treaty of 1784,* William Faden, 1793 (Library of Congress, Geography and Map Division); *flower,* details of Crown Imperial Fritillary, by Pierre-Joseph Redouté and Henry Joseph Redouté, 1827 (rawpixel .com/Cleveland Museum of Art); *sky,* detail of *The Return,* Thomas Cole, 1837 (Corcoran Collection, gift of William Wilson Corcoran, National Gallery of Art)
Cover design: David Fassett

To the American Philosophical Society,
an institution whose mission is as inspiring today as it was then

❖ CONTENTS ❖

Part IV. Legacies Lost and Lasting

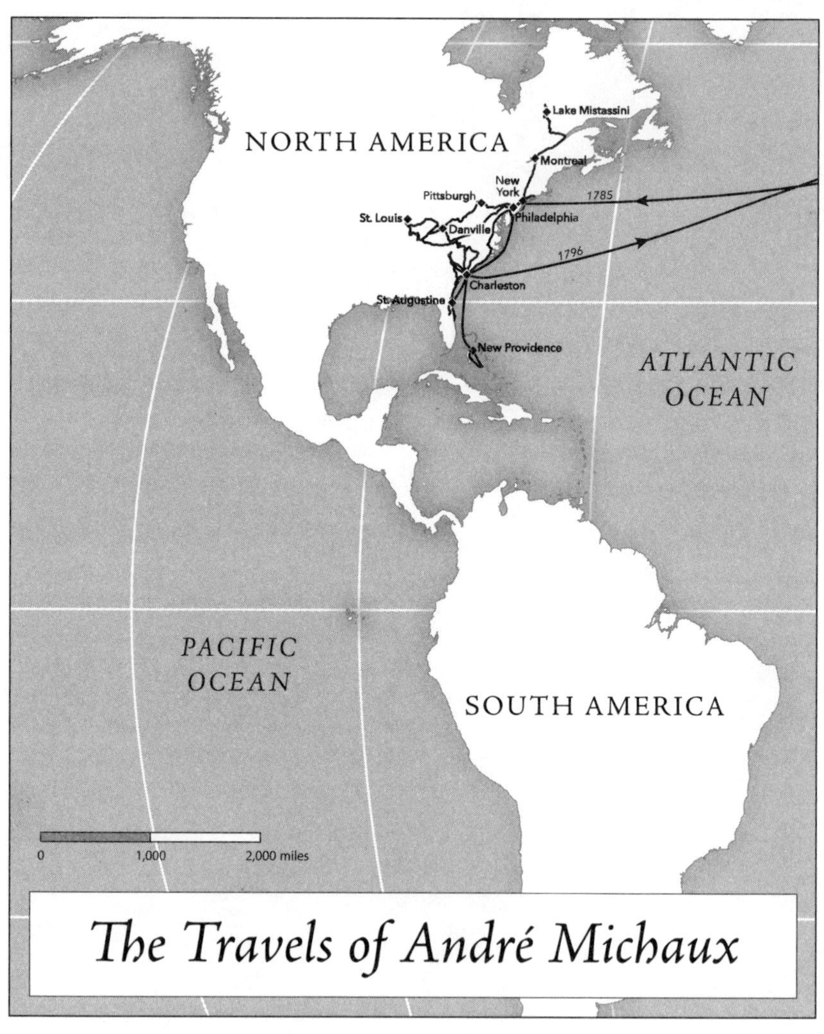

MAP 1. ANDRÉ MICHAUX'S GLOBAL TRAVELS. André Michaux's expeditions took him around the globe. He conducted scientific research throughout Europe, the Middle East, North America, and Africa. (Map by Nat Case, INCase, LLC)

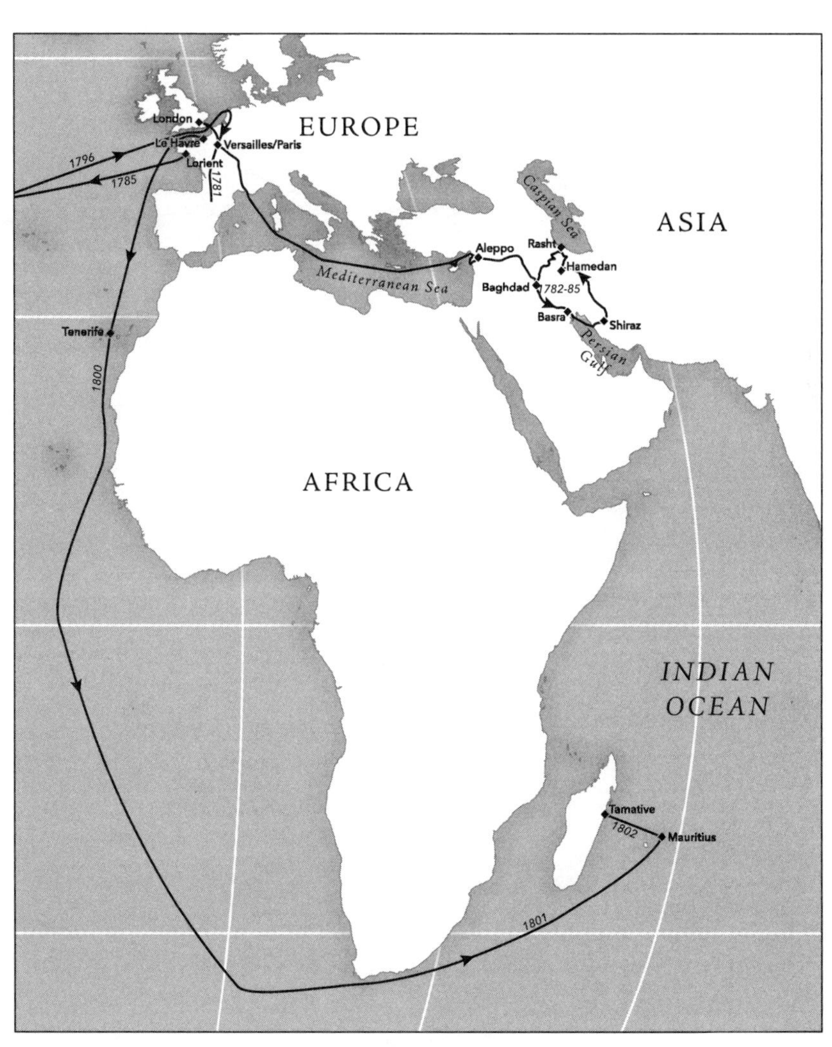
EUROPE
London
Le Havre
Versailles/Paris
Lorient
1796
1785
1781
Caspian Sea
ASIA
Aleppo
Rasht
Hamedan
Mediterranean Sea
Baghdad
782-85
Basra
Shiraz
Persian Gulf
Tenerife
1800
AFRICA
INDIAN OCEAN
Tamative
1802
Mauritius
1801

THE SCIENTIST TURNED SPY

❖ PROLOGUE ❖

Investigating a Legend

This book began as an investigation into a legend. Though I was unaware of it at the time, my quest began soon after I arrived in Philadelphia in 2015 to become the librarian of the American Philosophical Society (APS). Founded by Benjamin Franklin and other civically minded individuals in 1743, the Philosophical Society is the oldest learned society in North America. Its mission, as written by Franklin, is "promoting useful knowledge." Over time, it has amassed an enormous and remarkable collection of original manuscripts and rare books, all housed in Library Hall, only a few steps from Independence Hall, the site where the Declaration of Independence and US Constitution were signed. Today, the Society's collection contains more than fourteen million pages of manuscripts and close to three hundred thousand books. It is home to the papers of Benjamin Franklin, the journals of Lewis and Clark, and one of the largest collections in the world of endangered Native American languages. And the APS continues to collect, especially in the history of science, stewarding the papers of seven recent Nobel laureates, perhaps the largest single collection of any independent research library. As librarian of the Society, my great honor and privilege was to oversee this remarkable collection.

With a history like that, and a collection to complement it, legends are bound to develop, and the APS is rife with them. Everyone at the APS was eager to share their favorite anecdotes with me soon after I started. Some even handed me manila folders filled with pages of tales told by past librarians in the hope that I would continue to pass them on. There's the story of the Society's president dying during a scholarly meeting in 1931 while sitting center stage in a chair once owned by Benjamin Franklin. After removing the body, the Society's leaders decided that the pursuit of knowledge was more important than mourning, so they carried on as planned. In what one of the Society's chroniclers called "the cruelest of ironies," the talk that followed his death was called "Lengthening the Span of Life." Then there's the story of human remains buried in Philosophical Hall, the Society's headquarters. In 1937, Judson Daland left the APS a bequest to support medical research. The terms, though, called for his remains to be interred in the Society's building. The Society agreed to accept his ashes so it could better advance its mission to support science. While everyone at the Society knows of the gift, no one today is quite sure which wall Daland haunts.[1]

One piece of lore particularly captured my attention. It had to do with a single document stored among the millions held at the APS. Called the "Michaux Subscription List," this large eighteenth-century manuscript is so important that it rests permanently encased in a special glass frame designed to protect it from light and climatic changes. Its home is on the Society's "Treasures Cart," which holds items that are deemed of immense value, not just because of their potential financial worth but also because of their scholarly and cultural significance. Other items on this special cart include Thomas Jefferson's handwritten draft of the Declaration of Independence, Benjamin Franklin's annotated copy of the US Constitution, Thomas Paine's *Rights of Man* with Edmund Burke's marginalia in it, Charles Darwin's handwritten mock-up of the title page of *Origin of Species,* original photographs of the moon landing, and more. Most days, the cart sits quietly and securely in the library's vault, but every once in a while, it is wheeled out for distinguished visitors. The items for these "Treasures Tours" are often tailored to match guests' particular interests. The Michaux Subscription List, though, was always on the cart because I knew that everyone would be astonished by it and its story.

Here's the legend of the Subscription List that I first heard, one that I began repeating on every tour. In the early months of 1793, André Michaux, a French botanist studying American flora and fauna, approached Thomas Jefferson, then the secretary of state of the United States and the vice president of the American Philosophical Society, with a proposal of grand

Whereas Andrew Michaux, a native of France, and inhabitant of the United States has undertaken to explore the interior country of North America from the Missisipi along the Missouri, and Westwardly to the Pacific ocean, or in such other direction as shall be advised by the American Philosophical society, & on his return to communicate to the said society the information he shall have acquired of the geography of the said country, it's inhabitants, soil, climate, animals, vegetables, minerals & other circumstances of note: We the Subscribers desirous of obtaining for ourselves relative to the land we live on, and of communicating to the world, information so interesting to curiosity, to science, and to the future prospects of mankind, promise for ourselves, our heirs executors & administrators, that we will pay the said Andrew Michaux, or his assigns, the sums herein affixed to our names respectively, one fourth part thereof on demand, the remaining three fourths whenever, after his return, the said Philosophical society shall declare themselves satisfied that he has performed the sd journey & that he has communicated to them freely all the information which he shall have acquired & they demanded of him: or if the sd Andrew Michaux shall not proceed to the Pacific ocean, and shall reach the sources of the waters running into it, then we will pay him such part only of the remaining three fourths, as the said Philosophical society shall deem duly proportioned to the extent of unknown country explored by him, in the direction prescribed, as compared with that omitted to be so explored. And we consent that the bills of exchange of the sd Andrew Michaux, for monies said to be due to him in France, shall be recieved to the amount of two hundred Louis, & shall be negociated by the sd Philosophical society, and the proceeds thereof retained in their hands, to be delivered to the sd Andrew Michaux, on his return, after having performed the journey to their satisfaction, or, if not to their satisfaction, then to be applied towards reimbursing the subscribers the fourth of their subscription advanced to the said Andrew Michaux. We consent also that the said Andrew Michaux shall take to himself all benefit arising from the publication of the discoveries he shall make in the three departments of Natural history, Animal, Vegetable and mineral, he concerting with the said Philosophical society such measures for securing to himself the said benefit, as shall be consistent with the due publication of the said discoveries. In witness whereof we have hereto subscribed our names and affixed the sums we engage respectively to contribute.

Go Washington one hundred Dollars
John Adams Twenty Dollars
Benjamin Hawkins Twenty Dollars.
Ra. Izard — Twenty Dollars
Saml Johnston Twenty Dollars
Robt Morris Eighty Dollars
Jno. Henry — ten dollars
G Cabot — Ten Dollars
John Rutherfurd Twenty dollars

H Knox fifty dollars
Th: Jefferson fifty dollars
Alexander Hamilton Fifty Dollars
Rufus King — Twenty Dollars
John Langdon Twenty Dollars
John Edwards Sixteen Dollars
John Brown Twenty Dollars
Tho Mifflin Twenty Dollars

Jon.a Trumbull Twenty Dollrs
James Madison Jr. Twenty dollars
J Parker — Twenty Dollars
Alex White Twenty Dollars
John Page twenty Dollars
John Beckley 10 Drs
Wm Smith — Twenty Dolrs
Jere Wadsworth Thirty Dollars
Richard Bland Lee ten dollars
Thos FitzSimons ten dollars
Saml Griffin Ten dollars
Wm B. Giles Ten Dollars
J W Kittera Ten Dollars.

FIGURE 1. The Michaux Subscription List raised money to support André Michaux's transcontinental expedition. It is in Thomas Jefferson's hand and contains the first four US presidents' signatures. (Courtesy of the American Philosophical Society)

proportions, just the type of idea Jefferson liked to hear. Michaux wanted to undertake a scientific expedition across the North American continent, leaving from Philadelphia that spring and ending at the Pacific Ocean, but he needed a sponsor. Jefferson had long fantasized about such a trip, and he jumped at the chance to support Michaux. Within weeks, he mobilized the APS to launch an ambitious fundraising campaign to underwrite Michaux's plans.

To get the initiative started, Jefferson penned a long and formal outline of Michaux's proposal on a large document, what is now known as the Michaux Subscription List. He sent the Subscription List racing through his scientific and political networks, using it as a fundraising tool that electrified his friends in government, convincing them to open their wallets to support the project, and motivated the members of the APS to use their intellectual heft to back the mission. Jefferson's success is what makes the document so extraordinary. The signatures of all the donors rest at the bottom of the Subscription List. It's a veritable "who's who" of the founding era, including George Washington, Thomas Jefferson, John Adams, and James Madison, plus notable others like Alexander Hamilton, Henry Knox, and Robert Morris.[2] The story ends in vagueness, however, at least as it was relayed to me. Michaux's expedition never got off the ground because he became distracted by French revolutionary politics. I was told, essentially, what the APS relates on its website for the document: "Michaux was swept up in the political aspirations of Citizen Genet, who hoped to wage a campaign against the Spanish in Louisiana, and the expedition died quickly."[3]

There are two other breathtaking facts about the Subscription List. First, it may be the only document that holds the signatures of the first four presidents. Neither the Declaration of Independence nor the Constitution has all four. The second story relates the document's "discovery" at the APS. While the creation of this list and its text was known to scholars, the location of the original in Jefferson's hand and with these original signatures remained a mystery until 1979. In the summer of that year, an intern who was tasked with the drudgery of cleaning out an old storage vault in Philosophical Hall, the Society's oldest building, found a large box wrapped in brown paper. The words "Treasurer's Reports" were scrawled on top. Inside this nondescript package he found numerous documents. Most of them were, as the label indicated, rather bland accounts from long ago, but there was an older box bound by a red string that seemed different. Intrigued by what secrets it might hold—but fully aware that opening the box was outside his job description—the young man rushed across the street to Library Hall and the librarian's office. Whitfield Bell, the librarian at the time, untied the ribbon, opened the box, and found an old scroll. He unfurled the document and immediately realized that he had a national treasure in his hands. At least that's the story I was told. Having imbibed this account in 2015, I relayed it to countless others with great enthusiasm for five years. It was one of my favorite stories, especially the surprise ending about its rediscovery.[4]

Then, in 2020, our library, like the rest of the world, shut down because of the COVID-19 pandemic. Without a stream of visitors to greet and thus no longer able to recite these stories, I had the opportunity to do some of my own research into the legend of the Michaux Subscription List. I wanted to see if there was more to this story—or less.

I approached the project with these questions: Who was André Michaux, and what was he doing in America? What was the full story behind this Subscription List, and what does it tell us about the past? And what really happened to the expedition? As I pursued answers to each question, I came across fascinating characters and unearthed riveting stories with layers of complexity. Perhaps best of all, and to my great relief, I determined that what I was told—and subsequently told others—was true.

But I also discovered that there was a lot more to the story than just the usual tale. The brief ending about the failure of the expedition that often accompanied the telling of the story proved far more complicated and, I soon realized, important to the founding of the United States. As I dug deeper into Michaux's tale—in fact, as I was sucked into his story—I discovered the significant but little details that easily become lost over time. Michaux's life revealed a world filled with international intrigue, espionage, revolutionary ideas, partisan rivalries, geopolitical tensions, *and* science, all of which regularly mixed together to create a highly combustible environment in which the future was filled with uncertainty. When I put all these pieces together to create the whole picture, I was left awestruck by a story that changed what I knew about the nation's most formative period.

The pages that follow trace my exploration into those three core questions that initiated my research. I have thus organized the book into three sections, each almost a minibook unto itself that reveals the answers I found, plus a fourth section on the legacies of these disparate yet connected stories. While the narrative moves chronologically, each section focuses on one of those initial questions. The first provides a biography of André Michaux up until he encountered the APS in 1792. A man of Enlightenment science, Michaux was one of the greatest scientific explorers of his generation, a fact largely overlooked today. His exploits took him throughout the Middle East, Europe, most of eastern North America, and parts of Africa. In fact, he likely explored more ground in North America than any of his scientific peers.

The second section shifts to the story of the Subscription List and the 1793 plans for a transcontinental expedition. This part of the book focuses less on Michaux and more on the American Philosophical Society, the most important scientific organization in the new nation, and the scientific thought of Thomas Jefferson, then the secretary of state of the United States, as well as vice president of the APS and Michaux's primary backer. The APS's and Jefferson's involvement in the Michaux expedition make plain the somewhat obscure but powerful ways in which science, politics, and national interests fused during the country's founding to advance the nation's expansionary ambitions. By analyzing the details behind the Michaux Subscription List and the APS's support of it, I explore a cross-section of the young country's scientific community, examine their priorities (some of which might appear quirky to us today but were very serious endeavors then, including hunting for wooly mammoths and a rumored undiscovered species of llama in the American interior), and decode their motives.

The third section tells the oft-elided story of what happened to Michaux after the Subscription List was signed. My own archival expedition took a fantastical turn as I explored this part of Michaux's life. Events beyond his control soon transformed his trip from a purely scientific mission into a clandestine military operation in service of the French revolutionary government. While Michaux publicly maintained that the pursuit of botany was his reason for visiting Kentucky, his real objective, as dictated to him by the French government, was to organize a group of angry American frontiersmen to invade Spanish Louisiana, seize New Orleans, and erect a new, independent nation aligned with the French Republic. French strategists in Paris also hoped this military maneuver would provoke a conflict between the United States and Spain that would force the otherwise neutral United States into a military alliance with France.

It was a plan designed to take advantage of the political instability and combustibility that reigned on the North American continent, especially in its highly contested interior regions. Michaux's foray brought together all of the diverse and often competing forces in the early republican West: Native American groups asserting their sovereignty and forging diplomatic alliances with each other and with European nations to strengthen their autonomy; Spanish and French settlers trying to establish new toeholds in the American West after decades of losing ground; state, local, and national governments competing for power; individual American citizens trying to stake their own claims, not always in cooperation with their governments' wishes; and the collision of grand imperial strategies for dominance on the continent, all of which were combining in this moment to determine who might control the territory's future.

Much to my surprise, the French plan to capture Louisiana from Spain, and Michaux's role in it, was far more involved than most historians have acknowledged. It has also left several lasting, if underappreciated legacies, which form the subject of the book's final section. As this part shows, the Kentucky conspiracy of 1793–94 was no harebrained idea that wilted under the weight of its absurdity. Michaux's escapade to the West involved international jockeying, spying, diplomacy, divisive partisan politics, and, ultimately, a conspiracy that aimed at establishing an independent republic west of the Mississippi that, if successful, threatened to upend the American republic and reorder global geopolitics. More than that, it received widespread support from Americans, including, shockingly to me, surreptitious aid from several high-ranking US officials, including congressmen, senators, military officials, and even the country's own secretary of state, Thomas Jefferson. In fact, one historian has claimed that Jefferson's behavior during the episode was "near-treasonous." Such an audacious plot posed a grave threat to George Washington's first administration, one that forced him and others to confront the meaning of, and limits to, citizenship in a democracy. Washington knew that if he failed to navigate this crisis and avert a conflict, then the invasion of New Orleans by American citizens could easily shatter the foundations of the still fragile American republic.[5]

It is, to be sure, a most convoluted story, one far different from anything I had anticipated when I began my excursion into the archives, and one almost completely overlooked today. It is a hidden historical adventure embedded in a single document more than two hundred years old.

❖ **PART I** ❖

André Michaux

André Michau[x], born in Versailles to a farming family, and who[,] led by his love for the Sciences, has not ceased to take the most painful and most useful journeys in different climates, notably to Persia where he has just made a voyage of almost six years, the results of which attest to all that can be hoped for in new studies that he is ready to attempt anywhere where Nature's production gives him material.

—KING LOUIS XVI'S APPOINTMENT OF MICHAUX AS BOTANIST TO THE KING, JULY 1, 1785

❖ 1 ❖

The Education of André Michaux

1746–1778, France

André Michaux was born into a dilemma that followed him everywhere he went in life. He enjoyed a life of relative luxury, but it was not an easy one. Surrounded by extravagant wealth, he had little himself. Though he lived in a world in which individuals were freeing themselves of ancient and archaic dependencies, he always relied on the goodwill of others for his position. He could never shake the frustrations that accompanied his own lack of financial independence and subsequent life of dependence. Indeed, they would continue to shape, and upset, his work in one way or another as he traversed the globe in the service of science—and often, much to his consternation, in service to the whims of a patron funding his pursuits.

That was the situation that greeted Michaux as soon as he entered the world on March 8, 1746, on his family's farm outside Paris near Versailles. It was, on the face of it, a modest existence, but his father, also named André, was not just any farmer, and the plot of land upon which their house sat was no common farm. The Michaux family lived on the fertile plateau of Satory, a royal domain that abutted the grounds of the king's opulent palace at Versailles. The several hundred acres that Michaux Sr. plowed thus belonged to the king, and its produce served the needs of the royal table as well as the growing Michaux clan. The farm also provided benefits that few commoners in France could enjoy: a reliable income and long-term stability. It was a plum post, and Michaux's father dreamed of his son one day plowing the same ground, enjoying the same fruits of his labor, and sharing them with the same patron, the French monarch.[1]

Michaux Sr. did everything he could to prepare his son for this inheritance. When Michaux turned ten, his father sent him to a boarding school for the formal education that would befit a respectable middle-class Frenchman. Michaux excelled in the classroom. He learned Latin and devoured the classics. His imagination raced to the exotic foreign lands about which he read, and these dreams would become manifest in a ceaseless wanderlust that defined his adulthood. First, though, his father called him home for a different type of schooling. As Michaux entered his teenage years, his father wanted his son to begin to lay his roots deep in the family fields, so he decided to pull him from the classroom and instead train him in the demands of farm life. His father's new apprentice showed a natural aptitude for the work. "The young André," his friend and first biographer J. P. F. Deleuze noted, "acquired the most decided taste for agriculture."[2]

In fact, his productivity soon surpassed his father's. Michaux's natural inquisitiveness made him more than just a successful farmer who could till his fields as generations before had done. As he spent his days working the soil, he became intrigued with the natural world that surrounded him, so he carved out time for experiments and adopted new agricultural techniques that could improve his farm's yield. His research, as his early biographer recounted, focused on marrying theory with practice, a test-and-trial method that resembled the scientific method of today and showed something of Michaux's early aptitude for scientific research.[3]

Michaux continued on the path his father had laid out for him through his young teenage years, and when his father died in 1763, the seventeen-year-old Michaux and his younger brother took over the farm. It thrived, and the brothers supported their two younger sisters as well. His family expanded further when Michaux married Anne-Cécile Claye on October 17, 1769. The two shared a true and deep love, and they soon had a son, François André. Then tragedy struck, forever altering Michaux's life. His beloved wife died on October 24, 1770, only a year after their marriage and only two months after François André's birth, plunging the twenty-four-year-old Michaux into a depressive abyss.[4]

Michaux's sorrow was so deep that people worried that he might do something drastic. Several neighbors tried to help the inconsolable widower. Only one succeeded: his neighbor, the fifty-three-year-old bachelor Louis-Guillaume Le Monnier, who happened to be one of the leading scientific thinkers in France. He had started his career as a physicist, but his interests were too broad to be confined to a single subject. Le Monnier conducted electrical experiments using Leyden jars, visited mines to study geology, observed the weather, and practiced medicine. Botany, however, received his greatest attention. He took several botanical trips, including one with Carl Linnaeus, the Swedish botanist who designed a widely used system for classifying plants. King Louis XV was so impressed with Le Monnier that he appointed him a professor of botany at the Jardin du Roi, the king's official garden in Paris, known today as the Jardin des Plantes. Le Monnier also kept a house near Versailles outfitted with an experimental garden. All the while, he successfully practiced medicine—so successfully that King Louis XV made Le Monnier his personal physician.[5]

At some point, Le Monnier invited the grieving Michaux to his Versailles cottage. Perhaps Le Monnier was already familiar with Michaux's scientific proclivities, or perhaps what was intended as a simple kindness to a troubled neighbor led to the discovery of their common interest in studying plants. In any case, this shared passion laid the foundation for a lasting friendship that would change Michaux's life—and the world of science. Sensing scientific promise in his young neighbor, Le Monnier gave Michaux a botanical experiment to gauge his skill—and to distract him from his anguish. He asked Michaux to try to grow madder, a plant whose roots were used for orange dye, and a special type of barley on his farm. Le Monnier was right. The work consoled Michaux. It also consumed him.[6]

Michaux passed the test, and Le Monnier continued training his new pupil in botany. He also introduced his protégé to other members of the king's inner circle, including Charles-Claude de Flahaut de La Billarderie, better known as Comte d'Angiviller. Angiviller was the director of the king's buildings and grounds, one of the most important positions in the king's court. Botanical gardens fell under his purview and were among his top priorities. The king, and the advisors who surrounded him, viewed botany as a cutting-edge field of research that could transform their society. Famines still threatened eighteenth-century Europe, and botanical research, both through the discovery and cultivation of new plants and through the development of agricultural practices, could not only improve the bounty for French tables but also had the potential to boost the French economy by providing new exports. Botany, then, was not just a science; it was also of significant national interest. After hearing of Michaux's abilities, Angiviller decided that he too would offer a challenge to this promising young botanist. Angiviller wanted to know if French soil could support a special type of Ethiopian grass recently sent to him by a British explorer. Michaux accepted the assignment, and his success once again astounded his superior. It was the start of another close working relationship that would continue for decades.[7]

The buzz surrounding Michaux soon reached Bernard de Jussieu, another leading botanist in France and the manager of the gardens at Trianon Palace at Versailles. In 1777, Michaux quit his farm and took up quarters with Jussieu. Jussieu, like Le Monnier, came from a distinguished scientific family. His father, Christophe, was an apothecary in Lyon who had published a book on the use of herbs in medicinal cures. In fact, much of botany's origins rested in the knowledge of apothecaries like Christophe de Jussieu. They practiced what was called *materia medica,* or the study of herbs for medical purposes, a connection that continued into Michaux's time and carries through to this day in pharmacology. Three of Christophe de Jussieu's sons decided to dedicate their lives to the pursuit of plants, likely fueled by their father's interest in the natural world. They, however, were born on the cusp of the Enlightenment and helped transform the knowledge of apothecaries into the work of botanists. Antoine, born in 1686, became a professor at the Jardin du Roi, perhaps the most prestigious position a botanist could hold. His younger brother Bernard, born in 1699, followed Antoine's path, literally. He joined him on botanizing expeditions and later landed his own post alongside his brother at the Jardin. Joseph, born in 1704, was a polymath who undertook an expedition to Latin America in 1735 to make astronomical observations that would help scientists understand Earth's precise shape. Today, a visitor to the Paris garden would be hard-pressed to miss the name Jussieu. It is emblazoned on countless plaques and signs, a testament to this family's legacy in French botany. Lest one think they attained their positions solely through nepotism: Bernard de Jussieu turned down his brother's post after Antoine's death, insisting that Michaux's mentor, Le Monnier, was the better choice for it. And it was through Le Monnier that Michaux's own path brought him into their orbit when, in 1779, he relocated to Paris to study at the Jardin du Roi.[8]

In many respects, Michaux's journey from country farmer to professional botanist studying at the Jardin du Roi exemplified the shifting nature of science in the age of the Enlightenment. A profound change in science was happening as Michaux moved through life. Beginning in the seventeenth century but picking up steam throughout the eighteenth, a rising generation of European thinkers were questioning old scientific assumptions, discarding antiquated traditions, and replacing them with new knowledge forged through novel research techniques. Michaux, of course, would become a part of this transformation. He and others working in various fields were aided in their pursuits by the advent of innovative tools like the microscope and the telescope, along with improved experimental apparatus, that allowed them to better decipher the mysteries of nature. Many in the eighteenth century were optimistic that, for the first time, a real understanding of the natural world was within humanity's grasp. It was a time of great excitement and dynamism.

The sense of discovery permeated the age, and enthusiastic scientific leaders, driven by the desire to share and collaborate, often ignored national boundaries in an effort to advance what they saw as an international project. Other technologies helped individuals spread their findings far beyond their local communities. The printing press and the use of woodcuts and engravings, paired with more reliable means of distribution, allowed for the mass production of precise and uniform scientific images that could be widely circulated, thus vastly expanding access to scientific information throughout Europe.

This energetic spirit of cooperation also led to the formation of new scientific organizations throughout Europe whose primary purpose was to disseminate important new knowledge and to connect scholars. Institutions such as the Royal Society in London (founded in 1660) and the Academy of Sciences in Paris (founded in 1666) became essential nodes in the organization and spread of research within their respective countries and beyond. By the middle of the eighteenth century, almost every European country had its own academy of learning, sometimes several. These institutions served two important purposes (and still do). By electing leading thinkers and providing them with an intellectual home, these "societies" played an essential role in fostering their nation's scientific culture and setting its agenda while also collectively representing the caliber of their nation's scientific talent to the world. Their second purpose was to link each country's scientific community to similar communities in other countries by corresponding with learned societies scattered throughout the continent and the British Isles. Le Monnier, for instance, was elected to the French Academy in 1743, the Royal Society in London in 1745, and the Prussian Academy (founded in 1700) in 1746.[9]

By the time Michaux began his studies, these institutions had helped establish a coherent and connected scientific community within individual countries and throughout Europe. As these collectives grew larger and their influence stronger, their activities—whether through publication, support of research, or meetings—expanded access to knowledge and created opportunities for individuals like Michaux to pursue their own interests through more clearly established channels. These national academies also embodied one of the conundrums of the age, one that Michaux would regularly confront on an individual level: the exchange of knowledge they facilitated softened, but never erased, national distinctions. Despite extensive international cooperation, these institutions' emphasis on championing the work happening within their country encouraged a sense of national pride and prestige—and reinforced national boundaries as well.

Still, science in Michaux's day remained very different from science today. A key difference is revealed in something as simple as the way Michaux and his peers described their work. People like Michaux and Le Monnier never thought of themselves as *scientists,* though we would call them that today. Instead, these eighteenth-century protoscientists described each other as *natural historians.* While the title may be foreign to us today, it nicely encapsulated the efforts of those who bore it. Natural historians aimed to document the natural world by recording all that was in it and explaining how it worked, just as historians were documenting the human past to explain when events happened and why things occurred. Natural historians were thus observers and collectors who generally focused their efforts on areas such as botany, geology, geography, climate, and what was called "animal history." Often, natural historians studied all of these together—when they were in the field, they collected plant and animal specimens, recorded weather data, observed geological formations, and mapped geographic information. Natural history was an all-encompassing concept, one unlike the more professionalized and specialized scientific world of today in which science is separated into clearly defined and discrete disciplines.

To confuse matters further, there was another group of scholars whom we would also call scientists today but who were called *natural philosophers* at the time. Though distinctions between them and natural historians could be blurred, in general, natural philosophers differed from natural historians in the focus of their inquiry. Whereas natural historians were documenters of the environment and its functioning, natural philosophers worked in more theoretical fields like math or physics to explain what we sometimes call "the laws of nature." Benjamin Franklin was often called a natural philosopher because of his attempt to explain electricity and its properties.[10]

Michaux and most botanists fell firmly into the category of natural historian because their discipline was focused on identifying and categorizing plants. As these scientists made advances in the eighteenth century, and as institutions of learning grew in prominence, the work of science itself began to change. The discoveries made in the eighteenth century revealed that the natural world was far more complex than anyone had fully realized; whether it was scientific research identifying microscopic life, describing the laws of physics, or classifying the various individual elements that composed matter, the world became at once more knowable but also more perplexing. Every new discovery made clear that there was even more that was unknown and encouraged deeper research to solve these riddles. To interrogate these findings further—and to answer the questions they raised—individuals increasingly focused in more formalized and specialized disciplines, fields familiar to us today as chemistry, astronomy, and botany. Eventually, later in the early nineteenth century, the new term *scientist* was created to describe someone whose profession was dedicated to pursuing knowledge in one of these fields.[11]

Still, even as the professionalization of science and increased access to knowledge opened doors for people like Michaux, traditional forms of patronage and dependence fueled the scientific system. Michaux, like those before him, relied on the ongoing beneficence of the French Crown for his advancement—each of his mentors had held a royal position, the greatest botanical gardens were funded by the king's coffers, and support for research flowed through the king's purses. At the same time, Michaux was himself the new model of a practitioner, a more formally trained botanist dedicated to the solitary pursuit of botany as a career. The resulting tension between being a scientist dedicated to his field and a subject of the French Crown who was reliant on patronage would follow, and frustrate, Michaux throughout his life.

Michaux's education, though dependent on staying in the good graces of the French elite, was nonetheless on the cutting edge for his day. Michaux studied under the tutelage of France's greatest botanical thinkers, and they were key figures in the wider European scientific community. His curriculum under these men reflected two of the central imperatives that drew so much interest to the field. The first was the desire to identify and describe as many plants as possible. Linnaeus, Le Monnier's onetime botanical companion, had played a key role in advancing this agenda. His Linnaean system created a uniform taxonomy through which all botanists could describe and document plants regardless of their own nationality. Its purpose was emblematic of the Enlightenment project. He hoped it would provide a means to unify scientific knowledge by creating a shared vocabulary that could transcend language barriers and let botanists speak across national boundaries. The Jussieus were practitioners of this system and even tinkered with it to improve its utility. Michaux proved adept at embracing these new modes of practice, and he spent hours in the gardens of Versailles and Paris memorizing plants and learning these novel categorization techniques. His goal with this deep study was to have the knowledge to identify any plant he encountered in the field and, hopefully, discover some that were unknown to science. For a potential new find, a trained botanist like Michaux could use these taxonomic systems to properly classify it and describe it to his peers in any nation.

The second imperative was a drive to import and naturalize in one's country as many plants from around the world as possible. Three impulses fueled this craving to acquire. The first driver was a practical concern. Botany in this era was considered one of the most promising fields of study because of its potential to improve life. Many policy leaders believed that studying and understanding plants, especially foreign ones that could increase agricultural output, could transform a nation's economy and the lives of all who lived within it. Michaux's early experiments were examples of this desire to import foreign plants to increase France's productivity, whether it was in growing new types of barley or introducing dyes for manufacturing materials. One of Michaux's botanical peers, Ambroise Marie François Joseph Palisot de Beauvois, nicely captured this zeitgeist. In an age in which scarcity loomed, natural history was, he wrote, "the source without interruption from which man can obtain abundantly all his needs." The second reason behind this collecting craze was scientific. Natural historians wanted to document all plants, not just those that could be imported from a foreign country and used to benefit society, because they found the pursuit of knowledge to be a reason unto itself. The third and final impulse was both ornamental and political. In this era, botany became intertwined with status. Public gardens filled with exotic plants sprouted throughout Europe, displaying to the world the opulence and majesty of the monarch who owned them—and often their imperial conquests around the globe. These lush public displays became marvels, bringing great pride to a nation and projecting its power to others.[12]

The race to identify and import foreign plants was a priority shared by all European nations. In fact, it fed into existing rivalries that would shape Michaux's own career. The French viewed their greatest rival, Great Britain, jealously. British agents and natural historians traveled throughout their global empire and sent home a plethora of plants for both practical and decorative purposes. The British Isles abounded with private and public botanical gardens that showcased the empire's vast reach, and London, with Kew Gardens and the British Museum as anchors, became an international center of botanical studies. Many in France saw the British gardens blossoming and fretted that they were losing ground, a further spur for patriots like Michaux. The competition, though, was not just confined to these two imperial rivals. Almost all European countries took part in this acquisitiveness. Botanical gardens dotted the European landscape with almost every country supporting several by the end of the eighteenth century.[13]

Across the ocean, Americans, too, were engaged in this scientific enterprise. Many of the leading figures in the new nation, such as George Washington, James Madison, and Thomas Jefferson, were active participants in the international exchange of seeds. They believed the importation of useful foreign plants could introduce crops that could strengthen the still fragile country's economic foundation. It would be hard to overstate the centrality of this international effort. Jefferson himself captured the weight given to botanical work in a revealing, if a bit egotistical, note he wrote to himself about himself. One day, Jefferson decided to list all of his major contributions to American society. He was, he recorded, the author of the Declaration of Independence and the force behind the disestablishment of the church in Virginia, the end of entails, the prohibition on the importation of slaves, and prison reform. At the end, though, he decided that none of these was his greatest achievement. Instead, he reserved that for his introduction of olive trees and African rice to the southern United States in 1789 and 1790. "The greatest service which can be rendered any country," Jefferson wrote, "is to add an useful plant to it's culture; especially a bread grain. [N]ext in value to bread is oil." Jefferson, conveniently, had done both.[14]

Michaux became immersed in this culture of competition during his education among members of the French court, and it certainly drove many of his decisions once he transitioned from being a student studying in royal gardens in France to a practitioner in the field trying to feed these gardens with new material. In fact, his training in the 1770s coincided with a moment of great political and scientific contestation between France and Great Britain that certainly influenced Michaux's own development. France was still reeling from their loss in the Seven Years' War, and Great Britain seemed to be making great scientific advances throughout the globe thanks to the James Cook expeditions that began in the 1760s. While Michaux certainly wanted to find new plants for knowledge's sake, the records he left make clear that he was always, and above all else, a patriotic Frenchman who wanted to strengthen his country and have his discoveries help French botany surpass its British opponent. His work was also bound to networks of patronage that reinforced his national loyalty. Throughout his life, Michaux never lost sight of the belief that his botanical research promised to bring glory to France and improve life within it, even if political upheavals in France profoundly changed the government he was serving.

There was yet another element to Michaux's botanical ambitions that made him particularly well-suited for the profession. He possessed a deep and abiding wanderlust, sparked first when reading the classics as a young boy, and one that only grew as he learned more about the natural world that lay beyond his small corner of the planet. It was a necessary attribute for an aspiring botanist. Michaux knew that a truly great botanist had to trek through distant lands in hunt of elusive plants. This search, though, meant that botanists were often putting their lives on the line as they faced a variety of dangers: hazardous environments, deadly animals, poisonous plants, foreign microbes and diseases, and unwelcoming local communities were all common. Michaux proved more than up for the challenge, eventually traversing through several continents and facing many of these deadly threats.

His first expedition, however, was not so glamorous, nor all that risky. It was, though, vital to his scientific development. In 1779, propelled by his need to travel and his desire to study plants and discover new ones, Michaux made his first foreign foray. He crossed the English Channel to visit France's great foe, Great Britain. There, he planned to study British gardens and meet Britain's botanical leaders. It was also the start of twenty years of ceaseless travel that would span the globe.

❖ 2 ❖

A Circuitous Route to America

1779–1785, London, the Pyrenees, and Persia

Andre Michaux's short and smooth passage across the English Channel paled in comparison to the risks he encountered in his future exploits. Nevertheless, Michaux's trip to London in 1779 came at a perilous time for a Frenchman. Britain's thirteen colonies had declared themselves independent in 1776, and in 1778, France had forged an alliance with these colonial upstarts in their fight against Great Britain. Science, however, remained mostly outside of the fray. While war raged between the two countries, their leaders agreed that scientific exchange should continue unabated. The British thus permitted Michaux to study in London, much as the French and Americans promised safe passage to the scientific voyage of James Cook.[1]

Michaux encountered a botanical culture in London unlike anywhere else in Europe. Interest in botany consumed British society. Although the elite pursued botany for the same reason Michaux and his French patrons did, interest in plants transcended the elite, perhaps more so than it did in France. Great Britain had a burgeoning middle class and a thriving merchant community deeply invested in the idea of their rising empire. Private gardens provided individual Britons with a way to project the riches of empire and give them a sense that they too were participants in this grand project. Displays of this botanical fascination, especially exotic flowers imported from all corners of the globe, were sprouting, literally, everywhere. For Michaux, the trip may have been brief, but his exposure to Britain's botany-obsessed culture was nonetheless profound.[2]

Michaux made the most of his time there. He toured the grand gardens in London. He visited the Royal Gardens at Kew, of course, but he explored other, smaller ones of great note as well. He also met leading natural historians, including perhaps the most influential man of science in Europe, Joseph Banks. Banks was born into wealth, and, much to his family's dismay, he dedicated his life to the cerebral world of science rather than to the increase of his coffers. As a young man, while many of his high-status peers traded on their family connections to enter the world of finance, he used his to land an appointment as the official botanist for James Cook's 1768 expedition to the South Seas. His marvelous accounts of foreign plants captivated the British imagination. It also established his reputation within the scientific community. He leveraged that experience—and his elite connections—to secure the position of president of the Royal Society in 1778 at the relatively young age of thirty-five. From that perch, he funded an enormous amount of research, often dipping into his own resources. He was also a central node—perhaps *the* central node—for scientific correspondence in Europe, receiving tens of thousands of letters from scientists updating him on their experiments and discoveries, including Michaux after 1779.[3]

Although we have no account of Michaux's meeting with Banks, it is clear their paths crossed sometime during Michaux's visit to London. The two botanists surely bonded over their mutual interests, but their relationship also represented a contrast that captured this transitional era in science. Michaux and Banks were about the same age—Banks was just three years older—but Banks was at the end of his exploring career, thanks, in part, to the opportunity his elite background had given him to pursue botany and establish his reputation at a young age. He would spend the next forty years planted in London as the president of the Royal Society, using his station to encourage research, often in service of imperial aims, through financial support. The Royal Society thus became an energetic patron of science separate from, though connected to, the British government and its interests. It provided scientists with an avenue to wean themselves off of the archaic dependencies of Crown patronage or the limitations of being beholden to the whims of a single benefactor. Michaux, on the other hand, was just beginning his life of exploration, one that was often hamstrung by the persistence of more traditional modes of funding and patronage in France.

Michaux made more of his trip than just a chance to see gardens and meet peers. He also turned it into a somewhat unorthodox botanizing expedition (*botanize* is the word botanists use to describe their fieldwork where they try to identify, study, and collect samples, especially of new plants). He returned to France with several saplings from London gardens that he believed were unknown to France's soil. These specimens soon adorned the garden of his mentor Le Monnier.[4]

He also brought back something less tangible but more important: confidence and determination. With years of training now completed, he felt ready to undertake the real work of a botanist: foraging for new plants in the field. His first real botanical trip, one in which he went out into nature, not the curated gardens of London, took him to the mountains of central France. He joined a group of more experienced botanists, including Jean Baptiste Pierre Antoine de Monet de Lamarck, who in 1778 had published one of the most significant studies of plants in France and who would gain greater fame for developing early theories of evolution. Michaux brought seeds from a cedar tree native to Lebanon in the hope that it would grow in these forests, and foraged for other specimens to bring back to Paris. After his excursion to central France, Michaux ventured farther afield, to the Pyrenees in Spain. He returned from both trips with the marks of success necessary to further improve his rising reputation: new specimens to add to French gardens.[5]

When Michaux's colleague J. F. P. Deleuze wrote a brief biography of the botanist years later, titled *The Annotated Memoirs of the Life and Botanical Travels of André Michaux,* he shared some of his fellow travelers' recollections of Michaux as a person. He would, they recounted to Deleuze, often strike out alone early in the morning, outpace the others throughout the day, and return after sunset laden with treasures he had found on his hunt. Michaux, they remembered, showed far more stamina than other members of the party, fueled, it seemed, by an unceasing desire to explore and collect. Their memories of Michaux's earliest trip are telling. Michaux showed these same determined and single-minded traits in accounts of his future expeditions. These were unchanging and inherent parts of his personality that lasted until the very end of his life.[6]

The depiction of Michaux as a solitary, dogged figure reveals more about the rest of his personality as well, an aspect that comes through in other sources. He was not an unpleasant man, but he was not a gregarious conversationalist, and he certainly was not a gossip. Simply put, he was taciturn. He only spoke when necessary, and it was almost always to aid his scientific research or help someone in theirs. He ignored what we would call small talk, avoided the chatter that could consume nights around a fire, and he made few close friends. The promise of his botanical work and the fervent pursuit of knowledge were what animated him. Or as Michaux put it himself in his journal when he mused about this first botanizing trip, "The passionate love of botany has led me to traverse the mountains of Auvergne, and to visit the Pyrénées and the mountains of Spain."[7]

Michaux's first taste of fieldwork left him unsated, however. In fact, it made him hunger for even more-distant vistas. "I burned with longing to undertake a journey into the most distant countries," he confided to his diary. He set his sights on a place that had captured his imagination as a student reading the classics: Persia (Iran today). It was more than just a desire to fulfill a youthful fantasy that drew Michaux to the East, though. He suspected that the climate around the Caspian Sea was conducive to plants that could also grow in France and add to its bounty. Reaching the southern shores of the Caspian Sea, then, was his main objective.[8]

In 1782, Michaux saw his chance to venture there when Jean-François Rousseau, a French consul stationed in the Middle East and the nephew of the political philosopher Jean-Jacques Rousseau, arrived in Paris for a visit. Rousseau regaled the French court with marvelous stories of Persian life and brought beautiful works of art that encouraged their sense of wonder and spurred their imaginations. Michaux seized on this excitement. He realized that Rousseau's planned return to the Middle East was his opportunity to launch his own much-dreamed-of Persian expedition, so he lobbied for royal support to join the diplomat's entourage. Michaux promised to return to France with exotic new items that would fill the royal gardens and add to the Crown's luster. His well-connected mentor Le Monnier did what he could to bolster his protégé's prospects, pleading with Marie Antoinette to grant Michaux's wishes. "He had decided upon Persia," Le Monnier explained to the queen when he asked for her favor, "knowing that the country produces the most beautiful trees, the best fruits, and the most beautiful flowers, and that they can thrive in France." Le Monnier made sure to couch the request in the deferential language required of the patronage system, one in which he cast the purpose of Michaux's expedition as one that served the Crown's own glorification. "He will consider himself too fortunate if the harvest of trees and plants which he intends to collect can give pleasure to Your Majesty and enrich the beautiful garden of the Trianon," Le Monnier promised the queen.[9]

Michaux, thanks to his mentor's connections, received permission to join Rousseau along with 1,200 livres given by the king's brother to underwrite costs. Michaux bolted into action as soon as he heard the good news. He acquired a wide range of equipment for the expedition, including fowling pieces, a telescope, a microscope, and other scientific accoutrements. He also had to worry about what he was going to leave behind, namely his twelve-year-old son, François André. He enlisted one of his three sisters, Marie Victoire Michaux, and her husband, Jean Charles Desaint, to care for him. Marie Victoire and Jean Charles Desaint, a printer and bookseller, had been married in 1779 and lived in Paris, where they plied their trade at 133, rue de la Harpe on the Left Bank. Although records on Michaux's personal life are scant, most especially for this period, the bits we have show that the Michaux clan was a close-knit one and that he had good relationships with his brother and sisters; for instance, he allowed his brother to take over Satory after he decided to pursue science, and he was a witness for his nephew's wedding. With the death of Michaux's wife, alongside the demands of Michaux's training, one can imagine that François André was raised through a collective family effort that included Michaux's two unmarried sisters, Agathe and Gabriel. We do know that the Desaint home became a place to which François André would return during his adulthood, suggesting that it had served as something of a primary residence for him. Such communal rather than nuclear forms of child-rearing were common in eighteenth-century families, especially where early deaths of parents were common, and the family may not have looked at Michaux's botanical quests as an abandonment as much as a means to provide for his family while other family members cared for his son.[10]

Indeed, though this Middle Eastern journey posed numerous known risks, including the possibility of leaving his son an orphan, Michaux harbored no second thoughts, nor did he show any signs of nerves. He was, instead, exuberant. Since discovering botany as his calling, this type of trip superseded all his other responsibilities. It was exactly what he had wanted to do with his life: "The desire to extend my knowledge and to contribute to the progress of natural history moved me to search for several years for the opportunity to travel into parts of the world which had not yet been visited for that purpose," he recorded in his journal just before he left Paris on February 2, 1782. Success, he knew, could establish his professional reputation, an achievement that would help his family as much as it would himself.[11]

Michaux spent the next three years doing exactly that—and more. It was, though, an arduous three years and never easy going. It began with a turbulent crossing of the Mediterranean Sea to reach southern Turkey. His disembarkation there proved a harbinger of the troubles that awaited him. When he stepped off his ship at Canton, today Iskenderun, Turkey, he and his shipmates were greeted by warfare that forced them to retreat to the safe confines of their ship. Once cleared to leave, he traveled with Rousseau and a consular caravan across the Arabian Peninsula, visiting Aleppo, Basra, and Baghdad.[12]

Trouble followed Michaux at nearly every turn as he made his way from the Mediterranean coast to the Red Sea. He was accosted by robbers, caught in hazardous sandstorms, and faced off with several dangerous and deadly animals in the wild. He traveled for the initial portion across modern-day Iraq as part of an armed consular mission. Throughout, though, he heard stories of violence that shaped his perceptions of the society, and he occasionally encountered its aftermath, including arriving in Antioch only eight days after a massacre of more than seven hundred people who had sought refuge from the internecine violence in a local mosque. "I still saw the streets stained with blood in several places," he recorded. "The intrigues, the cruelties and the internal wars between different parties who rise and fall just as soon because of multiple assassinations," he wrote to a colleague from Baghdad, "would alone make up a volume."[13]

The Frenchman, fearful of the society he traveled through, was nonetheless awed by the nature that surrounded it. "I cannot express to you the delight with which I run about the country here," he wrote to a colleague in Paris after he surveyed the territory; "What happiness!" He collected countless species, including irises that he eventually brought to North America and introduced to its soil. And it was not just the plants that dazzled him. He was taken by everything he saw, writing rampantly to his friends in Paris of all that impressed him: the fish, reptiles, snakes, birds, and other animals like jackals, lynxes, wild boars, and hyenas excited his curious mind. "At night I could not sleep but awaited the dawn of the day with impatience," he recounted.[14]

Thrilled at his opportunity to botanize in this foreign domain, he refused to let the dangers that accompanied his expedition interfere with his scientific aspirations. "Excursions are equally painful and dangerous," he reported back to a friend. Determined to forage, he forged ahead, adapting to his environment. "The traveler carries his provisions and sleeps on the ground," he recounted, and he learned to avoid large caravans when on his botanizing forays because large parties attracted thieves. He instead ventured out with a guard provided by Rousseau. He remained dogged in his pursuits despite the risks and discomforts, noting that "one would never go out if one wished always to be safe."[15]

After several months of successful collecting in his travels from Turkey to Aleppo, Michaux sent a large shipment of items back to Le Monnier in France. It included plant and animal specimens along with other artifacts, including sketches of some architectural remains he saw, many of which Michaux believed would delight inquisitive French minds. Le Monnier was blown away. "I cannot praise you enough," he told his protégé, "it seems to me you have many new things."[16]

In March 1783, after spending almost a year exploring the Arabian Peninsula, he set out from Baghdad for his ultimate destination: Persia. Once again, the water passage proved troublesome for Michaux. Soon after his ship left the port on the Red Sea on what was meant to be a short and straightforward trip, pirates attacked the boat and seized him as a prisoner. The British consul in Basra put aside national tensions and came to Michaux's rescue by negotiating terms of release, likely through a ransom payment. Michaux spent several months in the consul's care, waiting for more favorable conditions for his trip. Eventually, later in the summer, when the coast seemed clear of pirates, he tried again, only to be attacked and captured once more soon after his ship left port. Michaux lost several pieces of scientific equipment and most of his clothes in the ordeal. The British consul once more intervened and secured Michaux's freedom. Michaux, though traveling lighter than before, nonetheless remained undeterred and headed onward toward Persia. This time, to provide him with even greater security, the consul in yet another act of magnanimity provided the French explorer with his own ship. Michaux finally arrived in Bushire aboard the British vessel in September 1783.[17]

Michaux spent nearly two years in modern-day Iran. Unlike in the Peninsula, where Michaux traveled under the cover of Rousseau and benefited from the protection of the British consul, he was largely fending for himself. Fortunately, it was, Michaux noted in a letter home, a safer environment. "When one has arrived in Bushire, one no longer has anything to fear if one accompanies the caravan," Michaux wrote. By the summer, Michaux had made his way to the Caspian Sea. It was a journey of contrasts that had begun in the temperate southern shores and continued through a mountainous and barren terrain. He acquired numerous seeds in Bushire and Shiraz, including some used for medicines, and he made many observations on the geology of the region. The Caspian Sea surpassed all that came before, however, proving to be the botanical nirvana Michaux had imagined. "In Persia," he concluded, "only the northern provinces are profitable for researches in natural history."[18]

At the end of 1784, having reached the southern shores of the Caspian Sea, he finally began the trek home. He was spurred by a letter from his sister that had reached him in this remote region and asked that he return. The specific contents of the note remain unknown, but it is easy to speculate that something had changed in the family. One potential reason was that her husband may have become ill. We know that Marie Victoire Desaint would be a widow by 1790. The second potential reason is that his son required more direct paternal care. Perhaps it was a combination of both.[19]

There are strong hints in the few surviving records that François André struggled with his father's long absence, lending some credence to the idea Michaux was called back because of his son. Though Michaux's expedition took him far from home, he was able to stay in sporadic touch with his family by receiving mail through consular offices. At least two letters François André sent to his father, one in September 1782 and another in August 1783, found the wandering botanist and forced Michaux to (at least momentarily) shift his attention from the field to his parental duties. Michaux received the first letter sometime in the spring of 1783, likely while in Iraq near Basra, and the second in March 1784, near the city of Shiraz, Iran, when he was on his way to the Caspian Sea. While neither letter from the son survives, the father's two replies do. These highly personal missives represent a marked contrast from most of Michaux's other extant correspondence, the vast majority of which is primarily professional in nature and written to scientific colleagues. Indeed, these two letters provide one of the best glimpses into Michaux's home life and inner self.[20]

The man that emerges shows many of the traits Deleuze described in his posthumous depiction. Michaux was a demanding father. The letter Michaux penned to his son in May 1783 in Basra, written soon after surviving his captivity, combined firmness with high expectations. He began with something of an apology for a prior exchange between the two that has not survived. In that earlier letter, he had apparently chastised his son for some misbehavior, and the scolding had upset the boy, then living far from his father and longing for his father's approval. It is clear that the reprimand had so deeply affected François André that Michaux's sisters felt it necessary to send Michaux a separate letter to reassure the absent father that his son was well-behaved. Michaux realized that he may have been too harsh with his son. Even if he retracted his earlier criticism, he refused to yield on one point: his standards for his son. "I was upset to have made you numerous reproaches: However, you should be persuaded that it is only the desire for perfection in you which obliges me sometimes to make reproaches at all of the times when I believed it necessary," he wrote. As Michaux's life and record make clear, the pursuit of perfection was not just an expectation Michaux had for his son. It was a standard to which Michaux held himself as well.[21]

With that opening, the rest of Michaux's letter reads as if he wanted to impart fundamental beliefs and life lessons to his son in case he never returned. His words confirm what his companions had hinted at in their account of him to Deleuze. Michaux was a driven stoic. He was exacting and had little room for trivialities. In fact, Michaux's semi-apology was followed by a castigation. "If there are faults found in you it is necessary to make some efforts to repeal them and to recognize them without reproaches before God and men and towards oneself," he told his son. He went on to remind François André that he should not become a victim of youthful frivolity, instructing him that that "the tricks and jokes of schoolboys are not permitted in such that they do not compromise honesty and decency."[22]

Michaux's second letter, sent from Iran, only reinforced the high bar, perhaps an unattainable one, that he set for his offspring. Instead of enjoying the innocence of youth, he wanted his son to understand deprivation and sacrifice, both of which promised to make him a stronger person. Michaux instructed his son to practice a life of asceticism by shunning youthful folly and instead embracing "good habits, suppressing fantasies, suffering from deprivations, etc. etc." His reason was that such behavior laid the foundation for character traits that would aid him as he went through life. "When in youth, one gets used to great misfortunes, which can last throughout life, suffering is much easier to bear," he explained. Reading between the lines of the exchange, it is possible Michaux was trying to reassure his son that his father's extended absence, though painful now, would serve him well later in life.[23]

In any case, Michaux's overall message was clear. Sacrifice and self-control were more important than indulgence and pleasure. Rooted in both Christian teachings and interpretations of the ideals of ancient Greece and Rome, these characteristics, along with a sense of duty and honor, became defining elements for an idea of masculine virtue that circulated widely throughout eighteenth-century Europe and its colonies. Others, such as George Washington, tried to embody them. Michaux cultivated these attributes himself. Indeed, his sense of control and restraint is one reason his interior thoughts and feelings can be so elusive for biographers. He refused to allow passions or emotions to manifest themselves, at least publicly. His relentless work ethic, one that sent him far away from home during this exchange and would continue to for years to come, was the very personification of the advice he gave his son to avoid the wastefulness of play, which he associated with self-indulgent pleasure.[24]

As Michaux made his way back to Europe, he was surely proud of his accomplishments. "I can, with modesty and without conceit, congratulate myself upon having used my time well," he reported back to France in 1784. It was, to be sure, a success. One of his finds was a white flower that eventually bore the name *Michauxia campanuloides*. Exemplifying the wide-ranging work of a natural historian, Michaux's contributions to European knowledge expanded beyond flora, however. He was so taken by all the wonders he saw that he amassed anything he thought might be useful for science. He took geological samples, observed the climate, and returned with dozens of animal specimens and accounts of many more. In fact, one of the painful decisions he had to make in the field was to forgo collecting large animals because he decided they would take up too much space at the expense of botanical and mineralogical specimens. He also made a point to compile a record of the Persian language in what was perhaps the first French-to-Persian dictionary written. He was, then, very much the archetype of an eighteenth-century imperial man of science, a natural historian trying to acquire and document as much as he could.[25]

He also lugged back a mysterious stone that confounded French scholars for decades. The black rock was rounded into an oval and had elaborate cuneiform images carved into its top. Below that, someone had etched a series of tables filled with what were at the time indecipherable inscriptions. Known today as the Michaux Stone, the object is held by France's national library and is on regular display. For decades, no one was quite sure what its markings meant. Eventually, in 1856, a scholar successfully identified the language as Akkadian, an ancient Mesopotamian language, and deciphered it. The stone's text recorded a gift of property given by a father for his daughter's dowry, and the carvings on the top of the stone represented gods whose presence consecrated the text, making it a legal document. In practical terms, the stone, known as a "kudurru," likely served as both a boundary marker for property and as a deed. Subsequent research dated the object to the eleventh century BC, making it the oldest such stone acquired by a European explorer up to that point. For scholars, its content provided new insight into the history of this ancient civilization.[26]

When he reappeared at Versailles in June 1785 laden with all these treasures from the Middle East, the scientific elite greeted him with adulation. He had demonstrated that he was a botanist with intellectual agility and daring ambition, two attributes necessary to accomplish the grand goals of Enlightenment-era botany. The royal court was impressed as well. For his service, King Louis XVI appointed Michaux the royal botanist. The appointment meant that Michaux had found the same kind of stability his father had once sought for him at their Satory farm, though he had achieved it through far different means. Michaux had a salary, status, and a position within the French patronage network. He was now part of the scientific establishment. Louis XVI made this clear in his decree appointing Michaux, boasting that Michaux was "a subject who combines intelligence, ripened by experience, with the faculties and strength necessary to travel to any country whatsoever to study the productions and collect with care for his majesty plants, seeds and fruits of trees and shrubs, even herbaceous plants suitable for increasing the species of forage."[27]

Never one to linger, Michaux was ready to accept his post and return to the field immediately. His eyes remained set on the East. He wanted to push beyond Persia on his next trip and intended to head to Tibet and Kashmir, in what is today Pakistan and India. King Louis XVI had different ideas for his botanist, though, and in a world in which patronage reigned supreme, Michaux's future was ultimately the king's to decide. He agreed that Michaux should continue his impressive fieldwork, but his eyes were set in a very different direction. With the close of the American Revolution, the European scientific community was more intrigued by North America than ever before. The French saw a special opportunity. With eastern North America no longer in British hands, and with Americans having forged a special bond with the French through their wartime alliance, French natural historians had greater access to the eastern seaboard, formerly terrain controlled by their British nemesis, than ever before. Many suspected that these eastern lands held boundless botanical potential. King Louis thus wanted Michaux to head west, across the Atlantic, and explore the American woods.[28]

Louis XVI had another reason to send his botanist to North America: national security. After having fought a series of global wars beginning with the Seven Years' War in the 1750s and continuing through the American Revolution, the needs of the French military had consumed an enormous amount of timber, leaving French forests dangerously depleted. Facing such deforestation, the king wanted to know if he could fill his barren woods with trees from America that were at least as good as, and perhaps even stronger than, native French trees. "The scarcity of fully matured forests in France for many years," Michaux explained of the king's purpose, "determined the [king] to try to naturalize the various species of trees which grow in North America, whose similarity of climate made success probable."[29]

On July 18, 1785, less than six weeks after Michaux had returned from the Middle East, Louis XVI issued orders to Michaux to travel to North America. The king gave Michaux an annual stipend of 2,000 livres, a very healthy sum, and promised to cover all associated costs of travel and research. As the official decree stated, Michaux was to identify "trees and forest plants . . . which are of the greatest interest for works of art as well as for carpentry construction" and "to embrace, moreover, all the researches which relate to botany." Michaux was told that he was to send all his samples to Angiviller, the director of royal buildings who had trained the botanist years earlier. He was also permitted to send a few small shipments to his other mentor, Le Monnier.[30]

Angiviller, his supervisor, later sent even more detailed instructions that established Michaux's collecting priorities. Angiviller's orders showed the myriad ways in which governments considered natural history a national priority. National security came first. Michaux's primary task, Angiviller made clear, was to collect large trees that could replenish the French forests and seeds of crops that could improve husbandry. Living animals that could thrive in France and whose meat and furs could benefit France's economy came second. Finally, the lowest priority, but one still worth listing explicitly, related to the ornamental needs of imperial nations. He told Michaux to find exotic fruits and flowers that would be "interesting for gardens."[31]

At the time, Michaux would have preferred to return to the East, but he was both a loyal subject and dependent on the king for his position. "I was obliged to yield to his wishes," Michaux said of his assignment with a hint of resentment. And so he did. Little did he know that he would spend the next ten years running two botanical gardens in North America, taking a series of risky but fruitful scientific journeys, and, eventually, partaking in a clandestine military operation that threatened the foundations of the young US government.[32]

❖ 3 ❖

Making America Home

1785–1787, New York City to Charleston, South Carolina

Though initially reluctant, André Michaux came to embrace his charge with gusto. It was, he realized, an expedition of grand proportions and immense potential. Within days of his assignment, the newly minted royal botanist began amassing what he needed for his North American experiment. He also drew up plans to execute a sophisticated project. First, he intended to build a modern botanical garden in New York similar to the ones he knew in Europe. From this entrepôt, he would then launch botanical excursions throughout the North American forests, collecting all that he could. When he returned to New York from these expeditions, he would grow the most promising plants and export the healthiest ones to France for their cultivation there.

Such ambitious designs, Michaux knew, required more than just one person if he was to fulfill his orders. He managed to recruit Pierre-Paul Saunier, a trained gardener who had earned a solid reputation while working in the royal parks, to be his deputy. He also brought a young and unskilled laborer: François André. Michaux suspected that his stay in North America was going to be safer than his foray to the Middle East, so he was comfortable bringing his now fifteen-year-old son with him. In fact, it's clear that Michaux felt compelled to provide greater mentorship to his son. Just as Michaux's father had wanted him to follow in his footsteps as a farmer, so too did Michaux decide that he should train François André in his botanical methods so he could inherit the new Michaux mantle.[1]

Michaux spent August 1785 building his team and purchasing equipment, and near the end of the month, Michaux and his crew left Paris for

L'Orient, the main port for ships destined for North America. Having raced to launch his expedition, Michaux faced stiff headwinds when he arrived at the port on August 31. Unfavorable weather prevented ships from leaving L'Orient for several weeks. His frustrations only mounted once underway. Several severe storms in the Atlantic battered the ship and slowed its transit. Only on November 13, 1785, after forty-seven days at sea, did Michaux finally arrive in New York City.[2]

Wearied from travel but eager to seize the opportunity, Michaux started hunting for plants almost immediately. He spent most of his time trekking through northern New Jersey. Though much of the territory he covered has become the paved suburbs of New York City, the area in the eighteenth century was home to lush forests that proved fertile ground for Michaux's research. He collected as much as he could, digging up more than four thousand specimens. He also scoured still heavily forested Long Island for material. "Fourteen days have been spent in collecting seeds and digging up trees both on Long Island and in different spots of New Jersey," he reported to his mentor Le Monnier in his first surviving letter written from America.[3]

He also found his way to the French consul in New York, Louis-Guillaume Otto. When he appeared on Otto's doorstep, he was loaded with items ready to ship back to France. Otto beamed at the sight. Having already spent several years in North America as a diplomat, Otto had himself come to admire the same American environment that now captured Michaux's wonder. Otto was convinced that many of the plants surrounding him could prove useful to his native land. He had even sent some promising specimens to France to prod his superiors into investing in a mission much like Michaux's. When Michaux arrived at Otto's residence, the consul was thrilled to learn of Michaux's project. "I cannot tell you," Otto told Angiviller, "the satisfaction that the arrival of this botanist has given me."[4]

Unsurprisingly, the two men hit it off. Otto immediately endorsed Michaux's plan for a botanical garden in America. In fact, an ebullient Otto declared that Michaux should open not one but two gardens. Otto suspected that plants from the American South would prove particularly suitable for southern France, but he feared that the harsh New York winters would prevent Michaux from cultivating plants from these more temperate American regions. He was convinced that Michaux needed a southern outpost as well, so much so that even before Michaux had created his planned northern garden, Otto was lobbying French officials to fund a second

MAP 2. ANDRÉ MICHAUX'S NORTH AMERICAN TRAVELS. André Michaux took numerous scientific expeditions during his stay in the United States and traversed nearly all of eastern North America. He traveled as far south as Florida, as far north as Hudson Bay, and as far west as the Mississippi River. (Map by Nat Case, INCase, LLC)

one. "You will think perhaps appropriate," he suggested to Michaux's supervisor Angiviller, "to establish an analogous garden in the Carolinas for the trees and plants that live only in a warmer climate." In the meantime, Michaux and Otto started scouting for the right spot for Michaux's northern base of operations.[5]

Even though he was without a permanent home in New York, Michaux remained busy botanizing during the cold winter months. He sent five boxes of materials to France in December 1785 and twelve more in early January 1786. The shipments contained a plethora of carefully packed specimens. In his first report, he highlighted two items of particular interest. The cranberry, he noted, resembled a cherry and "is used for making jam here," and the sweet potato from Carolina was especially popular for eating. He sent several samples of each to France, thinking that they might be worth introducing into the French diet.[6]

The exacting and laborious botanical work made Michaux realize that he needed to establish his garden soon. If he had his own ground, he would better be able to control the growth of and care for his plants, something he explained to his mentor Le Monnier in an early letter. "We have been obliged to use sod or turf from the land, which is already frozen," he complained of the first shipment, "making the work painful, and the packing will not be as well done as it would have if we had had the facilities."[7]

With the winter weather making fieldwork difficult, Michaux undertook other tasks. Michaux and Otto spent January searching for a suitable tract of land for the garden. It was no easy chore, as they needed a unique piece of property that could serve as a farm, a laboratory, a warehouse, and a manufacturing hub all at once. The habitat also needed to support the survival of a wide variety of plants. After spending a month scouring the region, they found twenty-nine acres in northern New Jersey located on a tract of land nestled between the Hudson and Hackensack Rivers that met their demanding specifications.[8]

The plot seemed perfect. "The main advantages are," Michaux reported to his superior in France, "proximity to diverse woodlands for gathering seeds and pulling out young plants, . . . the proximity of New York and of the River for communication with the packet boats, and finally, the land's quality." Best of all were the different types of soil packed into this relatively small plot. Such diversity would allow Michaux to grow the wide range of plants he expected to find. "The highest part is of clay and substantial soil,"

Michaux described, "the middle part is of gray sand, and the lowest part is a woodland of aquatic cypress." Michaux snapped it up for a few hundred dollars.[9]

Securing the deed, however, proved far more difficult than a simple transfer of money. If Michaux bought the property, then that would mean that King Louis XVI would own American land, and New Jersey barred foreigners from owning land unless they swore allegiance to the United States. Michaux, the proud Frenchman in the employ of the king, refused to take any vow that betrayed his French loyalty. Instead, he decided to seek special dispensation. In a country that had just overthrown a monarchy, this was no small ask. The prospect of a foreign potentate owning a piece of American soil could prove quite unpalatable to the democratic tastes of Americans. Otto, however, was determined that Michaux acquire the land, so he decided to put his diplomatic skills to use. He lobbied the state government and convinced the New Jersey legislature to pass a special act permitting the sale of the tract to Michaux. Perhaps not insignificantly, Otto also benefited from unusually good access to the seat of power. He had married the niece of New Jersey's governor, William Livingston, creating his own Franco-American alliance of sorts.[10]

Aside from his having made an opportune marriage, a few trends shaping the early nation aided Otto in his efforts. Even though Americans fretted about the fragile independence of their country and were especially worried about foreign powers conspiring to upset their internal affairs and undermine their government, the French king still held a special place in the hearts of Americans because of the French aid during the Revolutionary War. Michaux played upon this relationship in his lobbying efforts by promising that his garden would cement a new scientific alliance of mutual benefit to both countries. His persuasion worked. "He wishes to establish," the law declared, "a botanical garden at about thirty acres to make useful experiments, with respect to agriculture and gardening and intends to make a depository not only of French and American plants but of all the productions of the World which may be drawn from the king's garden at Paris."[11]

Michaux's garden soon drew national attention. Newspapers from Charleston to Boston reported on Louis XVI's acquisition and boasted of its import to the country. "Mr Michaux, Botanist to his Most Christian Majesty is erecting a garden," a New Jersey newspaper announced in April 1786 after the law was passed, "which, for its magnificence will far surpass anything of the kind in America." This optimistic article, and others like it, captured the symbolic importance the garden held for a people who had only just recently secured their independence. It also captured one of the ironies of American independence. In what may seem like a contradictory formula, then, Americans trying to build an independent democratic republic also often tried to replicate, and improve upon, Old World institutions as a way to establish their status with the rest of the world. The United States thus depended on European recognition to establish its independence and emulated foreign practices to prove they were worthy peers on the global stage. A botanical garden was one such thing. As New York's *Daily Advertiser* declared in June 1787, Michaux's garden promised to "rival if not exceed the most celebrated gardens in Europe." That was the hope not just for Michaux's garden, but for the country itself. The further irony in this case, however, was that the success of this grand American garden was going to rely entirely on a Frenchman, wholly devoted to his own country, and whose project was, ultimately, in service of French imperial ends.[12]

Michaux also spent those first few months preparing for what he knew was likely going to be an extended stay in America. His first priority was to improve his English. While he probably arrived with some ability to read the language, he was by no means fluent enough to spend weeks traveling through small towns and the countryside talking to strangers. In December and January, he took steps to change that. He bought English dictionaries and hired a tutor, all with an eye toward acquiring the skills needed to embark on more ambitious expeditions after the spring thaw. As Michaux's newfound friend Otto relayed to his French colleagues, "Michaux . . . will learn to speak [English] this winter, and next spring he will be ready to travel successfully in the interior of the country." Michaux also made sure his son was taught the language, expecting that François André would be his traveling companion on many journeys through American society.[13]

Michaux was a quick study. By the end of March 1786, he had enough confidence to dismiss his interpreter. He also toured the surrounding area looking for plants and animals—and made observations about another curiosity: the people of this newfangled country who called themselves "Americans." Michaux was a great student of the natural world, able to identify most known plants and to make perceptive observations about the geology and climate in which they grew. He was also an occasional observer of the people and societies he encountered. On this count, though, Michaux seemed to lack the same perceptive powers he had for botany. Perhaps his reticence, coupled with his unassuming but determined personality, made making cultural observations more difficult than scientific ones. Perhaps he was more at ease away from others and occupied with his own thoughts. In any case, many of his statements about Americans simply reaffirmed general stereotypes already circulating in Europe without offering any new insights. The Germans in Pennsylvania, he wrote, were industrious. The Dutch of New York and New Jersey were particularly clean and neat. Michaux spent an extended stay in Connecticut, where he visited farms and studied local agriculture—as well as the Yankee culture. He developed quite a jaundiced view of their puritanical ways. "The farmers of Connecticut are prudes," he concluded.[14]

One type of American character drew Michaux's particular ire: the lackadaisical American. Michaux harped on the poor work ethic of the American worker. He complained that the prevalence of alcohol, the ease with which one could capture game, and the abundance of land had rendered Americans slothful. He regularly criticized those whom he hired for day jobs. They demanded high wages, always underperformed, left whenever they wanted, and showed an independent streak that frustrated Michaux. "People are so arrogant that the poorest believes himself dishonored to be working for another man," Michaux recounted to his friend and former teacher André Thouin.[15]

Most likely, Michaux's tribulations with his employees reflected something else: in a newly democratic country with greater property ownership and opportunity for free men than France or elsewhere in Europe, American laborers exhibited far less deference to employers than French laborers in the monarchical, hierarchical, and autocratic culture of Michaux's Bourbon France. A frustrated Michaux, in a December 1785 letter to Angiviller, drew this distinction, writing, "I am certain that, if I was helped by farm workers like we have in France, I would be able to send several ships completely filled with interesting productions every year."[16]

Adding to his growing uncertainty, even unhappiness, was the scientific community he met in the Northeast. He was, to say the least, underwhelmed. He met few knowledgeable botanists and was shocked that no one had yet built the decorative gardens common in Europe. "People are ice-cold here," Michaux complained of New Yorkers during the depths of his first winter, "and indifferent to everything except what will bring money." In short, he felt isolated and unaccepted.[17]

He harbored hopes that the American South would offer him a warmer reception, though. People told him that exotic plants and gardens thrived in the region and that the southern elite supported a botanical culture that was more like what he knew in France. "I hope I will be more pleased in this respect by the South," he confided to his mentor Le Monnier, "where there are wealthy people who have accumulated all the interesting productions in their gardens."[18]

In June 1786, after securing the tract for the northern garden, Michaux set out to see if what he heard was true. He departed New York for Virginia believing it might be a good location for a second garden. His plan was to travel to Philadelphia first, then head farther south to Virginia, where he hoped to meet George Washington, and return via the Appalachian Mountains, an ambitious trek for someone so new to the country. It was to be his first foray outside of the Northeast.[19]

Michaux's stop in Philadelphia changed his dour view of the United States. The city was the largest in the country and served as its cultural and financial center. It was also the home of Benjamin Franklin, the most celebrated American scientist in the world. Franklin had just returned from a stint in France as the American ambassador where he had become one of the most popular figures in the political and intellectual circles of Paris. Michaux carried a letter of introduction to the seventy-nine-year-old from one of Franklin's friends and former diplomatic counterparts, the Comte de Vergennes, the French minister of foreign affairs. Franklin greeted the botanist at his Market Street home and hosted him for dinner. Impressed with Michaux and his promise, Franklin offered to assist the Frenchman in launching a second garden.[20]

But what really captured Michaux's attention was the vibrant scientific culture in the city, especially surrounding botany. Unlike New York, Philadelphia was home to several leading scientific thinkers, such as fellow natural historians and botanists Benjamin Smith Barton and William Bartram. "Philadelphia deserves to be compared with the best cities of Europe after Paris," the always proud Frenchman boasted to a friend back home. It was, he quickly realized, the intellectual capital of the country, much like Paris was to France, and very unlike New York. "There are more enlightened and scholarly people than in any other areas of the continent," he said of Philadelphia.[21]

Michaux also forged a long and lasting bond with the city's leading botanist, William Bartram. Bartram managed his own botanical garden with his brother John on the western banks of the Schuylkill River, a couple of miles outside the city center. Their father, John Sr., had founded the garden in 1728, and through its bountiful harvests, the family became major purveyors of plants in British botanical circles. The Bartrams undertook numerous expeditions throughout North America, especially to the South. They collected intriguing plants they found in the field, brought them back to Philadelphia to cultivate them, and then shipped them to their peers in Great Britain. Their garden was not only the oldest in the country, it was also the largest and compared favorably to those Michaux had seen in Europe. In William Bartram, Michaux had found a true intellectual peer and scientific comrade.

As Michaux walked through the Bartrams' garden, studying the cornucopia of North American plants that surrounded him, he ran through the lists of plants he had memorized as part of his training and realized that he had already seen most of them. Only one he considered "interesting and new," the extremely rare *Franklinia,* a small tree that blooms a glorious white flower. The Bartrams had discovered the tree in Georgia and named it in honor of America's most revered scientist and fellow Philadelphian. Since the Bartram discovery, few other botanists had been able to find additional examples of it, and none other than the Bartrams had successfully cultivated one. The plant had, in fact, become one of the most elusive and captivating botanical prizes of the eighteenth century. Its allure inspired botanists, including eventually Michaux, to scour the Georgia countryside in search of living examples from which they could cultivate seeds that would propagate in foreign gardens. No one except for the Bartrams ever proved successful. Today, the wild *Franklinia* is considered extinct, and all those living today in gardens are thought to descend from the Bartram specimen Michaux saw.[22]

After spending a few days in Philadelphia, Michaux continued his trek south, toward Mount Vernon. Along the way, he studied the soil as he searched for a desirable spot for his second garden, and, of course, he collected plants and seeds. He was unimpressed with Maryland—"the most sterile of all the United States," he concluded. Northern Virginia's soil proved more promising, but it was also his first real exposure to chattel slavery. Michaux, a doer who experimented in his own fields to improve his yields, disparaged the practice. He concluded Virginia's agricultural potential was "wasted by the owners with large properties" whose reliance on slavery had bred sloth in planters, squelching their ambition and productivity, and that the labor system was inefficient. Of the plantation owners, he wrote, "They are very little active or hardworking and the earth is not cultivated in proportion to the number of slaves." Though he may have been unimpressed with Virginia's farming practices, and critical of the way slavery affected society, he offered no abolitionist or emancipationist sentiments; in fact, his later actions would show that while he may have been critical of slavery's social effects, he was no opponent of the system itself if it served his interests.[23]

Michaux arrived at one of those Virginia farms, George Washington's Mount Vernon, on the evening of Monday, June 16. It was Michaux's final planned stop before returning north. Washington was preparing for dinner when the Frenchman called. Washington, the hero of the American Revolution, had become used to welcoming unexpected visitors at inopportune times. In this case, Washington was pleasantly surprised to read the two letters of introduction Michaux carried with him. One came from the Marquis de Lafayette, who was one of Washington's deputies during the war and had become a close friend and confidante after it; some even say Lafayette was like an adopted son to Washington. The second came from the Duke of Lauzun, a French military officer who had fought under him. Lauzun's letter outlined the scope of Michaux's mission. The French botanist was on a "grand tour," Lauzun explained to Washington, and was to make "the most compleat collection in his power of trees, seeds and vegetals unknown in France." Upon reading these warm words of recommendation, Washington had a plate set for the French botanist.[24]

At the dinner table, Michaux sat opposite a man basking in what he hoped would be his permanent retirement from public life. After the Treaty of Paris ended the Revolutionary War in 1783, Washington had returned home to pursue his true passion, agriculture. Though the ineffectiveness of the national government created by the Articles of Confederation troubled him and he worried about the country's prospects under it, the American Cincinnatus, well-regarded as the general who had given up power and returned to his farm instead of seizing even greater authority, remained happily ensconced on his plantation, where visitors from all over regularly arrived to pay their respects—often to Washington's consternation. Some years, Washington personally hosted more than one hundred visitors and entertained guests on more days than not. Michaux was not to be one of those burdensome visitors. As they dined, Michaux entertained Washington with tales from his travels through the Middle East and excited him with news of his current mission.[25]

Part of Washington's interest in Michaux rested in Washington's own long-standing involvement in botanical research. Washington had transformed large portions of his Mansion House Farm into areas of experimentation where he planted new varietals to see if they would take root, similar to the way Michaux operated his Satory farm. Washington was, in fact, driven by many of the same goals for the United States that led France to finance Michaux's expedition to America. Washington's aim was to find and introduce new staples into American agriculture, believing that by increasing the productivity of American farms, the nation's independence would become more secure. After the Revolution ended, and Washington's networks expanded far beyond his Virginia home, he became an important node in the international circulation of seeds. Correspondents throughout Europe sent him seeds that they had received from their own contacts, and he sent his own supply back in exchange. He had even recently promised Lafayette that he would procure seeds from Kentucky—a region that held great fascination for farmers and natural historians alike because of its promise—for Louis XVI's gardens.[26]

Washington, and other Americans who joined in this trade, such as James Madison and Thomas Jefferson, imbued these transatlantic gifts of plants with important symbolism. Washington knew that by sending seeds to French colleagues, he might not only nourish his correspondents' own agricultural pursuits but also offer meaningful, even transformative, aid to another country and its people and cultivate international alliances. As Washington's seeds bloomed in France's official gardens, Washington meant for them to represent America's ongoing gratitude for the king's support of the American Revolution and the two countries' continued bond.[27]

Before their evening ended, in another act of botanical diplomacy, Washington volunteered Mount Vernon as a storage site for Michaux's plants. Michaux was thrilled with the offer, and before leaving for New York, he reciprocated with his own act of generosity. From his room in Alexandria, a few miles up the Potomac River, he sent Washington a gift that his fellow agriculturalist would appreciate: a number of foreign plants that Michaux had brought to America, including seeds for pistachio and cypress trees. Washington carefully planted the items a few days later, documenting precisely how many plants he set down and where. He also penned a letter to one of his French colleagues raving about Michaux and his mission and reiterating his willingness to help. "Any assistance in my power will be most chearfully accorded as a tribute to his merit," Washington assured the Duke of Lauzun.[28]

Michaux's return to New York was brief. The peripatetic botanist made a series of short excursions in the weeks that followed, returning again to Philadelphia to visit Bartram and botanizing in the greater New York City region. All the while, he continued planning for a second garden. Now, however, he set his sights farther south, on South Carolina, believing its more temperate climate was more conducive for his mission. On September 6, Michaux left for Charleston aboard a packet ship with his son and a personal assistant, both of whom appear to have maintained the New Jersey garden while Michaux traveled to Virginia.[29]

Two weeks later, Michaux and his entourage disembarked in the southern port and wasted little time getting to work. Michaux met with the governor, the mayor, and the French consul and spent every other day in the woods. The environment was exactly what he had wished. As he trekked through the lush vegetation, he discovered himself surrounded by, as he noted in his first report back to his superiors, "a great number of the most interesting trees and a great number of other plants." Such biodiversity convinced him that Charleston was the right site for his second garden. It was, he wrote, "the most interesting area of all of America."[30]

In early November, he identified the perfect spot to lay down roots, a 111-acre farm for sale located ten miles outside of Charleston in an area known as Goose Creek. The sprawling plantation had two homes and stalls for horses and other animals. There were also a number of outbuildings that were quarters for people enslaved by the plantation owner. Like the New Jersey nursery, the Goose Creek plantation's diverse topography could support a multitude of plants. The property sat between two rivers and contained about eighty forested acres, fifteen acres cut for farmland, some swampy wetlands, and a creek. Its size—almost four times larger than the northern venture—provided something else. Michaux had enough space to turn certain sections into an active farm, thereby creating a self-sustaining plantation that would also save him time and money. It was to be "a depot in the center of the country," he declared. Unlike in New Jersey, though, Michaux encountered no barriers when he purchased the property for what he considered a song, 100 guineas.[31]

The expanse of the South Carolina plantation also provided Michaux with a better chance to fulfill what he considered his familial duties. He wanted to train his son as he himself had been brought up and, in so doing, instill in François André the same work ethic that he had gained as a boy on the Satory farm. Michaux, perhaps influenced by his views of the American work ethic, had grown concerned that François André was developing the same lethargic traits he saw in Americans. He decided it was time to act on the stern advice he had given his son while writing from the Middle East. He wanted his son to toil in order to appreciate his privilege. "I do not see in him," Michaux confided to Angiviller, "either the energy or disposition for any kind of knowledge, and that, being obliged to work for a living, he will learn the necessity for it." Putting him to work in the fields, he hoped, would correct his son's laziness and instill in him his father's values. One cannot help but wonder if the teenaged François was as apathetic as his father perceived, or if his father's high bar, his demand for near-perfection in life, was impossible for anyone but Michaux himself to meet.[32]

For the next ten years, Michaux entrusted Saunier, the gardener who had crossed the Atlantic with him, with the management of the New Jersey nursery, while he made Goose Creek his primary base of operation with his son. Michaux never explicitly stated why he preferred to remain in the South, though he left many clues. First, there were the people. While he had found New Yorkers "ice-cold," the South Carolina elite treated him like a distinguished guest. "Most of the rich inhabitants of Charleston have made me most welcome as they all have homes in the country," he said of his new neighbors in Goose Creek. Unlike the greed he saw driving New Yorkers, the South Carolinians were generous. They welcomed him with open arms, helped him feel comfortable in the region, and exploited their system of unfree labor to help Michaux, something Michaux made clear in one of the early, glowing reports he sent to Paris. "They have invited me to visit them and have promised for the most part all assistance; either by getting me acquainted with local areas or by having their [slaves] accompany me into the inhabited regions," he recounted.[33]

Everything in South Carolina seemed better to Michaux. His house, for instance, was "in the neighborhood of better people, which is important"—and by that, he meant the plantation grandees who, as beneficiaries of the exploitative slave labor system upon which their society rested, had the time and resources to indulge in other hobbies, like amateur botanical pursuits. Another draw was the presence of a pronounced French émigré community in South Carolina. Generations earlier, French Huguenots had sought refuge in the region, founding towns such as New Bordeaux, and there were several prominent merchants with French ancestry. Even though Michaux was far from his native country, here, in the South, he could socialize with compatriots, speak his native tongue, and exchange gossip, all of which could help him feel some sense of connection to a homeland an ocean away. Instead of being isolated and excluded as he had felt in New Jersey and New York, he found himself feeling at home in South Carolina.[34]

Michaux also raved about the natural environment. "The beautiful woods" of the region supported a variety of plants, including some already imported from foreign regions. Such praise revealed something about Michaux's own botanical predilections. Michaux's tastes drew him to colorful flowers and exotic plants, and, as he noted in a letter, his new home offered more of that than the lush but mostly green northern woodlands. "I soon recognized that this southern part of the United States is the richest and most fertile in different productions and that the weather for collecting seeds is without interruption from the month of May until the month of December," he reported to his superior amid a mild Charleston December.[35]

Finally, there was the distinctive southern culture that may have appealed to Michaux's own personality. Michaux was raised in and accustomed to the deferential, refined, and patronage-bound world of monarchical France, something that was more akin to the South's hierarchical slave society. Given Michaux's constant griping about the indifference of northern laborers, Michaux may have found the South and its more stratified society—and, indeed, its slave-based labor system—more amenable. Inequality, a pronounced aspect of French life, was far greater in South Carolina than it was in New York or New Jersey, something Michaux noticed immediately upon arriving. Michaux, embraced by Charleston's elite and even supported in his research by grants of unfree labor from his wealthy neighbors, surely enjoyed sitting atop the pyramid.[36]

Indeed, though unstated, the prominence and prevalence of slavery in South Carolina was likely a significant factor in Michaux's decision to lay down roots in a plantation society. The evidence, while not explicit, is strong. Free labor, at least the American version, confounded his scientific goals while in the North. Those complaints ended as soon as he landed in Charleston. The slave-labor system in South Carolina offered Michaux much more control than the labor system that had frustrated him in New Jersey. He took full advantage of it. Thanks to a federal census in 1790, we know, for instance, that Michaux held several people in bondage on his Goose Creek farm, some he purchased using funds from the French government, making them property of France, and others with his own funds.[37]

His botanical garden thus relied upon enslaved labor in a whole range of ways. Enslaved people manned the plows when Michaux was traveling, and, when he returned, they planted and cultivated many of the new species Michaux brought back. Their skilled but forced labor allowed his southern nursery to blossom and thrive, and their work provided the sustenance Michaux needed. It's important to remember and acknowledge that all of Michaux's accomplishments in North America depended upon his exploitation of unfree labor, something easy to miss if one were to rely solely on his diaries or correspondence because he elides his reliance on this system: in fact, in the eighteenth-century world, it was so commonplace and acceptable for someone like Michaux that he likely found it unremarkable. While the presence of the enslaved does not appear often in Michaux's records, there is a tangible record of their significance to his operations. One accounting of his South Carolina operations—done years later by the French Central Office of Accounting—estimated that 15 percent of his expenses may have gone to cover the costs of enslaved labor.[38]

As Michaux settled into this southern environment in the fall of 1786, a year after his arrival, there was no doubt that, after a slow and uncertain start, his American mission was beginning to thrive. Michaux had founded not one but two gardens in the king's name, one accumulating flora from northern climates and another from southern ones. Michaux busied himself filling the soil with the seeds and specimens he acquired. He also sent several shipments of material to France, meeting his mandate.

According to one estimate, he exported more than five thousand trees and several large batches of seeds in that first year alone. His collecting also included animals he thought might thrive in France and add to its culture. He captured ducks, turkeys, partridges, and other birds and carved out a half acre of land to breed them on his South Carolina plantation. As he planned his future work, he promised his superiors that he would expand his animal collection to include larger game, such as deer, and even vowed to search for a buffalo to export to France.[39]

Still, though Michaux had worked at a frenetic pace in his first two years in North America, he was never one to rest on his laurels or slow his speed. In April 1787, as spring weather awoke plants from their winter slumber and brought forth a bounty of colorful blossoms, Michaux's attention turned from setting up his operations to his primary mission. This was, in the words of the king's instructions, to "introduce [to France] . . . all of the trees and forest plants which nature has given, up to the present time, only to foreign lands." Sitting at his southern base and surrounded by this enticing environment, his imagination raced with what sat waiting for him to discover. It was time to strike out into these foreign lands.[40]

❖ 4 ❖

A Botanist Unleashed

1787–1791, The Southeast

"The base of my actions is to make abundant collections with the greatest possible economy," Michaux wrote from Charleston in December 1786. He would do just that in subsequent years, striking out into what he called "the most interesting area in all America; that is to say, Georgia, South Carolina, and North Carolina." Eventually, Michaux traversed more areas of eastern North America than likely any other person alive. What he discovered in his eastern travels, and the rumors of what lay just beyond, would eventually spur him to pursue even farther horizons.[1]

Michaux launched his first major botanizing foray on April 19, 1787. When he left Goose Creek, the country in which he now resided was in crisis. Americans from Georgia to Massachusetts remained torn over the best way to govern their new nation. Many, including Michaux's new friend George Washington, worried that the Articles of Confederation created an inadequate government, unable to meet the challenges of the nation. As Michaux headed into the forests, reformers like Washington were preparing to convene in Philadelphia to debate a change of government, a gathering that would, in a few months, produce the US Constitution. Michaux, though, paid little heed to the politics that surrounded him. Instead, while most Americans watched for news from Philadelphia, the botanist stayed focused on his mission. Michaux spent the winter months of 1787 at Goose Creek, planning for his venture to Georgia and the southern Appalachian Mountains.[2]

As he prepared for the trip, he realized that he would need more than just his own hands to collect and cart material. He decided to take his son, who had started to show a greater interest in his father's scientific pursuits, and an enslaved man as assistants. While the individuals whom Michaux brought with him would change in the years to come, the model Michaux created for this first expedition became the one he would follow in the future. He always traveled with a very small group, and he often relied on the labor of an enslaved person and the knowledge of local Indigenous guides to make his fieldwork successful. As Michaux's journal makes evident, the contributions of Indigenous guides and enslaved people to his work were vital to advancing knowledge, just as was Michaux's own training and leadership.[3]

Michaux did make one unusual decision on this first expedition. He invited another botanist to join his team: John Fraser from Scotland, who was then in South Carolina conducting his own research. At first, it appeared like a smart choice. Fraser had already spent several years in the country, so Michaux assumed his local knowledge would prove a boon to his first expedition. He soon regretted his decision, however, finding Fraser's training woeful. "His lack of knowledge in natural history, in areas he wanted to collect, especially plants and insects, made him collect in large quantities objects of little value and already well-known," Michaux vented to his diary. Fraser, it appeared to Michaux, was nothing but a poorly trained hack.[4]

Michaux, though, hid his frustrations and maintained a cordial relationship with his apparently inferior partner. The group traveled extensively throughout eastern South Carolina and Georgia. Michaux filled his packs with the species he collected and diligently recorded all he did in his journals. He had one special objective in these early days: finding the rare *Franklinia* that he had seen in the Bartrams' garden. All the *Franklinia* seeds French botanists had planted had failed to thrive, so Michaux's superiors asked that he find a living specimen in its natural habitat to see if its seeds might have better luck in French soil. At one point in southern Georgia, when Michaux suspected that they were close to the home of the rare plant, he urgently sent his son, his enslaved laborer, and Fraser to comb the area in search of the tree. Michaux, meanwhile, remained laid up at an inn nursing a badly infected insect bite. The scouts returned empty-handed, and the *Franklinia* remained elusive.[5]

Michaux's infection was serious. He almost never slowed, but this ailment kept him confined for several days. It was but one of several tribulations

Michaux encountered in this hunt for plants. He faced off with snakes, dealt with pestering insects, had his horses stolen by rogues, and confronted other dangerous beasts. "Alligators," he noted at one point on the trip, "are in abundance in the rivers, torrents, and swamps of Georgia and even in the Carolinas." While all these obstacles threatened to end the journey, the loss of his horses on May 15 provided Michaux with an unexpected piece of good fortune. When the group awoke that morning, they found their horses had vanished. At first they were unsure whether the horses had escaped or been stolen, but then they heard about a gang of horse thieves led by someone named "the Captain." The Captain was killed by vigilantes a few days after he stole Michaux's horses, but many of Michaux's horses fled during the melee, leaving Michaux unable to recover his property. Nonetheless, the theft did have one advantage for Michaux. Without enough horses for all his crew, he found a reason to part ways with Fraser in Augusta, Georgia.[6]

Fraser was unfazed by the change of plans and continued to collect on his own. And, as it turns out, Michaux, always the perfectionist who preferred solitary work, may have been a bit too harsh on his fellow traveler. Fraser was already well-known in Great Britain when Michaux met him, but he achieved even greater acclaim in the years that followed because of his botanical discoveries in the Carolinas. He brought more than thirty thousand specimens back to London and identified several plants for the first time. He even won the confidence of Michaux's supervisor, Comte d'Angiviller, who asked him to introduce a new species of grass into French gardens. Fraser's collecting, too, was not for science alone—something Michaux might have failed to grasp. He established a large and successful commercial nursery in London that, much like the Bartrams' garden in Philadelphia, boomed as the hunger for foreign plants grew among the middle and upper classes of Great Britain. The demand for Fraser's plants was so great that he eventually opened his own four-hundred-acre garden in South Carolina to grow plants for his British customers, essentially a botanical manufactory that fueled his London operations. Future botanists inspired by his exploits named several plants in his honor, most notably the Fraser fir, which graces many American homes at Christmastime today. Even though their partnership failed, that a Scotsman and a Frenchman, aided by a young boy and an enslaved man, ventured into the backcountry of the United States tells us much about the international and intercultural nature of eighteenth-century science and the range of people involved in the enterprise.[7]

After parting from Fraser, Michaux spent the next four weeks scouring western Georgia and the mountains of southwestern North Carolina for new plants. He now traveled unimpeded by his disappointing Scottish counterpart. Instead, he was aided by two Native American guides whom he recruited to add a new, and more useful, knowledge base to his crew. The complicated negotiations that Michaux went through to hire these Indigenous escorts further displays the polyglot, often contested, but also potentially collaborative nature of eighteenth-century science on the borderlands of North America. On June 9, Michaux met Louis Martin, a fellow Frenchman who had established himself within South Carolina's hierarchy. He now served as a deputy surveyor for the state and, through that, had an intimate awareness of the terrain and its people. Martin brought Michaux into the mountains that, Michaux noted, "separate the state of Carolina from the Indian nations of the Cherokees, Creek, Chickasaw, etc." Michaux's objective was to venture into this foreign territory, but he realized that he would need escorts to help him navigate both the physical and political landscape of a country controlled by Native Americans.[8]

To do so, Michaux decided to recruit local Native American guides. Martin introduced Michaux to two Indigenous men whom he thought might provide Michaux with the assistance he needed, but the men balked at what they considered his paltry offer. Instead, the two sides agreed to meet the following day to see if they could hammer out an agreement. Although Michaux never identified the Native nation with which he was working, it was most likely a Cherokee band, given the location in which he was operating. In a clear signal of their suspicions of Michaux and his intentions, the potential guides arrived to the meeting with a large retinue, including their chief, who was to serve as their community's negotiator. This larger group likely included elders in addition to their appointed spokesperson, and their involvement was meant to make sure key leaders heard directly from Michaux so that they could collectively agree on their community's willingness to support him and to set the parameters of his trip.[9]

At this June 10 meeting, Michaux outlined his objectives to the Native American leader and his prospective escorts. "I wanted to visit the sources of the Keowee River and the Tugaloo River that unite, forming the Savannah River, . . . and that I wanted to go as far as Tennessee," he told them. In response, the chief asked for fair compensation for their time and knowledge: a blanket and petticoat and six dollars a day for each guide. Their terms also exposed Michaux to the distrust that had developed between Europeans and Native peoples after nearly two centuries of colonization. The chief demanded that Michaux provide half of the pay in advance "because many other white men had deceived them." Michaux acquiesced. The next day, before heading off, he added another key companion to his expedition, a young Carolinian man who had lived among Native communities and was fluent in their languages and customs. He would make sure Michaux could communicate with his guides and others they met along the way.[10]

With the team assembled, Michaux headed into the Appalachians and spent until June 19 exploring the area, traveling through several Native American villages, collecting material, and recording observations. Along the way, he learned about the strife between Native peoples and European colonizers, as well as rivalries between Native nations. When he arrived back in Charleston, for instance, he noted, "I learned upon my return of the hostilities begun between the Nation of the Creeks and the Georgians." The white elites of Charleston shared local gossip that the Cherokees with whom he had just visited were now poised to join with the Creeks in an alliance to fight back white settlement. Michaux's first venture into the southern interior, then, introduced him to the violence, uncertainty, and fear that defined many interior regions—a combustible combination that Michaux would encounter again in a few years and that he would try to leverage to advance his country's geopolitical interests.[11]

Michaux also learned another important lesson on this trip. He would have to use Indigenous knowledge if he was to be successful in his future treks. Though Michaux rarely wrote about the Native Americans he knew, his diary and financial accounts show that he hired Native individuals for most of his journeys and relied upon them for safe passage. In fact, there are strong hints that Michaux's aptitude with linguistics meant that he learned some Native American languages, an advantage that further aided his research. His Indigenous guides often shared their own knowledge of plants and their usefulness with Michaux, and Michaux would pass on some of their medicinal remedies to his colleagues in France. Such contributions by Native Americans were essential to eighteenth-century natural history, but, as is evident in Michaux's own case, these individuals rarely received credit for their work—and, indeed, often went unnamed in extant records.[12]

Although Michaux's company may have improved with the loss of Fraser and the addition of expert Indigenous guides, when Michaux finished his work in June, he concluded that his venture into the Appalachian Mountains was a bust. "Not only did I have the displeasure of finding few new plants in these mountains in comparison with those collected recently in Georgia, but I didn't see a single bird of interest," Michaux griped. Disappointed but undeterred, he continued his work, heading next to Philadelphia, where he met with the city's French consul and talked about his recent travels with his friend William Bartram. He then went to New Jersey to inspect his operations there. Always the perfectionist, Michaux had some complaints about Saunier's work, and the two seemed to clash over how to operate the garden. After his visit, Michaux confided to a French colleague that whenever he made a suggestion to Saunier, "he shouts and makes a sermon that I can trust him that he will do the work and I should not even think about it." Michaux's approach to his management problem in New Jersey was to largely ignore it and instead focus on his Goose Creek plantation, so he left Saunier in charge and returned to his southern base in September. By the time Michaux arrived home, he had traversed more than two thousand miles, more than six hundred of which were in the field as he conducted research. Along the way, he had collected enough material to send several boxes back to France, including hundreds of trees carefully packed in pine needles, an innovation he developed to better protect live trees making the rough Atlantic crossing in the holds of ships.[13]

Michaux's travels in 1787 established an annual pattern. Every year, he set out in the spring on a major expedition to explore areas of North America, mostly in the South. He then returned to his Goose Creek home, where he would study and cultivate the plants he had found. Each excursion is worthy of its own book because of the risks he took and the discoveries he made, but, as is typical with the stoic Michaux, the commentary in his journal entries is so straightforward that his adventures appear rote and almost unremarkable. The editors of his journals noted, for instance, "he probably had a sense of humor, but, unfortunately, it appears in a very few places in his journal." Only by reading more deeply into his notes and finding other sources documenting the importance of his research and the travails he faced along the way does the true significance of his fieldwork become apparent.[14]

His next trek began in February 1788, when he headed farther south to Florida, into what was then East Florida and in Spanish hands. The Spanish

Crown was controlled by Bourbon relations of King Louis XVI and closely allied with France, so much so that they joined France in aiding the Americans during their revolution against Great Britain. Perhaps this connection made Michaux's travel into what was considered foreign territory easy; there is no evidence that he encountered any trouble in crossing the border and he traveled freely. Perhaps, also, these borderlands were so permeable that such ease of movement was common, at least in this period of relative peace. In any case, he was unimpeded in his pursuit of his main objective to explore the area around St. Augustine. Once again, he brought along his son and a small group of enslaved men, some whom he enslaved himself and others whom he "rented" from his neighbors. He ended up spending almost six months in the field, traveling in dugout canoes on the coastal waterways and inland rivers and by horseback through southern Georgia. Michaux was enamored with what he saw.

Though it was relatively easy for Michaux to enter Florida, he still needed to perform the kinds of diplomatic gestures expected of someone traveling on an international scientific expedition. On April 18, soon after Michaux arrived in St. Augustine, he called on the Spanish governor, Vicente Manuel de Céspedes, to let him know about his mission. The governor showed great interest in Michaux's work and supported it, so much so that the governor paid Michaux a personal visit on April 20 to review Michaux's collections. The governor was so impressed that, later that day, he invited Michaux to dine with him to continue the conversation, and Michaux enjoyed an afternoon "in the gardens of His Excellency with the hospitable ladies of his family." Michaux, in turn, gave the governor a box of seeds meant for the royal gardens in Madrid, another act of botanical diplomacy, and one that also, perhaps, symbolized the familial ties of the Bourbon Spanish and French Crowns. It was a connection that was, unbeknownst to both men, about to sever. Later, after his travels in Florida, he gave his new friend another gift. He named a new genus of flowering shrubs, *Lespedeza,* that he found after the governor (the genus's name was a misspelling of Céspedes's last name).[15]

But in the meantime, the approval of the governor opened other doors. Michaux also visited the lush garden of the self-taught botanist, sometime pirate, and overall eccentric Jesse Fish. He was awed by what he found in this remote outpost. Fish's life trajectory mirrored the ever-changing, dynamic geopolitics of North America—and the way some people could cash in on this instability. Fish was born into relative anonymity in New York in the 1720s, and, after taking to the sea for an opportunity to improve his lot, he landed in Florida in his teenage years and never left. When Michaux met him in 1788, Fish lived alone on Anastasia Island and had managed, through various legal and illegal means, to become one of the richest men in the region. His island (he owned the entire spit of land, along with additional acreage on the mainland) sat opposite St. Augustine and served as a barrier between the intercoastal waterway and the Atlantic Ocean. Fish's success was a remarkable accomplishment for someone who lived in one of the most tumultuous regions of North America. In his almost fifty years of living in Florida, he had endured at least three changes of government, from the Spanish control he knew when he arrived, to British in 1763 after their victory in the Seven Years' War, and then back to Spanish after the British defeat in the American Revolution. In between, a new nation had formed to the north in the area of his birth. He had done more than survive the chaos, though. He had thrived. Hustlers like Fish always seemed to do so in these nebulous regions where law and governance were at their weakest.

A character such as Fish was sure to develop into a legend, and indeed, he did. He amassed great wealth and land, and there was likely truth to rumors that he accomplished his success through cunning and backroom dealing. "He emerges as a sinister figure, an insidious schemer characteristically involved in contraband commerce, sedition, and illicit land transactions," writes Robert Gold, a historian of what he has dubbed "the Fish legend." Gold, after digging through the archival record, found that there was a far more complicated story to Fish. Rather than simply a daring pirate and profiteer, Fish was an astute and calculating businessman who succeeded in spite of—or perhaps because of—the volatility that defined this area of imperial contestation. To have thrived in this environment, to have navigated the turmoil and the swift succession of different political regimes, was a mark of distinction.[16]

Michaux's firsthand account also painted a far different picture than the legend. To Michaux's eyes, Fish was a sophisticated and self-taught botanist who turned his island into a massive botanical entrepôt filled with exotic plants imported from around the world. "This man, who was the most hard working and most industrious in all of Florida, had turned his place into a paradise despite the several pillages by pirates to which he had been exposed and the revolutions that he had twice experienced," Michaux commented after spending a day with Fish on his island and hearing about his time living through two turbulent transfers of power. His island was lined with groves of olive trees, dates, lemons, and oranges, all of which were native to areas far beyond North America. Here, on the very fringes of European settlement in North America, Fish's garden displayed the truly international nature of eighteenth-century botanical exchange and how this enterprise involved so many types of people, not just the elite-born. Fish's operations proved a great success. His produce, much of which he exported to the United States, gained great renown. His oranges, the seeds of which he had received from India four decades before Michaux's visit, were so memorably sweet that François André Michaux still raved about them years later. His father was left in awe.[17]

Fish was just Michaux's introduction to Florida. The entire region captivated Michaux, and its biodiversity almost overwhelmed him. On a Sunday about halfway through his travels, he took stock of his accomplishments. It was an impressive haul: 105 plants or trees collected since March 1; of those, he noted, "40 species whose genera and species are known to me," "36 whose genera are well known to me but whose species are doubtful or unknown," and a whopping "29, the greater part are unknown or could not be determined." As always, Michaux's travel was often difficult. Alligators, bad water, weather, and thick plant life plagued the expedition. At one point, Michaux and his men took to eating cabbage palms so they could preserve their bread for more desperate times. But he persevered and returned to his Charleston home loaded with living plants and seeds that he planned to cultivate in his garden and send to France. One of the many plants he brought back was the rare *Illicium parviflorum,* a decorative shrub that emits a wonderful fragrance and is also known as the yellow anise tree. It was quickly adopted by his neighbors in South Carolina and proliferated throughout the region. By November, he had packaged at least three separate shipments of material to France that held more than one thousand different specimens, many of which were drawn from his Florida trip, including species of magnolia, rose, hibiscus, plums, and several types of trees.[18]

The next year, in February 1789, he traveled even farther afield. Michaux knew that the Caribbean had its own unique microenvironments, and he expected that its islands were home to plants undocumented by

Europeans. On February 16, 1789, he left Charleston's wharves aboard the schooner *Hope* and headed for the British-controlled Bahamas. He landed ten days later at New Providence and beat a quick path to the governor, Lord Dunmore, to explain his mission and receive permission to travel unencumbered. Dunmore's path to the Bahamian governorship was, much like many of the elite Michaux met, shaped by the changes wrought by the revolutionary age. Years earlier, while serving as the royally appointed governor of Virginia, Dunmore played a central role in the opening salvos of the American Revolution. Fearlessly faithful to King George III, Dunmore received the ire of the revolutionaries for his offer to free enslaved people in exchange for their fighting for the British. He was chased out of Virginia, but for his loyalty to the Crown, he received an appointment as the royal governor of the Bahamas.[19]

Now, more than a decade removed from the turbulent events in Virginia, Dunmore enjoyed his Caribbean paradise and showed little ill will toward a Frenchman living in the former British colonies. He, like the other governors Michaux had met, welcomed the botanist to his home and told him he could explore the island freely—so long as he shared some of his findings with Joseph Banks of the Royal Society, a requirement Michaux gladly accepted.[20]

Michaux, as usual, went straight to work. He was guided in his Bahamian forage by the writings of an earlier pioneer, British natural historian Mark Catesby. Catesby had explored the British colonies in the 1720s, on a mission very similar to Michaux's. Like Michaux, he chose Charleston as his base, and he traveled throughout southeastern North America, including the Bahamas. After returning to England in 1726, he spent seventeen years documenting what he saw in a series of meticulously illustrated volumes titled *The Natural History of Carolina, Florida and the Bahama Islands.* Catesby's London-based publisher, recognizing the internationalism of Enlightenment science, published the text with two columns, one in English and the other in French, a language that often served as the lingua franca in Europe. By the time Michaux arrived in Charleston, he had devoured Catesby's work, now almost sixty years old but still considered the definitive account of the region's flora. Michaux had in fact made references to it on his earlier trip to Florida, comparing species he observed in nature to those he had seen in Catesby's work. As he embarked on his Caribbean expedition, he harbored hopes that he could supersede, or at least add significantly to, Catesby's work. Doing so would establish Michaux's name alongside that of this botanical legend.[21]

By March 8, Michaux had amassed a collection of 860 trees. He spent the next month bouncing between the surrounding islands. When he left New Providence for Charleston at the end of March, he carried seeds from at least seventy-five species and carefully shipped around 1,500 living trees to his South Carolina nursery. Though the numbers may seem impressive, his excursion proved to be something of a disappointment for Michaux. "I recognized," Michaux reported to Angiviller, "all the trees cited by Catesby, with the exception of only two or three species." Catesby's work, a disappointed Michaux recognized, remained definitive.[22]

In addition to these ambitious expeditions into foreign territories, Michaux regularly took several shorter jaunts in the southeastern United States, including one in June 1787 to the hills of northwestern South Carolina, near the North Carolina border. In a roundabout story that nonetheless encapsulates the type of work Michaux performed on all his expeditions, Michaux discovered a plant nearly as elusive as the *Franklinia.* Its scientific name is the *Shortia galacifolia,* but it is known more colloquially as the Oconee Bell, a name that refers to the region in South Carolina in which it is found and the drooping shape of its white flower, which resembles a small bell. His discovery of it, just one of hundreds of new species Michaux identified during his tenure in North America, went largely unremarked by Michaux at the time. Long after his death, however, its rediscovery in Michaux's files would spur a botanical quest for a living example that would consume several decades of scientific inquiry in the nineteenth century. A nineteenth-century botanist called it "perhaps the most interesting plant in North America." Some even dubbed finding the *Shortia* in nature "the botanical equivalent of the Holy Grail."[23]

Michaux's discovery of this unusual plant near the Keowee River provides a snapshot of the work an eighteenth-century botanist undertook. Nature itself was a botanist's laboratory. Trekking across terrain, enshrouded by a leafy canopy, a botanist was enveloped in his study—perhaps even overwhelmed by it. Michaux had to sift through all the data surrounding him, inspect dozens of leaves, trees, weeds, grasses, and flowers as he walked, and keep his eyes open for the unusual in this sea of green. On the Keowee River that day, Michaux's years of study served him well. He recognized that the flower now known as the Oconee Bell was an undocumented species as soon as he saw it.

Michaux carefully cut a leaf and stem and preserved the specimen in his herbarium. Herbariums were the most important tool for botanists working in the field. A herbarium was usually a bound volume filled with blank sheets of paper. In it, botanists affixed carefully dried leaves, petals, and other evidence to document a plant's physical characteristics. They also provided a written description of the plant and, if it was new, tried to appropriately classify it according to the emerging standards. Michaux's herbarium was thus more than just a collection. It was his legacy. It created an official record of his work, and its content would form the foundation for the book he intended to publish. He expected this publication to be the most complete account of North American flora ever compiled and that it would place his name among the pantheon of great natural historians. Ultimately, his herbarium contained more than two thousand species, of which this yet-to-be-named flower would be one of the several examples previously unknown to European eyes.[24]

After Michaux placed a specimen of the plant in his herbarium, however, it failed to attract much attention among all of his other discoveries. The herbarium itself eventually landed in a Paris library. In 1839, an aspiring young American botanist named Asa Gray visited the library and changed the history of botany. As he thumbed through the volumes, he recognized nearly all the plants Michaux collected. Then Gray came across an unusual plant, the one Michaux had captured by the Keowee River. Although it was decaying, there was enough left for him to be sure that it was unknown to him and to science. Gray became obsessed. His rediscovery of the plant set off a race to find a living specimen of what he called *Shortia galacifolia.*[25]

Determined to find an example himself, Gray followed Michaux's only clue, a vague note that he had found the plant in the "high mountains of Carolina." In 1841, Gray spent weeks hiking throughout the 5,000-foot-high elevations of western North Carolina with two friends. His efforts proved futile, and in the three decades that followed, dozens of people scoured the mountains for the Oconee bell. The hunt, driven by Michaux's clue, focused mostly on the high elevations of North Carolina. Eventually, in 1877, a seventeen-year-old boy accidentally rediscovered the *Shortia* along the Keowee River in the much lower elevation of Oconee County,

South Carolina. It turns out that Michaux's phrase "high mountains" was relative—likely, in his earliest voyages, the 1,000-foot hills he encountered set against the Keowee River Valley seemed large.[26]

Even if *Shortia*'s story is one of rediscovery, its initial acquisition encapsulates a truism of Michaux's work, something that his journals and correspondence make clear to anyone who reads them. He was voracious, scooping up as much as he could, and he remained driven to identify and discover as much as he could for science. Every year he sent shipments of live plants and seeds to his superiors, including dozens of unclassified plants similar to *Shortia,* fueled always by the twin goals of adding to knowledge and bolstering his country's standing in the world of science. Michaux's nationalistic and competitive streak appeared regularly in his reports. He paid attention to European rivals, at one point worrying about "two ignorant men sent by nurseries" in England, "who pick up everything and send some also to Mr. Banks." Such rivalries also fueled his sense of urgency. "I would like that France beat the English in publishing these discoveries," he confided to his friend and mentor André Thouin after traveling with Fraser.[27]

Michaux's seemingly contradictory position on scientific pursuits—one that embraced internationalism while also holding onto nationalism—reveals a key aspect of scientific culture driving research during the age of the Enlightenment; indeed, forces that may still shape science today. Michaux was, on the one hand, a natural historian who wanted to share knowledge across national boundaries. Not only did he invite Fraser on his trip in 1787, he also readily sent seeds to Banks after he heard that the Brit was interested in what he was finding. Nonetheless, national rivalries spurred a competitive race to receive credit for original discoveries as a way to boost the reputation of one's nation. Indeed, in November 1789, Michaux learned that his efforts at advancing knowledge by identifying new plants had borne fruit. An international group of scientists recognized one of the plants Michaux had brought back from his Persian expedition as a new species. As a result, its genus would carry Michaux's name. Perhaps even better, people in France were enamored with the flower. "You have probably learned," André Thoiun, Michaux's teacher, wrote to him, "that botany has a new genus that bears your name (Michauxia). It is your beautiful Campanula, which you brought back from the Near East and which we cultivate in our gardens."[28]

In that same letter, Michaux received other news that would forever alter his mission's direction. The French Revolution had broken out. His friend in Paris assured Michaux, an ocean away, that little would change for him, boasting of the Revolution's principles and raving about the country's prospects. The Revolution had, he told Michaux, "shaken its fist at the ministerial despotism." Thouin was thrilled to see that the nobility had their "aristocratic privileges" stripped and that the church had been compelled to cede its property to the new government. Most of all, he noted, "this memorable revolution was accomplished with hardly any loss of blood." The future, he predicted, was bright. "When you return to your country," he promised Michaux, "you will not recognize anything; everything changes and thank God to the satisfaction of the good patriots."[29]

Thouin was right. Everything was about to change for Michaux.

❖ 5 ❖

Revolutionary Disruptions

March–December 1792, Charleston to Hudson Bay

The initial cheerful reports of the French Revolution proved far too optimistic. The French Revolution, and with it the overthrow of the Bourbon dynasty, put Michaux's mission in deep jeopardy. Under the old regime, Michaux had no trouble receiving money from French consuls in the United States or drawing on credit backed by the French Crown. With the rise of the National Assembly in 1789 and the uncertainty that followed, Michaux's sources of funds dried up in 1790. His dire straits forced him to halt his botanical excursions. Things looked even bleaker at the start of the next year. "If the difficulties continue," Michaux complained in January 1791, "it will be necessary for me to return to France." The difficulties would continue, but so would his travel, and those expeditions would, in turn, spark grand new ideas for his scientific mission.[1]

At first, though, the uncertainty surrounding the French Revolution and Michaux's finances forced him to pause his costly annual expeditions. Instead, he turned inward, to his garden, and cultivated the plants he had already acquired. His nursery blossomed, and Michaux invested more energy in it than ever before. Michaux kept a detailed account of all the seeds he planted in 1790. It was an extensive and diverse list that included specimens he received from as far away as China. Like so many other southern plantations, though, its success and productivity relied upon the steady work of enslaved people. The federal census of 1790, taken during Michaux's sedentary turn, captured the size of his plantation operation. Michaux used at least twenty-four enslaved people to work his land, and the census recorded that a woman also lived on the grounds—her identity remains a mystery. Michaux certainly owned several of those twenty-four slaves, while he may have borrowed or leased additional hands from his slave-owning neighbors, a common practice. His accounts show that he also regularly employed day laborers and others to help in the field.[2]

Indeed, the importance of enslaved labor is subtle but always present in Michaux's journals and was certainly a major part of his daily life. In some cases, for instance, Michaux would make no comment about his fellow travelers when he left on an expedition, but their presence and various roles would gradually become apparent through passing references to them in his journal. "I continued my explorations while my black man was busy digging up the trees I had shown him," Michaux recorded on December 5, 1788, while traveling through Georgia, for example. Though Michaux was in his fourth week of fieldwork when he wrote those words, that entry was the first time he noted the presence of at least one enslaved man in his expedition. And then there are other entries in which he uses the royal "we" without clarifying who composed his small exploring group or that he "sent someone" to perform an important task. Such references, scattered and vague though they may be, collectively show all the ways in which Michaux regularly and systematically depended upon enslaved people to conduct his science.[3]

The census also captured an important absence at his home. His son had returned to France in February 1790, due to a gruesome eye injury. On September 20, 1789, while François André was on a walk near their Goose Creek farm, a hunter aiming at a partridge misfired and hit him in the left eye. Michaux summoned the best doctors available to try to save his son's eye. First, one doctor bled François André in an attempt to purge any infection from his body and reduce swelling. Draining his veins, though, had no effect on treating his eye. On September 30, ten days after the accident, François André remained in debilitating pain and the irritation around his eye had gotten worse. Another doctor came and this time made an incision in the eye, reducing the inflammation and perhaps saving the eye. Concerned that his son might lose his sight, Michaux sent François André back to Paris to receive the best medical care. His son would remain in France and witness the French Revolution firsthand. His departure, though, left Michaux short of a key staff member and even more reliant on his enslaved laborers, who had no doubt also become well-trained experts in botany.[4]

To the north, Michaux's relationship with Saunier remained sour. Michaux eventually used the strong-arm tactic of threatening to fire Saunier in order to cow his recalcitrant employee into compliance. "He does not consider himself under my direction," Michaux groused; "only when I gave him the choice of quitting the service or following my instructions did he behave better." Saunier was not an explorer like Michaux. He was more an overseer, and because of his experience working for the Crown in France, he may have dismissed Michaux's expertise, believing that he was superior. Michaux, nonetheless, would send him seeds he found to grow and would try, with obvious difficulty, to direct Saunier's priorities. Their personal relationship aside, Saunier did continue to produce. During the 1780s and early 1790s, Saunier sent shipments of material from his garden both to France and Charleston.[5]

The disruptions of the French Revolution eventually reached American shores and interfered with Michaux's well-honed nursery operations. In 1791, Angiviller, Michaux's mentor and supervisor, advised his protégé to sell the two nurseries and return to France. Michaux decided against the recommendation. He refused to abandon the "rare collections" that he had risked his life to acquire. Closing his gardens would have been, he recounted years later, a travesty for science. It would have left his country "deprived of the fruit of expenses which had been incurred for several years." Michaux thus took the tack that many do when their superiors make a suggestion with which they disagree: he ignored it. "As this order was not officially communicated to me," he confessed several years later, "I eluded it."[6]

Without money, however, Michaux struggled to keep his South Carolina nursery afloat. Eventually, the intendant of the civil list, operating under the direction of the French revolutionary government, sent him unambiguous orders that he had to sell the farm and return home. Because he could not ignore these instructions, he instead sought delay. He pleaded for more time, explaining that he needed only a few months to complete his work. In the meantime, he received encouraging reports that some members of the National Assembly wanted to save his two gardens. Michaux, still short on funds, managed to stave off a sale by negotiating a cost-sharing arrangement with an agricultural society in Charleston. He promised to share exotic seeds, plants, and fruit trees with the society and publish a memoir on how to grow these plants in exchange for funds to maintain the garden. They also made him a member of their honorary society, a roll that included other luminaries like Thomas Jefferson and George Washington.[7]

The State of South Carolina went even further in trying to retain Michaux and sustain his garden. They likely recognized the important role the garden played for their state, similar to what New Jersey had made clear in the special law they passed permitting Michaux to open a garden in their state. Michaux had introduced new species into the landscape, become enmeshed with the elite, and established a botanical garden that raised the reputation of South Carolina on the international stage. The state government, thus wanting to formally and permanently integrate Michaux and his talents into their community, offered to fund the garden if Michaux agreed to become an American citizen. It would be a patronage relationship similar to the one Michaux had with the king of France, though with a different provider lording over him. Always the Frenchman first, however, he refused to renounce his allegiance to France.[8]

Loyal though Michaux may have been, France's revolutionary government paid little heed to their devoted citizen posted to the American countryside. Members of the French Assembly were focused on internal affairs and advancing their agenda to radically reform French governance. If they were focused on international matters, it was in the realm of diplomacy and strategy, not funding a natural historian to conduct botanical expeditions on remote shores. Michaux's hopes that the government would restore his position were further dashed when Comte d'Angiviller, his supervisor, primary supporter, and main correspondent, fled Paris, perhaps in response to King Louis XVI's failed attempt to escape the angry mobs in Paris. The continued uncertainty surrounding Michaux's position made it impossible for him to secure any funds from his usual sources. The French consul in Charleston, always Michaux's first stop for cash, turned down his requests for money because he too was unsure about the future, and American financiers refused to accept notes offered in the king's name because they worried that they would never be repaid. Short on cash, Michaux eventually had no choice but to put the Charleston garden up for sale in March 1792. Only a friend's generosity preserved it. A fellow French émigré, the Charleston-based merchant Jean Jacques Himely, purchased the farm and gave it back to Michaux as an act of charity. To the north, Saunier managed to keep the smaller New Jersey garden alive, likely by commercializing some of his work. He also appears to have secured the independence from Michaux that he had long sought: after 1792, there are no records of him sending any shipments of plants to France.[9]

Aside from dealing with the financial fallout of the French Revolution, Michaux also had to confront the political changes wrought by it. It appears that Michaux's initial impression mirrored that of his peers. In letters back to France, he professed sympathy for the revolutionaries and embraced their republican values. Some biographers have speculated that his immersion in democratic and republican American society may have conditioned him to embrace the French Revolution. We know that he hobnobbed with many veterans of the American Revolution, both among the elite in the seaports and on his travels throughout the American woods. Michaux was clearly impressed with what he saw in the young United States, a society bubbling with ideas very similar to those put forward in the early days of the French Revolution. He, like Americans reading reports from Paris from afar, assumed in these heady early days of the French Revolution that his countrymen were simply establishing what he saw and enjoyed in the United States.[10]

At the same time, because Michaux left so few pieces of clear evidence, there is an alternative reading of his apparent and quick embrace of revolution. Rather than an ideologue, Michaux might have been a pragmatist. For one thing, despite his admiration for leaders like Washington and some elements of American society, he was also critical of some outcomes of the American Revolution, like the irreverent free laborers who had frustrated him in the Northeast. He himself had matured and thrived in a world in which deference to authority was the means to acquire patronage, and patronage was necessary to make a living, or at least to pursue one's work at the highest levels. What we might consider sycophantic today was what one needed to do to receive backing from kings and courts. Michaux displayed a talent for these performances of obsequiousness. Prior to Michaux's departure for America, there is no hint that he ever questioned the monarchy. Indeed, the evidence is quite the opposite. He praised and embraced it—and the French Crown rewarded his efforts. Michaux offered no hint of any frustrations with the French monarch after arriving in the United States. In fact, he continued to send special gifts to members of the king's family to show his appreciation for their support. It would only follow, then, that his continued reliance on the government for funds meant that Michaux would profess the same devotion to the French Republic as he had to the Crown.

Ultimately, given the scant evidence, we may never know Michaux's inner thoughts, especially in the earliest period of the French Revolution, though it seems probable that he, like many of his peers in America, held out hope for the prospects of a French republic. What we can say for certain is that Michaux's commitment to his scientific mission never wavered in the face of revolutionary tumult. Even as revolutionary forces buffeted him and jeopardized his mission, Michaux remained devoted to botanical research. In fact, the uncertainty wrought by the French Revolution created an unexpected opportunity for the intrepid explorer. Indeed, the government's inattention freed Michaux from the strictures of supervisors and the constraints of patrons, and an independent Michaux was finally able to pursue his own priorities. His unfettered actions say a great deal about what drove the man. Rather than rest on his laurels or stay planted and immersed in his botanical gardens, Michaux decided to strike out on his own to continue his scientific explorations—indeed, he became even more ambitious. It should be noted, though, that even if his status in the French government remained uncertain, Michaux nonetheless remained devoted to his country. When he traveled, now unencumbered by official orders, he still acted with France's interest in mind, writing to colleagues about what he found and trying to advance knowledge and increase his country's scientific prestige.

As Michaux took stock of his work, he noted a serious shortcoming. Like Catesby before him, he had focused most of his work on the southeastern regions of North America. He had traveled throughout Georgia, Florida, the Carolinas, and Virginia. He had even toured parts of the Caribbean. He had covered New York City and the northern New Jersey region well. He had also seen, and been uninspired by, parts of New England. Looking at a map, though, a large swath loomed unexplored, the area once called New France but known then, as today, as Canada. The allure of traipsing through territory largely untapped by other Enlightenment-era natural historians beckoned the ever-curious Michaux. In March 1792, he "set out without delay," as he recounted years later, "for those countries bordering upon the arctic pole." It promised to be his longest and most dangerous expedition yet in North America.[11]

After setting his sights on Hudson Bay, Michaux began a mad scramble to find funds, something in very short supply for the Frenchman who had lost his royal patron. Michaux headed first to Philadelphia. As usual, he visited the Bartrams' garden and spent an evening with some of the leading scientists in America, including Benjamin Rush and Benjamin Smith Barton, two fellow natural historians with deep interests in botany. But no support materialized. He then traveled to New York, where he found his financial situation to be as dire as in Charleston. The French consul and other financiers turned him away. Finally, he decided to call in some debts, including a very old one. During the American Revolution, Michaux had invested in a Boston-based firm that transported arms to the American rebels. He was supposed to receive a third of the profits, a whopping £28,000, worth the equivalent today of perhaps £3.7 million in 2023 currency. The money had never been paid, so he planned to call upon his partners now. Once again, he struck out. There is no evidence that he ever succeeded in recouping his investment.[12]

Having failed to acquire the support needed for his Canadian expedition, Michaux turned to his last possible source: his own coffers. Some of Michaux's own personal capital was bound up in the humans he enslaved. Just as the labor of enslaved people had allowed Michaux to collect and grow a huge variety of plants in South Carolina, they now provided Michaux with the money he needed to continue his scientific research. "I sold three of my blacks, acquired with my own money, in order to pay the expenses of a journey to Canada," Michaux recorded in his journal.[13]

After the sale of the men, Michaux traveled to New Haven, Connecticut, in early June to meet with Peter Pond (sometimes referred to as "Pound"), a man whose experience he admired and who could give Michaux guidance on his impending journey. Pond had, as Michaux related, "lived nineteen years in the interior of America," traveling extensively throughout Canada. Pond and Bartram were correspondents who exchanged scientific information, and it is likely that Bartram told Michaux to visit the trader to better understand the needs involved in trekking to Hudson Bay.[14]

Pond had bad news. If Michaux had planned to join fur traders, he had missed his window. They always left Montreal by the end of April. Michaux remained resolute, however, and left for Canada a few days later, on June 7. He headed up the Hudson River at his own pace, always carving out time to study his surroundings for new plants. By July, traveling variously by boat, foot, and canoe, he reached Montreal. Michaux once again entered a city whose inhabitants were still reeling from the political tumult of the preceding decades. It was a polyglot culture, much like the sites of his previous expeditions in Spanish Florida and areas of the United States itself. It was filled with French people who had settled when it was French Canada, but, since 1763, it had been governed by the British, whose cultural influence was growing and mixing with the French. Of course, Indigenous peoples were the largest single population and had a significant presence inside the colonial cities and largely controlled the areas outside of them. In short, while the specific languages and cultures may have changed, the need to navigate many different cultures and peoples remained constant from Florida to Canada. These were skills that Michaux had gained in his first expedition to the Middle East and had honed further during his earlier North American journeys.

As usual, the Montreal elite treated Michaux like a foreign emissary whose mission made him worthy of official recognition and special attention. He met several dignitaries, observed British troops mustering, and became acquainted with locals who dabbled in natural history. He then headed farther north to Quebec. There, a doctor who shared Michaux's interests taught him a trick that improved his ability to study flowers. Dr. John Mervin Nooth, an amateur natural historian living on the fringes of European settlement in North America, showed the far better-trained and cosmopolitan Michaux how to transform a telescope meant to study the heavens into a microscope that could capture the minute details of a flower's surface and its reproductive elements. He was, like Jesse Fish in St. Augustine, an international man of science who performed innovative research but was living in what, to Europeans, seemed like a backwater.[15]

Michaux also made an important hire in Quebec. He needed an Indigenous interpreter to help him negotiate the cultural barriers that he was sure to confront as he headed farther into the interior. Most Native peoples in this area spoke a dialect of the Algonquian language family, and Michaux, while likely conversant in some Algonquian languages in the Southeast, was starting from scratch with these groups. He realized that he needed help, just as he did when he traveled in the Southeast. In Quebec, as he planned for his larger expedition, one of his contacts introduced him to a young boy—probably a teenager—who was of European and Native descent and conversant in both his Indigenous language as well as French. Throughout North America, there was a long history of children being raised with fluency in both worlds precisely so that they could serve as cultural go-betweens. Michaux thought the boy would be perfect for the trip and offered him a job.[16]

Michaux and his interpreter left on July 31 for what Michaux called "the trip into the interior," meaning the area north of Quebec to the southern tip of Hudson Bay, a region that had remained largely unexplored by a trained botanist like himself. Michaux knew that he needed more than just an interpreter for this leg of his journey. He needed guides who could navigate the rugged northern landscape. He headed to Tadoussac, a prominent fur-trading village a bit farther north than Quebec on the St. Lawrence River, where he hired three additional and experienced Native American guides who were also likely Algonquian speakers.[17]

Michaux consulted with his expanded team, and they devised a strategy for surviving the dangerous terrain that lay before them. The safest passage, his guides assured him, was by canoe along rivers and streams that connected Tadoussac to Hudson Bay. After determining the route, Michaux decided that they could make it there and back in one season, forgoing the prospect of wintering somewhere. Such a short timeline, though, meant that it was critical that the team keep to a tight schedule. If he and his men took too long, winter weather would set in and could prove deadly—such mistakes had and would continue to cost the lives of intrepid Europeans venturing to the Arctic.

The Canadian expedition was by far Michaux's most daring gambit yet—and perhaps too ambitious. His objective was still to fulfill that original charge to document as much of North America's natural history as possible, though now, without a Crown lording over him, his drive to discover compelled him northward. It was surely the greatest test yet of his expeditionary skills. He gave himself only a couple of months to paddle about one thousand miles with just four other people. His journey resembled that of another Frenchman who had successfully undertaken a similar expedition before: Father Charles Albanel, who had done so more than one hundred years prior, in 1672. As with Michaux in the 1790s, French interest in understanding the North American continent spurred Albanel's mission. In this earlier case, the French governor of New France, Jean Talon, wanted to explore Hudson Bay for cartographic knowledge and to see if it could prove useful for two of France's imperial aims: trade and conversion.[18]

It is unlikely Michaux knew much about this earlier journey. If he had, then he would have known that Albanel's journey took significantly longer than Michaux had planned for his own, and Albanel's entourage was much larger, including two other Europeans, sixteen Native guides, and three canoes. Michaux's Native American guides, though, were surely aware of the risks and shared them with Michaux. Still, Michaux remained confident and left for Hudson Bay in early August. Soon after leaving, however, he confronted the dangers of such travel. One of their first challenges was to navigate treacherous river rapids. He survived unscathed in large part because of the knowledge of his Native guides. "They are skillful at avoiding the dangers at being carried away or knocked against the rocks or finally being overturned," Michaux said of his crew's canoeing skills afterward. As they surmounted numerous hazards, including racing rapids, waterfalls, long portages, and other obstacles, Michaux took a private dig at his European peers who might imagine that they could do the same. "The trips are frightening to those who are not used to them, and I would counsel the little dandies from London or Paris to remain at home," he confided to his journal. Perhaps these cautious words—some of the most pointed Michaux ever expressed in his journals—suggest that he, too, was more nervous than usual.[19]

Throughout, Michaux always found time to botanize. He had brought along his journals and herbarium, carefully wrapped in sealskin to protect its priceless contents from water. He recorded observations on almost every day of the journey. As they floated past riverbanks, he noted species and took excursions into the woods to explore. He was disappointed in what he found. Just as in New York, he found these northern climes lacking in novel or interesting vegetation. "As to plants," he summarized in a report written afterward, "I did not find an abundance of new species, as in more temperate latitudes."[20]

Other aspects of his expedition proved more rewarding. He saw a plethora of new-to-him animals: reindeer, beavers, muskrats, and many different birds. More than anything, though, the grandeur and sheer beauty that surrounded him was unlike anything he had seen before. His journal entries throughout the journey are longer and more descriptive than ones from earlier trips. His prose, too, had an almost literary tone, a sign of his rapture with the natural wonders he saw. "It would be difficult to form an idea of the majestic perspective of this one," Michaux wrote of a waterfall the group encountered deep in the Canadian interior. "It is a natural amphitheater in whose bottom we can only see trees, as well as on its sides, and it enlarges at its base to about 1,600 feet and with a depth also of 1,600 feet. One can see countless rocks in the midst of the disturbed water, broken and reduced to fog like thick smoke."[21]

As the group made their way farther north, the weather began to change and pose a grave threat to the expedition's future. Michaux had left Quebec knowing that he had a very brief window in which to make his sprint to Hudson Bay, but that window closed even sooner than he had anticipated. By the end of August, usually among the warmest times in South Carolina, hints of winter appeared. "The cold was bitter, the sky overcast for the last two days, and the rain like melted snow," he noted on August 31. A few days later, the first snow fell. Morning frost soon became a regular impediment. Michaux, accustomed to warmer weather, struggled with the cold. "Although I was better dressed," he wrote one night, "I still found the cold unbearable and had a fire made."[22]

On September 2, after suffering through a daylong hailstorm, Michaux and his team decided they needed to pick up the pace. "The Indians and I wanted to get to Mistassini as soon as possible for fear that the snows and cold would become worse," he noted in his journal. At Lake Mistassini, the Native guides promised, they would find swift rivers that could carry them north into Hudson Bay.[23]

The group covered more than two hundred miles in the next four days, an impressive clip. They made it to the lake and then headed northwest, still believing they could arrive at their intended destination in time. On September 5, they camped near what Michaux called the Atchouke River. No European map has ever contained such a name, so it was surely a phonetic spelling of what his Native guides told him. In 1948, a French botanist fascinated by Michaux's story explored the remote region to determine how far he reached. He concluded it was likely a tributary of the Rupert River near the 51st parallel. Wherever precisely Michaux was, we do know that he was tantalizingly close to Hudson Bay. Michaux's guides estimated it would take four more days to reach its shores, but there was a catch. Because the currents of the river ran northerly, their return trip would take ten days. With snow and hail falling almost daily, they told Michaux that the next leg was too risky. Instead of forging ahead, the group turned around.[24]

Years later, when Michaux recounted the decision to turn back, he explained that his companions refused to plow ahead. He cast himself as the resolute explorer frustrated by unwilling escorts. "I was extremely desirous of extending my researches to the sea," Michaux wrote, but "my guides represented to me that the country would soon be covered in snow, and our return, if delayed, rendered dangerous, and perhaps impracticable. I yielded to these representations."[25]

His journal tells a somewhat different story. His daily logs are filled with accounts of bitter cold, horrible weather, and constant precariousness. The entries he made, just a few days before the group decided to return, captured the looming dread enveloping Michaux and his companions. "It was overcast in the morning but developed into a melting sleet. The cold was less intense," he wrote on September 2; "despite the hailstorm that went on all day, we continued our journey as the Indians and I wanted to get to Mistassini as soon as possible for fear that the snows and cold would become worse. We had to cross three lakes and traveled about 25 miles."[26]

The next day was little better. "The frost was approximately a line ($^3/_{32}$ of an inch)," he noted the morning of September 3. "By midnight I saw white frost on all the shrubs and plants near the hearth where we were camping. The weather appeared better at least during the day, but around seven o'clock it became cloudy, and we had rain, alternating with hail and snow with intervals of radiant sunshine." With winter fast descending on them, the group raced back to French settlements. They set their sights on Lac Saint Jean, the northernmost trading post in Canada. If they reached it, then they knew they would find safe harbor. On their outgoing leg, it had taken them fourteen days to travel from Lac Saint Jean to Lake Mistassini. They covered the same distance on their return in seven days. Michaux, though traveling at a speedy clip, still found time to collect or observe. Once at Lake Mistassini, they shifted their sights farther south, to Tadoussac, the large trading community on the St. Lawrence where Michaux had hired his guides a few weeks earlier. They arrived safely on September 19, and all presumably returned to their homes, including Michaux.[27]

He considered the journey a success, if only as a way to tempt others to explore. He amassed a large herbarium, though he suspected many of the samples he had collected were already known, and he also had what he described as "a rather nice collection of live plants" that he planned to ship to France, a sign of his continued devotion to his country even if his official status remained unclear. More than anything, he hoped that his expedition would encourage others to follow and explore more. As he recounted to his son, perhaps to prod him, "there are hundreds of unknown lakes." "It would be interesting to know the botany of this extremity of America," he continued, knowing that there was much more to do. Still, he knew that he would not be the one undertaking that arduous expedition. "I am happy to have visited these distant regions," he concluded, "but one makes this kind of voyage only once."[28]

Though Michaux always seemed to work at a frenetic pace, botanizing even under duress in Canada, he took his time returning to the United States, a sign, perhaps, that he needed to recuperate. He spent about two weeks in and around Tadoussac, two weeks in Quebec, and then another two weeks in Montreal. He botanized and socialized, likely enjoying the still strong French culture in Canada. He crossed the border into the United States on November 15 and arrived in New York on December 2. Four days later, he set off for Philadelphia to boast of his adventure with his friends there.

Michaux arrived in Philadelphia with more than just the tale of his Canadian expedition. He also carried an idea even bolder than his Arctic jaunt. As he returned from his trek in Canada, he reflected on what was left undone and set his sights on a more distant vista. The West beckoned. "Having visited the southern portions as well as the mountains of North America from Cape Canaveral in the south to Lake Mistassini in Canada," he explained to a colleague, "it remains to complete the task that I have imposed on myself and to complete my research to know the portions west of the Mississippi." He knew that this vast territory contained an unimaginable amount of information unknown to Europeans, and he knew that if he could be the first to collect and document the area, then his name—and that of his country—would find a permanent place in the pantheon of great scientific explorers.[29]

Michaux had begun formulating his plan almost as soon as he returned from the Canadian woods. While in Canada, he had interrogated Native and European fur traders about what they knew about the interior. What he learned only intrigued him more. "I spoke to Canadians who have seen the source of the Mississippi," he related to his son. "They met natives who had never seen a white man or Europeans, and other natives who brought them gold bells taken from the neck of cows from the areas established by the Spanish." The fur traders had also given him some alluring hints of the natural history finds awaiting whoever could successfully cross the continent. "They brought back to Montreal last summer two skins of a mountain lamb, which they say belongs to the genus of the llamas," he continued. All of these reports enticed Michaux's always inquisitive mind and fueled his perpetual wanderlust.[30]

Michaux, as before, remained financially strapped and was incapable of funding such an ambitious expedition himself. He knew, however, that Americans were captivated with the idea of the West—as were many in Europe. As Washington's promise to send seeds from Kentucky to his French friend Lafayette showed, Michaux's scientific peers in both Europe and America were fascinated by the bounty of new plants and animals awaiting discovery. They also harbored hopes that these finds could change current understandings of the natural world.

When it came to Americans' interests, there was more at play than just science, however. There was also lust for land and power. European nations had vied for control of the North American interior for decades. In the Seven Years' War, France and Great Britain clashed near modern-day Pittsburgh in a contest over control of the Ohio River, the main artery connecting the eastern seaboard to the interior. During the American Revolution, Americans, many from Virginia, pushed settlement into the fertile Ohio River Valley. When Michaux entered Philadelphia, the federal government had just established Kentucky, the new state abutting the Mississippi River. To the west lay Spanish Louisiana, a region previously controlled by France. Now, many Americans eyed the region jealously. They believed that the destiny of the young and growing nation rested in conquering this territory and expanding their republic westward. They were, in short, eager to conduct reconnaissance west of the Mississippi for the purposes of political conquest as well as scientific research. Michaux, armed with tales of his travels to the remote reaches of Canada and aware of these geopolitical and scientific concerns, planned to convince the intellectual elite of Philadelphia to invest in his new plan because it would serve these twin interests.

Within two days of arriving in the city, he was pitching his idea to members of the American Philosophical Society, the leading scientific institution in the new nation. Michaux had become friends with many of its most active and prominent figures, people like Benjamin Smith Barton and William Bartram. Enamored with Michaux's proposal, these APS members quickly introduced Michaux to perhaps the only person in Philadelphia who could turn his vision into a reality: Thomas Jefferson, secretary of state for the United States and vice president of the American Philosophical Society.

❖ PART II ❖

The Subscription List

My funds had at this time considerably diminished; and as I was anxious of continuing my travels, to complete the plan I had formed, I appealed to several members of the philosophical society of Philadelphia, and communicated to them my wish of travelling over land to the Southern Ocean.

—ANDRÉ MICHAUX

❖ 6 ❖

The Promise and Perils of the West

December 1792–April 1793, Philadelphia

Thomas Jefferson was many things: author of the Declaration of Independence; ambassador to France; the first US secretary of state; John Adams's vice president; and a two-term president of the United States. Throughout, he was also something else: an internationally renowned natural historian. Jefferson's mind exemplified the expansive character of natural history in the eighteenth century. He worked across many overlapping fields. He was a noted mathematician, an astronomer, a geologist, an inventor, an architect, a linguist, and an inveterate collector. He has even been dubbed the "father of American vertebrate paleontology" because of his research into fossils. As a plantation owner like Washington, he was also a practicing botanist and agriculturist who kept a detailed farm journal, regularly experimented with plants, and was an active participant in the international seed exchange.[1]

Jefferson's intellect was so impressive that the members of the American Philosophical Society, a body composed of the greatest American thinkers of the day, elected him to their Council in 1781 and eventually made him their third president in 1797. As such, Jefferson followed in the footsteps of Benjamin Franklin and David Rittenhouse, a polymath who was considered Franklin's heir as the leading American scientist. When the Society notified Jefferson that he was their choice for president, they explained that they desired to have Jefferson's "genius and knowledge" guide the institution. Doing so, they knew, would ensure that "our national name will preserve a distinguished place in the annals of science." Jefferson, after learning of the appointment, described the honor as "the most flattering incident of my life." Jefferson held the position until 1817, serving in the post at the same time that he was vice president and president of the United States.[2]

Michaux almost certainly had heard of Jefferson before he came to Philadelphia in 1792. In fact, some of Jefferson's closest French friends in Paris were Michaux's mentors, leading some to speculate that the two may have even known each other there. There is, however, no concrete evidence that they had ever met before this point, and, as it turns out, Michaux was barely in France when Jefferson was—he was either in Persia or in America. In any case, when Michaux entered Philadelphia on December 8, 1792, Jefferson was primed to hear his idea. At the time, Jefferson was engaged in a heated and protracted transatlantic debate with several of Michaux's scientific peers about the essential nature of the American environment. Jefferson had long fumed over the theories promulgated by the French natural historian George-Louis Leclerc, the Comte de Buffon, in the 1750s. Buffon claimed that the healthy European climate fostered larger, more advanced creatures, whereas the American environment produced smaller, weaker plants and animals. Implicit in Buffon's thesis was a commentary on societies and people. Many of those who embraced Buffon's arguments about plant and animal life also took it to mean that humans born in America were bound to be inferior to those in Europe. Buffon's provocative ideas, perhaps unsurprisingly, gained traction in Europe, especially in France.[3]

Jefferson, inflamed by Buffon's critique of America, made it a personal crusade to disprove his theories. Jefferson may have been a fervent Francophile, but he was always first and foremost an American nationalist. Buffon's thesis upset Jefferson so much because it struck at the heart of his political ideology. Jefferson saw the republican United States as a rising nation, purer than the corrupted monarchies of Europe, and believed the country was filled with an as yet untapped potential for greatness. Rather than a place of degeneration, as Buffon claimed, Jefferson believed it was an area of great growth, health, and even generation—where the seeds of the best ideas from the Old World, freed from the toxins of decadent Europe, could blossom in the unique American environment. He distilled his beliefs in his *Notes on the State of Virginia,* the only book Jefferson ever published. Jefferson penned this treatise in 1781 in response to queries from another French natural historian, François Barbé-Marbois, who, like so many other Europeans, wanted to learn more about the climate and culture of North America. In it, Jefferson chronicled the dynamism of his home state's environment, geology, and horticulture, clearly trying to undermine Buffon's argument. Jefferson continued to tweak the text until he finally published it, not coincidentally, in 1784 in Paris. His intended audience was clear. He wanted to change the minds of the French cognoscenti.[4]

Michaux, Jefferson realized, could serve his interests. Michaux's plan to explore the West promised to produce even more fodder for Jefferson's rebuttal to Buffon. One of the reasons Jefferson became fascinated with the American interior, at least for his scientific purposes, was because he had faith that the evidence he needed to prove the superiority of the American environment was awaiting discovery in the West. Since at least the 1760s, European travelers to the Ohio River Valley, primarily traders and diplomats, had returned to the East with large bones that belonged to gigantic animals that no one had ever seen. The idea of extinction as a phenomenon had yet to gain traction, so Jefferson believed that such enormous skeletal remains came from undiscovered animals still roaming the American interior. These fossils provided Jefferson with evidence to disprove Buffon, but Jefferson wanted more. What he really sought was living proof of these species, and Michaux's trip could furnish just that.

There was, of course, more than just science driving Jefferson's interest in the West. Politics also infused his imaginings. At the very moment that Michaux returned from Canada, America's first party system was forming. It was a strange situation, pitting old revolutionary allies against one another and, in this case, members of the same presidential administration. In one camp stood Jefferson; in the other stood Washington. Although Jefferson served in Washington's administration, he had grown wary of its policies. He hated many of Washington's centralizing economic plans that strengthened the hand of the executive branch and empowered the federal government. He saw Alexander Hamilton's creation of a federally supported national bank as betraying the democratizing principles of the American Revolution. Instead of creating institutions that dispersed power, wealth, and influence to the people, the bank seemed to be focusing such things in the hands of the federal government and among the few. It was a system that to Jefferson resembled the worst of what he had seen in Europe and one that he thought the American Revolution had rejected.

Jefferson had a different vision for the country. The decadence and luxury that he observed in European cities were a sign of a decaying society. Instead, Jefferson and his compatriots believed that a republic needed to encourage small farmers—"yeomen," as they were called then—to check the tendencies of the mercantile and financial elite centered in the eastern seaports. A country filled with small farmers tilling their own ground, according to Jefferson, would produce greater levels of equality and guarantee the personal independence of citizens. Such widespread but relatively equal property ownership, Jefferson held, was necessary to sustain a democracy. Indebted citizens dependent on commercial trading, he feared, would never be free from external influences that might affect their pursuit of the public good. For Jefferson, then, the future of the young United States did not rest in the financial power of a national bank or in a trading empire based in the port cities but in its land. In fact, Jefferson had become so disheartened with the Washington administration that he was quietly forming a faction in Congress led by his protégé James Madison to oppose the very administration he served.

At the same time, Jefferson knew that his vision faced a dilemma. With a fast-growing population, he realized that land, though seemingly plentiful, was certain to become a scarce commodity. As population density grew, he feared that all the ills of urbanity would creep into American society. The West solved Jefferson's problem. That vast territory could serve as a different sort of bank, the type that would support and preserve his vision for the American experiment by providing a safety valve for Americans anxious to secure their own piece of ground. Michaux's trip could thus provide Jefferson with much-needed reconnaissance on what this promising territory offered. In Jefferson's mind, scientific exploration was essential to this expansionary vision of the United States' future. Michaux's expedition was thus a potential means by which Jefferson could advance his agenda.

It is unclear when, precisely, Jefferson first learned of Michaux or his proposed western expedition. Michaux's often meticulous journal becomes frustratingly confusing in the early days of this visit to Philadelphia. When Michaux was in the field, he made near-daily entries that noted every species he saw and recorded other important observations that might be useful to him or other scientists later. Sitting in Philadelphia, unable to conduct his botanical work, he put his diary aside—at least, that is what it looks like to scholars trying to make sense of it. His entries are sparse and often misdated. Most likely, he backfilled entries, conflating timelines and events when he did so.

What is clear is that Michaux shared his idea to make a western voyage with his friends at the APS very soon after arriving in Philadelphia. He knew three things when he met with APS members: he was short of money; he wanted to continue his scientific pursuits by heading west; and his excursion would take around two years and would thus need financing. He also realized that the APS and its members might have the wherewithal to back his expedition. It is unlikely that he made a formal presentation to the APS, as the early minutes of the Society make no note of it, and they are usually quite accurate. Instead, he probably sounded out his close friends and fellow botanists, people like Benjamin Rush, William Bartram, and Benjamin Smith Barton, who were also among the most active and influential members of the organization. "My funds had at this time considerably diminished," he recounted, "and as I was anxious of continuing my travels, to complete the plan I had formed, I appealed to several members of the philosophical society of Philadelphia, and communicated to them my wish of travelling over land to the Southern Ocean," meaning the Pacific.[5]

When Michaux approached his scientific colleagues, he recognized that many of the APS members were fueled by the same impulses as Jefferson. As natural historians and as US nationalists, they were driven to explore the natural world in order to discover new knowledge that could also benefit their country. Many, if not all, shared Jefferson's vision of the nation as a growing one, and they knew that scientific expeditions were a key step toward doing so. Michaux thus directed his appeal to the APS members' sense of national interest when he asked them for support. Having been trained in the ways of patronage, he knew he needed to serve his funder's interests in order to accomplish his own personal goals. He therefore cast the operation as one of mutual benefit, one in which the expedition would produce new information useful to the country's expansionary interests while also advancing Michaux's reputation. "I proposed to several members of the Philosophical Society," he recorded in his journal soon after meeting with his friends, "the advantages for the United States to have geographical knowledge of the country west of the Mississippi and asked that they subsidize my journey."[6]

His pitch resonated. Word of it soon spread throughout the membership. By the end of December 1792, Jefferson had learned of it. He was thrilled. Jefferson himself had long pondered such an expedition. In 1783, as the

Revolutionary War came to end, Jefferson immediately turned his sights on the West. After winning a war largely fought along the eastern seaboard, the West was, in his view, where American attention needed to shift. He feared that the British had their own designs for capturing it and hemming in American ambitions, and he suspected that the British were organizing scientific expeditions into the territory as a front to surreptitiously establish claims to the territory. "I find they have subscribed a very large sum of money in England for exploring the country from the Missisipi to California," he confided to George Rogers Clark, a Virginian who had launched a successful offensive during the Revolutionary War that secured areas of the Ohio River Valley for Virginia and who would soon become entangled with Michaux. "They pretend it is only to promote knolege. I am afraid they have thoughts of colonising into that quarter," Jefferson concluded.[7]

Jefferson decided to beat the British at their own game, and he thought Clark the best-equipped person to do it. Clark had launched a successful offensive into the territory east of the Mississippi during the Revolution and seized the land for Virginia. After the war, he settled on the conquered ground in an area that became Kentucky, where he established a plantation and dabbled in natural history. Jefferson wanted Clark, a battle-proven leader of men and a fellow natural historian, to venture west with his own exploring expedition in order to stave off the British, an early display of how Jefferson's scientific interests were interwoven with his expansionary ones. Jefferson lobbied his friends in government for support but was disappointed in the "feeble" response his proposal received.[8]

Jefferson pursued an expedition into the American West with even more gusto in 1786, when he met an ambitious and daring American explorer in Paris named John Ledyard. Ledyard was born in Connecticut in 1751. Finding no inspiration in the New England countryside, he took to the seas. He spent most of his life traveling the world and even volunteered for James Cook's 1776 expedition to circumnavigate the globe. After Ledyard returned to Europe, US naval hero John Paul Jones, then living in France, introduced him to Jefferson, then stationed in Paris as a diplomat. Jefferson was amazed by Ledyard's stories and impressed with his wanderlust. Together, they hatched a daring plan for Ledyard's return to the United States. Instead of taking the easy route across the Atlantic, they decided he should return via Siberia and cross the North American continent from the west to the east. Ledyard set out for Russia from France in 1787. He made it to

Siberia before Russian officials, concerned about the intentions of a foreigner traveling in their midst, arrested him and sent him back to Europe. While Ledyard's Siberian excursion was a remarkable accomplishment in its own right, his adventure failed to meet Jefferson's primary goal. Siberia was not what most interested Jefferson. It was the interior of North America that excited him.[9]

Jefferson's vision remained unfulfilled, but the idea persisted. Finally, in June 1792, back in the United States and with the country on firmer footing, Jefferson lobbied his fellow APS members to back a transcontinental endeavor. Jefferson's idea gained traction, and some of the most prominent APS members reached out to their contacts to see if they would be interested in the project. As Caspar Wistar reported to a fellow natural historian in June 1792, "Mr. Jefferson and several other gentlemen are much interested and think they can procure a subscription sufficient to insure one thousand guineas as a compensation to any one who undertakes the journey and can bring satisfactory proof of having crossed to the South Sea." At some point in that same year, a young Virginian named Meriwether Lewis heard about Jefferson's plans and volunteered to undertake the journey Jefferson envisioned. Jefferson rejected Lewis's offer. He was, Jefferson estimated, too young and inexperienced.[10]

Jefferson, though, was ecstatic when he heard about Michaux. The French botanist fit Jefferson's bill better than any of his earlier options. Michaux's Canadian trip demonstrated to Jefferson that Michaux was capable of undertaking an ambitious expedition with very limited manpower. Even better, Jefferson realized that Michaux's nationality provided something that other options like Meriwether Lewis and George Rogers Clark did not: political cover. Navigating relations with Native nations in the West was one of Jefferson's primary concerns. When he considered Lewis's offer, he feared that an expedition led by an American would appear like an official state-sponsored trip and escalate tensions with Native American groups who would suspect the excursion was, in fact, an incursion into their territory. Even before Michaux came onto the scene, Jefferson had decided that whoever undertook such a voyage should travel very light, so as not to raise worries. "I told him it was proposed that the person engaged should be attended by a single companion only, to avoid exciting alarm among the Indians," Jefferson recounted of his rejection of Lewis's inquiry.[11]

As it turned out, Jefferson and Michaux were of the same mind when it came to conducting the voyage. Michaux planned to travel with a small party led by Native guides as he had done many other times. This time, he looked for men who could escort him to the Rockies (he referred to the mountain range as the Shining Mountains, the colloquial term that the Canadians used for it), a vantage point from which he believed, too optimistically as it turned out, that he could spy a clear path to the Pacific. "To accomplish this journey, I propose to ascend the Missouri from the Illinois Territory as far as the Point-Mahes," he wrote after meeting with APS members. "With guides of that nation I would reach the Shining Mountains and it is probable that on the point of elevation I would discover the rivers which flow westward to the Pacific Ocean." In short, Jefferson found Michaux perfect for the job.[12]

In the days that followed, Jefferson worked feverishly to make Michaux's idea a reality—dashing off letters, ideas, and instructions to friends. There was a reason for Jefferson's rush, aside from his general enthusiasm. A delegation of Native American leaders from Kaskaskia, a Native community near modern-day St. Louis, had just arrived in Philadelphia to meet with the federal government. These spokesmen came to strengthen relations with the United States while also securing their sovereignty. They worried about American encroachments on their land west of the Mississippi and wanted to talk to Washington about it. Jefferson, though, also saw in their visit an opportunity for Michaux. If the diplomats left Philadelphia happy, Jefferson speculated that they might be willing to escort Michaux. "The return of these Indians will afford Mr. Michaux an excellent opportunity of being conveyed to Kaskaskia in perfect safety and without expence," Jefferson told Barton, noting that "such a lift as this should by no means be neglected."[13]

Jefferson had reason for such optimism. One of the Native leaders in town was someone with whom Jefferson had forged a personal bond over a decade earlier. Their first meeting came at one of Jefferson's lowest points during the American Revolution. Jean Baptiste Ducoigne, one of the spokesmen for the Kaskaskias, was also one of the first people Jefferson ever dealt with in an official diplomatic capacity, a sign of the centrality of Native American relations to American geopolitics. Their first meeting came in 1781 at Jefferson's Charlottesville home. Ducoigne's twisting path to Monticello is emblematic of life in the interior and its politics. Ducoigne was likely born in the 1740s to a Rene Ducoigne, a Frenchman who had once been captured in war by the Cherokees and worked as an interpreter, and Elisabeth Michel Rouensa, the daughter of the Kaskaskias' chief. The Kaskaskias lived along the Mississippi River Valley and were a part of a much larger Native coalition known as the Illinois Confederacy. The Illinois were historically closely aligned with the French, distrustful of the British, and highly protective of their sovereign rights, especially to land.[14]

Ducoigne grew up in the Mississippi River Valley and rose to prominence in the 1760s, becoming a chief around 1767. Yet Ducoigne's own group's fortunes waned as a result of internecine struggles, conflict, and disease. The Illinois Confederacy's population had dwindled from a height of around 10,000 to 2,000 by the 1760s and perhaps as few as 700 people by 1775. The Kaskaskias were among the most numerous within the Confederacy, accounting for perhaps a third of the Illinois's numbers in the 1760s, but they too experienced a similar trend of population decline.[15]

Ducoigne, facing the onslaught of imperial powers, spent years leading his people in search of a more secure homeland. Unhappy with British rule, he took them to Spanish territory along the Arkansas River. When the American Revolution erupted and split American colonists from the British Empire, Ducoigne realized that he might be able to use the conflict between these two groups to his advantage and bring his people back to their ancestral homeland. Perhaps because he inherited French sympathies from his father, and with many larger and rival Native groups siding with the British, Ducoigne decided to throw in his lot with the Americans, hoping that an alliance with them would strengthen his position in the Illinois Country if the Americans proved victorious. His warriors defended American forts, provided material aid, and served as important emissaries to other Native groups. They worked closely with George Rogers Clark, the Virginian who in 1777 led a band of militiamen into the regions that are today Ohio and Illinois to confront the British and assert both American and Virginian rights to the land. Clark's success meant that Virginia now claimed control of the region, making the governor of the state the chief diplomat to several Native groups. For the Kaskaskias, Clark's victory had served Ducoigne as he had wished—Ducoigne and the Kaskaskias were now aligned with the predominant foreign power in the region.[16]

In 1781, Ducoigne decided to meet with Virginia's current governor to cement the alliance between the state and his people. He left his home near the Mississippi River with a small delegation that included his family and traveled four hundred miles to Jefferson's home at Monticello. By the time Ducoigne arrived, Jefferson was facing perhaps the gravest crisis of his governorship. British troops were bearing down on the state, and many, including Jefferson, feared that the capital might fall into enemy hands. Indeed, the situation was so grave that the Assembly had fled Richmond and resettled in Charlottesville, near Jefferson's home. A besieged Jefferson nevertheless found time to welcome Ducoigne at Monticello. He knew that the immediate press of events did not outweigh his long-term interest in the West.[17]

Perched high on the hill upon which Jefferson's manse rested and joined by their two families, the men opened discussions. Ducoigne began by recounting to Jefferson the history of his people and outlined their strategic desires. Jefferson responded with a speech that historians have regularly analyzed for what it says about Jefferson's views on American independence and his nascent views on Native relations. While Jefferson used some choice phrases, such as "We, like you, are Americans born in the same land, and having the same interests," the fact is that the bulk of their conversation was focused much more on the very practical and very pressing situation in the area Clark had recently claimed. Ducoigne declared his willingness to ally with Virginia and outlined the terms upon which he wanted to cement this relationship. The heart of the matter rested on mutual protection: Ducoigne offered to provide Clark with support if he needed it and, in turn, expected that Clark would help Ducoigne if need be.[18]

The ceremonial passing of the peace pipe that ended their conference symbolized their mutual affection and the alliance between the two groups. In a further gesture of goodwill, Ducoigne named the newborn son he had brought with him "Louis Jefferson." It was, the editors of *The Papers of Thomas Jefferson* noted, "perhaps the earliest among a great many namesakes." Their meeting went so well that Ducoigne may have even joined his Virginian allies in battle soon thereafter. We do know that he stayed in the region until the Battle of Yorktown in October, and Ducoigne, the records show, later served as the messenger who relayed news of the British defeat to Clark, then stationed in the Ohio River Valley.[19]

Jefferson, for his part, continued to remember Ducoigne and their meeting fondly—as well as its timing so close to his forced evacuation. When he heard of Ducoigne's arrival in Philadelphia in late 1792, he wrote to his daughter about it, reminding her of their earlier interactions. "One of the Indian chiefs now here, whom you may remember to have seen at Monticello a day or two before [British Lieutenant Colonel] Tarlton drove us off remembers you and enquired after you," Jefferson wrote. Jefferson also proudly and prominently displayed several decorative skins Ducoigne gave him in the foyer of Monticello. He did so, he told Ducoigne, "in remembrance of you and your nation."[20]

When Ducoigne and Jefferson met again in Philadelphia, the political situation for both men had changed dramatically, but the underlying issues that had brought them together in 1781 remained the same. In 1781, Ducoigne had been negotiating with the new government asserting dominion over the region in which he lived: the state of Virginia. The Northwest Ordinances passed by the Confederation Congress in the 1780s changed the power dynamics, removing the competing claims of various US states to the region by placing ownership in the hands of the national government. The adoption of the US Constitution in 1789 and creation of the federal government only strengthened this nationalizing trend. Ducoigne and his people thus had to deal now with the national government in their attempt to contain the Americans' expansionary impulses.[21]

Still, while the US government claimed to control the region, Ducoigne and others knew that there was a ferocious contest among various nations for ultimate dominance. Michaux, in fact, was about to enter one of the tensest and most complex geopolitical situations in North America. Americans asserted sovereignty over much of the region, but their hold was tenuous. Native warriors there likely outnumbered American troops. Great Britain, meanwhile, maintained its own strong presence in the region by manning forts in the Great Lakes region, contravening the terms of the 1783 peace agreement that had ended the War for American Independence. The British, desperate to reclaim their lost lands, used these installations as bases from which they could build alliances with Native groups in the Great Lakes region and undermine American authority. Their strategy was meant to strengthen their hand in the event of another war with their former colonies, something many assumed was inevitable.

Meanwhile, Spain possessed the territory west of the Mississippi, known as Louisiana. Worse, from the perspective of western Americans, Spain also controlled New Orleans and, as a result, the commercial use of the Mississippi River. For Americans newly settled in Kentucky and Tennessee, the Mississippi River provided the best outlet to ship their goods to market, and New Orleans was the main port from which they could export their products abroad. Spain, meanwhile, knew that the Americans sitting on the eastern banks of the Mississippi jealously eyed the fertile lands of Louisiana. The Spanish decided to contain this land hunger by placing high export tariffs on American products, essentially sealing the port off from American farmers looking to export crops abroad. Their hope was, in part, to discourage American settlement by making farming the land for profit less viable. Meanwhile, a cadre of French traders still lingered in the region, their allegiances always unclear, if they had any at all. Rumors constantly circulated that they wanted to foment rebellion so that the French government could reclaim the territory.[22]

While European nations competed for control, Native American nations tried to fend off these grasping hands and maintain their authority and autonomy. Multiple nations with their own distinct cultures and histories called this region their home. Some allied with the Spanish, others remained independent, some wished for a return of the French, while others leaned toward the British. Since the end of the American Revolution, several Native nations in the Ohio River Valley had joined in military alliances to resist the expanding American state. For about ten years, the region was marked by periods of great violence as Native nations tried to defend their lands and sovereignty against US encroachments. In fact, in 1791, Native American warriors dealt the American army led by Arthur St. Clair a devastating blow. It was one of the worst losses in US Army history and made clear the weakness and fragility of American power. The region Michaux was about to enter was, in short, a powder keg.

Of all imperial powers vying for dominance in the West, American authority was perhaps weakest of all. Reeling from St. Clair's loss, its few fledgling vestiges of authority, its army forts and small towns, were in constant danger of total collapse. Worse, the United States' ability to strengthen its position was hindered by Spain's control of New Orleans. Cut off from easy trade routes down the Mississippi, Americans' fertile fields might as well have been fallow. Many Kentuckians fumed that the federal government was too passive. To them, it appeared as if officials based in Philadelphia were unaware of, or at least unconcerned with, the issues citizens living in the West confronted. In truth, policymakers in Philadelphia were acutely aware of the troubles out West. They worried that the nascent American state was on the verge of crumbling on its frontiers and that, if that happened, Americans throughout the country would lose faith in the young federal government. The West embodied the hopeful future of the country for people like Jefferson, and losing control of it posed an existential threat to the nation itself for those trying to govern it.

The geopolitical jockeying in the region and among the people there was premised, then, on seemingly contradictory impulses. Great Britain, Spain, and many Native groups feared the rising power and long-term intentions of the Americans, who were seemingly amassing along their borders, primed to cross into and claim new territory. But the Americans themselves felt hemmed in, insecure, and under threat from the various forces surrounding them. Americans living in the Ohio River Valley and on lands abutting the Mississippi River, meanwhile, were bitter because they felt as if their federal government was ignoring them, while the federal government itself desired, but struggled, to establish its own authority in the region.

Ducoigne, for his part, had seen his own influence wane in the years since meeting Jefferson. He was still a chief of the Kaskaskias, but other Native groups, some relatively new to the region, like the Shawnees, took a more active and assertive role. Nonetheless, Ducoigne's embrace of the United States had paid some dividends. In 1791, a special act of Congress granted the Kaskaskias 350 acres in their ancestral homelands in what is today Illinois. Ducoigne wanted his trip to Philadelphia in the winter of 1792–93 to further solidify this alliance and bolster his people's standing—or at least provide them with a measure of protection. Of particular concern were the American settlers flooding into the Kentucky territory—they were, Ducoigne would say, "like mosquitos, and try[ing] to destroy red men." He knew that as Americans pushed onto land, tensions and conflicts increased. He had a solution, one simple to articulate but hard for the American government to follow. Ducoigne wanted clear borders to divide the two and for the US government to enforce them. "Keep them then on one side of the line, and us on the other," he told Washington in a bid to maintain peace.[23]

Jefferson, meanwhile, had gone from being a novice diplomat in 1781 to a master of the trade. After leaving the Virginia governorship, he had replaced Benjamin Franklin as the United States' ambassador (technically, minister plenipotentiary) to France from 1785 to 1789. He had then returned to the United States to serve as the nation's first secretary of state. One of his first acts was to sign, along with Washington and Secretary of

War Henry Knox, a treaty with the Creeks, who came from the Southwest (what is today parts of Georgia and Alabama) to New York in 1790 to receive better recognition of their land and sovereignty. This treaty was the first one signed under the US Constitution and a sign, much like Jefferson's meeting with Ducoigne in 1781, of the centrality of Native relations to the United States. Indeed, for grand strategists crafting the United States' future, Michaux's foray could provide them with useful reconnaissance that would help them devise strategies for expansion through diplomacy, acculturation, or, if need be, conquest.

Ducoigne's pending return home thus played perfectly into Jefferson's then-forming plans for Michaux. Jefferson knew Michaux was heading straight into a brewing maelstrom in which Native, Spanish, French, British, and US interests all vied for control. Given his experience with Ducoigne, Jefferson was confident that he could recruit this Native leader with diplomatic skills to escort Michaux. "To the town of Kaskaskia, the society will procure you a conveyance in company with the Indians of that town now in Philadelphia," Jefferson promised Michaux. Ducoigne offered something more than safe passage to the Frenchman. Ducoigne, it was hoped, would provide the French botanist with a tutorial on the dangerous animosities that existed in the Illinois Country. Making matters even easier for Michaux was the fact that Ducoigne could likely provide this education in Michaux's native tongue. Given his French father, Ducoigne was likely fluent in French as well as several Native American languages and conversant in English. Such linguistic skills reflected the variegated nature of life in the interior and were essential to those who achieved success in it.[24]

Before Michaux could depart with Ducoigne, though, he and Jefferson had to address several other pressing issues. The most immediate one was money. Without it, there would be no expedition. Jefferson knew he had to raise an enormous sum to support such an ambitious and risky initiative. On this front, Michaux's timing was just as serendipitous as Ducoigne's presence in the capital city. Many of Jefferson's closest confidants and professional colleagues sat primed to open their wallets for Michaux. Jefferson, as the person who most straddled the worlds of government and science, also sat perfectly positioned to launch a fundraising campaign of grand proportion and national import.

❖ 7 ❖

America's Scientific Institution

1743–1793

While Michaux's idea met with a warm reception when he pitched it to APS members in December 1792, enthusiasm alone cannot make something happen. That, in fact, is why Jefferson's earlier attempts to finance such a mission had faltered. Intrigued though Michaux's colleagues may have been, they nonetheless realized that the scope of his vision, and its price tag, were far beyond their individual means and grander than anything the APS had ever backed. The Society's largest endeavor up until this point had involved an experiment to introduce silk production into Pennsylvania in the years immediately before American independence. Even though that undertaking had received significant government and individual support, it ultimately failed. Much had changed since the 1770s, of course, and many APS members were eager to see their institution do more to advance knowledge that could shore up the foundations of the young nation. Michaux gave them the opportunity to see if they were up to that task.[1]

Thomas Jefferson was one of the most enthusiastic of these energized members. In 1792, Jefferson, alongside his duties as US secretary of state, also served as vice president of the Society. While it was the federal office that drew the Virginian to Philadelphia, it was the Society that captured his imagination once there. Jefferson was fresh off a four-year stint as the US minister to France. He had spent his years in Paris basking in the salon culture of the European Enlightenment, where intellectuals often met in private homes to talk big ideas. In Philadelphia, the Society's regular meetings created the same atmosphere as the gatherings he savored in Paris. An

APS meeting usually involved at least one presentation of important scholarship, likely a report of work done by a fellow member or experimental data that one of the members had received through their correspondence network, followed by discussion and much conviviality, often over dinner.

Michaux's arrival in town gave Jefferson a chance to harness the buoyant spirit of inquiry fueling the APS. Jefferson had two entwined reasons for wanting the APS to take charge of Michaux's mission. One was to serve the interests of the institution. If the Society could launch this expedition, and if it were successful, it would cement the APS's reputation as the central institution for American science. The other was political. Jefferson also saw the APS as part of a nation-building project. If the United States wished to match its European peers, if not to surpass them, then it needed to build flourishing institutions that mirrored those in Europe. In the same way that newspapers boasted of Michaux's New Jersey garden because it promised to rival the botanical gardens prominent in Europe, so too did Jefferson want the APS to establish itself on par with the Royal Society in London or the Academy of Sciences in Paris. With these twin objectives in mind, Jefferson started lobbying his fellow members to join him in supporting Michaux in what would be the Society's grandest undertaking to date.[2]

In many respects, Jefferson's vision for the future of the APS and its role in American society was the same one its founders held when they formed the organization in 1743. The 1740s were a propitious time for the British colonies. Colonists, having established the foundations for their society in the preceding decades, began building institutions to sustain their burgeoning communities. Schools blossomed; newly founded universities enrolled their first students; libraries opened their doors and lent their books; hospitals started operating; fire companies formed; fledgling outposts turned into bustling towns. The colonies also housed a vibrant, though nascent, community of natural historians like the Bartrams who explored the natural world around them. When Benjamin Franklin drew up the outlines of the APS, he explained that the time seemed ripe for it. "The first drudgery of settling new colonies," Franklin noted in his proposal to create the Society, "is now pretty well over."[3]

Though Franklin and his colleagues were creating a new institution in America, their core idea was in no way pioneering. They aimed to emulate the flourishing academies they admired in Europe. Like its European analogues, this American body was to serve as an information clearinghouse through which new ideas could be shared, debated, and disseminated to fellow members and other learned societies throughout the Atlantic world. As its mission stated, its primary purpose was "promoting useful knowledge," and its members, people Franklin called "the virtuosi or ingenious men residing in the several colonies," formed the heart through which these ideas flowed.[4]

By maintaining what Franklin described as "a constant correspondence," these members would solve a key problem hampering the advancement of knowledge in North America: dispersion. As Franklin complained, "from the extent of the country such persons are widely separated, and seldom can see and converse or be acquainted with each other, so that many useful particulars remain uncommunicated, die with the discoverers, and are lost to mankind." Its function was to ensure that any member's discoveries would be preserved and disseminated to others. These exchanges would, in turn, expand the collective knowledge of its members, who could then apply what they learned to their local community. For Franklin, then, the *American* Philosophical Society was a means to knit these disparate British colonies together to advance their mutual interests—a prescient, if not yet revolutionary, idea to unite the colonies.[5]

While Franklin established this organization in 1743, the truth is that the APS struggled to find its footing until after the American Revolution, largely because it proved too difficult to transcend colonial provincialism. Local Philadelphia members met in fits and starts during the 1740s and 1750s, but the APS never cohered as an active body of continent-wide members. Rival bodies sprang up sporadically because of the APS's inactivity. Eventually, in 1768, the APS merged with one of these competitors in what is considered its second founding. For most of its early history, then, the Society existed more as an interesting concept than a real thing. The idea of a continental association lacked cachet for colonists who were deeply loyal to the British Empire. Instead, most American thinkers still looked east, across the Atlantic Ocean, to British colleagues for advice and validation rather than to their colonial neighbors. Only in the 1760s, after facing the weight of a more assertive Parliament, did colonists begin to look to the north and south and start to think of one another as brethren.[6]

The tumult of the Revolution only made matters worse. The Society went completely moribund for much of the war, but that compelling idea first formulated in 1743 never died. In 1780, as prospects improved, the old members reinvigorated the organization by electing a new class meant to embody the future of the country. It was a bumper year: George Washington, Alexander Hamilton, Thomas Jefferson, and John Adams were among those welcomed to membership.[7]

After the Revolution, the APS's mission took on new meaning and greater importance. The Society's members realized that if the institution was to represent American science to the world, then it needed to function like its European counterparts. Its reinvigorated membership started to hold regular meetings. International correspondence increased, fueled by the connections forged between Americans and their European allies during the war. Jefferson and Franklin, both ambassadors to France and with an extensive correspondence network in Europe, were particularly active in this international outreach.

The creation of the federal government and its move to Philadelphia from New York City in 1791 only amplified the Society's growing influence. Its new headquarters, built in 1789 and partly financed by Franklin, added to its standing. The large red-brick building occupied a prominent place near the halls of national power, sitting on the eastern side of the State House yard; its northern walls abutted the Supreme Court building, and it was adjacent to Independence Hall, where the Congress met. This location provided the Society with the veneer of state sanction, and even those in government whose names were not on its membership roll knew of it and its activities.

The federal government's relocation also meant that many of its members, usually dispersed throughout the country, were now just a few steps away. Virginian James Madison, for instance, was in town as a leading member of Congress, but he had been an active, if distant, member of the APS for years. Though rarely noted by his biographers, who rightly focus on his political accomplishments, Madison was also deeply immersed in natural history, especially botany, and was very engaged in the international exchange of seeds. Madison was a proud APS member (elected in 1785). He even undertook an expedition with Thomas Jefferson on behalf of the APS in 1791 to study the Hessian fly, a scourge that had destroyed wheat crops in New York and New England. Today, the Society's Library houses Madison's farm journal, a gift from his wife, Dolley, and a sign of the significance of the APS to the Madisons.[8]

Many other APS members were elected because of their natural history pursuits and were also in Philadelphia on government business. There was, of course, Jefferson. And there was also Michaux's new friend Washington. Washington, in fact, remained devoted to agricultural experimentation even as president. He turned sections of the Presidential Mansion, located a few steps from Independence Hall at the corner of Sixth and High Streets, into a botanical research center. The manager of Mount Vernon sent Washington seeds for him to use, as did others in town. The natural history work he did in his Philadelphia garden likely offered Washington an escape from the pressures of the presidency. It also allowed him to make his Philadelphia residence resemble Mount Vernon, the place to which he regularly expressed a longing to return.[9]

The list goes on. John Adams of Massachusetts occupied the vice presidency of the country. His election to the APS in 1780 had left a mark on him. He was so impressed with the Society after being elected that he encouraged the formation of a peer organization in Boston, the American Academy of Arts and Sciences. Washington's attorney general, Edmund Randolph, another Virginian, was elected in 1791. New Yorkers Alexander Hamilton (secretary of the treasury) and John Jay (chief justice of the Supreme Court, who was among those elected in 1780) were on the member rolls; Bay Stater and Secretary of War Henry Knox joined the membership in the same year as Randolph.[10]

With the fusion of government, policy, and science in Philadelphia, the Society's most active members realized that their institution was uniquely positioned to support the nation's strategic interests. They began offering "premiums," prizes for scholars who provided the best answers to pressing societal needs. Their contests were a mix of applied science, practicality, policy, and institution-building. One call asked innovators to create a safer and more efficient fireplace, while another requested reformers to design an educational system best suited to sustain a democracy. All were meant to better American society through the creation and application of knowledge.[11]

Michaux, versed in the ways such organizations functioned in Europe, recognized the APS's burgeoning role and the opportunity it presented him, but there was another element shaping the Society's activities to which Michaux's proposal spoke. A study of the Society's members shows that while there were some very prominent Federalists, most of its membership, especially its most active Philadelphians, were of Jefferson's political persuasion. It's unclear why so many APS members were Jeffersonians. There are, however, several possible explanations. For one, Jefferson's presence and personal friendship surely carried influence. More than that, the perception that the Washington administration's agenda emphasized industry, urbanization, and oceanic trade may have struck natural historians as at odds with their own priorities. They were, like Jefferson, less interested in the world of finance and more interested in the life of the mind. They wanted to discover more in the natural world in North America, not conquer foreign markets, and many of their experiments were meant to improve agriculture and husbandry. An agricultural republic, rather than a mercantile and commercial one, was more aligned with their own research interests; in fact, there was likely a relationship between their scientific agenda and their vision for the country. Another core tenet of Jeffersonianism was an abiding fear of government becoming too active in private affairs. Instead, Jefferson and his acolytes believed voluntary associations composed of citizens, rather than federal dictates, should marshal resources to promote civil society, something demonstrated by the APS's "premiums." The members were proud of this autonomy, so when Jefferson heard of Michaux's proposal in 1792, he felt that it was incumbent on the APS, rather than the federal government, to back the endeavor.[12]

With the APS poised to act, Jefferson and his allies got to work in January 1793. They knew that Jean Baptiste Ducoigne and the other Native envoys from Kaskaskia would return home in the early spring, so they had only a few months to complete three essential tasks: raise the funds needed to underwrite the expedition, establish the scientific priorities of Michaux's mission, and create a plan for its operation. It was no small task. Jefferson's first step was to forge agreements with Michaux on money and priorities, a challenge for two very independently minded men. In early January, Jefferson asked his fellow APS member and natural historian Benjamin Smith Barton to start initial negotiations. Later in the month, as the sides came closer together, Jefferson joined the conversation. They quickly identified three thorny issues that they needed to resolve.

First, Michaux dropped hints that he desired to return home to South Carolina to check on his Goose Creek plantation before heading west. Jefferson feared that if he left Philadelphia, they would miss their window of opportunity with Ducoigne. Barton rushed to Michaux's place to convince him to stay. "I visited M. Michaux. He assures me that he will relinquish all thoughts of his journey to S.C., and that he will engage in his scheme, as soon as you think proper," Barton reported back to Jefferson. Michaux, an experienced traveler, recognized the unique opportunity presented to him. "He seems much pleased with the prospect of having so valuable a guide, to Kaskaskia, as the one you have pointed out, and will be happy to have an opportunity of conversing with the Indian, whenever you shall appoint a time, for the purpose," Barton continued.[13]

Then there was the matter of money, often the most difficult issue to work out. In this case, Michaux's price tag seemed reasonable. Barton once again received good news from Michaux. He wanted little, at least as it appeared to Barton. "I have ventured, this morning, to be very explicit with my friend on the pecuniary head. He seems content to undertake the arduous task (for such it, undoubtedly, is) with a very moderate assistance in the off-set," Barton assured Jefferson.[14]

Yet Barton's initial optimism proved overly so. Money became a real sticking point. The proud Frenchman grew concerned that the revolutionary French government might view any remuneration he received from a foreign entity as a treasonous act. Michaux also wanted to operate without external orders—what he saw as constraints—by Jefferson or others. As he told Jefferson, "In order to have more freedom to act and to take the course that will be imposed on me by circumstances, I would prefer to undertake this expedition at my expense."[15]

Michaux, cash poor but richly motivated, still knew that he needed at least 3,600 livres (French currency) to underwrite the expedition's start-up costs. Although it is hard to put that value into current currency, one livre was approximately what a laborer could expect to earn in a day in 1789, so it was equal to 3,600 days' work, or more than ten years of labor (a goldsmith could expect five livres a day, in comparison). For Michaux, it was a healthy sum, but no windfall. Barton hit upon a novel solution. Instead of offering Michaux APS funds directly, the institution would instead loan Michaux the back pay that Michaux believed the French government owed him for his recent work. Receiving this sum became a non-negotiable point for Michaux. "If I am not assured of the sum before departing Philadelphia, I will not undertake this expedition," he stated in unequivocal terms to Jefferson.[16]

Although Michaux was nervous about collecting anything that might look like a salary from the APS, he showed no scruples when it came to accepting a large cash prize from the organization if he proved successful. He was taking an enormous risk, and he welcomed a reward for accepting—and surviving—that challenge. Michaux told Barton of his hopes. "Upon his return, he supposes (provided he shall make discoveries of interesting importance) he shall be entitled to something handsome," Barton related of his discussions with Michaux. With that, the general outlines of the expedition's financing took shape, balancing Michaux's desire to appear independent of the APS with a desire to also potentially profit from his success. The APS would raise funds that Michaux could use. This initial start-up funding would come in the form of a loan backed by what the French government owed him and that Michaux would presumably repay, but he would also be entitled to some extra dividends if he succeeded in the form of a prize.[17]

The third sticking point was perhaps the most important: who owned the knowledge Michaux was sure to uncover. This part of the negotiation revealed a great deal about the priorities of the two sides. Michaux made the first offer. "All the knowledge, observations, and geographical information will be communicated to the Philosophical Society," Michaux promised Jefferson. That offer spoke to one of Jefferson's overriding goals. Such geographic data was key for the United States' expansionary dreams. Knowledge about waterways, mountains, soil, and other information would inform the decisions of those crafting the nation's grand strategy for the West. In exchange for this information, Michaux insisted on owning and having the rights to the natural history collections he made. For Michaux, the object of the expedition was to receive recognition for the plant and animal discoveries west of the Mississippi. If he succeeded, then his name was sure to grace the pantheon of great natural historians. During his negotiations with Jefferson, he made it clear that, while he intended to share whatever he found with the rest of the world, he wanted the credit for himself alone. "The other discoveries in natural history," he told Jefferson, "will be for my immediate benefit and then destined for the general usage."[18]

By late January, Jefferson and Michaux had reached agreements on all these points, so Jefferson set out to codify the terms in what we now call the Michaux Subscription List, that treasure that today sits securely in the APS's vault. The document served two roles. First, it was a quasi-contract between those who were to pledge money and Michaux. Second, it was a fundraising tool meant to entice donors with its bold promises. Because of its latter purpose, Jefferson wanted it to look appealing to potential donors. He carefully wrote out the entire agreement on a large piece of parchment.

He made sure each line was perfectly straight and carefully crafted each letter of all four-hundred-odd words. That Jefferson took the time to carefully write it out in his own hand—something surely any potential subscriber would recognize—was a testament to his support for the endeavor.

"Andrew Michaux," the document began, "has undertaken to explore the interior country of North America from the Mississippi along the Missouri, and Westwardly to the Pacific Ocean." The text then went on to lay out the financial terms that Michaux and Jefferson had negotiated. The final arrangement turned out to be far more complex than initially imagined—as is often the case when it comes to money. The simple part was that if Michaux made it to the Pacific, he was entitled to the large prize promised by the subscribers. If he only made it part of the way, then the Society would prorate the sum based upon the distance he did travel.[19]

The most complicated section of the financing surrounded the money meant to fund initial operations. Michaux and Jefferson created terms that protected both the Society and Michaux. The agreement that emerged differed slightly from what Michaux and Barton had discussed. Instead of a loan, the APS gave Michaux the ability to draw upon one-fourth of the prize money as an advance for his journey. Meanwhile, these first funds were secured by the back pay Michaux claimed France owed him. If Michaux failed, or died, the APS would have the right to try to recoup their losses from the French government. If he succeeded, he simply would receive the prize money, less these start-up funds. Therefore, Michaux, for his part, could claim that the initial money was simply an advance of a promised prize. That arrangement meant that he was never in the employ of a foreign entity and any remuneration he received was purely an acknowledgment of his accomplishments.

When it came to Michaux's request to retain the rights to discovery, Jefferson largely, but not completely, acceded to Michaux's demands. The document called on Michaux to report *all* his findings to the APS immediately upon his return, implying Michaux had to share his natural history discoveries along with the geographic information he had offered. "On his return," the subscription stated at the outset, "to communicate to the said society the information he shall have acquired of the geography of the said country, it's inhabitants, soil, climate, animals, vegetables, minerals, and other circumstances of note." Later in the document, however, Jefferson gave Michaux the exclusive right to publish these findings in his own name. But there was a catch here, too. Michaux had to work in "concert" with the APS on the publication, language that suggested Jefferson expected the Society to publish Michaux's discoveries, so that the institution would receive due credit as well. The ambiguity surrounding what we might call intellectual property rights today became a sticking point that would linger as Michaux's potential departure neared in the weeks ahead.[20]

Jefferson finalized the Subscription List sometime in late January 1793. Interestingly, even though Jefferson was touting the APS's involvement in it, he never officially received the institution's approval of it. That small detail did not deter him, at least for now. Instead, he began lobbying for money with abandon. His first target was obvious: George Washington. Though the two-party system was then forming and bitter political disagreements were beginning to divide American society, the president's luster still shone. His command of the Continental Army during the Revolutionary War and his decision to resign his post after victory was secured endeared him to more Americans than any other revolutionary figure. Though many Americans in Jefferson's camp questioned several of the administration's policies, Washington remained above the fray and largely immune to their assaults—Alexander Hamilton, in fact, became the proxy for attacks instead. Securing the backing of the most admired American, Jefferson knew, would almost guarantee the success of the initiative. Jefferson even reserved a special place for the president's signature: the very top of the document.

On January 22, Jefferson sent a courier carrying the perfectly drawn Subscription List to the President's House. Tobias Lear, Washington's closest aide, greeted the messenger and took the package. Jefferson's cover note stated that he would visit the following morning to discuss the proposal and answer any questions the president might have. It was an unnecessary gesture. Lear delivered the package to Washington later that day. He read it—perhaps remembering Michaux's visit in 1786—and responded immediately. "Nothing occurs to me as necessary to be added to the enclosed project," Washington replied to Jefferson in a letter written that same day; "I would readily add my mite to the means for encouraging Mr Michaud's undertaking—and do authorize you to place me among, & upon a footing with the respectable sums which may be subscribed."[21]

Beneath his name, Washington also listed his pledge: one hundred dollars—the most any one subscriber would offer and around twice the average annual income an American could expect in the era. It is hard to make modern-day equivalences, but one calculator placed it at $130,000, comparable, again, to twice the average citizen's annual income. Sure enough, with Washington's name attached to the project, money poured in from all corners. John Adams, the vice president, placed his signature beneath Washington's with the promise of twenty dollars; Adams possessed a great mind but not great wealth. The column goes on to list gifts from seven senators. Prominent names include Ralph Izard, a senator from South Carolina, and wealthy business magnate Robert Morris, the "financier of the Revolution," who was then a senator from Pennsylvania.[22]

The second column held an equally impressive list of powerful officeholders. Henry Knox, secretary of war, placed his signature at the top, just above Jefferson's own pledge of fifty dollars. Alexander Hamilton, secretary of the treasury, and a great rival of Jefferson, placed his beneath Jefferson's. New York senator Rufus King, one of Hamilton's closest friends, signed below Hamilton, followed by the president pro tempore of the Senate, John Langdon of New Hampshire. Thomas Mifflin, the governor of Pennsylvania and the Society's patron, signed his name at the bottom of the column.

The third column contained pledges from thirteen members of the House of Representatives. Party, once again, posed no barriers to supporting the cause. Speaker of the House Jonathan Trumbull Jr.'s name graced the top of the column. Beneath this Federalist signature rested that of Jefferson's political ally and friend James Madison. Madison's hand, and surely Jefferson's quiet influence, whipped the Virginia delegation into particularly good order; seven representatives from the state committed to the project. While Virginia's support was notable, it, as with the rest of the pledges, was not partisan. Three of the seven Virginia subscribers were allied with Washington and the Federalists, while four were more closely allied with the opposition then forming around Madison and Jefferson.

The fervor for the project exceeded Jefferson's expectations—or at least the space he had reserved for pledge—and many were not even APS members but government officials who supported the initiative. Enthusiasm was so great that signatures soon overran the front, and Jefferson turned the document over for the latecomers, most of whom were APS members far less well-known today but influential in their own time. Aside from one House member who must have been late to sign, the rest of the names on the back were Philadelphia-based APS members. In total, the fundraising drive secured promises of $870, equivalent to about $1 million of income today. The sum attested to the significance of the proposed expedition for the nation. It also recognized the personal risk that Michaux was undertaking. The farther he traveled from the safe confines of the East, the more he placed his life on the line. The reward needed to reflect that gamble as well.[23]

Combined, the names lending support to the cause represented a wide swath of the country and the government. Eleven of the thirty US senators subscribed. Fourteen members of the House added their names, including the Speaker of the House. Three of the most powerful cabinet officials, along with the president and vice president of the United States, all publicly endorsed and funded the project. Indeed, the majority of the initial signers were not even APS members. Of the thirty-eight signatures, fewer than half (sixteen) were APS members. Signatories also came from all over the United States: men from North Carolina, Kentucky, New Hampshire, South Carolina, Pennsylvania, Maryland, Massachusetts, New Jersey, New York, and Virginia all signed.

Most of the supporters shared one other attribute: an active interest in natural history. This was as true of the political leaders as it was of Society members. Virginia representative John Page, for instance, had founded the Virginia Philosophical Society on the eve of the American Revolution, modeled in large measure on the APS. Rufus King, the senator from New York, amassed one of the largest personal libraries of the era. Benjamin Hawkins, one of North Carolina's senators, was deeply interested in Indigenous languages and cultures. Others were innovative agriculturalists. Jeremiah Wadsworth of Connecticut was noted for introducing improvements in animal breeding. Wadsworth also corresponded with Virginians George Washington and Richard Bland Lee, another signer of the Subscription List, about British techniques that Americans might adopt to increase the reproductive capacity of their livestock. Many of the subscribers, then, not only knew each other in politics but also in science. As a group, they were active participants in projects meant to understand and ultimately control the natural world in order to improve their country and its output. Michaux's proposal thus fit their own broadly shared scientific pursuits and interests.[24]

Science in this case was also meant to serve an explicitly political purpose. For those in government backing Michaux, their support was driven by national interest as much as it was for the advancement of knowledge for its own sake. They wanted Michaux to discover new things, to be sure, but, most of all, they wanted him to conduct reconnaissance for the potential future settlement of the continent. They were intrigued, perhaps even desperate, to know what lay beyond their current national borders. They could use such information to develop important strategic decisions, craft foreign policy, and shape their diplomatic—or military—approach to Native American nations. Their science and philanthropy were thus interwoven with the desire of many in this group to expand the United States' territory.

This amalgamation of signatures, then, captured a key, if somewhat hidden, aspect of early national politics and the zeitgeist of the elite who were driving policy decisions. Jefferson and Washington may have disagreed on profound political matters, with Jefferson preferring a smaller, passive federal government and Washington a more energetic one, but on one point, they shared a nearly identical vision: the United States was going to expand West. Both parties, then, agreed that they had an obligation to understand the North American continent. Jefferson used this unanimity to his advantage in organizing the Subscription List. By presenting a list of subscribers who represented all facets of government and all regions of the country, the document cast the campaign as an almost official government initiative. The Subscription List thus made clear a truism of the American founding. At a time of great political division, the two nascent parties agreed on almost nothing except for the fundamental assumption that the nation's future rested in settling the interior.

As Jefferson built enthusiasm for the mission and signatories lined up, Michaux apparently remained mostly unaware of what Jefferson was doing. His diary remains sparse during this period, though it is clear he traveled to New York City sometime in March, perhaps to inspect his New Jersey garden nearby, and returned to Philadelphia in early April, settling into the home of Philadelphia merchant and French émigré Charles Homassel. In any case, on Tuesday, April 9, Michaux was back in Philadelphia. Tired of waiting for news and growing anxious about his future, he showed up on the doorstep of David Rittenhouse, the Society's president.

"Mr. Misho called on me Yesterday, he wishes to know whether he is to prepare for his journey, and that instructions be prepared for him if he goes," David Rittenhouse informed Jefferson on Wednesday morning. It was time for Jefferson and the Society to turn the words on the page and the promises made on the Subscription List into reality.[25]

❖ 8 ❖

America's Scientific Community

April 1793, Philadelphia

André Michaux's visit to David Rittenhouse's home spurred the Society's president to act. But he was unsure what to do. Backing an expedition like Michaux's was an entirely new type of undertaking for the organization, so Rittenhouse reached out to Jefferson the very next morning for guidance.

"Will it be proper to call a meeting of the Society, or shall we have a meeting of a few individuals who are interested in this business?" Rittenhouse asked Jefferson.[1]

Jefferson offered a quick and adamant response. "It would be better to have a meeting of the society that they may accept the charge proposed to them by the subscribers," Jefferson advised Rittenhouse, responding within hours of receiving his inquiry. "I hope you will attend and have the thing done right," Jefferson curtly ended his instructions. The institution's involvement was essential to Jefferson's plan. Its support would cement the APS's reputation as the country's leading scientific organization. More than that, Jefferson was worried about a very practical matter. The subscribers had joined because the subscription agreement said the APS would provide oversight. He knew that promise mattered to donors. Indeed, though Jefferson was presenting the APS as the sponsoring institution to potential supporters, he had gotten a bit ahead of himself. He had yet to receive official institutional approval, even as the document asserted that the APS would oversee operations. Surely, he had confidence that it would agree to do so because he knew how much sway he had with the institution, but it was clear there was no official sanction.[2]

The heated political debates then swirling in Philadelphia may have influenced Jefferson's somewhat unorthodox approach. As historians have shown, partisan behavior was taking hold at this very moment, and the role of government was one of the chief points of division between the Washington and Hamilton–led Federalists and the emergent Jeffersonian Republicans. One of the core tenets that Jefferson and his supporters held was that government should respond to citizen-led initiatives, and he criticized Hamilton for taking the opposite, top-down approach, in which a strong central government dictated policy meant to shape individual behavior. When it came to the Subscription List, Jefferson may have seen it as a chance to make a statement about funding science through individual initiatives and voluntary associations rather than expecting the federal government to act. In essence, Jefferson wanted individual subscribers to show their collective support for a project and then present it to an institution for endorsement, not the other way around, an approach implicit in his turn of phrase to Rittenhouse that he wanted the APS to "accept the charge proposed to them by the subscribers."

Rittenhouse, the Society's president, followed Jefferson's orders, a sign of just how much influence Jefferson had on the institution. The Society met on April 19, a few days after Michaux called on Rittenhouse. Society members must have had advance notice of the weighty agenda. Eighteen people showed up at its headquarters, far more than was typical for a regular business meeting. Jefferson was unable to attend, possibly due to inclement weather. He had recently moved from a townhouse at 274 High Street, a location in the heart of the city and a few blocks from the Society's building, to a large house on the eastern banks of the Schuylkill River, about two miles away. Located near the Bartrams' garden, Jefferson preferred his new home's bucolic setting, but it made it harder for him to pop into the APS—perhaps, also, he did not want to appear to interfere with a decision in a matter in which he was so centrally involved.

At the meeting, APS members rushed through the regular business, tabling several items for a future meeting so they could get to the main issue: how the Society should respond to the subscription. The decision was clear. "The Society will patronize this undertaking, according to the terms and conditions expressed in said subscription," the minutes record.[3]

After taking ownership of the project, the Society formed three committees to manage various aspects of its planning. First, there were the financial obligations. Michaux had made clear what he expected from the Society. "He says 3 or 4 Hundred dollars put into his hands at present will be sufficient," Rittenhouse reported of his conversation with Michaux. Given that the Subscription List pledged to give Michaux a quarter of the amount raised in advance, an advance of four hundred dollars meant that their ultimate goal now had to be $1,600. The APS therefore tasked one committee with soliciting new subscribers to meet that new goal. The idea with this campaign was to secure commitments of $1,600 and then call on the subscribers to contribute a fourth of their promised contribution up front to provide Michaux with the money he needed, a strategy that also allowed contributors to hedge their risks. It then fell to the second committee to collect and keep the money pledged. Finally, for the expedition itself, the APS created a third committee, the weightiest of the three, to draw up detailed instructions for Michaux that would embody what the APS—and through it, the nation—considered the expedition's most important scientific priorities.[4]

Many of the people appointed to these three committees are names largely unknown today. At the time, though, they represented the scientific firmament of the young United States. Indeed, the collective biographies of these committee members provide a revealing window into the nature of American science and a representative cross-section of the varied backgrounds of many Americans involved in scientific endeavors during the eighteenth century. Their various, often meandering, paths to APS membership also capture the country's own recent turbulent journey to independence and its aftereffects on the pursuit of knowledge. It is, then, worth taking some time to resurrect their biographies to help us understand the nature of science at this foundational moment.

The committee appointed to raise money had a mix of people whose experiences made them particularly well-suited for the task. They were civic leaders, powerhouses within the APS (four of the five held an elected office in the institution), prominent doctors and natural historians, and financial gurus—most possessed several of these attributes at once.

James Hutchinson, a name long forgotten today, was perhaps the most prominent of the group at the time. After Hutchinson received his degree in Philadelphia in 1775, just before the advent of American independence, he followed the path of many aspiring colonial doctors. He went to England to receive training at the best hospitals and universities in the

British Empire so he could bring the latest, cutting-edge methods back to the colonies. Upon his return to the newly independent nation, Hutchinson helped establish the foundations of American medicine. He practiced and taught medicine and chemistry at the University of Pennsylvania's recently founded medical college, the first of its kind in the country. He was a chief force behind founding the College of Physicians in 1787. The College was an honorary society for doctors that was meant to strengthen the American medical establishment by creating for doctors what the APS did for intellectuals writ large. He also held a number of public health positions in the city meant to strengthen and improve medical services for Philadelphians. Meanwhile, at the APS, he was appointed a secretary in 1782, an important position because holders kept the official records of the institution. His experience, network, and role at the APS made him perfect for the committee meant to secure commitments and keep track of the records.[5]

Caspar Wistar brought something else to the committee: some of the deepest roots in the city of Brotherly Love and a gregarious personality perfect for fundraising. Only thirty-one years old at the time of Michaux's proposal, Wistar was the youngest person involved in the expedition, and perhaps the youngest APS member at the time. He was an emerging star in the field of medicine and natural history. Like Hutchinson, he had sought training in Great Britain, but he did so after the Revolution, a sign of how dependent Americans remained on their former metropole—and a reason people like Hutchinson wanted to build American institutions to strengthen the United States' medical infrastructure. When he returned to Philadelphia in 1786, Wistar opened his own practice and quickly secured a position at the University of Pennsylvania's medical school, working alongside Hutchinson and others. With Hutchinson, he was an early member of the College of Physicians and was himself elected to membership in the APS in 1787 at age twenty-six. In January 1793, just as Michaux's plans took hold, he was elected a "Curator" of the Society, a role that meant he oversaw the care and acquisitions of the institution's growing collections.[6]

Though a successful doctor—perhaps the most popular practitioner in the city—Wistar was better known among his APS peers for his expansive interests in natural history. He presented a paper with his friend and APS colleague Timothy Matlack on an enormous fossilized thigh bone discovered in New Jersey. The two protopaleontologists speculated that the bone, measuring more than four feet long, belonged to an enormous elephant-like creature. Today, though the bone is lost, scientists suspect that they may have been the first to describe a dinosaur specimen in America, possibly the *Hadrosaurus*. Wistar dabbled in botany as well, and his reputation in the field eventually led to a colleague naming the flowering plant *Wisteria* in his honor.[7]

John Vaughan possessed perhaps the most complicated background of them all; surely, he had traveled the most tortuous path to the APS. Vaughan was the son of Samuel Vaughan, a wealthy British merchant, Caribbean plantation owner, and parliamentarian. His older brother Benjamin Vaughan was a noted doctor and natural historian who became close friends with Franklin when Franklin was in London in the 1760s. He would later serve opposite Franklin as a member of the British delegation negotiating the end of the Revolutionary War. His father's politics certainly influenced both his sons—or perhaps his sons influenced the father. In any case, the elder Vaughan sided with Edmund Burke in the debate over the American Revolution, expressing regret for Parliament and the Crown's treatment of their colonies. He called for reconciliation.[8]

John Vaughan followed a different path. Though interested in science and politics, his chosen profession was trade. Vaughan built upon his family's substantial business interests in the Caribbean and became a noted merchant with strong connections to Europe and the Americas. In 1776, when the colonies declared themselves independent, he was stationed in Jamaica. He then relocated to France, a strategic place for a British merchant planning to maintain his trade with North America because he could skirt British embargoes. Vaughan used Nantes as his base, the primary port from which American agents shipped much-needed supplies to Revolutionary troops, and became close to several American patriots stationed there. In March 1781, Vaughan let Franklin know that he wished to take a dramatic step. He wanted to renounce his loyalty to Great Britain and become an American citizen. In 1782, as his brother Benjamin crossed the English Channel to take a seat on the British diplomatic delegation tasked with negotiating a peace treaty with Franklin, Vaughan was busy setting up shop in his newly adopted home, Philadelphia.[9]

Leveraging his existing connections in Europe and beyond, he became a noted importer, specializing in French wine but dabbling in far more, including books and even silver taken from the deposed French monarchy.

Perhaps his love of wine and books brought him to the attention of the APS; in any case, in 1784 the APS members added him to their rolls. Certainly, these two passions laid the foundations for his lifelong and close friendship with Jefferson, which ultimately included Vaughan becoming Jefferson's official wine buyer and a regular book trader. He served as the APS treasurer from 1791 until his death in 1841 and became the Society's first official and permanent librarian in 1803. He and Wistar were a wonderful complement. For instance, later, in the nineteenth century, Wistar would hold Saturday-evening parties for intellectuals in Philadelphia, and Vaughan would hold a Sunday-morning breakfast. They both were outgoing characters and great connectors of people, attributes important for the committee's task.[10]

Jonathan Williams had perhaps the weakest link to Philadelphia, but one of the city's most distinguished bloodlines flowed through his veins. Williams was Franklin's grandnephew, and the two had grown particularly close during the Revolution. Though Williams was from Massachusetts, the grandson of Franklin's sister Anne, the two forged a close bond when both Franklin and Williams lived in London during the 1770s. In 1776, as Franklin assumed his post in France, Williams settled in Nantes, where he oversaw crucial shipments to North America and likely crossed paths with Vaughan. On the side, Williams studied military engineering and, inspired by his great-uncle's own scientific work in meteorology, made weather observations. When he returned to North America in 1785 alongside Franklin, he finished a degree at Harvard and then took up residence in Philadelphia so he could help his aging great-uncle conduct experiments. He undertook research on sugar production, publishing an article in the APS *Transactions,* but his main contributions were to climate science. In 1793, he published another article in the Society's *Transactions* that reported on the work he did with his great-uncle chronicling oceanic temperatures. He published a monograph, *Thermometrical Navigation,* in 1799, a major expansion of his earlier essay.[11]

Not surprisingly, with Franklin as his advocate, Williams was admitted to the APS in 1787, in the same class as Caspar Wistar. He and Jefferson became close friends, a bond that would last through Jefferson's presidency of the United States. In January 1793, just as Jefferson's fundraising got underway, Williams's fellow APS members elected him a secretary of the Society.

With such a strong link to the institution's founder and a current holder of a key office within the organization, Williams's profile added a certain cachet to the operation that could surely aid in recruiting new donors.

John Nicholson, an ardent Jeffersonian and the final member of the fundraising committee, certainly had the least scientific background, but he had something vital to the committee's charge: deep pockets and a great deal of experience convincing people to part with their money. Nicholson had served as comptroller general of Pennsylvania after the Revolution, equivalent to the state treasurer, and his task had been to make sense of the financial mess created by the Revolutionary government. While in office, Nicholson started to speculate in land, which his political rivals considered a conflict of interest. He amassed a huge portfolio; the company he oversaw held an interest in at least six million acres of land spread throughout Pennsylvania, Virginia, and beyond. Nicholson had been elected to the APS in July 1791. He was the only member of the committee who did not hold an office within the APS, but he was a stalwart member, attending many meetings and participating in the life of the Society. Though Nicholson showed little direct interest in scientific pursuits, he used his wealth to back innovation, or what we might think of as applied "useful knowledge." He sponsored experiments, including James Fitch's work on a steam-powered boat, advocated for new canal and transportation systems, established mining operations, and opened several factories. His financial acumen and powerful connections to the world of finance surely made him a valuable appointee to the committee.[12]

The second committee separated the work of securing pledges, the salesmen of the operations, from those doing the collecting, or the enforcers. On this committee sat Charles Willson Peale, John Vaughan, and Nicholas Collin. The members on this committee shared attributes similar to the first. Vaughan, as treasurer, was appointed again. The others were noted natural historians who knew how to get people to give them money.

Charles Willson Peale was one of the most dynamic figures of his day. He was a preeminent portrait painter whose work enshrined the defining images of the leading figures of the revolutionary generation. He was also an innovator, entrepreneur, natural historian, and collector. He combined all of these attributes to launch the first successful museum in the country. His mission was to use his gallery to document the natural and political history of the United States by showcasing animals prepared by taxidermists from all over the continent and by displaying the portraits of those who shaped the nation. Peale's ambitions were fueled by both the Enlightenment project to document and organize nature and the patriotism and nationalism prevalent in the Revolutionary era. He designed innovative displays to lure in audiences, such as filling a room with what he called "moving pictures with changeable effects," essentially a device that used light and transparencies he drew to tell cinematic stories, perhaps akin to cartoons today. By 1793, he was a well-known figure about town with a reputation that increasingly extended far beyond it, a profile perfect to convince others to support Michaux. "That of Mr. Peale in Philadelphia," fellow committee member Nicholas Collin observed of Peale's museum in 1789, "is by his laudable care coming into reputation both at home and abroad." Peale also had a vested interest in Michaux's mission. Michaux's discoveries could prove profitable to Peale's own collection.[13]

Nicholas Collin, Peale's admirer, rounded out the committee. Collin's primary day job was to serve as the rector of the oldest Swedish parish in Philadelphia, a community with roots that traced back to the short-lived colony of New Sweden founded in 1638. His passion, though, was natural history, and this was likely the reason he won election to the APS in 1789. As with many of his scientific peers at the time, he had a roving, inquisitive mind. The various presentations he made to the Society showcased his curiosity: a model for a fire escape, a talk about lead-glazing techniques, a proposal for an elevator, and a discussion of linguistics. He also made weather observations, experimented with plants, and maintained a sizable botanical collection. After being elected, he became one of the most active APS members, attending most meetings and sitting on countless committees. Collin also served another important if informal role for the Society. He remained in touch with Sweden's scientific community and created a connection between the APS and its peer institutions in that country.[14]

Collin was an obvious choice for the committee for another reason. His first presentation to the Society, made in April 1789, offered a full-throated case for launching a project just like Michaux's. The lecture, "An Essay on Those Inquiries in Natural Philosophy, which at Present are Most Beneficial to the United States of North America," outlined a bold and ambitious scientific agenda for the country that comported with much that Jefferson and others at the APS also advocated. In this wide-ranging talk, Collin argued that in America, natural historians should pursue science to improve agricultural techniques. Doing so, he said, would give the country a competitive advantage over their more elitist European rivals, who considered inquiries into such everyday matters beneath them. He touched on medical opportunities and anticipated the Industrial Revolution by advocating developing machines to mechanize labor. His talk, covering so many fields—fields that we see as separate today but that were interwoven in the minds of eighteenth-century natural historians—so embodied the zeitgeist of the Society that when it came time to publish their 1793 volume of *Transactions,* the very year of Michaux's proposal (the Society published its *Transactions* sporadically; the previous edition came out in 1786), they selected Collin's piece as the lead article and titled it "Introduction to the Third Volume," thus making it appear as an institutional statement on American science that would be read widely at home and abroad.

The largest section of the essay bore directly on Michaux's proposal. When it came to "Inquiries in Natural Philosophy," Collin offered an impassioned plea that the United States explore the continent's interior four years before Michaux's proposal arrived at the APS. "What treasures may we not then expect in this new and vast division of the globe!" he exclaimed. Collin, a Swede by birth, even called upon that country's greatest scientist for inspiration. "I often heard the great Linnaeus wish that he could have explored the continent of North America; may this wish animate American philosophers," he recounted of his fellow Swede.[15]

Collin boasted of the many different plants and animals awaiting discovery in the interior. His prose burst with excitement as he did so, bouncing from snakes, to fish, to quadrupeds, to medicinal and edible plants. "General knowledge of fishes," he noted, "is very limited and confused; of those in the western waters we have here only reports." Though he was frustrated with the lack of knowledge, he was quick to excite the reader's mind with what may await by sharing a credible report of one-hundred-pound catfishes—a spur for action, he surely hoped. He moved on from fish to the land. "The great herds of buffaloes in the Western country, are a valuable national possession; a wanton destruction of them should be checked," he anticipated, "and trial of domestication would perhaps be both practicable and useful." As Collin's choice of the words "practicable and useful" made clear, for him and most others in the APS, so much of natural history, including the scientific exploration of the West, was about applying new knowledge to advance the nation's future glory—and its inevitable expansion.[16]

Botany, Michaux's own field, received special attention from Collin. Anticipating the bountiful arrival of new discoveries, Collin implored his fellow APS members to create a botanical garden similar to what Michaux had established. "Seminaries of learning," Collin said, meaning learned societies, "should immediately form botanical gardens, on a plan so liberal as gradually to receive all the trees, shrubs, and plants most valuable in every respect." It is no surprise that the Society made such an advocate the chair of the committee to collect funds.[17]

Taken together, the profiles of the APS members serving on the fund-raising and fund-collecting committees create a composite of the men involved in the pursuit of science in the young republic. There was one Brit turned American (Vaughan), and two were London-trained doctors (Hutchinson and Wistar) who were involved in new civic institutions meant to establish an American medical community. One was deeply involved in public health (Hutchinson), while the other (Wistar) pursued a wide range of natural history research, sparked, in part, by his medical background. There were two businessmen (Vaughan and Nicholson) who used their resources to support the advancement of knowledge and one (Peale) who used his entrepreneurialism to advance one of the grandest natural history projects in the new nation. Then there were two with careers quite outside natural history, who nonetheless became noted natural historians, one who focused on climate and the other on botany (Williams and Collin, respectively).

These men and their two committees sprang into action as soon as the April APS meeting adjourned. Their task was the crucial first step. Without money, there would be no need to write instructions for Michaux's expedition. Sitting in Philosophical Hall with Jefferson's subscription agreement before them, the APS members-turned-fundraisers realized that the original list was their best marketing tool. Around the time of the Society's meeting, Collin, who had already placed his name on the back of the original agreement, sat down and drew up a copy of Jefferson's agreement, making sure to list the big names who had already signed it. That document and all the ensuing records also sit in the APS's vault. Though Collin's copy is in no way as elegant as Jefferson's—the paper is cheaper, and Collin's handwriting is much poorer—it nonetheless followed Jefferson's original design and purpose. Anyone who saw it would feel compelled to join such an illustrious group.[18]

As the now APS-sanctioned agreement made its way through prominent Philadelphia homes, money flowed in. Most of the new signers were fellow APS members who placed their names near the top of Collin's copy, suggesting the new list passed first through the APS rolls. Society president David Rittenhouse offered fifty dollars. Collin enlisted at least twenty-two other APS members. It included leading state figures as well. John Penn, the former colonial governor and a descendant of William Penn, offered twenty dollars. Thomas Mifflin, the current governor and business partner with Nicholson, offered ten.

The five charged with securing pledges clearly used their wide networks to cajole friends outside of the APS to support the endeavor as well. The weighty names of those who had pledged support was surely an inducement for these new enlistees. Benjamin Franklin's grandson, Benjamin Franklin Bache, though not a member, nonetheless pledged eight dollars. John Nixon, also not an APS member but famous in Philadelphia today for reading the Declaration of Independence outside Independence Hall on July 8, 1776, offered ten dollars. Several emerging natural historians added their names; at least two would later become APS members. By the end of April, the committee members had secured commitments from thirty-seven new subscribers, nearly doubling the initial thirty-eight Jefferson had received. The final combined list was a veritable who's who of Philadelphia high society, federal and state governments, and American science.

They were also a charitable group. Although the fragmented nature of eighteenth-century accounting makes it hard to say with certainty, it appears that they secured at least $689 more, bringing the grand total for the prize to at least $1,559 and perhaps as much as $1,609, or, according to one estimate, the equivalent of $1.75 million in income using today's dollars. A quarter of that sum was almost exactly what Michaux had told Rittenhouse he needed to start. The committee had hit their target.[19]

With the pledges received and Michaux waiting for his start-up funds, Rittenhouse sent Collin a note on April 23 instructing him to have the collecting committee start its business. They got right to work, pounding the pavement and asking people to pony up. They worked so furiously that Peale enlisted his son Rembrandt to help. By April 25, just six days after the APS meeting that had set the fundraising drive in motion, the committee had received $128.25 dollars from twenty of the subscribers, more than a quarter of the amount due for the initial $400 installment Michaux desired. Washington and Hamilton were among those who paid their quarter share.[20]

Jefferson was surely pleased with the results. By receiving such an enthusiastic response from a wide range of individuals, the subscription showed the strength of support for the mission among America's elite. That's exactly what Jefferson wanted to see. For Michaux, the whole process must have looked very different from what he knew in France. There, he had sought the king's patronage and relied on his court to fund his scientific expeditions. Even institutions similar to the APS in France often depended on the Crown for their funding. In Philadelphia, Michaux saw a more democratic process unfold, one that, ultimately, was able to raise more money than Michaux needed. Here, without a central body that dispensed funds to favorites, citizens could endorse projects based on the merit of the idea. It was an emerging model for funding science, one built for a different type of society, a democratic one.

With the fundraising success, the third committee, the one tasked with the weighty responsibility of creating instructions for Michaux, became activated. It was perhaps the most important, for it was to provide Michaux with instructions that were to guide his mission. For that reason, the Society appointed some of its most substantial members to this vital body: Rittenhouse himself, along with William Smith, John Ewing, Thomas Jefferson, Benjamin Rush, and, once again, Caspar Wistar. What separated this group from the other two committees was the members' level of seniority and scientific accomplishment. There were no business leaders, nor were there any amateurs. Four held appointments as professors—and Rittenhouse had once held such a position and no longer needed it. The committee also had representatives who crossed generations. Three committee members (Rittenhouse, Smith, and Ewing) were in their sixties and had all been elected to the APS in 1768, at the time of its second founding. They brought to the committee the wisdom often conferred by age and the regard earned by illustrious careers. The other three, meanwhile, represented the future of American science (Jefferson, Rush, and Wistar). In some ways, the members of this committee had less exciting life stories than those on the other committees, in part because their careers were largely dedicated to the life of the mind. That cerebral lifestyle, however, was the very reason the APS appointed them to the committee charged with the most cerebral task. Together, these six men were to set the scientific agenda for Michaux's mission. While the backgrounds of those on the fundraising committee reflected the diverse interests many American natural historians possessed simultaneously, such as being a minister as well as a botanist, these six dedicated their lives primarily to science, and their accomplishments reflect the cutting-edge work of their day.

Rittenhouse was in many respects Franklin's heir, not just as the Society's president after Franklin's death in 1790 but as the nation's most accomplished scientist. He first gained international attention in 1769, when he observed the Transit of Venus. In that year, European astronomers and institutions all raced to document the phenomenon. These observers hoped that, with the advent of new telescopic tools, they would be able to document this rare occurrence better than ever before and, with their results, better understand the heavens. The Royal Society in London even sent James Cook to Tahiti to witness it. Rittenhouse spearheaded observations in Philadelphia, and he and other colonial scientists published their findings in the Society's *Transactions,* creating a sensation that established the APS's bona fides among its European peers. Rittenhouse also designed intricate scientific instruments and became a sought-after surveyor because of his mathematical acumen and his finely made surveying tools. Mason and Dixon used his work for part of their landmark survey, for instance. Aside from the APS, he also served on the Board of Trustees at the University of Pennsylvania, and Washington appointed him as first director of the US Mint in 1792. For Michaux's project, his scientific knowledge was essential to his instructions, but so too was his position as the Society's president.[21]

Two of the other appointees were, like Rittenhouse, senior scholars whose names and contributions added intellectual heft to the project. Rittenhouse's friend and occasional collaborator John Ewing was an ordained minister like Nicholas Collin and known to be a mathematical genius. In addition to serving as a Presbyterian minister, Ewing was a professor of ethics and natural philosophy at the University of Pennsylvania. He had joined Rittenhouse on several surveys, including the controversial and difficult survey to locate the border between Pennsylvania and Virginia. In 1793, the sixty-one-year-old was in his thirteenth year as provost of the

University of Pennsylvania, essentially the equivalent of the modern president of a college.[22]

William Smith brought a similar background and, at age sixty-five, even more seniority to the committee. Smith was regarded as one of the most distinguished minds in the nation and an institutional leader. An Anglican minister and more of a humanist than the others on the committee, he served as Penn's first provost and is today considered the person who built the foundation upon which the modern university sits. He continued institution-building in 1780, when he helped found Washington College in Maryland. Smith, and other like-minded early American leaders, wanted to expand the country's higher education infrastructure because they believed an educated citizenry was key to sustaining a democracy.[23]

These three committee members, all in their sixties and elected to the APS in 1768, brought the seniority needed. The other three, meanwhile, represented the rising generation of scientific leaders. Jefferson was the oldest at fifty. His wide-ranging intellectual pursuits included Indigenous history and languages, botany and agriculture, paleontology, mathematics, and astronomy. Wistar, the youngest at thirty-one, shared Jefferson's natural history inclinations, especially two of particular potential relevance for Michaux's expedition: botany and paleontology.

Benjamin Rush, meanwhile, was the most noted physician in America. The forty-eight-year-old held a professorship in clinical medicine at Penn and was the single most important person training the rising generation of American physicians. Rush's own research interests never veered far from medicine, but within this field, his work was considered the cutting edge of the time. He also studied race, became a pioneering advocate for mental health, and wanted to learn more about Indigenous practices and beliefs. On the last of these items, he and Jefferson shared an intellectual bond. Both believed that by studying Indigenous cultures, they could learn more about human civilization and its evolution. Where Jefferson sought information on languages, Rush focused on health. As early as 1774, Rush had delivered a lengthy talk about Indigenous health and medicine to argue that a comparative study of Native American and European practices could prove enlightening. He remained interested in the topic, and Michaux's expedition promised to provide new data.[24]

With the money flowing into APS coffers, this third committee felt confident enough to draft instructions for Michaux. It was the final step before

Michaux could launch his westward trek. Michaux's request for instructions, and the Society's desire to give him a set, though, meant that he and Jefferson were about to confront a conflict that had sat latent all this time, obscured by the swell of enthusiasm surrounding the expedition. As a Frenchman cut loose from his government salary, Michaux needed to negotiate terms that comported with his values. The APS, of course, had its own concerns. As the third committee sat down with Jefferson at its head in late April, they started to outline plans for the expedition that revealed much about the priorities of American science at the founding—and about Michaux's loyalties.

❖ 9 ❖

American Interests and Scientific Priorities

April 1793, Philadelphia

With the mission funded and the committee preparing his instructions about to meet, Michaux, the otherwise intrepid explorer, was having second thoughts. He still seemed unconcerned with the risks posed by the expedition. Instead, he now questioned his reliance on the APS and what it meant for his obligations to his home country. Subtle signs of Michaux's uncertainty had appeared even in his earliest negotiations with APS representatives. When Benjamin Smith Barton opened discussions in early January, Michaux asked if the expedition could wait until after he had traveled to Charleston. He had said he wanted to check on his Goose Creek nursery, but he was also likely anxious to see if he had received news from France about his reappointment. While Michaux decided to stay in Philadelphia, the new French consul in Charleston, Michel-Ange-Bernard Mangourit, shipped Michaux his mail so he could stay abreast of the news. As he opened his letters, he found tantalizing hints that his prospects in France were improving.[1]

Michaux, in fact, never gave up hope that his own country might fund his trip into the American West. Even while seeking money from the APS in January, he was simultaneously lobbying French officials for support, showing that he preferred, always, to work for France. Michaux had even broached the idea of the expedition in his very first contact with the new French consul in Charleston. Writing on January 15, he explained that the western voyage was the last piece he needed "to complete my research." A man constantly driven to work, Michaux complained that without cash he was "exposed to wasting my time." His only recourse, he lamented, was to seek funding from the APS. He let the consul know that he preferred to have the French government underwrite the project. "I do not know if the administration can be concerned now with this objective and subsidize these voyages," Michaux inquired.[2]

Michaux found a firm ally in the new consul. Like Otto in New York City, Mangourit agreed that Michaux's work was of national import and sent letters to the revolutionary government demanding that its members act quickly to patronize the botanist, lest they lose the country's investment in him. "You will not allow that his useful establishments pass into foreign hands," Mangourit told his supervisors in France. He also warned that Michaux's deepening poverty posed a threat to French interests: "This fellow citizen was obliged to put his hand out so to speak to the individuals in Philadelphia to continue his voyages of discovery."[3]

In March, as Jefferson was busy collecting pledges, Michaux learned that the French government had indeed reappointed him. He received a new commission from the interior minister along with the charge to, in his words, "continue collecting all natural history objects for the natural history collection of the republic and the Jardin des Plantes." Michaux was thrilled. Freed from the earlier requirement that he send massive numbers of living trees to France to replenish its forests for strategic reasons or to follow the orders of his superiors, Michaux felt liberated to advance knowledge for its own sake. It was, in fact, the job he had always wanted. He was able to serve both science and his country without either being in conflict with the other. "Probably I will obtain more ample collection than ever," he enthused to a colleague soon after receiving his new orders, "not having specific work to take up my time, like cultivation that I had to do under the Old Regime."[4]

With these instructions and the prospect of a new stipend, Michaux was no longer in limbo and once again in the formal employ of France. This change in status, however, jeopardized his deal with the APS. If Michaux had struggled with balancing the needs of two masters before the French Revolution (the Crown's needs and science's), he faced an even more challenging dilemma as he weighed his ties to the APS alongside his obligations to his country. He worried that the French government might look askance at a French official who received money from an institution that had such a strong relationship with the US government. Still, he realized Ducoigne's impending departure presented him with a unique opportunity. Unsure of what to do, he wrote to the consul in Charleston for advice while continuing to plan to join Ducoigne if he received no news. "I will do everything to wait for your response," he assured Mangourit on March 5; "nevertheless, I would like to benefit from the escort of friendly Indians who have to leave in a few weeks from Philadelphia."[5]

It was amid this uncertainty that Michaux, eagerly awaiting guidance from the APS, paid a visit to David Rittenhouse on April 9 to seek an update. Knowing that Ducoigne and his party were planning to depart soon and that his escort was essential to Michaux's success, Michaux wanted to read the APS's official instructions. Their orders, he suspected, could clarify matters. It was Michaux's request that spurred the APS into action—officially endorsing the expedition, creating committees to launch it, and, ultimately, drafting up instructions that would guide him.

Meanwhile Jefferson, unaware of Michaux's growing doubts, continued to strengthen his relationship with Ducoigne. On April 13, just a few days after Michaux's impromptu meeting with Rittenhouse, he purchased a rifle, powder flask, clothes, and other items as presents for Ducoigne. Such objects had great value and use to Ducoigne. Arms and ammunition were essential to life in the interior, but, more than that, they carried great symbolic meaning, one both Jefferson and Ducoigne knew. To exchange weapons meant the two were trusted friends and allies, not enemies. Jefferson provided no commentary on the gifts in his account book, aside from noting that he gave them to Ducoigne for his son, presumably the one who bore Jefferson's name. By giving these presents to his son, Jefferson was likely also indicating that he intended this friendship to transcend generations. In any case, it was clear that Jefferson and Michaux's joint plans depended upon Ducoigne ushering the Frenchman into Indian Country, and these items only further cemented their bond.[6]

At nearly the same time as he was giving these gifts to Ducoigne, the third committee, the one tasked with writing instructions for Michaux, began to meet. Though Jefferson missed the original APS meeting in which the committees were created, he made sure to attend the meetings of this more substantive committee. As a sign of just how involved Jefferson became, this group's final product—the official and very specific instructions meant for Michaux—is in Jefferson's own hand, just like the Subscription List. Jefferson's authorship shows how much ownership over the project he wanted—perhaps like the Declaration, he even penned the draft himself and then solicited comment from the committee, thus providing the framework through which the discussion would happen. In any case, today, the sprawling, four-page-long document is pasted into a volume in the Caspar Wistar Papers in the APS's vault. Its contents reflected an agenda shaped by the intellectual currents swirling among natural historians on both sides of the Atlantic. More than that, since it was composed by this elite group of six American thinkers and policymakers, it constituted a significant statement of the United States' scientific priorities. The advice conveyed to Michaux captured what the leading thinkers of the day believed they knew about the West, and their requests for Michaux's research show what they most wanted to learn about the territory. Significantly, the text provides clear evidence of the ways in which these priorities were inextricably tied to the United States' expansionary dreams.[7]

These six APS luminaries made explicit the overriding priority of US expansion. Above all else, they wanted Michaux to discover the fastest riverine path to the Pacific for commercial purposes and to conduct reconnaissance along the way for the potential future settlement of the territory. "The chief objects of your journey are to find the shortest and most convenient route of communication between the US and the Pacific ocean," they stated in the opening, "and to learn such particulars as can be obtained of the country through which it passes, its productions, inhabitants, and other interesting circumstances." By finding the most direct route to the Pacific, this ostensibly scientific expedition promised to provide traders with advantageous knowledge that could open new markets and introduce new goods into American life. The natural history information—the "productions" of the soil—would serve the agricultural interests of Americans by letting farmers, hungry for more fertile land, know what crops they might plant and grow. The reports on the Native peoples, meanwhile, would provide planners with useful intelligence on those who stood in the way of future American settlements.[8]

While the goal of finding the fastest and most direct route to the Pacific comported with US national interests, it was at odds with Michaux's own priorities. He was, at his core, a botanist who wanted to pursue knowledge of the natural world for its own sake, all the more so now that he had received such open-ended encouragement from the French government. For Michaux, crossing the continent remained a secondary consideration, and finding the fastest route to the Pacific struck him as less important. Collecting specimens was what drove his agenda. "I intended for a long time to go

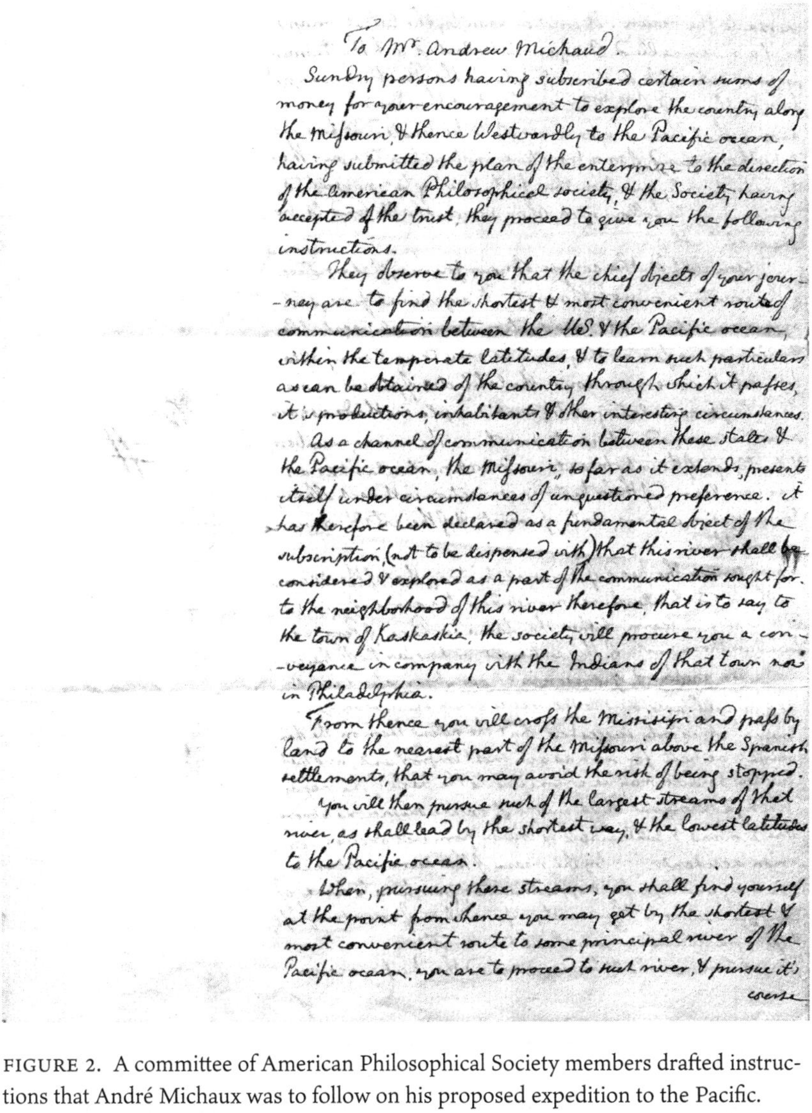

To Mr. Andrew Michaud.

Sundry persons having subscribed certain sums of money for your encouragement to explore the country along the Missouri, & thence Westwardly to the Pacific ocean, having submitted the plan of the enterprize to the direction of the American Philosophical society, & the Society having accepted of the trust, they proceed to give you the following instructions.

They observe to you that the chief objects of your journey are to find the shortest & most convenient route of communication between the US. & the Pacific ocean, within the temperate latitudes, & to learn such particulars as can be obtained of the country through which it passes, it's productions, inhabitants & other interesting circumstances.

As a channel of communication between these states & the Pacific ocean, the Missouri, so far as it extends, presents itself under circumstances of unquestioned preference. it has therefore been declared as a fundamental object of the subscription, (not to be dispensed with) that this river shall be considered & explored as a part of the communication sought for. to the neighborhood of this river therefore, that is to say to the town of Kaskaskia, the society will procure you a conveyance in company with the Indians of that town now in Philadelphia.

From thence you will cross the Missisipi and pass by land to the nearest part of the Missouri above the Spanish settlements, that you may avoid the risk of being stopped.

You will then pursue such of the largest streams of that river, as shall lead by the shortest way, & the lowest latitudes to the Pacific ocean.

When, pursuing these streams, you shall find yourself at the point from whence you may get by the shortest & most convenient route to some principal river of the Pacific ocean, you are to proceed to such river, & pursue it's course

FIGURE 2. A committee of American Philosophical Society members drafted instructions that André Michaux was to follow on his proposed expedition to the Pacific. Written by Thomas Jefferson, the manuscript is part of the Caspar Wistar Papers that now reside in the Society's vault. (Courtesy of the American Philosophical Society)

and visit the far-reaching areas to the west," he wrote a friend in April, "but since I have no other objective than to acquire the largest number possible of objects in natural history, I will decide depending on the circumstance for this goal." Therein lay the dilemma for the two sides.[9]

The tension between an organization that wanted to direct an expedition it funded and a scientist who wanted to pursue his own agenda continued as the instructions went on. The committee members decided to delve into the minutiae of the mission and provide detailed orders on the specific route they expected Michaux to take. Their course, and the assumptions that underlay it, reflected their collective knowledge of the American interior as well as the degree to which they wanted to manage Michaux's trip. The Missouri River was of particular interest. Exploring it, they said, "was a fundamental object of the subscription." Again, the priorities of the United States drove this aim. The Missouri was important because many suspected it was going to be a key artery that connected the western regions to the Mississippi, much as the Ohio River had done a generation earlier for the eastern seaboard. Aware that Spanish settlements jealously guarded the confluence of the Missouri and Mississippi Rivers, they advised Michaux to pass to the north, so "that you may avoid the risk of being stopped" by watchful and wary Spanish rivals.[10]

Michaux, himself, had started to sketch his own anticipated route. He imagined a similar path and was aware of the dangers that imperial jealousies posed, but he said much less about the specific waterways he intended to travel. "When I will be in Illinois," he wrote to a colleague in Paris in early April, "if I do not anticipate obstacles from the Spanish government from Lower Louisiana, I will go there easily."[11]

When it came to telling Michaux what to do beyond that river, Society members recognized the limitations of their knowledge. They had studied various maps that depicted the interior territory, some held by the Society. These cartographic studies were often produced by Spanish or French authorities, and several sketches made the Oregon River appear to be the most viable way to reach the Pacific after the Missouri. The committee also knew that, if anything, these maps were reliably unreliable. They therefore gave discretion to Michaux to make decisions. "The Society is aware that these maps are not to be trusted so far as to be the ground of any positive instruction to you," they wrote of the Oregon River; "they therefore only mention the fact, leaving yourself to verify it, or to follow such other as you shall find to be the real truth."[12]

Still, just a few words after apparently giving Michaux the freedom to act, they could not resist giving him more specific guidance and, in so doing, reaffirmed their interest in navigational information above all else. Even though they admitted they knew little of what lay beyond the Missouri River, members reminded Michaux that his decisions should always be informed by the APS's objective of finding the shortest route to the Pacific. "You will then pursue such of the largest streams of that river, as shall lead by the shortest way, and the lowest latitudes to the Pacific ocean," they dictated.[13]

Of Michaux's personal and primary pursuit, botanical research, there is but little. One sentence lists "vegetable" as one of the objects of interest to the Society, but it is surrounded by many more items. They asked him to observe "the country you pass through, its general face, soil, rivers, mountains, its productions animal, vegetable, and mineral." Their directives made it clear that while they shared Michaux's interest in natural history, their primary objective with this information was for reconnaissance purposes and not the pure natural history research Michaux sought.

Then there were the items of specific concern to the APS, topics toward which Michaux had historically shown little curiosity. The APS leaders demonstrated their deep desire to learn more about the Native cultures Michaux encountered by listing the very specific information they sought. They asked Michaux to observe "the names, numbers, dwellings of the inhabitants, and such particularities as you can learn of their history, connections with each other, languages, manners, state of society and of the arts and commerce among them." Michaux, of course, had met many different Native American peoples throughout his travels, but he had shown little interest in observing their ways for scientific purposes. He likely learned useful words and phrases in various Native languages, for instance, but he did not document any, at least as far as we can tell, like he did in Persia. APS members like Rush and Jefferson, though, sought out concrete documentation of Indigenous peoples and their cultures.

There were at least three reasons for this priority. First, there were geopolitical concerns at play. Such intelligence would shape strategies that policymakers developed as they plotted the nation's move into western territories—up to and including military conquest. Another was scholarly. For their own nation-building purposes, Society members wanted to document Indigenous groups and uncover elements of their distant past. They were especially fascinated with the mound-building cultures that had once dominated the Mississippi Valley region. For Jefferson-minded Americans, the great mound-builders provided evidence to refute Buffon's claims about the inherently inferior nature of peoples who inhabit certain climates. Finally, there was a more practical reason for their interests. Rush and Jefferson and many others knew that European colonization often displaced Native peoples and threatened their cultures. Observations taken now could preserve what once was; it was, perhaps, a precursor to what became known in the twentieth century as "salvage anthropology." Rush made this explicit at a 1774 APS meeting, two years before American independence. "We may venture to foretell, that, in proportion as the white people multiply, the Indians will diminish; so that in a few centuries they will probably be entirely extirpated." Michaux's instructions, then, were a tacit acknowledgment that his foray was on the vanguard of what Rush predicted would become an "entire extirpation." Rush and Jefferson thus wanted Michaux to record what he saw before American expansion altered the demographic landscape.[14]

Jefferson was especially interested in languages. For years, he had used his political offices and connections to compile one of the largest collections of Native American linguistic material ever assembled. He gave word lists to diplomats, military officials, traders, and others who ventured into Indian Country. He intended to compile his data and publish the results for posterity. This scholarly endeavor was, to Jefferson, an important part of natural history, and he documented and categorized Indigenous words in a manner that resembled what botanists were doing with plants. Jefferson collected with more than just preservation in mind. He planned to compare the languages with each other and theorized that he could unlock the deep historic connections of separate Native American groups by finding commonalities in their languages.

It was also part of his project to use natural history for nation-building. Identifying and tracing these long-ago connections would help him uncover the history of the continent before European contact and show the evolution of Native peoples. A nation, for those like Jefferson, needed to know its entire history and, ideally, celebrate it. These word lists thus represented two important elements for Jefferson. On the one hand, they preserved for posterity languages that some like Rush speculated were likely to be destroyed by the inevitable weight of colonization; on the other, they provided a window into the past that Jefferson hoped could show the dynamism on the North American continent before European colonization. There was embedded in Jefferson's approach an unsettling contradiction: he wanted to prove the historic vibrancy of Native American cultures at the same time he expected these cultures to fade away under pressure from the colonization efforts he was endorsing.[15]

Next on the list were the Society's very peculiar requests for what they called "Animal History." "That of the Mammoth is particularly recommended to your enquiries," they instructed Michaux, "as it is also to learn whether the lama, or paca of Peru is found in those parts of the continent, or how far north they come." The hunt for a mammoth and search for a North American llama may sound downright strange to us today, but they were very real and very important in Jefferson's day. Once again, the Society's concern with these two animals interwove national interests with those of American natural historians.[16]

Natural historians had long speculated that an as yet undocumented large, wooly beast roamed in the American interior. For decades, traders and travelers to the West had returned with bones from the Ohio River Valley that belonged to animals far larger than anything known to live in North America at the time. As natural historians pieced together these skeletal remains, the outlines of a large elephant-like creature emerged. In the late eighteenth century, the concept of extinction had little salience among American scholars. In fact, the very notion that something like extinction could occur was only just emerging among European thinkers. For many, the idea that a species could vanish seemed ludicrous, perhaps even heretical, because it ran counter to the Bible's claim that God created all the species and that his work remained unalterable. Even Jefferson, a religious skeptic who questioned the supernatural stories in the Bible, rejected the concept in his *Notes on the State of Virginia:* "Such is the economy of nature, that no instance can be produced of her having permitted any one race of her animals to become extinct; of her having formed any link in her great work so weak as to be broken."[17]

Instead, he and others were convinced that the mammoth had simply migrated to unexplored regions. The prospect of finding this large beast fueled the imagination of people like Jefferson. If such a creature still lived in the West, what else might they discover? Many dismissed the search for the animal as a waste of time. Jefferson refused to relent and even marshalled evidence gleaned from his contacts in Indian Country to buttress his claims that it still existed. "The traditional testimony of the Indians [attests] that this animal still exists in the northern and western parts of America," Jefferson told readers in *Notes;* "he may as well exist there now, as he did formerly where we find his bones." Discovering such an animal in North America served another very important purpose for Jefferson. Proof of its existence would add, quite literally, large and compelling evidence to Jefferson's refutation of Buffon's theory that plants and animals in North America were inherently small and inferior.[18]

The quest for the North American llama was a more unusual, perhaps even perplexing, item. There are no known mentions of the llama in the previous writings of those sitting on this committee. Its presence, then, appears anomalous, almost bizarre, and has gone largely unremarked by historians as a result. This addition, though, has a fascinating origin owing almost certainly to Michaux's friendship with Benjamin Smith Barton. Barton had heard of a large, wool-bearing animal west of the Mississippi from his correspondent Peter Pond, the same trader Michaux visited in Connecticut before embarking on his Canadian excursion. Intrigued, Barton dug deeper and read reports from Jesuit missionaries that claimed a llama lived somewhere around the Rockies. Barton was skeptical that the animal was in fact a llama, but he was convinced from the various accounts that a mysterious "wool-bearing kind inhabits these unexplored regions."[19]

Soon after arriving in Philadelphia, Michaux gave Barton the best confirmation yet that such an animal existed. During a meeting with Barton, perhaps the very one in which he pitched his westward expedition, Michaux regaled his friend with stories of the Canadian expedition, including an account of the hide of a "mountain lamb" that he saw in Montreal. It was, he reported, twice as large as a regular sheep and lived near "the Stony, or Shining Mountains" (the Canadian Rockies). "I have lately received from a friend of mine," Barton relayed to another friend in December 1792, "that last summer, the skin of one of these animals was brought to Montreal, from whence it was sent to England—I am inclined to think it is the Pacos." Almost certainly, Barton's source was Michaux. Barton's vague but consistent accounts of such an animal were almost certainly references to bighorn sheep, a species that Lewis and Clark gained fame for documenting on their expedition ten years later. While Lewis and Clark have received credit for making that discovery, the inclusion of the llama in Michaux's instructions provides clear evidence that knowledge of something like it existed in the scientific ether and that Michaux had contributed to the knowledge of its existence.[20]

In any case, the committee's desire to find this animal shows that a combination of practical and theoretical science played into the United States' national interests. Wool was a vital part of American life. Yet, Americans relied on foreign imports of woolen goods, especially those produced in Great Britain. Such economic dependence posed threats to their national independence. To combat this trend, Americans increased their flocks and developed homegrown industries. Washington, for instance, doubled the number of sheep at Mount Vernon in the decades following the Revolutionary War.[21]

Many natural historians speculated that the continent contained a native species that produced wool better suited for the North American environment. Thus, the committee sought proof of the mysterious North American llama. If Michaux discovered llamas naturally living in the Northern Hemisphere, then Americans could exploit this domestic source of wool. Notably, Jefferson, as chair of the committee, confided to Washington on June 28, 1793, just a couple of months after this meeting, that he was directing new attention toward increasing American wool production, perhaps as a result of the discussions this committee had about llamas. Jefferson's interest continued in the following years. When he was president, he turned the grounds of the White House into a menagerie of wooly and exotic animals, including several Peruvian llamas that were sent to him as diplomatic gifts. "At the time the grounds of the President's House were in a state remarkably rude," a visitor to Jefferson's White House noted, "and were full of Arabian steeds, of Cashmere goats, and Peruvian lamas, sent to Jefferson by foreign potentates."[22]

These, then, were the highest priorities the Society had for Michaux. His main objective was to find the most navigable way to the Pacific, and he was never to veer from it. He was to observe all he saw along the way, paying special attention to Indigenous peoples and the potential for future white settlement. And, if there were any other clear and specific priorities, he was to find a wooly mammoth and a llama. The instructions clearly reflected the interests of the committee and Jefferson in particular. Botany, Michaux's primary interest, as well as his charge from his own nation and primary employer, France, was only a small piece of the mission, seeming almost an afterthought in the instructions.

The instructions ended with some final advice to Michaux on how to manage his travels—as if he needed that. Their first concern was preserving the knowledge Michaux acquired. Knowing the perils Michaux faced, they asked that he tattoo his skin with the most important information he observed. Therefore, should his papers be lost or destroyed, but he returned safely, his body would have stored his most important finds. This unusual request was almost certainly made at the suggestion of Jefferson, who had made an identical request of John Ledyard before his similarly risky expedition to Siberia. In fact, Ledyard may have sparked the idea for Jefferson. Ledyard had received tattoos while in Tahiti sailing with James Cook, and his inked skin had created a stir among the elite who saw him after his return. The technology likely gave Jefferson the idea for its potential utility beyond just the decorative.[23]

Their second piece of advice, perhaps more practical, and certainly less painful, was that Michaux use birch bark paper for a journal rather than the rag paper used by Euro-Americans. Many Native groups used birch bark for recording their stories and observations. There were two reasons behind this suggestion. The first was practical. Birch bark was far more durable. The second was pragmatic. Those on the committee knew of Native people's distrust of Europeans. Indigenous Americans had grown particularly wary of writing tools. They rightfully associated pen, paper, and ink with the surveying and mapmaking practices that Europeans used to undermine Indigenous claims to sovereignty. Birch bark, the committee suspected, might be less likely to raise hackles. "Details may be committed to the bark of the paper birch, a substance which may not excite suspicions among the Indians," Jefferson wrote, "and little liable to injury from wet, or other common accidents."[24]

The document's concluding section reiterated several points that surely increased the French botanist's already simmering angst. It stated in no uncertain terms that his primary charge was to find the shortest route to the Pacific, not to document natural history. "The first of all objects," they reminded Michaux, "that you seek for and pursue that route which shall form the shortest and most convenient communication between the higher parts of the Missouri and the Pacific ocean." Perhaps worst of all, they made explicit what had been otherwise implicit: Michaux's scientific mission was to serve the interests of the United States and its citizens. "Consider this," they wrote of his mission, "not merely as your personal concern, but as the injunction of science in general which expects its enlargement from your enquiries, and of the inhabitants of the U.S. in particular, to whom your report will open new fields and subjects of commerce, intercourse, and observation." As Jefferson inked these words on the paper, they also became etched in his mind—they would be fulfilled, as we shall see, a decade later when Jefferson had a second chance to launch such an expedition. This second time he would have the weight of the federal government behind him.[25]

Finally, the instructions reopened the thorny issue of who had the rights to Michaux's discoveries. In their instructions, the committee members told Michaux that they expected him to provide "a full narrative of your journey and observations," while acknowledging that he retained the right to publish them. That implied that they expected Michaux to share all his natural history finds with them, alongside the navigational observations he had promised them.[26]

Unsurprisingly, the instructions displeased Michaux when he received a draft of them near the end of April. Although we do not know when the committee met, we do know that by April 29, Michaux had received a copy of the instructions. When he read the terms, he felt that the APS intended to treat him more like an employee who was expected to do their bidding and serve the United States' priorities than an independent explorer pursuing his own inquiries. On April 29, he let the committee know it. "Bound by all manner of considerations to my country," he informed the Society, "the primary objective of my researches on natural history is to fulfill my obligations in this regard." "The second objective," Michaux pointedly wrote to the APS, "is to be useful to America."[27]

Michaux, always anxious about the financial relationship he had with the APS, also took issue with the responsibilities that came with accepting APS funds. His recent reappointment by the French government only heightened those concerns. More than ever, he wanted to follow his own instincts and interests in the field rather than feel bound by instructions from the APS. He thus indicated he no longer sought any remuneration. "In accepting financial help," he wrote to Rittenhouse, the Society's president, "I would impose obligations upon myself, and in a dangerous undertaking I wish to be free of such considerations."[28]

Finally, rights to discovery remained an issue for Michaux. In his reply to the instructions, he reassured APS members that he intended to share all geographical and navigational observations with them because he recognized their potential utility to the Society and to the country's commercial and expansionary aspirations in particular. He was adamant, though, that the natural history discoveries were his alone.

A day after drafting his firm response to the APS, Michaux's reservations continued to mount. Before he sent off his letter to the Society, he appended a postscript reiterating his refusal to be bound by the Society and to be considered in its employ. There is also a hint that, as enthusiasm built within the APS and the halls of the US government, he was growing nervous about the expedition itself and meeting the large expectations of the Society. "It is in every sense of the word in order not to give rise to too high hopes, and knowing how limited is my information, that I desire to be free of obligations to fulfill," he added. He was thus asserting himself as an independent explorer who traveled under his own steam and guidance, much as he had on his Canadian trek. Still, he let the APS know that he remained committed to the expedition in principle. "But I will devote myself to this without reserve," he promised at the very end of his addendum.[29]

As April turned to May, matters remained at loggerheads. As time wore on, the odds of Michaux undertaking the expedition seemed to decrease. On May 9, Ducoigne and nine other Native delegation members departed Philadelphia in two horse wagons. Michaux remained in Philadelphia, hoping that something might change. "The repugnance I felt at receiving assistance from strangers made me delay in employing the first sums that were subscribed," he recounted years later; "I wished to be alone indebted to my country for the means of exercising my zeal." Earlier, Michaux's entire timeline was dependent on receiving Ducoigne's escort. That he watched them leave was a clear sign of the serious doubts he harbored. The APS, meanwhile, seems to have been waiting patiently—there are no records of any response to Michaux's concerns. Another reason for the silence might have been that events were suddenly about to change for both Philadelphia and the nation, pushing the expedition to the side and altering Michaux's mission.[30]

"Things remained in this state when I received intelligence of the arrival of the minister Genet at Philadelphia," Michaux recalled. Edmond

Genet, the newly appointed French minister plenipotentiary (essentially, the chief diplomatic official, comparable to an ambassador today), changed everything. His orders were to transform Michaux's plans and undermine the work of the Society. Had the Society and Michaux been able to work things out sooner, had the Society been more sensitive to Michaux's national loyalties, and had they taken a lighter hand in their instructions to Michaux, then there is every reason to believe Michaux would have left with Ducoigne before Genet's arrival in Philadelphia on May 16. Instead, Michaux was in town to meet Genet, from whom the loyal Frenchman received entirely new instructions. Within a month, Michaux the botanist would embark on a clandestine mission to the West, but instead of serving the United States' national interests, this one threatened to undermine the young nation and upend geopolitics in North America. And, rather than Michaux feeling that his western journey was testing his national loyalties, Michaux's new expedition would try Jefferson's.[31]

❖ PART III ❖

The Expedition

I saw minister Genet at Philadelphia in April 1793. On the information which I communicated to him respecting Canada and the French Illinois territory, he entrusted me with a secret mission.

—ANDRÉ MICHAUX

❖ 10 ❖

Enter Edmond Genet

March–May 1793, South Carolina to Philadelphia

After seven long and tortuous weeks at sea, the French ship *Ambuscade* pulled into Charleston's docks on March 7. When Citizen Edmond Genet walked down the planks to greet an expectant crowd, no one knew that the handsome, blue-eyed, gregarious twenty-nine-year-old French ambassador carried secret instructions that, if pursued, threatened the new American republic. His public mission was to establish a strong bond between the United States and newly republican France. His private orders, so extreme that they appear ludicrous to some today, were very real. He was to recruit Americans to harass British ships in the Atlantic and launch an invasion of Spanish-controlled Louisiana from Kentucky (and, if possible, of Florida from South Carolina). As his instructions stated, Genet was going to spread revolution throughout North America by making "the principles of the French revolution germinate in Louisiana, in Kentucky and in the other provinces which neighbor the United States."[1]

Genet's path to Charleston was a circuitous one and, on the face of it, unlikely. Genet was, by all accounts, a true believer in the French Revolution when he arrived on American shores. Genet's upbringing, however, had been anything but radical. In fact, it was downright conservative. His father, Edmé Jacques Genet, was the chief of the Bureau of Interpretation, an important diplomatic post in the ancien régime. The elder Genet dreamed of his son following in his footsteps and did everything he could to encourage it. Edmond received a formal education, learned at least seven languages, and, thanks to the doors his father opened for him, socialized in the upper echelons of French society, all necessary preparation for a career in the foreign service. He, like so many others of his class, also found time to dabble in science. Hot air ballooning, a phenomenon that delighted the French public in the 1780s, caught his fancy. Fascinated by the new technology, he presented a paper to the French Academy of Sciences, the APS's peer organization, that proposed a novel way to propel the balloons through the sky. The family's position rose higher under King Louis XVI thanks to the patronage of Louis's wife, Marie Antoinette. She chose the elder Genet's daughter as a close confidante. Genet's clear path continued when his father died in 1781, and Louis XVI named the nineteen-year-old Edmond as his replacement. Later, Genet secured an appointment to the court of Catherine the Great in Russia. It was while he was in St. Petersburg that the National Assembly seized power from the king, starting the French Revolution.

Even though it is impossible to say precisely why Genet, a diplomat whose career and service had depended upon the French Crown, decided to embrace the French Revolution and its republican ideology, his background provides several hints. His father's diplomatic work required him to translate fiery American political pamphlets that justified their revolution. Genet thus imbibed the ideas of liberty that fueled this earlier revolution. He also met with American diplomats in Paris, including Benjamin Franklin, and learned from them the principles that drove their cause. Perhaps, also, his distance from Paris at the beginning of the French Revolution meant that his early exposure to events came by way of idealized reports, much like Michaux's. In any case, his fervor ended up costing him his appointment in Russia. Catherine the Great denounced the French Revolution and sent Genet, a vociferous advocate of it, packing.[2]

When Genet returned from Russia in September 1792, he sought a position in the revolutionary government, then controlled by the moderate Girondin faction in the National Assembly. Genet had already come to their attention because of his friendly reports from Russia that displayed his strong support for the French Revolution and the Girondists. Those in power were duly impressed with the young diplomat's ardor and realized that his skills could be useful to them. With his fluency in English and knowledge of America gleaned from his previous work, they appointed him the first ambassador that the French Republic sent to their sister republic, the United States. It was an important post; with many European monarchies uniting in opposition to the French Revolution, relations with foreign governments, especially those that might be sympathetic to the French cause, were essential to securing a republican form of government.

A combination of realpolitik and ideology drove the Girondin government's approach to foreign policy, both of which combined to guide Genet's mission to the United States. North America had assumed a central place in the Girondists' geopolitical strategy. While moderate in their domestic policies—many, for instance, wanted to exile the king rather than execute him, though ultimately a more radical contingent prevailed and ordered the execution in January 1793, a few months before Genet arrived in the United States—they were far more immoderate in their view of the Revolution's international goals. They believed that the French Revolution was a continuation of the American one and that it was the next step in a global movement that was going to tear down monarchies throughout the world and replace them with republican governments. Shaped by their messianic view of their revolution's destiny, the Girondin officials saw both Spanish and British colonial holdings on the American continent as vulnerable targets for fomenting new republican revolutions. This vision, of course, threatened the stability of almost all of the major European governments as well as the geopolitical landscape of North America.

Girondin objectives in North America also carried, not coincidentally, a more strategic and practical purpose. Spain and Great Britain had united in war against France in 1792 and 1793 to protect their status quo. When Genet arrived, the three countries were locked in battle on the European continent and the high seas. If France could turn Louisiana (and maybe Florida) from colonial holdings into republican strongholds, or at least launch a serious attack on these territories, then they could force Spain and Great Britain to divert resources away from the European front to defend their North American colonies. More importantly, they believed that if the French acted in North America, especially if with the aid of Americans, Great Britain and Spain would consider the United States as playing a part. If France's enemies duly blamed and declared war on the United States, circumstances "would inevitably force America to take [France's] side." It was a calculating geopolitical strategy for the French government, then trying to shift the balance of power against its two powerful European rivals.

The French laid out their audacious—and overly confident—plan for transforming North America in a document titled "Plan for a Revolution in Louisiana." In it, they outlined the surreptitious means by which they intended to turn Louisiana into a sister republic. The French were sure that the Spanish had a tenuous hold on this formerly French territory, stating that their sources estimated that the Spanish had only 1,500 troops in the region and, better yet, that many of those bearing arms were in fact Frenchmen with weak ties to their Spanish overlords. The French thus hoped to organize an invasion of the vulnerable territory by having Genet entice Frenchmen living in the United States—likely Philadelphia, a home to many French immigrants—to support the cause. Their plan called for these recruits to head west to Kentucky, where they would convince Americans, especially Kentuckians and French émigrés living there, to join them. In Kentucky, this enlarged group was to form military units under the guise of a defensive force intended to protect communities in the event of war with Native American groups, not as a body preparing to launch an offensive against Spain. Doing so, the French believed, was less likely to raise any concerns with US government officials. Then, after the militias had formed, they would launch an assault on Spanish Louisiana before the US government realized their true intentions. They named General James Wilkinson, an American, and a French trader named Barthélemi Tardiveau as possible collaborators Genet should seek out.[3]

The document ended with a few key conclusions, the first of which embodied the confidence of the French revolutionary government: "the proposed expedition is an easy and inexpensive expedition." All of it was to be done, they said, without the knowledge of the US government because American officials were sure to oppose such an action. American political leaders in the federal government had lost, the French feared, the fiery spirit of revolution that had once animated them and that now animated French citizens. Their "Plan for Revolution" bemoaned this lack of enthusiasm: "Pleasure has made them calmer, they no longer treat liberty like a lover but like a husband, everything with them is calculated, mixed together: Reflection guides them well, but freezes them." The tepidness of the Washington administration worried French strategists. It seemed to the French that the American government wished to avoid any engagement with a cause that the French saw as transcendent. The French therefore decided that they needed to force the Americans' hand to support what the French considered a global revolution to remake the world, a movement they believed was sparked first by the Americans themselves. Much, also, was left to Genet to determine once he was stationed in Philadelphia and could better assess the situation.[4]

An unlikely source provided French policymakers with further encouragement: General George Rogers Clark. Clark, a leading figure of the Revolutionary War in the West and someone whom Jefferson had earlier approached about leading a transcontinental expedition, had soured on the country he helped forge. Stationed in Kentucky, far from the seat of federal power, he, like most other Kentuckians, felt that the US government had neglected their needs by failing to secure Americans' free and unfettered use of the Mississippi River from Spain. There was another, more personal, reason for Clark's disillusionment. In the years following the Revolutionary War, he had begged both Virginian and federal officials for land in recognition of his accomplishments. After being denied at every turn, he felt so unappreciated that he decided to turn on the United States. "My country has proved notoriously ungrateful, for my services, and so forgetful of those succesful and almost unexampled enterprizes which gave it the whole of its territory on this side of the great mountains, as in this my very prime of life, to have neglected me," a disenchanted Clark explained to a French minister.[5]

Around Christmas of 1792, just as Michaux was meeting with APS members in Philadelphia, Clark huddled with his son-in-law James O'Fallon, a surgeon and fellow veteran of the Revolution who had become similarly unhappy with the United States. Given both their own and their fellow frontiersmen's complaints, the two struck upon an idea. Since their own country seemed so disinclined to support them, they would, with a little French aid and the support of fellow American veterans, attack Spanish Louisiana, capture it, and turn the territory into an independent republic.[6]

O'Fallon reached out to fellow veteran Thomas Paine with this truly radical, even revolutionary, idea. Paine, the author of *Common Sense* and other influential tracts that had energized the American Revolution, had recently decamped to revolutionary France. A freethinker who believed in ideas above all else, he wanted to follow the spirit of the American Revolution when he crossed the Atlantic and bring the same zeal to the French Revolution that he had shown in America. Once there, he quickly fell into the Girondin camp. In a rather remarkable turn of events, French revolutionaries, who were thrilled to have a legend from the American Revolution like Paine among them, decided to elect this British-born Quaker turned intellectual leader of the American Revolution to the French National Assembly.

Knowing of Paine's vaunted status, O'Fallon sent Paine a proposal that fed into France's dreams for North America. Though O'Fallon's original missive is lost, other similar proposals survive. Based on the evidence and Paine's reply, it is nearly certain that O'Fallon's father-in-law, Clark, offered to swear allegiance to France, muster a militia of angry frontiersmen, capture Spanish New Orleans, and turn Louisiana into a republic. In exchange, he expected funds, a military commission, and significant land grants in the newly acquired territory, the very things the American government had denied him. Those, at least, were the terms of a letter sent to another French minister at about the same time.[7]

Clark's proposal received a warm welcome in French circles. Paine let O'Fallon know that the executive council of the French Republic had reviewed it and responded positively. More than that, Paine implied that the existing French diplomat in Philadelphia, Jean Baptiste Ternant, a person whom Paine referred to as "the Resident" and who had fought with the Americans during their Revolution and returned to America as a diplomat in 1791, had sounded out the idea with Thomas Jefferson, the US secretary of state. According to Paine (and confirmed by later events), Jefferson indicated that he too wished to see Spain and its monarchy vanquished from North America. Jefferson also apparently vouched for Clark's suitability as a commander. "Mr. Jefferson's private sentiments respecting him, which the Resident has, as I understand, transmitted, and the reliance I have in your narrative," Paine wrote to O'Fallon in February 1793, "which confirms the whole, will excite every exertion on my part, to have the expedition promoted as you wish."[8]

There is some discrepancy in the records about when Paine turned Clark's offer over to French officials. It is unclear whether it was before or after Genet left France, whether it directly informed their instructions to Genet or was a happy coincidence that followed them. Either way, the ministry gave Genet unambiguous—though secret—orders to put these plans in motion as soon as he could. "The Executive Council therefore authorizes Citizen Genet to maintain agents in Kentucky, to send also to Louisiana, and to incur such expenses as he deems fit to facilitate the execution of this project," the French government instructed their ambassador before he left.

It is also clear that Paine played a prime role in helping his friends Genet and O'Fallon put the plan in motion. Paine had apparently given Genet a list of potential allies in America to consult, and he let Genet know about O'Fallon as a possible friend, a recommendation that likely happened separate from O'Fallon's inquiry on behalf of Clark. "He is my sincere friend," Paine said of Genet to O'Fallon, "and your name is already made known to him by me."[9]

Seven weeks later, Genet arrived on American shores. His original destination was Philadelphia, but as his ship neared the coast, he directed it to Charleston instead. Ostensibly, Genet's hatred of Great Britain, a popular sentiment among French revolutionaries, spurred him to visit the southern city. He had heard of the British occupation of Charleston during the Revolution, and he wanted to visit a city that had suffered under British rule—presumably because he assumed the citizenry would harbor the same resentments toward the British as Genet and therefore be receptive to his mission. "I recognized Charleston and I could not resist the desire to see this city so famous for all the cruelties which the English exercised there," Genet recounted.[10]

There was surely another reason for Genet's decision. Landing in this southern port would better serve his secret mission. First, he could distribute letters of marque in the port. Such appointments turned merchant ships into privateers that sailed under the flag of whatever country issued the letters and authorized them to harass enemy ships. The sailors' compensation was the booty they captured in their attacks. Ambitious American ship captains embraced the opportunity. Within days of Genet's disembarking, several American vessels flew French colors and patrolled the Atlantic seaboard in search of British prizes, eventually taking several. Genet also met with the French consul stationed in Charleston, Michaux's new friend Mangourit, to plan for an invasion of Florida. Perhaps, too, while meeting with members of the South Carolinian elite or with Mangourit, he heard about a French botanist who roamed North America in search of plants and maintained a sophisticated garden outside the city.[11]

After distributing the letters of marque and meeting with Mangourit, Genet departed the southern city for the federal capital in an elaborate four-horse carriage owned by Thomas Pinckney. Pinckney had no use for the carriage himself. He had recently left for London after Washington appointed him ambassador to Great Britain; he would, however, play a small but important part in the events to come. Riding in style, Genet took his time on his trip north, visiting small towns and cities along the way. The French government had sent Genet reports indicating that the French Revolution remained wildly popular with most Americans, even if the Washington administration seemed hesitant to embrace the French cause openly. His goal was to test the intelligence he had received about the American public's strong support of the French cause.[12]

As Genet traveled from Charleston to Philadelphia, the temperature of the American people proved very warm indeed. Genet met one cheering crowd after another as he bounced from one town to the next. Many towns hosted grand events to celebrate the arrival of their distinguished guest. To Genet's eyes, the apparent adoration that followed him confirmed that the American populace shared the same messianic zeal for the French Revolution that he and his superiors in the French government possessed. Emboldened, he decided that, if necessary, he could appeal directly to the American people to combat their government's policies that harmed the French cause—what today we might consider foreign interference in domestic politics. In fact, those giving Genet orders predicted that he might have to do just that in order to accomplish the Girondin goal of forcing the United States to join France in its war against Great Britain and Spain. "As this plan would be carried out by the Citizens of the United States, it would eventually drag them into the present war; for I say it frankly, as a free country the United States should help you in the generous efforts you are making for universal freedom against universal despotism," they advised Genet.[13]

Genet's inflated sense of importance only grew greater when he arrived in Philadelphia on Thursday, May 16. City newspapers had followed Genet's every move, noting the jubilation that greeted him and reprinting the speeches made by leaders in various towns. As Genet neared the city of brotherly love, Philadelphians realized it was their turn to do the same, and, being the nation's largest and capital city, they knew that their welcome needed to exceed all the others. The event began at 1:00 p.m., when the *Ambuscade*—the ship on which Genet had arrived in Charleston was now moored in the Delaware River awaiting Genet's arrival by land—announced his approach with roaring cannons. Moments later, Christ Church's bells tolled. The signals sent throngs of Philadelphians racing to Gray's Ferry on the western outskirts of the city, near where Jefferson lived, to welcome the Frenchman.[14]

Hosting the city's official reception was seen as a civic act, so municipal leaders called a public meeting at 6:00 p.m. outside the State House to discuss what Philadelphia should do next. That night, a large crowd gathered in front of an observation deck that the APS had built in 1769 to observe the Transit of Venus. In the following years, the stage had become the main site for holding public events like this one, including the first public reading of the Declaration of Independence. The meeting on the night of May 16 continued that tradition. A committee of city elders sat on the platform and discussed what the city should do to welcome Genet. They ultimately decided to appoint a committee to prepare an address to Genet that would be delivered the next day.[15]

This new committee's task was particularly important, as it would set the tone for the minister's stay. Therefore, the most prominent members of the city were selected. All were APS members who knew each other, and several had worked together to get Michaux's scientific expedition off the ground. They were also a decidedly pro-Jefferson, pro-France contingent. At the head sat APS president David Rittenhouse. Also appointed were James Hutchinson, the doctor who sat on the fundraising committee for Michaux, and Benjamin Smith Barton, the natural historian whom Michaux had first approached with his idea for a western expedition. Fellow APS member Peter DuPonceau also joined the group. DuPonceau, a Frenchman who fought in the American Revolution and stayed in Philadelphia, was a leading lawyer and linguist who shared Jefferson's fascination with Indigenous languages—and his political beliefs. Alexander Dallas, the secretary of state for Pennsylvania, was a recently elected APS member who was also firmly of the Jeffersonian political persuasion; indeed, he would eventually serve variously as James Madison's secretary of treasury, war, and state. Rounding out the committee was Jonathan Dickinson Sergeant, a prominent Philadelphia lawyer, and George Fox, a physician close to William Temple Franklin, grandson of Benjamin Franklin.[16]

The next morning, the committee convened at Charles Biddle's house to draw up a response. Each member had spent the night crafting their own version of the speech they thought the committee should deliver. When they met the next day, they compared their efforts and undertook the difficult task of massaging several drafts into a single consensus. That night, a larger crowd gathered in the State House yard to hear the result of their work. "This interest of freedom and equality," the address stated, "adds to the force of our affections, and renders the cause of France important to every republic, and dear to all the human race." There was little debate and easy approval from the crowd as they heard the words read aloud. For Rittenhouse and his committeemen, and those in the audience hailing their work, their speech made clear that the French and American Revolutions were bound together in a cause they hoped would sweep the globe.[17]

A mass of people, propelled by the speech and their fervor for it, then marched to the City Tavern, the place Genet was staying near the Delaware River and about four blocks east, to present it to him. As one newspaper described the scene, "an immense body of citizens" walked three men abreast that spring evening. Many in the promenade were decked out in French regalia and cheered on the French Revolution as they proceeded. One person counted more than a thousand in the crowd, while Alexander Hamilton, perhaps the most cynical of the observers, placed the number at a still impressive five to six hundred. To place Hamilton's more jaundiced estimate in perspective, the total population of the city was perhaps fifty thousand, meaning that he estimated 1 percent of the population turned out to cheer on Genet. Today, in a city of 1.5 million, that would amount to fifteen thousand people, no small gathering.[18]

Genet was overjoyed with what he heard. The statement read that night reaffirmed Genet's impression of widespread support for the French cause. It created a lasting impression, one that would guide his behavior in the weeks and months to come. He responded with an extemporaneous speech delivered from his window. The mass assembled in the street below endorsed his words with three ebullient cheers. The next day, when Genet had more time, and as his head cleared a bit from the previous evening's celebration, he penned an official reply. He delivered it to the city's committee at noon, and its text soon appeared in city newspapers. In it, he noted that Philadelphia's enthusiastic response reflected the mood of the country. "In every place the general voice of the people convinced me in a most sensible manner of their real sentiments and sincere and friendly dispositions toward the [French] nation," he boasted, "and the advancement of that common cause which she alone supports with so much courage."[19]

The fetes continued in the days that followed. The German Republican Society issued its own statement welcoming Genet. French Philadelphians, led by DuPonceau, did the same. On May 19, an elaborate "Citizens Dinner" commemorated the ties between France and America. The event included fifteen toasts, including one to "the valiant defenders of French liberty by sea and land" and a chorus of revolutionary songs. As the evening of good cheer drew to a close, a liberty cap, the symbol of the French Revolution, was passed from one head to the next. The city's artillery was even involved in the fanfare. The battery fired a salute after each toast was read.[20]

On June 1, the Philadelphia elite held yet another private dinner, this one at Oeller's Hotel. A more exclusive affair than the earlier soirée, attendees paid a high fee to attend. Enthusiasm, though, remained strong, and more than two hundred of the city's elite turned out. As one attendee reminisced, reports of the festivity "created a great sensation throughout the country." The evening was marked by food, drinks, many toasts to Genet and the French cause, and even a group sing-along to the French Revolution's anthem "La Marseillaise" in French and, thanks to DuPonceau's linguistic abilities, in English. One toast connected the two countries in common cause. "The spirit of *Seventy-Six and Ninety-Two,*" they shouted, "may the citizens of America and France, as they are equal in virtue be equal in success."[21]

Michaux's journal is once again painfully quiet about his activities during this period. We know that he had joined a French society in Philadelphia that was inspired by the French Revolution in February 1793. He was also enmeshed with members of the APS, and he clearly had extensive connections to the French émigré community in Philadelphia, so it is entirely possible—perhaps even likely—that he partook in some of these events himself.[22]

Regardless of Michaux's participation, the organizers of the Philadelphia celebrations had two attributes in common that proved important for Michaux and Genet's plans. Most were ardent Jeffersonians, and many were members of the APS; in fact, increasingly, the APS was morphing into a Jeffersonian institution. This politicization—and polarization—reflected a broader trend then shaping American society. As Genet made his way north, holding rallies everywhere he stopped, the Washington administration was locked in a bitter feud over its policy toward the country Genet represented. At issue was whether the United States was bound by the Treaty of 1778 that established the Franco-American alliance. Genet and soon Michaux would soon become embroiled in this dispute—and use it to their advantage.

No one in the cabinet wished for war, but that spring they debated what they could, or should, do for a fledgling fellow republic. Jefferson and his pro-France allies found themselves, as they often did, at odds with Washington's trusted aide Hamilton. Jefferson, a strong supporter of the French Revolution, wanted the United States to recognize the French Republic and its prior treaties with France, thus keeping trade open between the nations. He also made a constitutional argument. Reflecting his interpretation of the distribution of power in the government, he contended that the US Constitution placed decisions like war, peace, and neutrality with the US Congress, not the president. No other cabinet member agreed with Jefferson's constitutional argument that Washington lacked the authority to act, but there were divisions within the cabinet about the position that Washington should take toward France. On the other end of the spectrum sat Hamilton. He argued that the country should disavow its earlier treaty since it had been signed with a now overthrown government, something he knew might implicitly benefit the naval superpower Great Britain.[23]

While the cabinet's deliberations focused on law and policy, there remained a much deeper issue at play: the meaning of the American and French Revolutions. As Thomas Paine declared in his dedication to George Washington in *Rights of Man,* one of the most strident defenses of the French Revolution offered to the Anglophone world, he wished Washington would "see the New World regenerate the Old," thus drawing a direct connection between the American and French Revolutions. Those who agreed with Paine, those who offered toasts to 1776 *and* 1792, felt that the Americans and French were allies in an ideological battle to secure universal rights for individuals and establish republican governments throughout the world. American citizens in this camp, and they were plentiful, not only embraced Genet but believed their government should as well. In fact, those in this camp, whether French, American, or otherwise, would call each other "citizen," such as "Citizen Genet" or "Citizen Rittenhouse," to indicate their shared belief in equality and republicanism and to show that these ideas transcended national boundaries.

Others, though, feared that the French Revolution, with its emphasis on the destruction of traditional institutions and radical egalitarianism, threatened their understanding of liberty. News of massacres, mass arrests, and, in January 1793, the execution of King Louis XVI confirmed their suspicions that the French Revolution was far too radical and that the United States' best course of action was to keep its distance. Hamilton was among the leading voices counseling caution. "The cause of France is compared with that of America during its late revolution," Hamilton wrote to a friend when Genet arrived. "Would to Heaven that the comparison were just. Would to heaven that we could discern in the Mirror of French affairs, the same humanity, the same decorum, the same gravity, the same order, the same dignity, the same solemnity, which distinguished the course of the American Revolution. Clouds & Darkness would not then rest upon the issue as they now do."[24]

Genet's tour gave Americans an opportunity to debate this issue in ways that seem, on some level, much like political campaigning today. Historians have often debated when American political parties first emerged. Some have said this occurred as soon as Washington announced his intention to retire, opening up jockeying between factions competing for who should next take the reins of power. Several have pointed to the Jay Treaty of 1794, which many Americans opposed due to its pro-British terms. Others have noted Genet's arrival. While the wide variety of opinion suggests the ultimate futility of trying to say precisely when parties formed, Hamilton, an astute political observer, noted that Genet's arrival elicited an organized and loyal opposition—what he called "a curious combination"—that in his descriptions bore the hallmarks of a party. "They were the same men who have been uniformly the enemies and the disturbers of the Government of the U[nited] States," he wrote to a friend a few days after Genet arrived in Philadelphia; "It will not be surprising if we see ere long a curious combination growing up to controul its measures, with regard to foreign politics, at the expence of the peace of the Country—perhaps at a still greater expense."[25]

Hamilton worried that the large public events held in support of Genet might do exactly what the French policymakers hoped: pressure Washington to side with France. "Public manifestations even of strong wishes in our citizens in favour of any of the contending parties might interfere with this object; in tending to induce a belief that we may finally take a side," he warned in a piece he intended to publish in newspapers. Hamilton's fears were right. Elite Philadelphians organizing these huge celebrations knew that they were in the nation's capital and their literal parties (of the festive sort) were meant to show government leaders the depth of popular support for the French Revolution. It was party behavior even if Americans were reticent to call it such.[26]

In fact, the debate over the meaning of the French Revolution helped the opposition find its voice. While stark divisions on a range of policy decisions were emerging between the Jeffersonian party, soon to be known as Republicans, and the Washington administration, known as Federalists, the French Revolution became one of the clearest lines demarcating these differences and, most important of all, the easiest way in which political differences could be expressed in public. Hamiltonians chafed at outside criticism of the Washington administration's domestic policies, as implied in his quote above. Hamilton and others claimed that their opponents undermined the government itself simply by challenging Federalist policies with which they disagreed, such as the assumption of state debts and creation of the national bank. For those critical of the federal government, therefore, foreign policy could provide safer ground upon which disagreements could emerge. Rallying around the French Revolution was a less obvious challenge to the stability of the federal government, though everyone knew it was a tacit critique of Hamilton's desired foreign policy. Jefferson's nascent opposition party thus took the opportunity of Genet's visit to mobilize around a topic safer than criticizing policies closer to home. As Genet's tour to Philadelphia and the embrace of him there had shown, people were hungry to let their voices be heard.

Washington sat in the middle of these debates. As president, he would make the ultimate decision on the country's foreign policy. He was, unlike Hamilton, no Francophobe. He counted several Frenchmen among his closest friends, none more so than the Marquis de Lafayette. When Washington first heard of the French Revolution, he was optimistic that events across the ocean could follow a course similar to those in the United States. He remained hopeful, though increasingly wary, as news of disorder arrived on his desk. His uncertainty grew greater as word of the king's execution reached American shores in March 1793, just as his administration's debate about neutrality was picking up speed.[27]

Washington eventually crafted a position that he hoped would permit the United States to maintain relations with both nations and stay out of the conflict itself. On April 22, four days after Genet left Charleston for Philadelphia in his four-horse carriage, and just as the APS put the final touches on plans for the Michaux expedition, Washington issued the Neutrality Proclamation outlining the United States' stance. The proclamation made clear that the country refused to become embroiled in any aspect of the war.

Washington vowed that the United States would treat any warring nation the same and that its ports would remain free and open to all. His caution was guided most of all by realpolitik—the United States depended more on Great Britain than France economically, and the young nation's fragile finances could ill afford a war, either military or economic, with Great Britain. The decision, however, likely fueled the passions of Philadelphians who hoped that their fervency for Genet might persuade Washington to reconsider.[28]

Genet had his moment to convince Washington to change his mind on May 18. Genet entered the meeting after having met impassioned Philadelphians on May 16 and 17 who gave him confidence that he might be able to sway the administration's position. On May 18, the French minister secured his first official meeting with the American president. Although Hamilton had urged Washington to refuse to receive the minister on the basis that France had yet to establish a legitimate government, Washington listened to Jefferson's advice and received Genet as France's official ambassador. He may have received him, but Washington's demeanor inside the President's House struck the ever-impressionistic Genet as cool compared to the jubilation he saw in the Philadelphia streets.

Washington's feelings were chilled, in part, by Genet's outfitting of American ships as French privateers in Charleston. Several British prizes had already sailed into American ports, including one sent to Philadelphia that the aptly named *Citizen Genet* had captured. The seizures created a major diplomatic row between Washington and the British ambassador, George Hammond. The British held that permitting American ships to be outfitted as privateers in American ports was tantamount to an act of war. Washington, of course, feared that American citizens were going to do the very thing the French hoped would happen: draw their own country into the conflict against the government's wishes. Washington had already made his views on the privateers clear to Jefferson. "It behooves the government of this country to use every means in its power to prevent the citizens thereof from embroiling us with either of those powers," Washington had written to Jefferson in April. Little did Washington know that while he was fuming at Genet's use of privateers and fearing that they may force the United States into a war he wished to avoid, Genet—with the aid of Michaux—was about to unleash an even greater threat to Washington and his administration.[29]

❖ 11 ❖

A New Mission

May 1793–July 1793, Philadelphia

Amid all the adulation, Edmond Genet found two things awaiting him: a letter from George Rogers Clark offering his services and a French botanist eager to explore the very region in which Clark lived. This happy coincidence provided Genet with the perfect means to carry out his secret orders to attack Spanish-controlled Louisiana.

Clark's letter, written to Genet's predecessor but now delivered to him, made clear that he was itching to organize angry American frontiersmen in aid of France's aims. Clark promised the French that he, and perhaps he alone, could succeed in such a risky gambit. He cited his service in the American Revolution as evidence that he could now help this new revolutionary movement: "This wish, this inclination, Sir, are actually as strong and vivid in my bosom, as they ever were for the cause of this my own native country during the most critical periods of the last American war," Clark wrote to the French ambassador, "and the means of powerfully assisting yr country's cause, in the actual crisis of contest between it and Spain, are (I verily believe above any one private person on earth) actually in my power." Clark's appeal, referencing his dedication to the "cause," tapped into the French revolutionaries' own fervor to see their revolution connected to the American one and part of a larger movement to spread republican government throughout the world.[1]

Aside from sharing ideological principles, Clark also shared a plan similar to the one Genet carried with him. He told Genet that he had a network of spies who fed him information about Spanish defenses. This intelligence assured him that New Orleans was vulnerable. The population of Louisiana,

Clark noted, was predominantly French or Indigenous, and neither group had any real affection for their current governors. Spain's hold was so weak, he told French officials, that he could easily capture all of Louisiana. His plan was to first seize St. Louis and then travel downriver to New Orleans. The only thing he needed was some funding and a few French ships (or, conveniently, privateers) that could blockade the New Orleans port. "In Illinois I can (by my name alone) raise 1500 brave men, or thereabouts," he promised. "With the first 1500 alone I can take the whole of Louisiana for France. I would begin with St. Louis, a rich, large and populous town—and by placing only two or three Frigates within the Missisippi's mouth, (to guard against Spanish succours) I would engage to subdue New Orleans, and the rest of Louisiana."[2]

The only thing he asked of the French Republic in return was 3,000 livres to cover expenses, a generalship, land in the newly acquired territory, and French citizenship, because he intended to renounce his allegiance to the country that had so disregarded him. By becoming a French citizen, he also expected, probably naively, that the Spanish would view his actions as independent of the United States. "For our pay and gratifications in land, (as we abandon our own here) we shall confide in the Justice and generosity of the great nation we shall serve, after our labours are over," he wrote. "To save congress from a rupture with Spain, on our accounts; we must first expatriate our selves, and become French citizens. This is our intention."[3]

Clark's fluid conception of citizenship may strike us as surprising today, especially coming from someone so central to establishing an independent United States, but it was a common feeling among American settlers on the frontiers of North America. In these areas in which government controls were weak and individual ambitions were great, revolutionary ideas swirled, ideas that empowered individuals to reject governments with which they disagreed and assert their own ideas of autonomy and independence. Along the Mississippi River where Clark lived, Spanish, French, British, American, and Indigenous peoples intermingled and competed for control, and this instability gave some individuals the ability to choose the government that most suited their interests. Many Americans who had recently gained their freedom from Great Britain believed that if they could renounce their allegiance to a monarchy they could do the same in a republic if that government wasn't meeting their expectations. In fact, as citizens, rather than subjects, they felt freer to act however they wished. Rumors—real and imagined—regularly circulated that western Americans were negotiating pacts with Spain and other powers. These rumors were driven by the reality that the promise of the Mississippi River and the land west of the river beckoned enticingly while the promises of the federal government in the east continually fell short.[4]

On May 18, two days after Genet had arrived to such jubilation in Philadelphia, André Michaux called on his compatriot, a meeting that set the wheels for Clark's scheme in motion. Michaux introduced himself to the French diplomat by delivering a long report that outlined all that he had done. Michaux also told the ambassador about his previous negotiations with the APS and his uneasiness with the terms the organization had offered him for his westward expedition. "Toward the end of March," he summarized for Genet, "it seemed to me by the instructions given concerning the journey that I was considered as completely foreign to my own country and employed exclusively for the advantage of the Philosophical Society." Instead, he assured Genet that his loyalties were with France and that he would rather serve its interests than those of the APS. "Dedicated to my mission in the service of the Republic, I wish to be employed in the way most useful to my country," Michaux vowed. Genet was thrilled to hear Michaux's offer, though his response was surely not what Michaux had expected or sought.[5]

Michaux's ardent patriotism, fused with his natural history background, meant that this botanist possessed everything Genet needed to launch his clandestine project in Kentucky. "I cast my eyes on Citizen Michaux," Genet reported to his superiors in Paris; "He is active, circumspect, loyal, and dedicated to the glory of his country; he speaks English, he knows the language and customs of the Indian nations." Michaux's years of North American expeditions had thus provided him with skills now unexpectedly useful for this military operation. Genet decided that Michaux should travel to Kentucky as soon as he could, ostensibly to conduct natural history research but, secretly, to initiate the plan to invade Louisiana. It was the perfect ruse. "As he is accustomed to travel in the hinterlands of America, his departure can be suspicious to no one," Genet boasted to his superiors in Paris of his newly found deputy.[6]

An excited Genet took Michaux into his close confidence. By May 22, Michaux's attentions had shifted away from the APS, and he was committed to plotting a new western expedition with Genet. On that date, Genet officially appointed Michaux as "political agent of the French Republic" whose job was, in keeping with the French Revolution's goals of displacing monarchies around the world, "to deal with the French of Louisiana and the Indian peoples west of the Mississippi in order to restore freedom to the inhabitants of New Orleans." Genet drew up his specific instructions in a detailed document that Michaux and Genet deliberated over for days. The final document called on Michaux to travel with all possible dispatch to Clark in Kentucky. Along the way, Michaux was to seek out Benjamin Logan, another general from the American Revolution, who was rumored to harbor sympathies similar to Clark's. Michaux was then to find Clark and hammer out details with him. If they came to an agreement, Michaux had the authority to commission the American as a commander in chief in what Genet called the "Revolutionary and Independent Legion of Mississippi." Genet also told Michaux to recruit others to join the cause, including potential Native allies, and appoint officers as he saw fit. All the while, Michaux was to continue to act as if he was a natural historian collecting botanical specimens.[7]

Michaux accepted the charge. Still, even Genet, who was known to see only the positive, noted some subtle reluctance in the natural historian. While Genet had full faith in Michaux's "zeal," he also detected the stubborn independent streak that had guided Michaux through most of his life, and that now came across almost as hesitancy to follow what amounted to orders. "He felt all the advantages of it and despite his love for independence he promised to fulfill this mission with the most ardent zeal," Genet recounted after meeting with Michaux. The French botanist always strove to pursue his research freed from external strictures, but he had also almost always depended on others to underwrite his work. After having received word from the National Assembly that he was reappointed, Michaux had thought he was finally free to follow his own agenda. Now Genet, as other French officials had done before him, asserted control. It was a compromise Michaux had navigated most of his life. In this case, his new directives were taking him further afield than ever before. This dedicated natural historian now had to launch a covert operation to organize an invasion of Louisiana as a means for him to botanize in Kentucky.[8]

Genet and Michaux conferred several times in the weeks that followed to finalize details. As Michaux's departure neared, Genet grew anxious.

Genet's initial fears of the Washington administration's disfavor proved all too true. While pro-French Philadelphians welcomed the diplomat into their fold, the Federalists proved no friends at all. Genet knew that their animosity could pose problems for Michaux, a relatively unknown Frenchman traveling through the hinterland—perhaps Genet's opponents would suspect he was indeed a foreign agent meant to upset politics.[9]

Jefferson, as usual, was the outlier in the Washington administration. He and Genet became fast friends. Throughout May and June, Genet and Jefferson wrote dispatches to each other—by the end of June, Genet had sent Jefferson about twenty pieces of correspondence; Jefferson had sent his French counterpart eight. By the end of the year, Genet had written Jefferson close to eighty letters, and Jefferson responded with more than fifty of his own. That steady exchange made Genet Jefferson's second-most-frequent correspondent during this period, after only Washington. These letters were more than just diplomatic dispatches. The pro-French Jefferson saw Genet as an ideological comrade. "It is impossible for anything to be more affectionate, more magnanimous than the purport of his mission," Jefferson enthused to Madison soon after meeting Genet. "In short he offers everything and asks nothing."[10]

Soon, though, Genet was asking his friend for favors. During a private meeting in June, Genet told Jefferson about Michaux's pending trip to the West. We do not know how much Genet confided in Jefferson about his orders for Michaux (we do know he spilled much more later), but we do know he asked Jefferson to recognize Michaux as a French consul for Kentucky. Such an appointment would have justified Michaux's presence in the region and permitted his free movement in it, but it would also have set a new precedent in US diplomatic affairs. European consuls were common in many port cities because of the international commerce that happened in them, but there were none in the interior. Assigning one in the interior would set a new precedent, one Jefferson disliked. He turned down Genet's request because he feared it would lead to a swarm of foreign agents filling the American interior. Jefferson knew that these men would be hard for the US government to control and could prove particularly dangerous to the stability of the nation in these areas of limited government power.[11]

Jefferson wanted to help his friend, though, so he suggested a compromise that could serve Genet's purpose. Jefferson offered to write a letter of introduction vouching for Michaux as a natural historian. Genet accepted the offer. Jefferson drafted a letter addressed to the governor of Kentucky, Isaac Shelby, on June 28 attesting to the French botanist's skills and need to conduct research. Genet was delighted. Short of the official appointment Genet sought, a letter of introduction from the US secretary of state to a state governor was tantamount to a government-issued passport.[12]

As Michaux's departure neared, Genet remained nervous, so he requested a private summit with Jefferson in early July. The meeting, he told Jefferson, was not an official one. He wanted to talk to his friend as two private citizens who shared a common cause, not as a foreign representative to the secretary of state. "He said he communicated these things to me, not as Secy. of state, but as Mr. Jeff," Jefferson recorded in his journal.[13]

On July 5, a frenzied Genet arrived at Jefferson's house on the Schuylkill. Jefferson recorded the scene in great detail in his diary, capturing the ambassador's frenetic state. "Mr. Genet," he recorded, "read very rapidly instructions he had prepared for Michaud." Genet held nothing back. As his words spewed forth, he confessed everything, including the confidential details of Americans already involved in the plot. "It appears that besides encouraging those inhabitants to insurrection, he speaks of two generals at Kentucky who have proposed to him to go and take New Orleans if he will furnish the expedition about 3,000 sterling," Jefferson summarized.[14]

Genet sensed Jefferson's concern and echoed Clark's position that the intended raid posed no threat to the United States. He assured Jefferson that these military maneuvers would occur outside US borders, and this technicality, Genet claimed, absolved the federal government of any perceived complicity. It was, he insisted, a legitimate action of an independent group committed to fighting for universal equality. That they happened to be former US citizens, he claimed, was irrelevant.

For a historian looking back at the moment, Jefferson's response to Genet's information is shocking. After hearing of Genet's goal to raise a militia of Americans in order to attack Spain, a country with whom the United States was then locked in delicate negotiations to open the Mississippi, Jefferson, the secretary of state of the United States, did little to stop him. Indeed, Jefferson took issue with only one part of the plan. His one concern, he told Genet, was that Americans would likely face execution by the federal government if the scheme failed. "I told him that his enticing officers and soldiers from Kentucky to go against Spain, was really putting a halter about their necks, for that they would assuredly be hung if they [commenced] hostilities against a nation at peace with the U.S.," Jefferson recorded in his journal. What Jefferson said next gave Genet the impression that he was otherwise fine with the mission. "That leaving out that article I did not care what insurrections should be excited in Louisiana," he assured Genet. Although we do not know precisely what "article" Jefferson meant, it is likely that Jefferson was implying that though he did not want American citizens involved, he was comfortable with Michaux mobilizing disaffected Frenchmen, Native Americans, and others in the region for the cause.[15]

As if the secretary of state giving his tacit approval to a foreign country that was plotting to attack another foreign country then at peace with the United States—an action that quite possibly could push the United States into war—were not shocking enough, Jefferson went on to do something even more dumbfounding. Genet, feeling emboldened by Jefferson's response, asked Jefferson for a new favor. Jefferson had written a letter of introduction for Michaux on June 28. Although concrete evidence appears lacking, it appears that on June 28, he believed Michaux was going to Kentucky only to conduct natural history research and was traveling on his own accord. In the original version, similar to the letters Michaux had carried to Washington and Dunmore earlier, Jefferson raved about Michaux's skills as a botanist but said little more, likely intending to assure those Michaux met, especially elite figures, that he was a legitimate researcher who should be welcomed and aided. While it was an adequate letter for Michaux's scientific purposes, Genet thought it insufficient for his political ones. He wanted Jefferson to add a clause that implied he knew of Michaux's real mission and endorsed it. "He now observes to me that in that letter I speak of him only as a person of botanical and natural pursuits," Jefferson wrote of Genet's reaction to his original letter of introduction for Michaux, "but that he wished the governor to view him as something more, as a French citizen possessing his confidence."[16]

What the sitting secretary of state of the United States did next, now knowing full well what Genet and Michaux intended, is inexplicable. Jefferson acquiesced to the French ambassador's request and revised his letter so it was more aligned with Genet's wishes. Jefferson's final letter maintained Michaux's cover as a botanist, stating that the primary reason for his visit was for research, something that Jefferson now knew was only partly true and surely the lesser of the two tasks Michaux had to perform. "Mr. Michaud is a citizen of the French republic who has resided several years in the US. as the Conductor of a botanical establishment belonging to the French nation. He is a man of science and merit, and goes to Kentuckey in pursuit of objects of Natural history and botany, to augment the literary acquirements of the two republicks," Jefferson began the letter to the governor.[17]

In his original letter, written after the APS had raised the money for Michaux's purely scientific expedition and before Jefferson had been fully briefed by Genet, he had encouraged Isaac Shelby, Kentucky's governor, to support Michaux in his scientific endeavors. His original letter read: "I take the liberty of making this gentleman known to you, and of recommending him to your notice, your counsels and good offices, as they may respect both his person and pursuits." After Genet voiced his concerns, Jefferson completely rewrote this sentence to make clear that Michaux was traveling with the support of the French ambassador and the knowledge of the American secretary of state. The new letter read: "Mr. Genet the Minister of France here, having expressed to me his esteem for Mr. Michaud and good opinion of him, and his wish that he should be made known to you, I take the liberty of recommending him to your notice, your counsels, and good offices." Although Jefferson no longer advised Shelby explicitly to support Michaux's "pursuits," it was nonetheless a major and more generalized endorsement that would ease Michaux's travels and his pursuit of both his scientific and military missions.[18]

Jefferson also gave Genet one other piece of assistance, perhaps inadvertently. After their meeting in June, he told Genet that he should seek out Kentucky's Senator John Brown, someone who had subscribed twenty dollars to the APS's Subscription List, for advice. He was someone Jefferson knew well. Before entering politics, Brown had been a lawyer whose early career was spent in Jefferson's Charlottesville law offices. Politically, Brown remained loyal to his legal mentor. He was also, like so many of his Kentucky neighbors, furious that the Washington administration had proven unable to gain control of the Mississippi River for American commerce. The historic record provides no evidence that Jefferson and Brown ever discussed Genet's true intentions regarding Michaux's mission, but Jefferson surely must have known of Brown's inclinations and realized that the senator better understood Kentucky politics and local dynamics than he did.

In the end, Jefferson's suggestion proved even more useful to Genet than his letter of introduction for Michaux. Brown offered Genet more help than he could have imagined. Brown, it turned out, was willing to do more than just write letters. He wanted to support Michaux's endeavors—*all of them*—in any way that he could. "He put me in touch," Genet recounted of Jefferson's advice, "with several congressmen of Kentukey and in particular with Mr. Brown, who convinced that his country would never be flourishing so long as the navigation of the Mississippi were not free, adopted our plan with as much enthusiasm as an American can manifest. He showed me ways of acting with success, gave me addresses of many dependable men, and promised he would apply all his influence to the success of our plans." Senator Brown thus proved one of the most valuable assets for Genet's plans to reconfigure North American geopolitics.[19]

Brown's own letter of introduction followed Jefferson's lead. He used Michaux's scientific pursuits as pretext for the botanist's travel to Kentucky, even though he knew Michaux's real intentions. "From long study and research he has acquired the reputation of being an able botanist and visits Kentucky in the hope that among the plants and other productions of that country hitherto unexplored by the skillful naturalist, he may be able to make many discoveries as curious as useful to society," Brown wrote in a letter of introduction addressed to Kentucky's governor, Isaac Shelby. But Brown did even more. In another letter, which he wrote to George Rogers Clark, he added words that implied he supported—or at least was cognizant of—Michaux's real objectives. "Any assistance you may be so good as to afford him in accomplishing his views, or attentions which you may please to pay to him during his stay in Kentucky will be conferring a favor upon a man *who deserves your confidence,*" Brown wrote to Clark. The italicized words (my emphasis) were likely meant to indicate his awareness and tacit approval of Michaux's confidential mission.[20]

With such sponsors, no one could question the motives of a Frenchman traipsing through the American countryside. While such letters assured the unsuspecting that Michaux was on a quasi-government-approved scientific mission, to anyone in whom Michaux truly confided, these letters easily signaled that this Kentucky senator and the US secretary of state were aware of the secret mission and perhaps even supported it.

Scholars have struggled to explain Jefferson's actions. There is, first, the issue of what really happened in his July meeting with Genet. To help, we have Genet's account, which jibes with much of Jefferson's. As the French diplomat reported to his superiors in Paris soon after the meeting,

Jefferson assured him that "a little spontaneous irruption" against Spain posed little threat to the United States, a summary similar to Jefferson's own note in which he recounted that he offered no objection to an "insurrection" so long as Americans were left out. While the leading historian of Genet's visit has dismissed Genet's account as exaggeration, there is nothing in his account that can be contradicted. In fact, his story parallels closely Jefferson's own account.[21]

Historians who have scrutinized the episode noted Jefferson's unusual decision-making, but they often also hesitated to condemn Jefferson. The editors of *The Papers of Thomas Jefferson* called his choice to keep Washington in the dark about Genet's true plans "a serious omission considering the diplomatic consequences that might have ensued from an attack launched from American territory on part of the Spanish empire." Early on, a leading historian in the mid-nineteenth century concluded that "the most ambiguous position in regard to the whole affair of Genet and his mission is that of Jefferson." Frederick Jackson Turner, in his study of the Genet plot, was equally puzzled. "Jefferson's position in 1793 is less easy to explain," he concluded. "It might be supposed," two of the more recent leading historians of the era, Stanley Elkins and Eric McKitrick, wrote of Jefferson's relationship with Genet, "that the Secretary of State would not henceforth have permitted any but the most narrowly correct official business between them. But this seems not to have been the case." "A near-traitorous action" is how the otherwise sober historian Harlow Giles Unger summed it up in probably the most pointed terms anyone has yet used to describe it.[22]

Indeed, one cannot help but wonder what Jefferson was thinking during this entire affair. As Unger noted, it would be unconscionable today if the secretary of state learned of such a conspiracy and said nothing; indeed, Jefferson may even have used his office to abet the initiative. Placed in the context of the early republic, however, there are several possible explanations for Jefferson's actions and inactions. In fact, there is probably not one single clear reason for Jefferson's behavior but instead a concatenation of events that all influenced his thinking, none of which necessarily absolve Jefferson of what might be considered duplicity.

First, at the time, there still existed a sense of a private and public self, and a holder of public office could easily separate these two capacities. Therefore, because Genet approached Jefferson as "Mr. Jefferson," not as secretary of state, Jefferson's duty was to maintain the confidence with which Genet entrusted him. Jefferson thus felt that it was honorable for him to listen to Genet as a fellow citizen of the world trying to encourage republicanism rather than a diplomatic official serving national interests.

Another factor at play was the developing party strife in the nation's capital. Up until this point, party politics remained controversial. Many Americans believed parties to be signs of corruption because, in the eighteenth century, political theorists argued that parties simply served private interests, not the public good. Evidence of parties or factions within a body politic were, according to this theory, a sign of illness. Four years into their untried republic, Americans were fast realizing that policy disagreements among a diverse and dispersed people were inevitable. Still, the idea of parties as legitimate forms of opposition remained taboo. That hostility toward dissent put Jefferson, a critic of the Washington administration's policies who was also a part of it, in a bind. Jefferson thus saw Genet as a proxy through whom he and his allies could safely voice their opposition, and, in this case, advance their interests in opening the Mississippi and perhaps encouraging American expansion.

There was more to Jefferson's embrace of the French minister than simple partisan jockeying, though. Jefferson's own deeply held beliefs surely influenced much of his behavior. Jefferson was an undeniable and fervent supporter of the French Revolution who, like Genet, saw the American Revolution and French Revolution as part of a larger movement that was going to transform the world. A key element uniting Jefferson's thinking about the American Revolution with that of the French revolutionaries was the absolute sovereignty of the people. One of the things that troubled Jefferson so much about Washington's view of the federal government was Washington's assertion of executive power that, to Jefferson's mind, took power away from the people and hinted at a slow return to a hierarchical, almost monarchical, government. At the moment Genet arrived, before the French Revolution's most radical and violent tendencies had yet to emerge fully, Jefferson saw Genet as a revolutionary brother-in-arms who could remind Americans of the spirit of 1776; his plot could help spread these principles farther across the continent.

In fact, the idea that Genet proposed—a body of men forming voluntarily to attack a monarchical power to establish a republic—seemed, to Jefferson's mind, an entirely natural occurrence in a global movement to expand republican principles. Such insurrections had occurred regularly in the years since the American Revolution. It was Jefferson, of course, who had made the famous quip in 1787 that "the tree of liberty must be refreshed from time to time with the blood of patriots and tyrants." Rebellions, he argued in that same letter, were useful and necessary. "What country can preserve it's liberties if their rulers are not warned from time to time that their people preserve the spirit of resistance? Let them take arms," he concluded. With his growing distance from and distaste for the policies of the Washington administration, perhaps Jefferson felt it was time that Washington be reminded of the power of the people.[23]

Finally, aside from Jefferson's ideological reasons, there was an element of callous strategic thinking. Jefferson already feared that war between the United States and Spain over the Mississippi was imminent and inevitable. "Spain is so evidently picking a quarrel with us that we see war absolutely inevitable with her," Jefferson confided to James Monroe on June 28, just about the time Genet was approaching him with his own scheme to antagonize Spain. Jefferson may have figured that, at a minimum, the United States might co-opt these mobilized militiamen if a war between Spain and the United States erupted. Even if war did not break out, if Clark launched a successful invasion of Louisiana, then the United States might gain the much-desired control over the Mississippi—and probably, over the long term, acquire the territory itself. In short, Jefferson may have truly believed that there was little risk to US interests if Genet managed to launch a successful invasion; to the contrary, he might have seen the possible advantages.[24]

One thing was clear. Genet was deadly serious about the Louisiana invasion, and his scheme's success was entirely plausible. The privateering venture he had started in South Carolina was proving a grand success, with news of American ships capturing British ships regularly arriving in Philadelphia. Some of the prizes themselves were even brought to Philadelphia in what many in the Washington administration viewed as an affront to their stated policy, leading the federal government to eventually seize them. Still, with American merchant ships waging a proxy war for France in the Atlantic, there was every reason to expect that Clark's foray on land could prove equally effective.

Rightly confident and newly empowered by a US senator and the American secretary of state, Genet went about acquiring more letters of introduction for Michaux. He created a list, likely based upon Brown's advice, of all the powerful figures in the West, mostly in Kentucky, who might be sympathetic to Michaux's real mission. By the end of June, Michaux had letters of introduction to some of the chief political players in Kentucky. In addition to the one to Shelby, Michaux carried at least twelve others, including to two sitting congressmen, three former generals, and several prominent lawyers. All appeared to either be aligned with the political party then forming around Jefferson or were vocal advocates for opening the Mississippi River. The letters also provided Michaux with an itinerary. His first letter was for a prominent attorney in Pittsburgh, Hugh Henry Brackenridge. His next letter was for Colonel Alexander Orr, a congressman living in Limestone, Kentucky, an important inland port along the Ohio River. After that, he had several letters for figures in Lexington, about fifty miles south of Limestone, and Danville, then a hub of political activity that sat about twenty miles farther south of Lexington. Of course, he also brought a letter addressed to George Rogers Clark of Louisville, his final and ultimate destination.[25]

With his journey mapped out and letters in hand, Michaux started packing his materials in early July. It was a massive amount of cargo. One receipt states he brought at least 550 pounds of baggage on his trip west. Though there is no itemized list of his goods, he likely carried his scientific instruments, herbarium, and tools. Michaux also managed to smuggle some arms and ammunition among the cargo as tangible proof to Kentuckians that France was ready to outfit them. While there is no direct evidence of how Michaux paid to outfit the expedition, it is almost certain that he was once again firmly in the employ of the French ambassador and Genet was able to provide him with the credit necessary to conduct his work. The APS, for its part, seems to have moved on from the expedition itself. The minutes are quiet in the months following April 1793, as if the entire campaign never happened. Indeed, the Society's involvement only reemerged years later when the institution undertook an accounting of their finances in 1799 and realized they needed to reclaim the money raised from the Rittenhouse estate.[26]

On July 15, ten days after Genet's unofficial meeting with Jefferson, Michaux was ready to depart. He met that day with Genet one last time to go over plans. Genet wrote up his final instructions and gave Michaux some final words of encouragement. "You will neglect nothing, Citizen," Genet advised Michaux, "when striking Americans with these powerful considerations and when convincing them that their glory wants, that their interests demand, that they liberate themselves from the diplomatic shackles that oppose their wishes, the timid conduct of the federal government, in going to occupy new Orleans which is almost defenseless and where the inhabitants await them with anxiety well convinced that once they are the masters no force will be able to dislodge them out and that France will support them."[27]

At ten o'clock that evening, as the moon lit the roadways and darkness cooled the summer day, Michaux started his trek west. Because Ducoigne and the Native delegation had long since left, Genet provided Michaux with two French army artillerymen to protect him and who could advise Clark on the assault. It was a small delegation so as not to raise suspicions and modeled on the same type of small groups Michaux always traveled with on expeditions. This time, though, rather than having Native American guides or some of his skilled slaves as his traveling companions, he had military men by his side—a sign of his true purpose.[28]

Armed with his letters of introduction and with his cargo of instruments—and some hidden contraband—in tow, he appeared to be a botanist laden with the tools of his trade embarking on a mission to observe the natural world and fulfilling his quest to advance knowledge. But the reticent and perhaps a bit quirky natural historian also carried clear but secret orders from Genet that his primary objective was to initiate the invasion of Spanish Louisiana. He did so with the full knowledge of the US secretary of state, Thomas Jefferson. It was, to say the least, an unexpected turn of events for a natural historian who had largely avoided politics his entire life. In a matter of weeks, he had gone from planning a transcontinental scientific expedition under the auspices of the American Philosophical Society to traveling west as a secret agent for the French government. While he had hoped his time in the United States might let him transform the world of botany, if he carried out this mission, he would transform geopolitics in North America.

❖ 12 ❖

Michaux's Dual and Dueling Expeditions

July 1793–August 1793, Philadelphia to Kentucky

Michaux headed west from Philadelphia on the night of July 15, laden with his instruments and other implements essential for his work, including, in this case, a secret cache of arms. Though the horse-drawn carriages surely labored under the weight of the cargo, Michaux and his entourage nonetheless traveled with great dispatch to Pittsburgh. He passed through Lancaster, about ninety miles west of Philadelphia and one of the most bustling inland towns at the time, on July 17, less than two days after leaving Philadelphia. He made it over the Appalachian Mountains by July 22. He then followed a string of forts that the British had built in the 1750s to ward off French attacks, before arriving at Fort Pitt on July 27. Pittsburgh was still a small outpost that served as a waypoint for those hoping to travel farther west or to ship materials east. It contained only a couple hundred homes, mostly clustered around the confluence of the Ohio, Monongahela, and Allegheny Rivers.

Michaux made excellent time getting to the town. He traveled between twenty-five and forty miles a day after leaving Philadelphia, making the three-hundred-mile-long trek in eleven days. As he made his way, he knew that he once again had to serve two masters. When he had worked for the ancien régime, he had to juggle his drive to explore and document the natural world with the French Crown's expectation that he collect and ship tens of thousands of trees across the ocean to replenish French forests. When he had negotiated with Jefferson and the APS, the sticking point had centered on a similar tension: the APS wanted him to serve their interests rather than let him follow his own botanical proclivities. Now, as he headed into forests that he suspected housed many undocumented species, he once again had to balance his deep desire to collect with the most unexpected, and certainly the riskiest, task he had ever been asked to fulfill for his country—and that is saying something for a life that had already seen its share of peril.[1]

Torn by these competing interests, Michaux let his desire to botanize overtake him only twice on the trip west. Michaux had to maintain his facade, after all. Now that he was traveling again, he returned to his daily journaling, and he noted interesting plant species outside Lancaster and again near the Juniata River. Even on those two days of research, he covered twenty-one miles. Such focus continued once in Pittsburgh. On July 28, the day after he arrived in what was then an American frontier town, he called on Hugh Henry Brackenridge. Brackenridge served as an important node connecting the East and West. He was a renowned attorney, a leading figure in his community, close with many politicians in the national capital, and a regular contributor to eastern newspapers, often offering the perspective of frontier people to seaboard audiences. Most recently, he had published the first installment of one of the first major American works of fiction, *Modern Chivalry.* Mimicking the formula of *Don Quixote,* Brackenridge's entertaining novel followed a frontier bumpkin traveling through Pennsylvania and rising in its ranks, often in spite of himself. Even though some literary scholars consider *Modern Chivalry* "the first great American novel," most Americans today have never heard of it.[2]

When Michaux showed up at Brackenridge's door, as many prominent travelers to Pittsburgh did in those days, he carried something that was sure to get Brackenridge's attention: a letter of introduction. Unfortunately, there is no record of who wrote it, but given Brackenridge's renown and connections, the recommendation likely came from Kentucky senator John Brown. If Jefferson had authored it, there likely would be some record of it in his extant papers, though it remains a possibility because the two also knew each other. In any case, Michaux, it is clear, held nothing back. As Brackenridge would later recount, "Michaud had a commissary's commission for the expedition which Genet had planned from the quarter against the Spaniards."[3]

Brackenridge had a reputation for moderation, and that certainly proved true when he sat down with Michaux and heard of his plans. He responded very coolly to the idea. In fact, Brackenridge had recently warned against

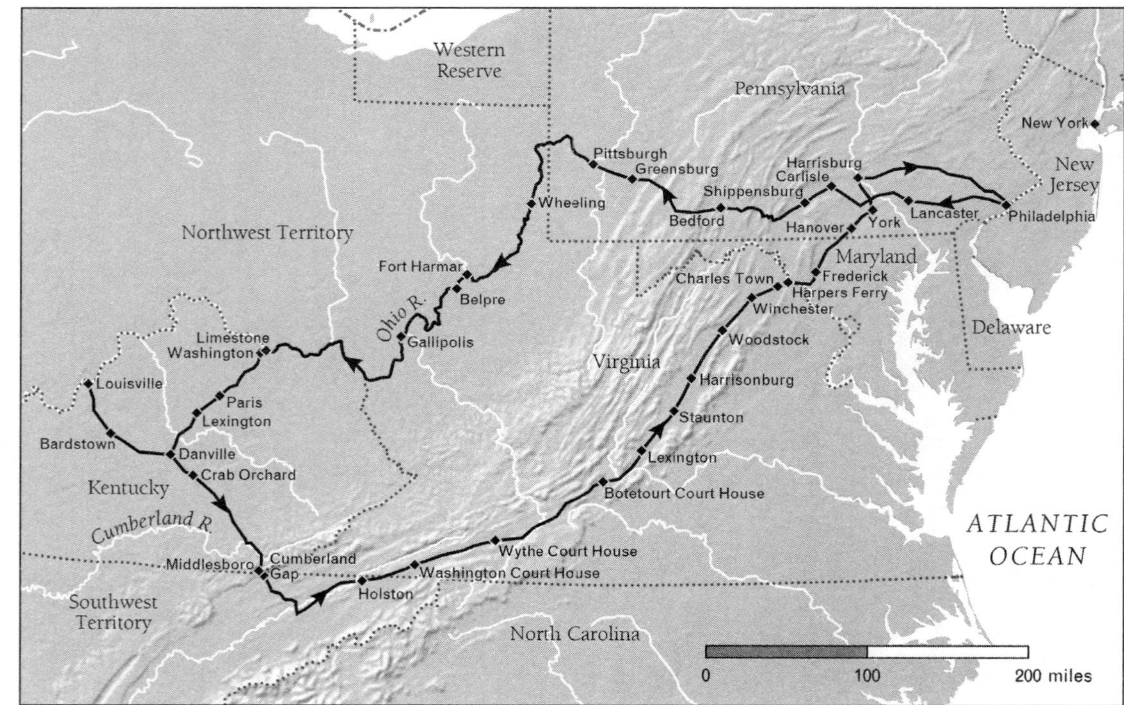

MAP 3. ANDRÉ MICHAUX'S KENTUCKY JOURNEY. In the late summer and fall of 1793, André Michaux traveled from Philadelphia down the Ohio River to Kentucky before returning on a more southern route. He traveled under the guise of science, but his real mission was to organize a group of Kentuckians to invade Spanish-held Louisiana. (Map by Nat Case, INCase, LLC)

such ploys. Rumors of Americans launching independent raids against foreign domains abounded on the frontier. Many of the more temperate frontiersmen, including Brackenridge, worried what this mentality might bring. He was so concerned that he expressed his fears in a newspaper report published a year before Michaux's arrival. "The time will be when the Western country will fall off from the Eastern," he fretted on the front page of the *National Gazette,* "as North will from South, and produce a confederacy of four."[4]

Such dire prognostications were common throughout the country as separatist movements ripened on the frontiers—indeed, their known prevalence encouraged the French to undertake this very mission. There were leading Americans, like Revolutionary War hero turned Kentucky politician General James Wilkinson, who were known to foreign governments because of their desire to sow division between East and West. Many of these individuals hoped that they could enrich themselves by aligning with a foreign potentate, and many western settlers were willing to forgo their allegiance to the United States if it meant they might have more economic opportunity under a different regime. Before Genet left for America, French government officials had even shared intelligence that echoed Brackenridge's words, and Wilkinson's name appeared in a number of planning documents as a likely ally. "By the gradual increase of this population the split between the Atlantic States and those of the West will be inevitable. The Americans know this and are doing their best to set back the era," the French ministry wrote in a brief for Genet.[5]

As the French dispatch noted, the Washington administration was well aware that American frontiersmen were dangerously disgruntled and that their growing disillusionment could threaten the union. Most of all, federal officials worried about alliances American citizens might forge with foreign governments, a phenomenon that may seem odd today but occurred with surprising regularity in the eighteenth century, as the Clark-Genet plot proves. Brackenridge, though, was not one of those frontiersmen. He was firmly committed to the union, so he ignored Michaux and offered him no direct aid. That said, he also did nothing to discourage Michaux or report the scheme to others.[6]

After leaving Brackenridge's home, Michaux found himself unexpectedly trapped in Pittsburgh. The Ohio River was the highway that transported travelers west to Kentucky. When Michaux arrived, the water was unusually low, and the deeper-bottomed boats he needed to carry his heavy material were unable to depart. With his political mission on hold, the ever-inquisitive Michaux turned to what he did best: exploration.[7]

The town, he learned, was home to one of the most significant, violent, and contested pasts in a country whose recent history was defined by those very things. Pittsburgh sat at the confluence of the Ohio, Allegheny, and Monongahela Rivers, with the Ohio serving as the main artery connecting the East to the interior. It stretched across what was then Virginia, Ohio, and Kentucky until it reached the Mississippi. For much of colonial history, the French and British eyed this spot because of its strategic importance. They both knew that whichever imperial power controlled this strategic point would control access to the interior of the continent. Nearly forty years earlier, the competition for its possession had sparked the first global war. In 1754, a young lieutenant from Virginia named George Washington had charged into these woods to confront a French Empire that claimed this same territory. The conflict, begun by Washington on the frontiers of North America, soon engulfed Europe in a conflict known as the Seven Years' War (1756–63), but when the American theater is included actually lasted nine years (1754–63).

As terms of peace, the British forced France to renounce its claim to lands east of the Mississippi. While the British hoped that would create a more stable West, it only unsettled matters further. Virginians and Pennsylvanians, each eyeing this valuable ground, fought over which colony could lay claim to it, sometimes violently. By the time of the American Revolution, Virginia firmly controlled Pittsburgh. Then, during the American Revolution, the British, aided by Indian allies, clashed with emboldened Americans who were now claiming ownership of this strategic piece of land and the waterways that surrounded it. In the midst of the maelstrom, Pennsylvania seized control of Pittsburgh from Virginia. Near the end of the American Revolution, as Americans sought to establish their dominion, they launched an offensive against Native people who also considered this territory theirs, leading to a stream of violent encounters, including the massacre of peaceful Moravian Indians at Gnadenhutten in 1782 by a Pennsylvania militia.[8]

Michaux, the Frenchman, saw remnants of this contested past all around him. In his journal, he recorded the various transitions of power, relating stories surely told to him by residents for whom this recent history was still very much alive—and kept even more alive by the ruins among which they lived. "We can still see the ditches that acted as an entrenchment for Fort Duquesne built by the French. Since then, the English built another fort, almost next to it, at the angle formed by the junction of the two rivers," he recorded in one of the longest entries in his journal; "the Americans had it demolished to use the bricks in the construction of houses that are being built daily at Fort Pitt." As Michaux was learning, the conflicts and volatility that had once defined this region had moved farther west to another water artery, the Mississippi, now at the core of his secret mission. There, Native, Spanish, British, American, and French interests all vied for dominance once again, knowing that whoever controlled that river would control the future.[9]

The recent history of imperial rivalries in this region may have been bloody and violent, but it also meant that people from many different backgrounds inhabited the area. Many white settlers were more interested in economics than hewing to the dictates of their national allegiances. Nowhere was that more evident than in the polyglot crew of three cargo boats that Michaux watched row into port on August 13. Thirty French Canadians from the Illinois Territory jumped off the vessels. The owner of the boat, Michaux learned, was Francis Vigo, one of the most prominent traders in the region. He was an Italian who had come to Spanish New Orleans in the 1770s. He entered the fur trade and eventually set up shop in St. Louis before moving on to British-controlled Vincennes. During the American Revolution, Vigo aided George Rogers Clark in his offensive into the Ohio River Valley. After the war, the Italian who had lived under both Spanish and British rule served in militias defending American territory.[10]

On August 13, the same day Vigo's flotilla arrived, Michaux encountered more evidence of this frontier internationalism when he paid a long visit to Pierre Audrain, a sixty-eight-year-old French merchant who had lived in the town since the mid-1780s. Audrain had come to North America in 1777, at the unusually old age of fifty-two and for reasons that remain obscure but may have had to do with the American Revolution. Once settled, Audrain used his French connections to develop a trading operation that stretched from Pittsburgh west to the Mississippi River and south to New Orleans.[11]

Audrain was up to more than trading. On the side, he and two other French émigrés, Barthélemi Tardiveau and Delassus de Luzières, were organizing a secret scheme to settle displaced French émigrés on the western banks of the Mississippi—the very region Clark hoped to possess through his own scheme with the French. Tardiveau was a merchant operating near St. Louis. He may have been a person the French government had identified a possible co-conspirator in their plot because this last name was mentioned in one of their planning documents. Barthélemi, however, had a brother, Pierre, whom Michaux would later meet in Kentucky, and the document may have referred to him. In any case, Barthélemi Tardiveau, like the Americans living along the banks of the Mississippi River, understood the potential of the land west of the river. De Luzières, meanwhile, was an exiled French aristocrat who had arrived in Pittsburgh only recently. He stridently opposed republicanism, remained faithful to the Bourbon dynasty, and had fled France because of his beliefs—and because he was found conspiring with British and Spanish forces in a planned British invasion of France from the sea. After escaping France, he made his way west, to Pittsburgh, where he established a home sitting on a bluff above the Monongahela River. There, he and Audrain became fast friends and created grander visions for themselves in the distant West.[12]

Spending their days at de Luzières's hillside home, the three gazed out toward a West that seemed to hold endless possibilities and plotted their ambitious scheme to colonize the very area the French government now intended to seize. Their plan rested on being able to recruit a group of five hundred French immigrants who had, like de Luzières, fled revolutionary France because of their royalism. In 1791, these exiles had founded a commune in Ohio dedicated to preserving the French way of life that the French Revolution had disrupted. They called their town Gallipolis, meaning "the city of the Gauls." Things quickly went south for the new arrivals. The land proved less productive than promised, and their titles to it were unclear in any case. The settlers had grown disillusioned and were slowly dispersing. The trio of Audrain, Tardiveau, and de Luzières, surely feeling their own sense of cultural isolation, were convinced that their fellow countrymen wanted to live with each other and that a royalist colony on the Mississippi River would appeal to this disaffected band. It was an almost utopian vision.[13]

Genet had his own utopian vision for the same territory. He wanted to seize it from Spain by force and establish a republic as part of an effort to extend the French Revolution into a global movement. These three took a different tack. De Luzières and the Gallipolis settlers were ardent royalists, happy to live under Spanish king Charles IV, a member of the same Bourbon dynasty that had ruled France. Driven by this combination of profit and political ideology, the three organizers decided to approach the Spanish government in New Orleans with their idea. Aware that Spain's control of North America was weak and their holdings in the West vulnerable, the Frenchmen made sure to offer something important to Spain's geopolitical interests. A large and loyal settlement, the men pointed out, could serve as a defensive buffer to possible rivals. A year before Michaux arrived, Tardiveau had even broached the topic with the governor of Spanish Louisiana, Francisco Luis Hector de Carondelet, someone who conveniently also had French ancestry. He made sure to remind Carondelet of the rising American threat on the Mississippi's banks and vowed his proposed community could retard its growth. "The central and urgent issue is to oppose the rapid developments of the Americans in the West and to erect a barrier between this bold people and the Spanish possessions," Tardiveau told the Spanish governor.[14]

When Michaux met Audrain that August, Audrain had recently returned from a yearlong scouting trip for the venture. The preceding fall, after Tardiveau had sent that letter to Carondelet, Audrain and de Luzières voyaged down the Ohio River to meet Tardiveau at his trading post along the Mississippi. Captivated with what they saw, they continued down the Mississippi to call on the Spanish governor. After a round of heavy lobbying, they convinced him that their plans were viable. Carondelet vowed to back the project with official sanction and funding.

One wishes for greater evidence of what Michaux and Audrain discussed when they met. Vague hints in Michaux's sparse journal entries suggest Audrain may have told Michaux of his plans. Michaux's journal noted that Audrain was "charged to send provisions of flour to New Orleans." Surely Audrain and other traders managed to conduct some trade from Pittsburgh to New Orleans, but the route was quite long and circuitous. More tantalizing is the possibility that this phrase referred to Audrain's role in the colonization project. One of the chief goals of the proposed French settlement was to create a highly productive farming community that would feed grain to the mills Audrain owned, meaning that he would control the flour trade between the imagined colony and New Orleans. Perhaps that is what Michaux meant to convey in the entry. Michaux was keeping a journal for himself, of course, not historians, and perhaps he elided details because he knew his memory would fill them in. Plus, because Audrain's plot was sure to upset American interests, Michaux must have known it would be best to be elliptical in this entry in case his journals fell into the wrong hands.

There is likewise a small hint but no real evidence that Michaux shared his secret mission with Audrian, for Audrain offered to give him a letter of introduction to someone Michaux simply described as "the leader of the post at Saint Louis." Though Michaux left the name unrecorded, it is likely that Audrain gave him the name of Tardiveau, who was at the time one of the chief traders in St. Louis. Clearly, Audrain wanted to assist Michaux in whatever it was he was doing. The offer of such a letter showed that, at a minimum, Audrain knew that Michaux intended to visit Spanish-controlled territory. More likely, though, Michaux maintained his cover with Audrain. Audrain was, after all, a royalist, and Michaux was now trying to advance the objectives of revolutionary France. Audrain could easily have been oblivious to Michaux's larger aims and simply wanted to help a fellow Frenchman in his scientific pursuits.

In any event, the meeting of these two men in Pittsburgh, with Audrain's scheme to establish a royalist French settlement under Spanish auspices and Michaux's mission to launch an invasion of Spanish Louisiana for the French Republic using American frontiersmen, demonstrates both the combustibility and promise of the West. In an area of feeble government and often reckless ambition, schemes and plots proliferated. Everyone was eyeing Spanish Louisiana, and the incredible uncertainty that surrounded the region created opportunities for people to craft bold ideas for how to seize power. At this point, no one was quite sure what was possible and what wasn't, and there was little to stop people from trying anything they wanted. This volatile environment was made all the more unstable by the easy mutability of people's loyalties. Individuals' affections for a distant government could often prove as fragile as the government's authority itself, a reality that underlay the assumptions of both Audrain's and Michaux's plans.

Michaux continued to discover this diversity as he spent more time in Pittsburgh, likely to his great delight. Audrain, Michaux learned, was only one of several prominent French expatriates in town. Michaux also heard about Audrain's co-conspirator de Luzières, lending some credence to the idea that Michaux may have learned of their scheme to settle the

West. Michaux noted that the two were connected in some way, writing "this man, Audrain, they say is an associate of a man named Louisiere." De Luzières's reputation preceded him. In his diary, Michaux recorded details of de Luzières's role in the failed plot to organize a joint British and Spanish attack on France. Michaux also heard of a prominent French attorney, Jean Lucas de Pentareau, who, it was claimed, was among the best frontier lawyers. He was also, according to Michaux's sources, an ardent "democrat," meaning a French republican and Jeffersonian. This was certainly true. Pentareau would eventually serve in the US Congress with the anglicized name "John Lucas" and support the Jeffersonian agenda.[15]

During his two-week stay in Pittsburgh, Michaux made sure to maintain his cover and undertook natural history research whenever he could. He wrote more about the soil of Pittsburgh than he had in other locations, perhaps to continue to serve the interests of his friends at the APS. He traveled to a new coal mine that had opened along the banks of the Monongahela River to inspect the region's mineralogy. As he walked to its mouth, he marveled at the abundance of the black rock—"15 feet thick of pure mineral without any mixture," he wrote. There, standing in this dark entryway, he observed a key resource for the industries that would define Pittsburgh in the years to come. Pittsburgh sat at the center of one of the largest coal beds in the country. It would serve to fuel the city's rise from a frontier entrepôt to an industrial behemoth.[16]

When Michaux visited, though, Pittsburgh struck him as just a small town. He estimated it had only about 250 homes. Instead, the lush forests and clean rivers beckoned his botanical curiosity, and the natural historian veered away from his covert mission to study them. Michaux spent six days walking along the riverbanks and exploring the woods, documenting all that he saw. One historian criticized Michaux's apparent procrastination, calling his scientific detour evidence of his "leisurely journey." That's unfair to Michaux. Michaux had been ready to leave on August 9, but the river was too low for safe travel. It took five more days before the river rose high enough to haul his enormous cargo. Indeed, these condition-induced delays allowed him to juggle the tensions inherent in his mission. He knew full well that his primary purpose was to find Clark and organize an invasion of Spanish Louisiana, but he was also well aware, and very happy, that he needed to appear to be an active botanist traveling in the service of science.[17]

After Michaux was finally able to depart Pittsburgh on August 14, the Ohio's currents carried him and his companions west at a healthy clip, usually more than thirty miles in a day. As he left Pennsylvania and entered Virginia (modern-day West Virginia) and then Ohio, he noted the sparse population. His journal records several days in which they saw no other signs of human life. When his company did spy an American community hugging the riverbanks, it often numbered no more than a dozen homes. The desolation Michaux witnessed was because much of this territory remained contested. Even though the United States had created the Northwest Territory in 1787, including the area that would become the state of Ohio in 1803, Native nations fought to defend their ancestral homelands, and the future control of the region remained uncertain. For Americans, laying down roots in the region remained a risky venture.[18]

Still, Michaux remained productive on the ride. He botanized on the riverbanks whenever he could, added several species to his collection, and made one extended stop at a village on the river. He spent three days in Gallipolis, the struggling community made up of French émigrés—perhaps more evidence that Audrain had confided in him. It was, he realized, a desperate situation. Only 150 people remained in what Michaux described as "this unfortunate colony."[19]

On August 27, almost two weeks after leaving Pittsburgh, Michaux finally entered Kentucky. Michaux and the two French artillerymen disembarked at Limestone just as dusk fell on the town. Here, Michaux's role as a covert agent would be put to the test.

❖ 13 ❖

Organizing a New Expedition

August 1793–February 1794, Kentucky

As Michaux made his way southwest along the Ohio River and he crossed into Kentucky, he noticed an important change. Rather than seeing sparse, often desolate towns like Gallipolis, he saw small but growing communities filled with men on the make. "Flourishing" was the word he used to describe one community. It was in these towns and among these men that Michaux hoped to organize an army to invade New Orleans.[1]

Kentucky was, as Michaux observed, a state in transition and very much on the upswing. Until very recently, it had been part of Virginia. Land-hungry Virginians, along with others, rushed to settle there after Clark's successful foray into the territory during the American Revolution. As the population increased and new farms stretched across the land, the federal government made it an independent state on June 1, 1792, just over a year before Michaux's trip. One of the reasons the government separated it from Virginia was that no one wanted a single state to be too large and therefore too powerful in the union. The second was that its settlers wanted a regional government closer to them.

This theme was a constant on the American frontiers. Though the images of hardy frontiersmen seeking autonomy have inundated our popular culture, elements of which were certainly true, it was also true that frontiersmen almost always petitioned for and sought to strengthen government and law enforcement. They just wanted it in their hands, not controlled by a distant, eastern federal or state entity. Of course, the one federal institution frontier people often welcomed with enthusiasm was the US Army and the defensive—and sometimes offensive—support it offered them against imperial rivals and Native American groups. Indeed, tensions between the military and frontier people could develop when the settlers perceived the army as being weak or ineffective.[2]

Michaux landed in Limestone in search of one of the proponents of this political culture: Alexander Orr, a congressman of the Jeffersonian stripe and someone to whom Michaux carried a letter of introduction. Michaux wasted no time in finding his first contact for his mission and paid Orr a visit the day after he arrived. While there is no known record of their interaction, the pair apparently hit it off. Historians have assumed that Michaux let Orr know of his real plans; certainly, if Michaux's meeting with Brackenridge was any indication, he did. In any case, Michaux told Orr that he planned to travel next to Lexington and then to Danville to meet with other weighty figures, all men Orr likely knew, including the state's first elected governor, Isaac Shelby. Hearing of Michaux's intentions, Orr volunteered to escort his new friend to Lexington to provide a personal introduction to these men, an offer Michaux happily accepted.[3]

Before leaving, though, Michaux switched his attention to his scientific purpose. He spent a couple of days in the field botanizing and examining the geology and soil of the region. He even found hints of wooly mammoths—one of Jefferson's personal priorities. "The bones of monstrous animals that are thought to be elephants are found nearby," Michaux noted. Michaux had his own ideas about these fossils. He disagreed with the emerging consensus, of which Jefferson was an ardent proponent, that these were bones of an elephant-like creature still alive and roaming the area. Instead, the "great abundance of marine life remains found in these parts" led him to conclude that the bones came from some sort of marine animal.[4]

After a few days, Michaux and Orr started the two-day, sixty-six-mile trek to Lexington, which Michaux dubbed "the principal city of the state of Kentucky." As Michaux headed south, he split off from his two artillerymen. He directed them northwest to Louisville, near where Clark lived, so they could conduct reconnaissance in advance of his arrival.[5]

Michaux's scientific instincts remained strong as he traveled south with Orr. A stream of observations filled his journal. The whole countryside, to him, exuded stability and security. He saw fertile farms, hot springs, saltworks, and welcoming homes lining the road to Lexington. The way he felt was perhaps the most notable thing about the journey. "Travelers can go without danger from Limestone to Lexington," he wrote. That he noted a sense of safety suggests just how different Kentucky seemed when compared to what he had just experienced as he floated down the desolate Ohio River and through areas that remained contested.[6]

Once in Lexington, Michaux followed the plan that he and Genet had hatched in Philadelphia. He arrived on September 5. He made his primary home with someone named "Mr. Cradicka" (probably Cradick) and, occasionally, "Proutte"—these names appear in later correspondence, but the identity of the men remains uncertain. Michaux got right to work the day after arriving. On September 6, he sought out two men for whom he carried letters of introduction. One of those, James Brown, was Kentucky's secretary of state and the younger brother of John Brown, the senator who had advised Genet on Michaux's itinerary. Although Michaux left no record of the meeting with this high-ranking state official, Michaux's reception in the days that follow suggest that Brown welcomed Michaux and his mission with excitement and enthusiasm. The other person on his Lexington list was Joseph Simpson, a local leader who was well-connected in the community. Genet had also provided Michaux with some initial funds, and it appears he also permitted Michaux to draw more funds in his name, so it is probable that Michaux also worked with locals to establish some sort of line of credit. Michaux, of course, managed to perform some botanical work amid it all, something important for both his own goals and to provide cover for his main mission.[7]

His next stop was Danville, a few miles southwest of Lexington. At the time, Danville was an important inland hub for the fast-expanding nation. Unlike Pittsburgh, which sat at the confluence of three waterways, Danville was located at the intersection of several key roads. It had developed into one of the most influential communities in Kentucky. At its center sat the Political Club of Danville, a powerful organization whose influential members advocated for the interests of Kentuckians. These civic leaders also had strong Jeffersonian inclinations, though their primary goal was to pressure federal officials for access to the Mississippi River. Michaux carried letters for several prominent individuals active in its affairs. While in Danville, Michaux also met with Pierre Tardiveau, the brother of Barthélemi, the man who was plotting with Audrain to create a French colony in Spanish Louisiana. This small frontier crossroad was, perhaps not surprisingly, a hotbed of intrigue.[8]

In between these private meetings, Michaux indulged his natural history inclinations. Much as Genet had hoped, Michaux's scientific work provided the cover the secret agent needed to assuage suspicious onlookers. In fact, while we have little evidence of what transpired when Michaux met with powerful Kentuckians, we have strong evidence of what Michaux told curious onlookers when he encountered them in the streets. When he was asked what he was doing in Kentucky, he may have even implicated the APS; what we know for sure is that he dropped Jefferson's name as his chief sponsor. General Arthur St. Clair, the federally appointed governor of the Ohio Territory, even alerted Thomas Jefferson to Michaux's claims, thinking the secretary of state might be upset. "Mr. Michaeu, at Lexington," St. Clair wrote to Jefferson, "gives out that he is employed by you to gather materials for a natural history of this country."[9]

While the subjects discussed in most of Michaux's early meetings are lost to history, we do know that he had a frank discussion with Benjamin Logan at his home outside Danville on September 11. This fact, along with Brackenridge's testimony, adds to the supposition that many of his conversations likely followed a similar line. Logan was, much like Clark, a highly regarded veteran of the Revolutionary War. In fact, he made his name serving as a deputy under Clark. In the years since, the retired general had acquired large swaths of land in Kentucky, including a primary residence twelve miles outside Danville and another large piece of property near Louisville. Genet had received some back-channel hints that Logan might be interested in the scheme alongside Clark, so Genet gave Michaux his name as a prime contact.[10]

Logan welcomed the Frenchman into his home, and Michaux spilled everything, much as Genet had done with Jefferson. Logan considered what he heard. Like Clark, Logan knew that Spain's defenses were vulnerable and its hold on the Louisiana territory precarious. He told Michaux that he thought the prospects for military success were good, but he also shared news from Philadelphia that deterred him from enlisting. Senator John Brown had sent the general a hurried note, likely well aware that Michaux would be visiting him, and warned him off the expedition. Something seemed to be happening in Philadelphia that was making Genet's former stalwart allies change their opinions, Logan warned Michaux. It was the first hint of possible troubles for Michaux and the larger plan.[11]

Michaux remained undaunted (and, as we shall see, Logan would reconsider his position). Two days after visiting Logan, the botanist was back in Lexington meeting with Isaac Shelby, the governor, to whom both Jefferson and Brown had written letters introducing Michaux in accordance with Genet's wishes. Again, there is no record of what transpired between the two. Some historians have suggested that Michaux shared nothing because Shelby made no move to stop Michaux or alert federal authorities. Based upon what followed, that possibility seems plausible, but the lack of evidence makes it hard to draw a firm conclusion. What we do know is that Shelby would learn of the plot soon enough, and his political opponents, along with a raft of historians, would eventually scrutinize—and criticize—his subsequent actions, or, rather, inactions.[12]

Finally, on September 14, Michaux headed to his ultimate destination, Louisville, the home of George Rogers Clark. Throughout his journals, it appears as if he traveled alone, though he may have had the two French artillery officers in tow. He arrived on September 16 and knocked on Clark's door the very next day. Michaux got right to business: "I gave him the letters of the minister and told him the object of my mission."[13]

Clark, somewhat to Michaux's surprise and consternation, appeared cool to the very idea that Clark himself had proposed just a few months earlier. "The enterprise in question was dear to his heart," Michaux noted of Clark's response, "but since he had written so long ago about it without any answer, he had thought the project had been abandoned." Michaux tried to explain away the delay and convince Clark that his services were still needed. Clark, however, remained ambivalent, hinting that the insider information Logan had received was circulating more broadly. "A new circumstance appeared to put an obstacle in the way," a reluctant Clark explained to Michaux.[14]

Michaux spent the next three days in Louisville, primarily in conferences with Clark, trying to sway him and rescue the faltering cause. Clark's concern went beyond fears of the federal government's interference. He also worried about funding. He had to acquire boats, outfit men, and provide pay for regular soldiers. He told Michaux all of that. Finally, Clark asked for fifteen days to mull it over.

With their negotiations at a standstill, Michaux left Louisville on September 20 and returned to Lexington. Never one to waste a moment,

Michaux took to the field. The Kentucky countryside proved fertile ground for his research. He identified flora new to him. He also made a connection with some of his earlier work that demonstrated his sharp memory and mental acuity. During one of his treks through Kentucky's woods, he spied a shrub (a species of *Fagara*) that resembled one he had observed in New York and another species he had seen in his Carolina treks. Even if his political mission was floundering, his scientific one was proving productive. "The surroundings are very interesting to visit for a botanist," as he put it in his usual matter-of-fact fashion.[15]

When not botanizing, Michaux tried to salvage what he could of his covert mission. Aware of Clark's money concerns, he sought out James Brown, Kentucky's secretary of state and brother to the US senator. This time, we know they talked about Michaux's mission, and Brown provided a sympathetic ear—and more. "Mr. Brown was very much informed of our affairs," Michaux reported to Genet. "He desires it could be effected." Brown then lobbied his wealthy friends to provide the financial aid Clark desperately needed. "Mr. J. Brown spoke for me to some Merchants of Lexington," Michaux let a wavering Clark know. "They have all promised to advance to me so much money as possible." The plot, which had received the tacit approval of high federal officials when Michaux had left Philadelphia, now also had the direct support of high officials in the new state of Kentucky.[16]

Still, Michaux started to grow nervous after two weeks had passed with no word from Clark. On October 7 and again on October 10, he dashed off letters prodding Clark. For his part, Clark was surprised to receive Michaux's anxious missives. He was back onboard with the plot and had even sent a letter on October 3 to that effect. That letter had gotten lost—or intercepted. In any case, on October 21, Michaux received official word from Clark that he was ready to commit to the endeavor. "I will surmount every obstacle and pave my way to Glory which is my object," Clark vowed.[17]

Weather, however, posed a problem. With the seasons changing and winter approaching, Clark argued that they should delay the expedition until the following spring. Michaux agreed. In the waning days of October 1793, Clark and Michaux had a furious exchange of letters in which they outlined the next steps each was to take to make sure the military uprising against Spanish Louisiana was ready to be carried out by the spring. Clark dedicated himself to raising men and outfitting the expedition. In fact, he was already well on his way. Volunteers were enlisting, and Clark made some initial appointments. "I am putting my machinery in motion and appointing emissaries in every direction," Clark gleefully reported to Michaux. Clark also got to work amassing the flotilla that he would need to travel down the Mississippi River. He ordered one of his newly appointed officers, Captain James Sullivan, to build a boatyard and to construct boats eighty feet long and eighteen wide—a not insubstantial vessel—that would compose their naval force. Records indicate that Clark would spend more than $1,000, acquiring massive amounts of food for his troops, two boats, clothing, and various other sundries. In fact, there is evidence that some of the recruits wore official uniforms.[18]

Despite this progress, Clark remained desperate for one crucial component for the expedition: armaments. He needed real military firepower, not just the long rifles common among settlers. He asked Michaux to get two small cannons that could shoot three-pound balls, smaller-bore mortars, and howitzers. He figured these artillery pieces were powerful enough to serve their purpose but also small enough that they could be hidden in common large trunks sent from Philadelphia, much as Michaux had done with the initial shipment of contraband he brought west.[19]

There was one other problem Clark foresaw, one more important than cannons: money. They needed much more. Genet had provided Michaux with about 3,000 livres (equivalent perhaps to about $750) to help get the mission off the ground. Clark found the sum adequate to recruit and outfit ships, but he knew their grandest plans required much more. Clark was, of course, heartened to hear of Michaux's budding prospects among the merchants in Lexington, but he pressured Michaux to turn promises into reality. "I hope you can get what money you want in Lexington," Clark told Michaux after hearing of Michaux's early successes, "without it our schemes may be ruined." Clark outlined these desperate financial straits in a letter sent directly to Genet that Michaux was to deliver. In it, he warned Genet that the mission would only succeed if he secured more money. "The fund you have appropriated for the fitting out this expedition may answer the present purpose but the future expense will depend on the success of which I have no doubt [you will secure]," Clark advised Genet.[20]

With so much energy going into organizing the project, Clark and Genet realized it was futile to keep up the veil of secrecy. The most prominent men in Lexington and Danville knew of the adventure, and some were trying to find more backers. Clark, meanwhile, was sending out feelers to possible recruits in his network. It seemed as if everyone in the region knew of the plan—and, remarkably, no one seemed to want to stop it. "I find that we can get as many men as we please," Clark happily reported to Michaux in October, "but it will be out of our power to keep our design a secret. It is generally known already but I don't know that it will damage the cause much."[21]

Clark was right. Open knowledge of the plot caused no damage at all. In fact, in the weeks that followed, enthusiasm for Clark's foray only grew. By the end of the year, Clark had amassed a formidable force and received promises of additional funding from dozens of people. Twenty-two Kentuckians organized a new subscription list. In this one, signers pledged to support Michaux's new military mission. Several high-powered individuals lent their names to it. The accounting record of the subscription is in British pounds, likely because they were trying to rectify it against a known European currency. It shows that the gambit attracted more than £100, probably the equivalent of about $400. John Bradford, publisher of the *Kentucky Gazette,* put his name on it. The Lexington-based lawyer Levi Todd, the grandfather of Mary Todd Lincoln, also promised money. There is a second Abraham Lincoln connection. Michaux carried letters of introduction for and met with James Speed, the grandfather of Lincoln's closest friend, Joshua Speed.[22]

In addition to those lending their financial wherewithal to Clark, dozens without the same fiscal resources but with bottomless ambition volunteered to fight. Such enlistments streamed into Clark's home throughout the fall and winter. Though the stories of these nameless volunteers are largely lost, a missive one of Clark's old war buddies, John Montgomery from Clarksville, Tennessee, wrote to Clark provides clues into the plot's enthusiastic reception among frontiersmen.

Montgomery, like Clark, hailed originally from Virginia, and he had served as one of Clark's colonels during the American Revolution. Afterward, like so many others who fought in the western theater, he headed out to stake a claim on the land he had conquered. He founded a town named after his old commander, Clarksville. When Montgomery heard of Clark's new expedition through a mutual friend, he seized the chance to rejoin his former leader. But more than that, Montgomery recruited others to serve under him. "I have collected the sentiments of a number of the principle inhabitants of this country relative to the matter, and find that it will be in my power to raise several hundreds for your Service in a very short period of time," Montgomery reported to Clark. Montgomery also decided to establish a fort on the banks of the Mississippi to aid the project. Its primary purpose in this early stage was to surveil travel on the river so as to prevent news of the plot from reaching Spanish ears. Later, it could be turned into a way station for the assault.[23]

Still, as Clark's preparations proceeded, supportive Kentuckians began to realize that this military sortie could create a massive political problem for them. Jefferson's early advice to Genet had indicated the harsh punishment that was in store for combatants should the scheme fail. The federal government, Jefferson knew, would consider an invasion of Louisiana by Americans a treasonous act, and any surviving participants would likely be subject to capital punishment. To counteract this possibility, frontiersmen marshaled legal arguments that justified their actions. At a moment in which Americans were still sorting out the meaning of citizenship and the role of government in their democratic society, frontiersmen held that their obedience to the US government and its policies ended as soon as they left US jurisdiction. Many on the frontiers argued that the proposed expedition—occurring, as it would, outside of US territory—was an entirely legitimate action, one well within their rights as free individuals. They staked their claim on the belief that outside the United States, they were no longer bound by, nor did their actions reflect upon, the country from which they came, especially if, as in the case of Clark, they also renounced their citizenship.

Clark used such a rationale explicitly when he laid out his new plans for the invasion to Genet in October 1793. "I find that I shall have to be very circumspect in my conduct while in this cuntry and guard against doing any thing that would injure the U States or giving offence to their Govt," he explained to Genet, "but in a few days after seting sail we shall be out of their Govermet I shall then be at liberty to give full scope to the authority of the Commission." Clark's interpretation of the law appeared to be the consensus among his peers. In fact, as word of the invasion traveled and support became widespread, men in taverns and around their hearths debated different legal strategies that would validate actions that many in the federal government considered illegal.[24]

Michaux took part in one of these brainstorming sessions at the home of George Nicholas of Danville, another former military officer who wished

Clark's endeavor would succeed. Now a frontier lawyer, Nicholas came up with what he thought was an ingenious legal loophole to circumvent any possible interference by the federal government—though, surely, if the Washington administration had heard it, they would have found the argument specious. He suggested that Genet should invert the sequence of events for the invasion. Rather than have Clark start the invasion upriver and then meet a French naval force at New Orleans, as Clark intended, Nicholas proposed that the French navy should start the invasion with a blockade of New Orleans. The French navy could then declare Spanish Louisiana conquered, at which point control of Louisiana would be thrown into legal limbo, and someone with Clark's leanings could easily say they considered Louisiana to be French territory by right of conquest. If Clark were to embark on his foray at that point and be attacked by the Spaniards, Nicholas argued, then Clark would have the right to claim self-defense when he answered their fire with his own. The ensuing melee might be seen as the fault of the Spanish, who were then conquered and had no rights to act militarily, thus leaving the United States out of it. "In this way the Spanish government would have no reason to complain to the United States against breaking the pact since the French Republic was said to be in possession of this part of the country," Nicholas explained to Michaux.[25]

Perhaps the most stunning proponent of this reading of international law came from the governor of Kentucky, Isaac Shelby. For most of the fall, Shelby claimed that he was ignorant of the potential assault on Louisiana, a somewhat dubious claim. His secretary of state was actively helping Michaux. Merchants offered aid to the Frenchman. Clark was amassing forces. It was, as Clark acknowledged, no longer a secret. Yet the governor reported to Jefferson in October that he had heard nothing of the plot. As Regina Crandall, a historian who closely studied this episode, noted with incredulity in 1902, "In October Governor Shelby would seem to have been almost the only personage in the West unaware of what was going on."[26]

When, a few months later, Shelby acknowledged that he was now aware of the operation, he relied on these same legal justifications to claim that he was powerless to stop it. "I have great doubts," as he put it to Jefferson in January 1794, "whether there is any legal authority to restrain or punish them." The state had little recourse to control its citizens so long as they followed the law, Shelby argued to federal officials, and there was nothing illegal about Clark's actions thus far. Acquiring arms, building boats, mobilizing ad hoc militias—these were all legal actions that any citizen could undertake, as far as Shelby was concerned, and the government had no standing to arrest anyone involved in such legal activities.[27]

He further claimed that even if he was aware of what the conspirators might do once they left US jurisdiction, he remained powerless to stop them because no crime was committed within his jurisdiction, and he did not consider a possible future act a crime until it had been committed. "For if it is lawful for any one citizen of this state to leave it, it is equally so for any number of them to do it," he argued. "It is also lawful for them to carry with them any quantity of provisions, arms, and ammunition, and if the act is lawful in itself there is nothing but the particular intention with which it is done that can possibly make it unlawful, but I know of no law which inflicts a punishment on intention only, or any criterion by which to decide what would be sufficient evidence of that intention." It was a convoluted argument made to justify his own inaction—and it served as tacit support for the mobilization. Shelby's reply also had embedded within it a tension between state power and federal authority. As Shelby described, he considered Kentuckians citizens of "*this state.*" Those in the federal government, especially someone like Washington, saw citizenship and loyalty differently. For them, citizenship was to the union, not to local authorities. Shelby's turn of phrase revealed a tension between federal and state power that would linger as events unfolded.[28]

Shelby offered other reasons for his inaction that suggest his legal arguments were but a veneer for his true sympathies. He was hesitant to wield his authority to punish his friends, he said. Kentucky was a small place with a tight-knit elite. With so many of his peers supporting Clark, including some he considered friends, Shelby feared the backlash he faced if he tried to stop something so popular. "I shall upon all Occasions be averse to the exercise of any power which I do not consider myself as being clearly and explicitly invested with, much less would I assume a power to exercise it against men who I consider as friends and bretheren, in favour of a man whom I view as an enemy and a tyrant," Shelby explained. His last point about the "enemy" and "tyrant" referred to the Spanish Crown and revealed his underlying motive. While the United States took a neutral position toward the French revolutionary wars and treated Spain as a trading partner, Shelby and other Kentuckians felt that the Spanish king was their true enemy for unjustly restricting American use of the Mississippi River. He used this same vein of reasoning to take a subtle swipe at the federal government's own inaction toward the Mississippi and its apparently friendly posture toward Spain. As far as he was concerned, the Kentuckians' independent action was to secure what he considered their fundamental right to use the waterway. "I shall also feel but little inclination to take an active part in punishing or restraining any of my fellow citizens for a supposed intention only to gratify or remove the fears of the minister of a prince who openly withholds from us an invaluable right," he continued.[29]

Another reason for Shelby's inaction was tactical. As one of his closest advisors, Kentucky secretary of state James Brown, pointed out to him, even if Clark's scheme was certain to fail, Shelby might use the threat of it to pressure the Washington administration to do more to open the Mississippi River for trade. "Such information might call their attention to our situation, and give our interests a place in their political deliberations," Brown advised Shelby. Years later, when Shelby ran for office again, his political opponents scrutinized his actions—or, rather, lack thereof—in 1793 and 1794. To rebut his critics, Shelby marshaled a public defense that echoed Brown's earlier advice: "The attention of the General Government being thus drawn to the Western country, I deemed it a favorable time to make an impression on their minds of the importance of the navigation of the Mississippi, and of the necessity attending to that subject."[30]

Here, then, on the frontiers and in Shelby's arguments, rested one of the gravest threats facing the United States' still very young federal government. In these areas of new settlement, governors, American citizens, and local officials assumed they all had the power to challenge the official foreign policy of the national government or, equally troubling, to completely ignore it. With a federal government that lacked the power to restrain their actions, citizens living on the distant fringes of the young country could reshape government policy to fit their own views and serve their own needs. There was, in short, no authority willing or able to stop Clark because the only real government in the region—the state government—sympathized with and even aided his effort.

With Clark making impressive headway and with no real impediments stopping him from launching an armada down the Mississippi except for the lack of funding, Michaux decided to return to Philadelphia in November to confer with Genet. His task was to convince Genet that they needed more money and more military supplies. One of the reasons for Michaux's departure was that he was experiencing his own fundraising problems in Kentucky. While the Lexington merchants had greeted the project with excitement, Michaux found it hard to turn their pledges into hard cash. These businessmen told the Frenchman that they were unable to produce the money fast enough—most likely, it was a case in which they were willing to support the endeavor in theory but actually unwilling to risk their own capital.[31]

Unbeknownst to Michaux and Clark, good news was on its way. In early October, Genet had dispatched a team of four French agents to the region to provide Michaux and Clark with additional expertise, supplies, and new instructions. The four men had their own responsibilities, each key to the mission's success. There was Charles DePauw, a merchant born in modern-day Belgium who had come to America alongside his friend the Marquis de Lafayette during the American Revolution. After the war, DePauw chose to stay in America. He leveraged his strong French ties to establish a trading house in New Orleans that also had outposts throughout the West. Genet asked this well-traveled sympathizer to escort the Frenchmen to Louisville. A carpenter with the last name of Mathurin joined him. He was to build the boats that were to "set fire to the vessels in the different ports of the country." The background and, indeed, true identity of a third man, Juan Pedro Pusgignoux (even his name is spelled various ways in the records; this is the version that appears in a deposition he gave), remains a mystery, though he eventually played a central role in the way events unfolded.[32]

The fourth, Auguste La Chaise, had perhaps the toughest task; certainly, it was the most secretive. He was to serve as the operation's Trojan horse. Genet appointed the elite Frenchman an officer in the army then forming on the banks of the Mississippi, and Clark promoted him to colonel once they met. La Chaise's instructions were to travel to New Orleans, publicly renounce his support of the French Revolution, and settle in the city with his exiled royalist family, who were already living there. Once safely ensconced, La Chaise was to gain the confidence of the Spanish governor by feigning his own royalist sympathies. Then, when the French navy bombarded the port from the sea and Clark's army laid siege to it by land, La Chaise was to burn the city from within.[33]

The foursome arrived in Limestone soon after Michaux had left. The place was abuzz with word of the invasion. Money, they learned, remained the chief problem. DePauw decided to tap into his deep resources to solve it. He auctioned off most of his inventory and donated the proceeds to Clark. Mathurin also got right to work constructing additional boats.[34]

La Chaise, meanwhile, secured the greatest victory yet: he convinced Benjamin Logan, the former general who had rebuffed Michaux, to throw his name behind the effort. Before meeting with the former general, the French-speaking La Chaise met with Pierre Tardiveau, Barthélemi's brother, for advice and ended up employing him as an interpreter in the region. With Tardiveau in tow, La Chaise called on Benjamin Logan in late December. Logan's perspective had changed after watching Clark's movement gain steam. In his letter to Clark announcing his decision to serve, he offered the same rationale that others used to justify actions that seemed to be independent from—even in opposition to—the foreign policy of the United States. "I have taken my leave of appointments in this state of the united states and do presume I am at liberty to go to any foreign country I pleas and intend so to do," he promised Clark on December 31.[35]

A few weeks later, on January 25, 1794, a recruiting advertisement for Clark's scheme appeared in the *Centinel of the North-Western Territory,* the leading newspaper in the region. The text was likely a reproduction of recruiting bills that littered the frontier and were likely hung from trees on roads, displayed in town squares, and posted in taverns. Eventually, a copy made its way to the editor. Mostly likely written by Genet, it exuded brash confidence. Clark, the piece announced, was now a major general in the French army and "Commander-in-chief of the French Revolutionary Legion on the Mississippi River."[36]

It went on to lay out in detail the project that Clark was leading: "For the reduction of the Spanish posts on the Mississippi, for opening the trade of the said river, and giving freedom to its inhabitants." It offered generous inducements for those considering the opportunity. Every soldier, the ad promised, would receive one thousand acres of land in the newly conquered territory; those who continued to serve after the capture of Spanish Louisiana could receive up to two thousand acres. Of course, the call for recruits made clear that all soldiers were also entitled to "All lawful plunder . . . agreeable to the custom of war."[37]

There is strong evidence that this recruiting worked. On the same day that the notice appeared in the newspaper, an anonymous source in Lexington sent Senator Brown secret intelligence outlining Clark's stunning success in very specific detail. It revealed exactly how advanced plans were and how serious the invasion appeared to outside observers. More than two thousand men, led by some of the most well-known figures on the frontier, stood ready to launch a coordinated attack within a month. As the informant wrote of the operations:

> General Logan has, I am told, embarked in the enterprize as second in command, and will unless prevented by the Federal Arm, proceed down the River before the last of February, at the head of two thousand men. Clark it is said has resumed his sobriety, and attention, & yet promises to renew his fame. Colo. Montgomery of Cumberland at the head of two hundred men has stationed himself at the mouth of Cumberland River with a view of interupting any Boats which might carry information to the Spainards of their designs. When you hear that Logan is among the adventurers you will easily conceive that a number of very influential old Buffaloe Hunters are engaged in it. Colo. Hall, Majr Lanier of Bourbon & some others of that County have nearly compleated the enlistment of a Regiment, & procure men with more ease than when the late Campaign was the object. So popular is the undertaking here that I fear Government will want power, either to prevent it, or to punish the adventurers.[38]

The report laid bare the dramatic situation then developing on the banks of the Mississippi. Kentuckians had managed to organize a large and complex military operation in very short order. The speed with which it was organized, and the size of the operations, reflected the very unsettled nature of life within the young United States, especially for those living in the West. The more than two thousand men who stood prepared to invade Louisiana were driven by a series of overlapping motives. They were frustrated by what they considered the inaction of the federal government to open the Mississippi. Some were spurred, as was clear with Clark, by a desire for greater martial glory. Many also had their own pecuniary interests in mind and liked the prospect of capturing new territory for themselves.

By the time of this report, the extralegal group of disillusioned and angry frontiersmen started to take on the shape of an unofficial government, potentially creating a legitimate challenge to the federal government. Troops mustered, decked out in official garb, arms were acquired, and leaders created forts meant to regulate travel in the area and control the flow of people and information so as to protect the mission's secrecy. As the letter writer bemoaned, one of the most troubling parts of the mobilization was that it was all done free from the federal government. Indeed, it appeared as if the national government was completely unaware of what was happening within its own territory. Even worse, the informant suspected that the federal government was so weak that, even when it did find out, there was little it could do to stop the invasion, a feebleness that the letter writer knew posed a serious threat to the stability of government and the future of the republic. Little did the informant know that when he confided to the senator from Kentucky, he was entrusting this information to one of the people who helped Michaux put these dangerous plans into motion.

Nonetheless, this report was one of many then circulating in Philadelphia, meaning that Clark's largely unimpeded effort to organize a legion of Americans for the French government was about to face a serious new obstacle: the US government. In fact, a hint of what was coming appeared just beneath Clark's recruiting statement. The newspaper published a second announcement that made clear that the federal government had received word of Clark's endeavor and was mightily displeased. Arthur St. Clair, the federally appointed governor of the Northwest Territory, published an official and stern proclamation that denounced the plot and ordered all American citizens involved to abandon it and return to their homes. St. Clair's address laid out the geopolitical situation and the established policy of the United States. He described the warring factions and made note that while the United States had an alliance with France from the American Revolution, in this conflict the United States was maintaining "an exact neutrality" that called on all Americans to treat each belligerent nation as "perfectly equal." He then made it very clear that Americans were to stand down, declaring that all inhabitants in the Northwest were "required and commanded to observe a strict neutrality towards Spain, to abstain from every hostility against the subjects or settlements of that Crown," and forbidding them to "aid or abett" any French officials trying to organize Americans for an invasion.[39]

St. Clair even identified by name the four newly arrived French emissaries as dangerous foreign agents and ordered American citizens to ignore their entreaties. He also instructed local authorities to arrest the men if they were caught trying to recruit Americans. In fact, the placement of this chastisement next to Clark's advertisement suggests that the editor of the newspaper wanted to warn citizens away from Clark's calls as much as broadcast them, and St. Clair himself may have facilitated the publication of the poster alongside his rebuke.

St. Clair included another piece of news that was surely meant to jolt the organizers. He reported that the US government had learned of these French operatives and of the proposed invasion from secret Spanish informants who were feeding them intelligence about the happenings in the West. Clearly, Colonel Montgomery's goal to create a base on the Mississippi that would prevent the flow of information down the river into Spanish Louisiana proved a futile endeavor. Someone had managed to leak news to the Spaniards. The Spanish, it was clear, were throwing up their own obstacles to fend off a potential invasion. Having themselves been involved in earlier plots that tried to bring Americans into their fold, they knew that the reports from Kentucky were a serious and legitimate threat to their colony. With Spain alerting the Washington administration of the plot, it was clear that the federal government was going to have to act to avoid a conflict that could upend their foreign policy and diplomatic relations.

As the plot received this unwelcome attention, Michaux, it seemed, had escaped the region just in time. He remained unnamed in all pronouncements and thus avoided the same public scrutiny as the newest arrivals in the area. Still, St. Clair's proclamation was a sign that while Michaux had been on his western expedition, something significant had happened in the East. Michaux was soon to discover all that had transpired in Philadelphia in the months that he was away.

❖ 14 ❖

The Return

August 1793–March 1794, Philadelphia

Michaux entered Philadelphia on December 12, after having traversed, according to his daily log, 746 miles via an overland route that took him south through the Cumberland Gap. A great deal had changed during the five months he had been away. In fact, dramatic changes began almost as soon as Michaux had left on his march west, changes that influenced events in Kentucky while Michaux was there and even more so after he left.

It all started to unfold a few days after Genet finished his blusterous speech to Jefferson on July 5 in which he outlined his designs for Spanish Louisiana. Frustrated by what he perceived as the Washington administration's hostility, the overconfident and always zealous French minister decided to try a new tactic to coax the obstinate Washington administration into rescinding its Neutrality Proclamation. Genet wondered if he might have better luck by appealing directly to Congress. The French ambassador lobbied Jefferson to convince congressional leaders to invite him to address the body. Applying the ideology of the French Revolution, and, to some extent, the Jeffersonian political philosophy, he believed that if he could speak directly to the institution that represented "the people," then he could persuade them to break the administration's stance on neutrality. Jefferson demurred. He was sure that Washington would see such an action as an assault on executive power.[1]

Genet's braggadocio continued, however, fueled by sympathetic local political leaders across the young country. The enthusiasm ginned up by his travel started to spread beyond the towns he had visited. In the summer of

1793, new "societies" sprang up throughout the countryside. Calling themselves either "Democratic Societies" or "Democratic-Republican Societies," each group formed in opposition to Washington's domestic agenda and in support of the French Revolution. It, indeed, was no coincidence that the first, largest, and most influential group formed in Philadelphia soon after Genet arrived. The atmosphere that surrounded Genet, the public displays of enthusiasm and boisterous partying along with the increasingly partisan feelings, naturally lent itself to the creation of such an independent body. It was also no coincidence that the Philadelphia Democratic Society included several APS members of the Jeffersonian persuasion who had supported Michaux's original expedition, including APS president David Rittenhouse. The Philadelphia group's rolls quickly mushroomed, eventually totaling more than three hundred people, and it served as the central society through which many of the outlying groups coordinated their activities.[2]

While Genet's role in forming this group remains unclear, Genet later claimed that he coined the name "Democratic Society of Pennsylvania" by convincing its organizers that their preferred name, "Sons of Liberty," was inappropriate. If true, his influence shaped national politics in ways that still reverberate today. The modern *Democratic* Party traces its roots to these organizations. The ultimate choice of name was more than just a name for a party. It was emblematic of a democratizing nation, something an outsider like Genet may have grasped more than the Americans. "The Sons of Liberty" harkened back to the American Revolution, when colonists formed such associations to protect their British liberties from a king and Parliament that seemed determined to infringe on sacred rights. They had been, essentially, organizations to preserve the status quo within the British Empire. In that earlier age, few people spoke of democracy, and, when they did, it was in hushed tones, for democracy meant anarchy. Americans spoke of creating a republic instead, a representative government formed by the virtuous, as a way to protect against the totalizing extremes of a pure democracy.[3]

But by the 1790s, in the wake of the French Revolution, the word *democracy* acquired more salience in polite society because its definition embodied concepts of egalitarianism and political participation rather than anarchy and destruction of property. Americans formerly leery of it now embraced it. In 1791, James Monroe, for instance, stationed in France and immersed in the rhetoric of equality, liberty, and fraternity that defined the French Revolution, realized that Americans (at least white male Americans like him), too, were democrats, even if they rarely said so. "The bulk of the people are for democracy," Monroe wrote from Paris to his friend Jefferson about his fellow Americans in 1791.[4]

Those who readily used the term did so for a very specific political reason. The word symbolized their rejection of the elitism, hierarchy, and aristocracy that defined the Old World. They believed that "the people" broadly construed had the right to shape policy at the ballot box, and they believed the best government served the interests of average citizens rather than those of the wealthy few. Many like Jefferson feared that the Washington administration's signal achievements—the creation of the national bank and the Neutrality Proclamation, which seemed to turn the country's back on the French—along with the growing influence of moneyed men meant that the country was mimicking the ways of Great Britain. The choice of name for the "Democratic Societies" thus stood for a new vision of American society, one diametrically opposed to the Federalist one. The articles of incorporation for the Philadelphia Democratic Society, for instance, articulated their more egalitarian values by emphasizing the power of the people to vote and their right to check the power of those holding offices.[5]

These voluntary associations, organized as they were to connect a dispersed group of like-minded individuals in opposition to an administration, served as an important step in the development of the first political parties. They adopted patterns of public behavior that encouraged and emboldened others to join their cause. Throughout the summer, as Genet tried to bend the Washington administration to his will, Democratic Society members flaunted their support of the French Revolution by strutting around town wearing symbols of it, items like broaches or cockades on their hats, much like the signs and bumper stickers that adorn our lawns and cars today. Such open displays of opposition served to legitimize political disagreement in America's political culture. They also sent a message to the Washington administration about the strength of the support the French Revolution enjoyed among the American people. The Kentucky branch added a specific local objective to their agenda: the need to open the Mississippi River. For Genet, the proliferation of these "Democratic Societies" only bolstered his certainty that the American public stood behind him, and not behind

Washington. Indeed, Genet had been the spark for this partisan activity; his arrival and tour through the East Coast had rallied people and provided them with an outlet to express their beliefs.[6]

The Washington administration, and especially Alexander Hamilton, considered these groups dangerous threats to the still young and fragile federal government. Whereas the Democratic Societies saw their actions as legitimate forms of protest, those in the administration acted as if these groups actually intended to topple the government. They feared that the presence of a coordinated opposition weakened their authority and rendered the nation and its new government vulnerable to foreign enemies or internal threats—fears that Genet seemed only to confirm. To those in the new nation's first administration trying to make sense of the changes in the Philadelphia streets, Genet's arrival fomented what appeared to them to be a quasi-rebellion. A foreign agent, they believed, was illegally interfering in domestic politics. Genet was doing so to sow discord among Americans and undermine the administration. He also seemed to be attempting to circumvent the executive to accomplish his aims, a diplomatic breach of protocol. "It is publicly rumored in this city that the Minister of the French Republic has threatened to appeal from the President to the people," Hamilton complained in an essay published in a newspaper that summer.[7]

Genet's behavior provoked heated responses from many members of the Hamiltonian faction in and around government, a group then cohering as the Federalist Party. In fact, Genet's presence accelerated the formation of the Federalists as an organized party just as much as it did the Jeffersonian Democratic-Republicans. In Genet, Hamilton and others now had a figure around whom they could focus their animus. During the summer, while Michaux was in Kentucky, Hamilton had written a series of searing newspaper editorials that painted Genet as an intemperate radical who threatened to bring the anarchy of the French Revolution to American shores. He also tarred his political opponents who allied with Genet. "Yet there are men among us, who call themselves citizens of the United States, degenerate enough to become the apologists of Mr. Genet," Hamilton declared in an anonymous essay that most people easily recognized as coming from his pen.[8]

Hamilton's barbs elicited strong retorts from Jefferson and only served to encourage more partisan behavior. As the secretary of state, Jefferson knew that he was unable to respond publicly to the attacks increasingly aimed at his political allies, who sat outside the administration he served. Though in an awkward and unusual position, Jefferson nonetheless refused to remain passive. He orchestrated a response behind the scenes by turning to his most trusted ally, James Madison. He begged Madison to go toe-to-toe with Hamilton in the press. "For God's sake," Jefferson implored his friend, "take up your pen, select the most striking heresies and cut him to pieces in the face of the public."[9]

Madison followed Jefferson's command, but the escalating war of words did little to alleviate Jefferson's more immediate concern. While Jefferson wanted his country to do more to help France and its cause, everything Genet did pushed the administration further away. Soon after that July meeting with Genet in which Jefferson had agreed to write letters of introduction for Michaux to meet Genet's specifications, Jefferson began to reconsider his once hopeful views of his French friend. After Genet's harangue, Jefferson warned the minister that his open defiance of the Neutrality Proclamation caused more harm than good. Jefferson had sensed this problem while sitting at cabinet meetings and hearing the debates. By doggedly supporting more privateers in the face of executive orders to stop, Genet had changed the debate within the administration from one focused on neutrality, something Jefferson wished to keep on the table so he might shift policies toward French interests, to a question of how to respond to a foreign diplomat interfering with domestic politics and official policies. "Never in my opinion was so calamitous an appointment made, as that of the present minister of France," Jefferson vented to his closest confidant, James Madison, on July 7. "Hotheaded, all imagination, no judgment, passionate, disrespectful, and even indecent toward the President."[10]

Washington, it was clear, needed to take a firm stance against this obstreperous French diplomat lest he and the executive branch appear weak and the government ineffectual. It was a battle Washington was unwilling to lose. At first, Jefferson thought he might be able to temper the minister. Yet as time went on, Jefferson realized there was no taming the passions of this revolutionary. "He does me justice personally, and, giving him time to vent himself and then cool, I am on a footing to advise him freely, and he respects it, but he breaks out again on the very first occasion, so as to show that he is incapable of correcting himself," he complained to Madison. By August, as Michaux made his way to Kentucky to follow Genet's orders,

Hamilton had convinced Washington that French-American relations had deteriorated to the point that the administration's only recourse was to demand Genet's recall. While Jefferson initially objected to such an act, eventually it became evident even to him that Genet's position was untenable.[11]

Washington tasked his secretary of state with drafting the request that the French replace their appointee. In early August, Jefferson got down to writing a long letter to Gouverneur Morris, the US representative in Paris, ordering him to request the recall of Genet. In it, he spelled out how the minister's insistence on arming privateers had doomed his mission. Rather than behaving like a diplomat, Genet had acted as if he was "a co-sovereign," meaning he was acting as if he could affect the policies of the government he was visiting or acting as if he had the authority of a separate government within the confines of another government. Such behavior was a serious breach of diplomatic protocol. "Mr. Genet, however, assumes a new and a bolder line of conduct," Jefferson summarized in the letter. "He proceeds to do what even his sovereign could not authorize, to put himself, within the country, on a line with it's government, act as co-sovereign of the territory, arms vessels, levies men, gives commissions of war, independently of them, and in direct opposition to their orders and efforts," he wrote of Genet's behavior. Likely this request would have proven unnecessary. In Paris, a coup had displaced the Girondists, the relatively moderate faction that had appointed Genet. The change in power marked the rise of Robespierre and the beginning of the Reign of Terror. As a result of the new French government, Genet would almost certainly be recalled in any case.[12]

For Jefferson, the entire Genet affair clarified something that had plagued him since he had joined Washington's government. He remained an outsider within the administration. Though Jefferson was charged with managing foreign relations, he felt that his opinions often carried less weight than he wished. He also disliked the administration's internal economic policies, and he distrusted the speculators and merchants who seemed to influence Washington's decision-making. All of these tensions within Jefferson came to a head with Genet's arrival and stay in Philadelphia. At the very time Washington decided to send Genet packing, Jefferson began considering his own retirement. On August 6, he told Washington that he intended to resign. Jefferson unloaded his frustrations in a private meeting with the president, one in which he articulated the essential beliefs of the then-forming opposition party. "I expressed to him my excessive repugnance to public life," Jefferson later recounted of his conversation with Washington, "the particular uneasiness of my situation in this place where the laws of society oblige me always to move exactly in the circle which I know to bear me particular hatred, that is to say the wealthy aristocrats, the merchants connected closely with England, the newly created paper fortunes."[13]

Washington wanted his secretary of state to stay onboard. With so much controversy swirling in the capital, Jefferson's departure would have rocked the administration at a time when Washington needed stability. So desirous was Washington to retain Jefferson that he paid a personal visit to his home to plead with him to stay on through the fall. Jefferson, reluctant but loyal, agreed. "He said if I would only stay in till the end of another quarter (the last of Dec.) it would get us through the difficulties of this year," Jefferson remembered of Washington's appeal.[14]

It was a good decision, for a second, closely related controversy was about to envelop the administration, one that could have irreparably damaged Jefferson's reputation had he not been there to manage the situation. While Michaux and Clark recruited with abandon in Kentucky, and a loose-lipped French minister operated in Philadelphia, rumors of the planned assault on Louisiana began to circulate in the federal capital. In late August, the rumors became a reality. A copy of a recruitment poster for Clark's military mobilization had worked its way back to Philadelphia—and into the hands of Spanish diplomats there. This clear evidence exposed the plot and implicated American citizens in it. Although the document was unsigned, previous historians suspected that the Philadelphia Democratic Society authored it. Its words were so inflammatory, its rhetoric so impassioned, and the plans so specific, that Thomas Jefferson pegged Genet as the most likely author. Michaux had likely brought copies of this broadside with him to recruit others to join up.[15]

The recruiting advertisement captured the revolutionary spirit swirling in the Atlantic. It exuded confidence and a sense of destiny. "The moment has arrived when despotism must disappear from the earth," it declared in its opening sentence. From there it went on for more than six pages, trying to stir up "the Frenchmen of Louisiana" to overthrow the Spanish government. It ended with a plea to join "the republicans of the western portion of the United States" who stood "ready to come down the Ohio and Mississippi in company with a considerable number of French republicans." The independent Louisiana republic, the proclamation then offered, would join with the United States and France to create "an alliance which will be the basis on which, henceforth, shall stand our mutual political and commercial interests." This final section, outlining as it did the invasion of Louisiana and creation of an independent republic, provided the official proof that Spain needed to show that Americans were conspiring with France to attack Spanish territories.[16]

On August 27, the Spanish consulate in Philadelphia, proclamation in hand, sent a dispatch to Jefferson officially alerting the secretary of state to their discovery. "We ask you to tell us whether such an offer has been made with the knowledge of your government, and if not, we do not doubt that your government will properly take measures to punish the daring of the man who has proposed, without any authority, to involve the United States so generously," the consul warned Jefferson. The news was something of a gift to Jefferson. It meant he could control the flow of information to Washington and protect his own potential complicity.[17]

With such hard evidence in hand, Jefferson had no choice but to bring it before the president—while making sure any hint of his own foreknowledge remained hidden. Washington read the consul's letter and the accompanying poster. Washington knew that the ploy threatened the ongoing and delicate negotiations to open the Mississippi River to the United States. His response was firm and clear. "The president would exercise all the power vested in him to prevent any Citizens of the U.S. from being concerned in any enterprize against the Spanish subjects," Washington assured wary Spanish officials. It may also have been at this time that Senator Brown from Kentucky also learned of the plot's exposure, perhaps from Jefferson as well since Jefferson had suggested that Genet should seek Brown out for advice, and that this news was what caused him to send an express to Logan that he should rebuff Michaux. Although we have no evidence to that effect, it would explain Logan's initial reluctance and his explanation that he demurred because he had received advice from Senator Brown to do so.[18]

Acting on Washington's orders, Jefferson dashed off a letter to Isaac Shelby, the governor of Kentucky, on August 29 alerting him to the scheme and giving him clear orders to use the state government to stop Clark if necessary. For Jefferson, someone who had privately known of Genet's plans since July and had even given Michaux a letter of introduction to Shelby that Genet had crafted, this letter to Shelby must have been an awkward one to write. "If you shall have reason to believe any such enterprise meditated, that you put them on their guard against the consequences, as all acts of hostility committed by them on nations at peace with the United States, are forbidden by the laws, and will expose them to punishment," Jefferson warned.[19]

Jefferson ended his missive to Shelby on an optimistic, if also cautionary, note. He hinted that negotiations with the Spanish government to open the Mississippi were progressing. In fact, as he confided to Shelby, they had reached such a delicate point that Jefferson worried that any reckless action by Kentuckians could set things back and undermine their own interests. "In addition to considerations respecting the peace of the general Union," Jefferson warned Shelby, "the special interests of the State of Kentucky would be particularly committed as nothing could be more inauspicious to them than such a movement at the very moment when those interests are under negotiation between Spain and the United States."[20]

In the middle of October, just as Michaux's operations in Kentucky were gaining steam, Spanish officials sent Jefferson more damning intelligence. One of the four reinforcements Genet had sent to aid Clark turned out to be a secret Spanish operative. Before leaving for Kentucky, the man known variously as Signeux, Pisgignoux, Pis Gignoux, or Gignoux informed Spanish diplomats in New York about the plot. Little is known of the informant's background. In a deposition taken later, the man's name was listed as Juan Pedro Pusgignoux, and he stated his hometown was Cahors in southwestern France (meaning that if true, his first name may have been a Spanish translation of Jean-Pierre). His motivations are also unknown—perhaps he wished to see the Bourbon monarchy restored, or perhaps he saw an opportunity to advance his interests by aiding Spain. The Spanish were clearly wary of him. While they were confident that his information was mostly true, they also worried that he might be a "double spy" and therefore detained him in southern Louisiana. In any case, these Spanish officials soon relayed his testimony to Jefferson, further escalating the pressure on the administration. It was likely Pusgignoux's information that informed St. Clair's proclamation denouncing the plot and demanding that American citizens disperse at once.[21]

Jefferson once again penned a stern note to Shelby that warned him of foreign agents and called on the governor to better assert his authority. "They were authorized by the Minister of France here to excite and engage as many as they could, whether of our citizens or others, on the road or within your government, or any where else," Jefferson informed Shelby in a November dispatch, "to undertake an expedition against the Spanish settlements within our neighborhood, and in event to descend the Ohio and Mississippi and attack New Orleans where they expected some naval cooperation." Jefferson called on Shelby to encourage his fellow citizens to exercise common sense, respect the authority of the federal government, and trust that it was serving their interests. "Their good sense will tell them that that is not to be effected by half-measures of this kind," Jefferson continued, "and that their surest dependance is on those regular measures which are pursuing and will be pursued by the general government, and which flow from the United authority of all the states."[22]

Jefferson's hint to Shelby that Kentuckians should have faith in the United States' diplomatic efforts was not merely lip service. Genet's actions were having one unexpected salutary effect on the federal government. In the spring, Jefferson had fretted that war with Spain seemed inevitable. Now, as geopolitics shifted, Spain's diplomatic positions weakened. With a war against France raging, the prospect of a second front in North America made Spanish officials realize that their strategic interest rested in assuaging the United States. The previously slow-moving negotiations about access to the Mississippi were picking up speed, and the United States' position was growing stronger.[23]

There was, however, one curious omission from Jefferson's warning to Shelby: André Michaux. In what can only be described as a stroke of good luck for Jefferson, the mole never mentioned Michaux's name to his Spanish handlers. Michaux, as an early emissary who traveled separately and under the cover of natural history, must have eluded the Spanish spy's knowledge, and no other reports linking Michaux to the plot had arrived in the federal capital. Jefferson could thus avoid exposing his friend. More importantly for Jefferson's own self-interest, by keeping Michaux's name out of it, any inaction—even complicit action—of Jefferson's could remain hidden from the president he was supposed to serve.

Thus, when Michaux entered Philadelphia on December 12, almost six months after leaving on his secret mission, he returned to an environment much different than the one he had left. In July, it appeared as if enthusiasm for France and Genet was strong and growing and Genet's scheme had the tacit support of some of the most powerful figures in government. Six months later, everything had changed. The federal government was aware of Genet's machinations in the West and was trying to end them. The once-popular French minister had become ostracized, his behavior deemed improper or even deceitful. At the same time, support for the French cause evaporated among most Americans as news spread of the Reign of Terror that had taken hold in France. Once tense Spanish-US relations were now thawing. And Michaux's scientific patron Jefferson was on his way out as secretary of state.

Michaux must have learned of these changes almost immediately upon arriving in the city. His first stop was at Genet's residence. Surely, Michaux updated Genet on the situation in Kentucky, and Genet must have updated Michaux in turn. Michaux's second visit was a meeting with both Thomas Jefferson and David Rittenhouse. Unfortunately, there are no records of what was said at these private meetings. We only know of them because Michaux recorded that they happened. He included no further description in his journal, and there is no known correspondence describing either event. But Genet, Jefferson, and Rittenhouse were all well aware of the changed environment, none more so than Jefferson, who appeared as the central node for all the information surrounding the events in Kentucky and within the government.[24]

We have little information on what Michaux learned or what he said over the course of the next weeks, but we do know a great deal about whom he met and where he went, clues that underscore Michaux's true interests. Natural history, once again, consumed his time. From his arrival on December 12 until January 10, Michaux made five visits to Genet and other French officials. He spent the other seventeen days doing scientific work, including "getting my Kentucky collection in order," a clear indication that his trip out west had served his natural history goal as well as France's military one. He also met with several APS members who had backed the original expedition that never happened. Though Michaux had known Bartram and Barton before the subscription drive, the people he called on now all appear to be people he had met because of the aborted transcontinental project. He called on Charles Willson Peale, the APS member who was the founder of the first successful natural history museum in the United States, and Nicholas Collin, the Swedish theologian with a large botanical collection. Both had served on the APS committees that supported Michaux's original expedition, and both were deeply immersed in the world of natural history collecting. He also spent time with his closest scientific confidant, William Bartram, and he made a second stop at David Rittenhouse's home. Although the Society never provided Michaux with funds, these visits show that Michaux had forged a bond with the scientific community that surrounded the institution. It also shows that he remained doggedly focused on his scientific research even as he tried to balance the new demands the French government had placed on him.[25]

His activities in town also suggest that he was expanding the scope of his research. Animal life had always been a side interest for the botanist, but during and after his Kentucky trip, Michaux began to study animals more formally. After spending a day with Peale, whose museum was filled with taxidermied animals from all over North America, Michaux tried practicing the art with squirrels. Peale was considered one of the finest taxidermists in America, and he likely imparted some of his techniques to Michaux when they met. Michaux also borrowed Benjamin Smith Barton's copy of Linnaeus and spent three days copying the section that categorized animal species.[26]

His immersion in Philadelphia's scientific community reinforced Michaux's natural inclinations. When he met with French officials on January 10, he expressed discomfort with his role as a secret operative. Genet was then in New York City trying to raise more support for the French cause, so he had delegated oversight of Michaux to one of his staff, Charles Bournonville. At their meeting, Michaux made it clear that he wished to return to South Carolina and his scientific research. "I told him that I wanted to employ my time as best as possible in research in natural history," Michaux recounted. Still, Michaux, always the good French patriot, assured Bournonville that if the French Republic still needed his services as an operative, then he would "devote myself to it."[27]

Bournonville must have sensed Michaux's reluctance. He let Michaux return to South Carolina so he could put his collections in good order. It was, however, to be only a brief reprieve. Bournonville also told Michaux that he would have to return to Kentucky to carry out their plans. To that end, he instructed Michaux to meet with Congressman Alexander Orr, the man Michaux had befriended in Limestone, and Senator John Brown, an earlier backer of the project, before he left for South Carolina. Michaux followed his orders. On Sunday, January 12, the three men met and strategized their next steps. All three seemed committed to the invasion, and their conversation that Sunday focused on what Michaux described as the "federal government's inclinations." Perhaps the biggest piece of news they discussed was that their onetime ally Thomas Jefferson had stepped down as secretary of state on January 1, 1794. He was replaced by Edmund Randolph, someone who shared many of Jefferson's political leanings but, having previously served as the country's first attorney general, was far more dedicated to asserting the federal government's authority.[28]

Unfortunately, the only record of Michaux's meeting with these political figures consists of Michaux's brief summary of it: "I visited Mr. Brown and Col. Orr, members of Congress, deputies from Kentucky. I conferred with them regarding the inclinations of the federal government and execution of the plan of Gen. Clark." This note, concise though it may have been, nonetheless clearly showed that these two elected members of Congress remained invested in the French plot even as news of it spread within the capital. In any case, whatever they did decide on that Sunday did little to slow down Michaux's work on organizing the assault in the days that followed. After meeting with these two sympathizers, Michaux sent a series of letters to his contacts in Kentucky. He also sent Clark at least $400 to keep his mobilization afloat. That cash infusion meant that the French Republic provided at least $1,150 to underwrite this American-led assault.[29]

About three weeks later, Michaux left for his garden in South Carolina. More than two years had passed since he was last there. In those intervening years, he had visited northern Canada, traveled to the Mississippi, and, most surprising of all, organized a military force in Kentucky to assault Louisiana. He seemed to want to make up for lost time on his journey south. He botanized everywhere he went.

Politics, though, proved unavoidable for the French botanist. Partisanship was enveloping the country, and the French Revolution remained one of the most contested issues. Michaux witnessed just how heated debate over the French Revolution could be when he stopped at a tavern near the border between North and South Carolina. On March 9, Michaux alighted at a small enclave filled with French émigrés on the banks of the Little River. Michaux described the community as filled with "French Democrats," meaning supporters of the French Revolution, and Michaux took pleasure in being able to relay to them what he described as "the latest favorable news" he had from Philadelphia—a small sign, perhaps, of his own political leanings. But as Michaux learned, not everyone viewed revolution so favorably. That night, a Frenchman named Jouvenceau, someone Michaux described as an "old soldier," perhaps a veteran of the American Revolution who decided to stay, talked politics over drinks with an American Michaux described as a "Tory," meaning someone who was pro-British. The American denounced the French Revolution, and the old soldier took it personally. Jouvenceau refused to take the insult and struck the man twice. The American responded by shooting his adversary twice in the stomach. A surgeon was called to tend to the French veteran, and, Michaux reported, he suspected the man would survive.[30]

On March 15, a month after leaving Philadelphia, Michaux arrived back at his South Carolina garden. While it is unclear who managed its operations during Michaux's absence, evidence suggests that at least two enslaved men played an important role in its upkeep. He returned with even more work to do. He needed to organize and cultivate the many new specimens that he had acquired in the past year, materials that came from as far north as Canada and as far west as Kentucky. Still, French politics occasionally intruded on Michaux's time. The French consul in Charleston, Mangourit, had been working diligently on a proposed invasion of Florida that was to coincide with Clark's foray. While Michaux steered clear of involvement in this other scheme, he still regularly discussed the potential Florida invasion when he met with his friend.[31]

Michaux, however, showed little desire to return to Kentucky, at least for the purposes of organizing a military invasion. When he left Philadelphia, it was clear that the federal government was preparing a major push to suppress Clark's activities, so he knew it would be dangerous for him to continue his own involvement. Further changes in Philadelphia strengthened Michaux's retreat. In late February, a new French mission led by Jean Antoine Joseph Fauchet replaced Genet. Fauchet quickly tried to restore relations with the Washington administration by repudiating Genet. Genet for his part absconded to a farm outside of Philadelphia before exiling himself to New York City. With Genet gone, Michaux had no one to push matters further, so he largely abandoned the plot that he had been instrumental in sparking. If anything, all indications were that Michaux was finally going to receive his wish and pursue his scientific endeavors freed from outside pressures. He had, after all, received an appointment from the revolutionary French government, and, this time, he believed it would allow him to botanize with abandon.[32]

In Kentucky, meanwhile, Clark and his men were largely unaware of all that had transpired in the capital and were instead anxiously waiting for Michaux's return. They continued to build their stockpiles as they looked for Michaux to arrive with Genet's final instructions and fistfuls of cash. As they waited, and as suspense mounted, they began to worry. Rumors circulated that Michaux was dead. Others said he was delayed and arriving in April. As April turned to May, they learned the real reason for Michaux's long absence.[33]

❖ 15 ❖

The End of an Expedition

Spring and Summer 1794

While Michaux hunkered down at his Charleston garden, matters back in Philadelphia were getting hotter, in large part because a steady stream of reports from Kentucky suggested that Clark's invasion of Louisiana was imminent. In fact, Michaux's escape from the capital had been as well timed as his departure from Kentucky. As news from the frontiers flowed into the Washington administration, the president and his cabinet analyzed every morsel of intelligence. Every bit of news confirmed that Clark's expedition was receiving widespread support in Kentucky and there was little anyone was doing to stop it.

Soon after assuming the post, the new secretary of state, Edmund Randolph, received several dispatches from American informants confirming the Spanish reports. In fact, if anything, Randolph's information painted an even grimmer picture. Clark had reportedly amassed an enormous arsenal. By the spring of 1794, he had secured several large pieces of artillery, including cannons, with even more on the way. Rumor had it that the commandant of Fort Vincennes promised to donate some of the fort's armaments to the cause. Money had also started to flow again. The arrival of a French agent, likely carrying the $400 Michaux had sent in January, provided the fiscal reinforcement Clark needed to alleviate his financial woes. Flush with cash, he made a massive purchase at the end of March—five hundred pounds of gunpowder and one ton of cannonballs. One letter writer informed federal officials that Kentucky iron forges burned brightly as their operators shifted their resources to smelt more cannons to meet Clark's demand.[1]

Even worse, local and state governments showed no interest in stopping what the federal government saw as illegal—indeed, even potentially traitorous—activities. "The measure of the expedition was openly advocated," a secret informant confided to Secretary of War Henry Knox, "and not opposed by any considerable numbers." Travelers noticed that while the federal government's stern proclamations against the attack circulated widely in Ohio, these proclamations were found nowhere in Kentucky. In a particularly ominous sign, several officers in Clark's regiment reportedly auctioned their Kentucky lands, an indication that they soon expected to move elsewhere. With anticipation mounting, reports to the federal government pegged April 15 as the day of departure.[2]

Spanish officials spent the winter and spring preparing for the attack, only further ratcheting up the tension in the region and in the halls of power. In internal discussions, Spanish military officers acknowledged that Clark's estimation of their weak defenses was correct. They suspected that a small but well-armed and dedicated group of American frontiersmen could easily overrun them. One Spanish officer predicted that if the situation remained unchanged, Americans would control the Spanish forts along the Mississippi by the start of summer. The Spanish had, he counted, a mere ninety soldiers to defend the vast territory and a measly two hundred in volunteer militias, many of French descent. The latter, he noted, "can be but little trusted."[3]

To buttress their position, Spanish officials took a new strategic direction. They worked to strengthen their military alliances with Native American groups in the region. In moments like this one, in which imperial powers competed against each other, their relationships with Indigenous nations were of paramount importance. A strong military partnership with a Native American power could provide one side with the additional force necessary for victory. In October 1793, just as Michaux and Clark were beginning to mobilize forces on the Mississippi, desperate Spanish officials concerned about a pending attack met with Native American leaders from the Cherokee, Choctaw, Chickasaw, and Creek nations at Fort Nogales, near modern-day Vicksburg, Mississippi. The Spaniards' objective was to secure a military alliance that could bolster their defenses. After days of negotiating, they succeeded.[4]

The terms of the treaty at Nogales captured the strategic complexities of diplomacy in these areas of contestation. First, the Creeks, Chickasaws,

Choctaws, and Cherokees all vowed to maintain "pacific intentions" toward the United States while Spain remained engaged in negotiations with the Washington administration. Spanish officials realized that maintaining the peaceful status quo was essential to their separate talks with the United States. Should the Creeks or another Indigenous group allied with Spain become embroiled in a war with the United States, then the United States could use that conflict to justify capturing Spanish territory, thus upsetting Spain's delicate diplomatic situation with the United States over the Mississippi.

In turn, Spanish officials at Nogales recognized the Native groups' territories as belonging to these Indigenous nations; such acknowledgments of sovereignty were paramount to Native American diplomats, who were trying to fend off the imperial ambitions of these European and American countries. An acknowledgment of their sovereignty by one European empire, such as Spain, could provide these groups with important leverage in their negotiations with other foreign powers. With the Spanish recognizing their land, the Creeks, Chickasaws, and Cherokees had a further incentive to avoid war with the Americans because, should the United States defeat them, the Spanish recognition would lose its significance.[5]

In exchange, these Native nations promised defensive aid to the Spanish should any foreign force attack the Spanish posts in Louisiana. Their assistance, Louisiana's governor Francisco Luis Hector de Carondelet realized, was the only way the Spanish could successfully protect their territory from Clark's invasion. He knew that Clark's intelligence was right. Spanish Louisiana could easily be captured by a small but determined force of American frontiersmen. "The advantages which result to Spain from this negotiation are so obvious," the governor boasted to his superiors in Spain, "we are able to avail ourselves of the nations mentioned, principally the Cherokees and Chickasaws, to oppose their attempts; whereas we neither have troops to oppose them, nor can count on the great part of the militia composed of Frenchmen." Without this treaty and the military alliances it promised, the governor was sure Spain faced a calamity. "I do not believe that the king can keep Louisiana or at any rate that its total devastation can be prevented," he predicted, should they lose these allies.[6]

With the treaty secured, Spanish officials shifted their focus and prepared for the expected onslaught. They buttressed their forts, especially the one at Nogales, increased their forces, and marched through villages, hoping that displays of their growing military might would cow any residents sympathetic to France.[7]

Back in Philadelphia, meanwhile, Washington knew that the country was teetering on the brink of war and that he had to take measures to avoid what he feared would be a disaster for the country. Just as Spanish diplomats had to think multidimensionally when negotiating with their Native partners, so too did Washington have to navigate complex diplomatic waters involving British, French, Spanish, and Native American interests. In fact, Washington's challenge was even more complicated. While Spain was in open conflict with France and in an alliance with Great Britain, Washington had to make sure the United States maintained its neutrality toward all three of these warring countries. That was a difficult position in the best of times, and with Genet still in the country he also had a French ambassador stirring up public opposition to his policies and trying to wage a quasi-war against France's enemies by outfitting American ships and arming citizens. Then, he had to worry about the sentiments of frontier people who demanded the free use of the Mississippi and were threatening an assault on Spanish Louisiana to get it.

On top of it all, Washington had to worry about Native American relations. North of where Clark was mobilizing, American forces and Native groups like the Miamis and Delawares (Lenapes) were locked in a standoff. The United States and Native American nations had been fighting over control of the Ohio Territory since the close of the American Revolution. At the moment, a tense armistice prevailed, and Washington was trying to formalize the peace through a treaty. Continued combat appeared likely, however, if this diplomacy failed, and Washington was simultaneously preparing for an offensive that could secure American dominance. He thus knew that he might have to call up local forces in case of a conflict, and Clark's gambit could rob the government of this potential manpower. Clark's proposed act of violence—even if aimed at the Spanish—could easily upset Washington's strategy and would surely upset the greater stability he sought for the region.[8]

With war possible on several fronts, Washington had to strike a delicate balance, one in which he maintained American neutrality with European nations and managed relations with Native American groups. A note Secretary of War Henry Knox wrote to General Anthony Wayne outlined the factors that went into Washington's decision-making and made clear the multidimensional strategic thinking at work. After a cabinet meeting in which it was decided that they needed to send Wayne reinforcements, Knox informed him, "Upon the most mature consideration of this subject, the President of the United States has conceived that the national interests and dignity are intimately blended with the measure of terminating the western Indian war during the course of the present year. The necessity of such an event is greatly enhanced by the consideration of the critical position of our affairs with some of the European powers." Washington, then, had to balance potential conflicts on multiple fronts, and a misstep on any one of them could result in warfare on all of them.[9]

As reports of American militias amassing on the banks of the Mississippi streamed into the administration, Clark's plot became a test of the federal government's domestic authority as much as it was an international crisis. Washington fumed to colleagues as he fretted about the country. He dreaded the prospect of war. Worse, he feared the dissolution of the union. Kentucky, he worried, was on the verge of independence, a grave threat to the stability of his government. If there was one piece of good news, it was that the new French ambassador, Jean Antoine Joseph Fauchet renounced his predecessor's actions and rescinded all appointments and orders. Washington knew, however, that Fauchet's symbolic diplomatic action might do little to stop the movement Genet had begun.[10]

The crackdown began in February 1794, when Edmund Randolph, the new secretary of state, sent a pointed letter to Kentucky's governor, Isaac Shelby, ordering him to use his authority to tamp down the rebellion. It continued on March 10, when Washington and his cabinet met to debate the best way to deal with Clark's potential invasion of Spanish Louisiana. Once again, the divisions between Jeffersonians and Federalists emerged. Washington agreed to take four actions to stop Clark's activities, three of which the Jefferson-influenced Randolph supported. Randolph agreed with his colleagues that the president should issue a proclamation denouncing the French agents and the mobilization. He agreed that a cabinet secretary should send another stern letter to the governor of Kentucky "upon the subject of his conduct," and he agreed that Congress should formally outlaw behavior such as Clark's. Randolph was the lone dissent on the fourth proposal: to have General Anthony Wayne send troops to a fort along the Mississippi and "intercept by force, if necessary," an American-led invasion.[11]

Randolph objected to the use of federal troops to stop American citizens, though he couched his opinion in terms far subtler than Jefferson had when he had disagreed with the president. His dissent, nonetheless, revealed the underlying differences between the Jeffersonian and Federalist vision of governing. Randolph opposed the fourth proposal on two grounds. One was tactical. He was afraid that Clark's men could interpret the preemptive move of federal forces as a hostile act that could escalate the situation, potentially triggering a bloody civil war and the West's "separation from the union."[12]

The second reason was constitutional. Randolph argued that the president lacked the authority to use federal force in such a way. He believed that the Kentuckians' actions constituted an internal insurrection, not an invasion from a foreign nation. Randolph, as the former attorney general, was well-versed in statutes, and he held that, according to the current laws of the nation, the president could intervene only if called upon by the Kentucky legislature or governor first, neither of which seemed inclined to do so. Randolph was not inherently opposed to Washington possessing the authority to undertake such an action; he just believed the president needed to establish the executive's right to do so through new legislation. He thus argued that Congress needed to first pass a new law that empowered the president to act in such circumstances. The difference between Randolph and the rest of the cabinet revealed the differences emerging among the parties. Randolph's argument deferred to local authorities and reflected a strict interpretation of constitutional power that left the executive weaker.[13]

Washington and his allies, meanwhile, adopted a far more practical and expansive approach to the executive's powers. His approach was guided, in part, by other events then unfolding in the countryside. Just as Washington had to think on multiple fronts when it came to foreign policy, he had to do the same when it came to domestic issues. In this case, the controversy over the use of federal power in Kentucky was happening alongside ongoing debates within his cabinet about assertions of federal authority in other parts of the country. In particular, Washington was juggling a parallel internal crisis in which a body of recalcitrant westerners refused to comply with federal taxes and whose open defiance also tested the mettle of the executive's authority. Since 1791, westerners, especially those in Pennsylvania around Pittsburgh, had opposed a whiskey tax, and their objections only grew more heated as the federal government refused to rescind the tax. In this Pennsylvania dispute, Washington was taking a light hand toward the protestors. He wanted to avoid an open conflict between the government and the people. He hoped instead that he could convince westerners to comply with the tax through appeals to reason and sent representatives from the federal government to the region to convince Pennsylvanians of their duty. Some in his cabinet, however, wished for military action so Washington could make a statement about federal authority that would reverberate throughout the nation. Washington had, up until this point, demurred, though he was also preparing for a possible military confrontation.

In Kentucky, however, Washington considered the situation graver. He believed he had to act forcefully and immediately and that he could do so without having to appeal to Congress or the Supreme Court because he considered it illegal for a group of citizens to organize an invasion of another country with whom the United States was at peace. He was determined to stop a small band of angry citizens from forcing the United States into a conflict it was trying to avoid. In contrast to the situation in Pennsylvania, the Kentuckians posed more of an immediate and fundamental constitutional threat, and, as far as Washington was concerned, he was duty bound to protect the Constitution and preserve the Union. Because of that obligation, he held that he had the authority to exercise executive power as necessary to maintain both.[14]

In the weeks that followed, Washington's administration rolled out these initiatives. William Bradford, Randolph's successor as attorney general of the United States, drafted Washington's proclamation. Hamilton, Knox, and Randolph then collaboratively revised the text before presenting it to the president. It was given to Washington on March 24, and he signed off on it later that day with only minor alterations. In it, he took a firm stance toward those involved in Clark's scheme. Titled "Proclamation on Expeditions Against Spanish Territory," Washington ordered all Americans involved to cease and desist. "I have received information," Washington began, "that certain persons in violation of the laws, presumed under colour of a foreign authority to enlist citizens of the United States and others within the state of Kentucky, and have there assembled an armed force for the purpose of invading and plundering the territories of a nation at peace with the said United States."[15]

Washington then made clear that he considered any such activities illegal—"criminal," he said—and used the proclamation to affirm the executive's right to stop citizens from interfering with the country's foreign policy. "It is the duty of the Executive," Washington declared, "to take care that such criminal proceedings be suppressed, the offenders brought to justice, and all good citizens cautioned against measures likely to prove so pernicious." Such declarations were vital as the federal government established its authority. Washington was not just asserting his rights; he was also educating his citizens on the constitutional powers that the president possessed. To make his position as clear as possible, he ordered every citizen to reject any future appeals to join Clark's effort and warned anyone who persisted that they did so "at their peril." More importantly, in response to Kentucky officials' inaction, Washington enjoined "all court magistrates and other officers" to "exert their powers" to suppress any rebellion and, most pointedly, "to bring condign punishment on those who may have been guilty" of organizing an illegal military action.[16]

Washington's proclamation was printed and shipped to General Anthony Wayne, then stationed in the Ohio River Valley, and other officials based along the western frontiers. They copied, posted, and distributed it throughout the region. Washington's actions had their intended effects in the capital city. Senator John Brown, an earlier ally of Genet and advocate for the invasion, shifted his position soon after hearing of Washington's reaction. Rather than encouraging the initiative among his friends and family in Kentucky, he began sharing intelligence from his local informants with the administration. His family, though, was divided. His brother, James, Kentucky's secretary of state, remained recalcitrant and continued to advise Governor Shelby to avoid interfering with Clark, describing state intervention as "impolitic."[17]

Meanwhile, on March 29, a few days after this proclamation, Edmund Randolph added to the federal response by directly addressing the defiance of Kentucky governor Isaac Shelby. Guided by Washington's firm proclamation, Randolph applied a heavy hand in a long letter that combined biting sarcasm with a dressing-down. He took direct aim at what he considered Shelby's specious argument that he, as governor, had no authority to intercede. In doing so, Randolph confronted some of the fundamental constitutional questions that the Kentuckians had raised, issues that dealt with the national government's role in a federated republic and the constraints that federal policy could place on individual citizens. At issue were two questions: Were Americans free to do whatever they wanted, so long as they broke no laws within their country? Did an American citizen's obligations to their government end as soon as one left the United States? Shelby's answer to both queries was an unambiguous "yes."[18]

Randolph used his letter to make it clear, in the most pointed terms possible, why Shelby was wrong. For Randolph, the most important question was, if a government is unable to restrain its citizens from launching an invasion that was sure to throw their country into a war, does the government really possess the fundamental power it claims to have? "What government can be so destitute of the means of self-defence," Randolph asked Shelby, "as to suffer, with impunity, its peace to be drawn into jeopardy by hostilities levied within its territory against a foreign nation, order to be prostrated at the will of tumultuous individuals, and scenes of bloodshed and civil war to be introduced?"[19]

Randolph took particular umbrage at Shelby's unwillingness to stop the four French agents who continued to recruit. Such direct foreign interference in American affairs, Randolph explained, was not only unprecedented but outside well-established international norms. "That foreigners would meddle in the affairs of a government where they happen to be, has scarcely ever been tolerated," Randolph exclaimed, "and is often severely punished." Echoing Washington's view on the stakes, the French activity in Kentucky, he told Shelby, was tantamount to an assault upon the United States' sovereignty that could not be tolerated if the United States was to be a free and independent nation. "That foreigners should point the force of a nation, against its will, to objects of hostility, is an invasion of its dignity, its tranquility, and even safety," Randolph explained to the obstinate governor.[20]

Randolph concluded his excoriation with a firm assertion of federal authority, one that perhaps went against his own personal inclinations but served the administration's position. He dismissed Shelby's claims of powerlessness. In what was surely a subtle dig at Shelby, Randolph acknowledged that the "civil arm may sometimes be unequal to the task of sustaining civil authority" in distant locales like Kentucky, a critique that Shelby likely read as a chastisement. When that occurred, Randolph explained, the federal government could intervene—even though he had earlier and privately questioned its right to do so. To make his point, Randolph sent a copy of a militia law that gave the president the power to use federal marshals or call on state militias when local governments appeared too feeble to ward off an invasion from external enemies or from "an insurrection" from within. Even though Randolph privately dissented from the administration's position, he nonetheless marshaled the argument he needed to serve the administration. He used the militia law to show Shelby that the president had the power to stop what the administration saw as a possible insurrection. It was a veiled threat, in which Randolph used the specter of federal officials taking control of local affairs, something that Shelby likely feared more than anything, to prod Shelby to use the levers of state government at his disposal.

Next, on March 31, just two days after Randolph wrote his letter, Secretary of War Knox ordered Anthony Wayne to establish a fort on the Mississippi River near Louisville that could block Clark's potential invasion, an action to which Randolph had objected. The orders themselves likely did not surprise Wayne. Knox and Wayne had previously discussed establishing such a fort for other strategic military reasons, but its erection was never a top priority. In the past, Knox had deferred to Wayne's on-the-ground judgment as to whether he had the resources to allocate for its construction. Now, with Clark's invasion apparently imminent, Knox told Wayne that he had to build the fort immediately. He also included "secret and confidential" instructions that authorized the lethal use of force against American citizens engaged in the invasion of Louisiana. "If notwithstanding every peacable effort to persuade them to abandon their criminal design they should still persist in their attempts to pass down the Ohio, you are to use every military means in your power for preventing them," Knox ordered. With these directives issued, Washington had authorized US forces to attack American citizens if they attempted their invasion of a foreign country.[21]

Wayne followed his orders. By the end of May, he had sent troops to establish the fort. Wayne assured Knox that he understood the "secret and confidential" instructions sent to him, noting that he entrusted the major overseeing the fort with "a literal copy of those you mentioned in your letter of the 31st of March." Similar commands were sent in May to Georgia's governor, once again over Randolph's firm objection, because the government had learned that Genet had a similar scheme afoot there as well.[22]

The debates that Washington heard among his cabinet secretaries, especially the objections of Randolph, convinced him that the federal government needed to take one more important step. Randolph may have failed to persuade Washington that the president lacked the authority to use federal forces, but his arguments did convince Washington that the government should more clearly establish that behavior like Clark's was illegal and that the federal government had the authority to stop it. Doing so would render arguments like Shelby's moot in the future. On May 20, Washington called on Congress to address the issue. He presented to both the Senate and House of Representatives the evidence of the invasion that his administration had accumulated. He ended with a call to action: "I am impelled by the position of our public affairs to recommend that provision be made for a stronger and more vigorous opposition, than can be given to such hostile movements under the laws as they now stand."[23]

Congress heeded his words. In an unusual show of unity and a telling sign of just how consequential Genet's brief term was in American history—and how serious the Kentucky conspiracy was—both houses passed sweeping legislation on June 5 addressing the central questions the controversy had raised. The entire Genet-Clark episode had exposed two vulnerabilities in the federal government that needed to be rectified. One was a challenge to its authority created by a foreign country trying to meddle in US domestic affairs. The other was a challenge posed by citizens who believed they were free to act however they wished outside the jurisdiction of the United States—whether on land like the Kentuckians or by sea through letters of marque. An Act in Addition to the Act for the Punishment of Certain Crimes against the United States addressed these two issues by giving the president clear and explicit power to intervene in such circumstances and by clarifying the rights, obligations, and limitations of citizenship. It said, for instance, "that if any person shall within the territory or jurisdiction of the United States enlist or enter himself . . . in the service of any foreign prince or state as a soldier . . . or letter of marque or privateer, every person so offending shall be deemed guilty of a high misdemeanor." Section 5 of the law took specific aim at Clark's expedition. It outlawed Americans from participating in or organizing "any military expedition or enterprise to be carried on from thence against the territory or dominions of any foreign prince or state with whom the United States are at peace."[24]

Initiating the passage of such defining and precedent-setting laws was a key part of Washington's tenure and his legacy. As Americans tried to establish the role of the federal government in their society, debates like the one between Randolph and the rest of the cabinet members occurred throughout the country. Washington knew that if a trusted advisor like Randolph had issues with what he assumed were inherent executive powers, then others certainly did, others perhaps less respectful and loyal than Randolph. By explicitly forbidding citizens to do what Clark was attempting, and by outlining strict punishment for anyone who supported an invasion of a foreign country such as Genet had encouraged by outfitting privateers, the law did exactly what Randolph had argued was needed in his earlier objections: name such behaviors as illegal and empower the executive to act accordingly. The law was so essential that, even though it was initially set to expire every two years, it was renewed until 1800, when Congress made it perpetual.[25]

While this law showed firmness, Congress took two other unusual steps to allay the Kentuckians' apprehensions and deescalate the situation. At the prodding of Kentucky's two senators, the Senate passed two additional resolutions, one on May 15 and another on June 5, that affirmed the United States' commitment to opening the Mississippi River to Americans. Washington worried that such resolutions might blur the lines of diplomatic authority between the executive and Congress, so the resolutions also acknowledged executive privilege and the need for secrecy surrounding the negotiations. "That as it appears from the communications of the executive, that the right of the United States to the free navigation of the Mississippi, is now the subject of negociation with the court of Spain; and as it is the interest of the United States, and every part thereof, to come to an amicable adjustment of the right in that mode," the Senate declared on June 5. The resolutions thus showed the way in which the early government—Washington and Congress—worked in unison to maintain the union by complementing each other's actions. In this case, on the same day Congress passed the law that outlawed Clark's actions, an act clearly aimed at reining in Kentuckians, the Senate also passed a resolution reassuring Kentuckians of the country's commitment to opening the Mississippi River without breaching any of the executive branch's rights.[26]

What Congress as well as Washington knew as they passed these resolutions was that the administration's diplomatic affairs were fast improving on several different fronts. The deportment of the new French ambassador, Fauchet, was far different from that of the brash, idealistic Genet. After arriving in the city and denouncing all that Genet had done, he also announced his intention to arrest the former diplomat and presumably send him to Paris if he could. In an act of great benevolence, Washington, however, granted Genet asylum in the United States and allowed the former diplomat to relocate to New York City permanently. Spain, meanwhile, showed a renewed interest in resolving the Mississippi dispute. Spanish ministers, aware of the growing tensions along the river's banks, realized that a peaceful resolution was preferable to conflict. Edmund Randolph had even confided as much to Shelby in March. In addition to his scolding, he had also let Shelby know that the Washington administration had men in Madrid actively negotiating to open the river to American goods. Although Randolph expressed reticence in sharing private executive business with the governor, he assured Shelby that everyone was confident that the United States was moving toward "a peaceable expectation of the result."[27]

The swift and coordinated actions of the federal government, along with these changes in diplomacy, brought about a rapid change in Clark's affairs. He was unable to absorb both the loss of French backing and the weight of the federal government bearing down on him. Many of the enlistees began returning to their homes. To add to Clark's woes, a new threat shifted Kentuckians' focus. The tense stand-off between American forces and Native groups in the Ohio River Valley grew hotter as the summer approached in 1794. Miamis, Delawares (Lenapes), and other Native American nations, aided by the British who constructed new forts in the Ohio, began preparing to militarily defend their sovereignty in the face of American settlers' encroachments.[28]

The direct involvement of the British drew American ire, especially given US neutrality. It seemed as if the British were taking advantage of the situation and trying to pick a fight. With a conflict brewing, Kentuckians turned from preparing for an assault on New Orleans to preparing for an attack on their own land, and General Anthony Wayne, who had prepared to squash the Kentuckians' attack on Spain with force, now wanted to call out Kentucky militiamen to help him defend American forts. Overtaken by this combination of events, Clark's scheme fell apart. Rumors of its potential reformation persisted throughout the summer, but nothing came of it. Clark instead stewed over the enormous bill he had racked up—according to his estimate.[29]

Despite the looming crisis in Ohio, Kentuckians remained politically motivated if not militarily mobilized around their goal of access to the Mississippi River. Instead of mounting an invasion of Spanish Louisiana, in June a large group of angry Kentuckians redirected their lingering frustrations into more legitimate channels by descending on Lexington to convene an assembly to discuss their shared concerns. They ended it by passing a series of resolutions that laid bare their grievances with the federal government.

In thirteen points, the protesters' screed made clear that the seeds of disaffection that had spurred their support of Clark's endeavor were still germinating. Most of their complaints, as before, focused on their inability to access the Mississippi River. To make their point, they declared that they were entitled "by nature and by stipulation" to "the free and undisturbed navigation of the river Mississippi."[30]

Their rhetoric also exposed a much deeper issue that could tear asunder the nation. Those frustrated Kentuckians accused the "general government" of failing in its fundamental duty to serve the needs of its citizens, a serious charge in an age in which Americans had used similar complaints as grounds for independence fewer than twenty years earlier. The petitioners took particular umbrage at what they saw as the government's regional favoritism. They pointed out that Washington's Neutrality Proclamation benefited "Eastern America" by serving the interests of merchants, traders, and industrialists in the country's port cities who relied on British trade. Meanwhile, the president, they claimed, ignored the needs of "western America."

This geographical and, in turn political, division ran throughout their resolutions. Repeatedly they complained of their position as "inhabitants of the Western Country" who were ignored by a distant, unfeeling eastern government that was focused on the separate and distinct needs of those living on the other side of the Appalachian Mountains, those who were also closer to the seat of power. In their final point, these Kentuckians' complaints verged on a threat to separate from the nation. "That the attainment and security of these our rights, is the common cause of the Western people, and that we will unite with them in any measures that may be most expedient for that purpose," they declared.[31]

After making their complaints clear, the group then passed two resolves that outlined their future action, both of which were meant to apply greater pressure on the federal government. They vowed to expand their organizing efforts beyond Kentucky to include "the other inhabitants of the Western Country." Locally, they called on men in every Kentucky county to form local groups committed to the same principles as the convention's. If the political situation remained unchanged, then these county groups were "to elect proper persons to represent them in Convention, for the purpose of deliberating on the steps which will be most expedient for the attainment and security of our just rights." Combined, these steps were meant to mobilize Kentuckians and others in the West into a more formalized political organization.[32]

The language of the last resolution—"for the attainment and security of our just rights"—contained hints of revolution that were easily recognized by those in Washington's cabinet, men who had fought to secure just such things from Great Britain a generation earlier. In fact, where Kentuckians saw their convention as a legitimate means of organizing a political protest, those in Washington's cabinet, many of whom had lived through the American Revolution, saw the creation of these extralegal organizations as dangerous and illegal assemblies that threatened the existing government. These bodies reminded those veterans of the American Revolution of the Committees of Correspondence that American patriots had formed in towns and counties before the thirteen colonies declared themselves independent. Such committees had been vital in bringing revolutionaries together in the lead-up to the Declaration of Independence. For a time, the committees operated as a shadow government, separate from the official British imperial government. Many in the East who read the Kentucky Resolutions feared that the organizers of the gathering now had similarly rebellious intentions. "The illegality," Secretary of War Knox concluded of the meeting, "seems to be unquestionable."[33]

Washington was unsure how to respond to the Kentucky remonstrance and resolves. He once again polled his cabinet. This time, their opinions were unanimous. As Edmund Randolph noted to Washington upon reading the resolutions, "The temper of that country is roused to an extreme." Randolph, like his colleagues, found the Kentuckians' expectations unreasonable, if not completely unfounded.[34]

One of the other issues that the cabinet focused on was executive privilege—a topic still very much in debate today, more than two centuries later. The Kentuckians demanded that Washington give them regular updates on negotiations to open the Mississippi River. While doing so might have appeased these furious frontiersmen, Randolph adamantly opposed such a gesture. He argued that sharing private diplomatic negotiations posed a dangerous threat to the executive, and to the government more generally, by establishing a "precedent for throwing open the archives of the executive to the whole world, on all occasions." Randolph, though perturbed by the request, also believed that the government had already adequately acquiesced to the Kentuckians in practice. His letter to Shelby on March 29 contained news of progress with Spain, as did the subsequent congressional resolves. Once word reached the Kentucky elite, he hoped reason would reign in Kentucky.[35]

Cabinet officials also fretted about the future of the federal union. They knew that Washington's reaction to the remonstrance would either cool or escalate tensions. At issue was Kentucky's sense of autonomy and what that could mean for the national government. "What if the government of Kentucky should force us either to support them in their hostilities against Spain or disavow and renounce them?" Randolph asked his friend and predecessor Thomas Jefferson in August. "The lopping off of Kentucky from the Union is dreadful to contemplate, even if it should not attach itself to some other power." Cabinet members worried that if Washington took a misstep by acting too forcefully, then Kentuckians, primed to fight, might respond with a violent defense of their rights that could lead to disunion. The cabinet thus recommended a moderate federal response for the moment, in part, surely, because they knew that the situation, while volatile, seemed to be settling down. "No notice be at present taken of the remonstrance & resolves," Knox advised. "But it would appear proper that at the meeting of Congress the President should take notice also in his speech of the resolves & remonstrance in a temperate but firm manner."[36]

Washington then shifted his attention across the Atlantic, to Madrid, believing the time was right to push the Spaniards to open the Mississippi. He dispatched a special envoy to negotiate a treaty in the summer of 1794. His first choice was a logical if somewhat surprising one: Thomas Jefferson. Jefferson's extensive diplomatic experience surely factored into Washington's request, but he also knew that many Kentuckians saw Jefferson as a political ally. His appointment would help assuage their fears and better establish trust between the West and the federal government. Jefferson's close friend and successor as secretary of state, Edmund Randolph, approached him to see if he would serve in the administration again, this time as a special envoy to Spain. Jefferson demurred. "No circumstances my dear sir will ever more tempt me to engage in any thing public," Jefferson replied to his friend. Stymied, Washington next asked Virginian Patrick Henry, another noted ally of the West. He too passed. Washington settled on Thomas Pinckney, a diplomat then stationed in London, whose coach, coincidentally, Genet had rented in his ride from Charleston to Philadelphia.[37]

As Washington and his cabinet sought a resolution to the crisis from the seat of US federal power in Philadelphia, Spanish officials in New Orleans made what was perhaps the most consequential decision in response to the Kentuckians' fervency. The Kentucky resolves had also landed on the desk of Carondelet, the governor of Spanish New Orleans. Aware of just how vulnerable Spain's grasp on the region was, and afraid of what the future might hold if the Mississippi River remained sealed off from these raging and volatile Kentuckians, Carondelet penned a letter to Madrid advising the imperial government that they needed to open the Mississippi quickly. "The circumstances are urgent," Carondelet reported, "as I do not doubt that they will begin hostilities at the end of the year, in case we have not then made a friendly agreement."[38]

In the meantime, as Carondelet waited for something official to happen in the halls of power across the Atlantic, he took a unilateral action meant to dilute the fury of the Kentuckians. He ignored Madrid's orders to enforce a 15 percent tariff on American goods arriving in New Orleans. His decision to cut the rate effectively gave Americans what they most sought: commercial use of the Mississippi River. The gesture, albeit temporary, was meant to dampen any lingering enthusiasm Kentuckians may have had for Clark's cause. "You will see," he told his superiors, "by what is happening what good reason I have had for suspending the execution of the Royal order regarding the reestablishment of the 15% duty on all products of Kentucky and other settlements of the West that come down to this Province by the Ohio; which would have hastened the hostile determinations of the same, inducing them perhaps to unite and help the French expedition of Gen. Clarck which he tried to form on the Ohio."[39]

Carondelet's decision meant that by the end of the summer, Clark's proposed expedition, initiated and facilitated by André Michaux, and from the French perspective a total disaster, was, in fact, a resounding success for the Kentuckians. A group of citizens, angry with what they saw as their own government's inaction, had managed to pressure both the Spanish government and the Washington administration to prioritize and in some ways accede to their demands. It is true that both were already working toward the solution that the Kentuckians desired, but the military mobilization on the banks of the Mississippi surely sped up the process. By the fall of 1794, Americans could trade on the Mississippi without any punitive tariffs. Within a year, their success would become even more tangible when Spain, battered by war with France and worried about their weak control on Louisiana, formally acquiesced to the United States' demands in the

Pinckney Treaty and officially opened the Mississippi to unencumbered trade. Although many Kentuckians showed themselves willing to take up arms and risk their lives to accomplish this goal, they ultimately accomplished their aims without having to fire one shot or suffer any casualties.[40]

In some measure, the affair was also a victory for Washington and his desire to maintain union. Through a combination of federal power and compassion, Washington managed to destroy the plot while also, he hoped, assuaging Kentuckians' concerns about his commitment to opening the Mississippi River. Washington had also taken an important step in his own evolution as an executive during the affair. Washington decided that in order to maintain the nation's security, and perhaps even its existence, he needed to wield federal authority in a way he had not yet done before, going so far as to authorize the use of the US military to tamp down citizens. Such a decision likely played into an even more well-known and indeed pivotal act he would soon take as president. When protests against the whiskey tax in Pittsburgh turned violent and deadly as federal marshals clashed with bands of armed and organized civilians, Washington was quick to take decisive action. Reports made it appear like a war zone, with organized militias targeting federal officials. This could not stand. In the fall of 1794, a few months after the Kentucky controversy, Washington mobilized federal militias and personally marched west to suppress what he saw as an internal rebellion. The Kentucky episode surely played a role in Washington's decision to act so forcefully against the whiskey rebels. Having almost deployed US troops on Kentuckians who threatened to upend the United States' foreign policy and having had to deal with a near attack on Louisiana, he realized that a symbolic assertion of federal authority was necessary if he was to keep the American West a part of the federal union.

One other figure deeply involved in the plot saw its end as something of a victory: André Michaux. Michaux managed to elude any notice of his involvement—thanks, in large measure, to his friend Jefferson, who likely kept Michaux's name out of the affair to protect his own reputation as much as the French botanist's. For Michaux, although the invasion of Spanish Louisiana fizzled, its demise proved to be a boon for his research. The botanist, always uncomfortable with his appointment as a secret military operative, could shift his attention back to his natural history interests. His real work, he knew, remained unfinished. He was ready to return to it.

❖ PART IV ❖

Legacies Lost and Lasting

To recapitulate. During eleven years, I have travelled through North America, from north to south, through the whole extent, comprising an extent of 23 degrees of latitude, or 575 leagues, as the crow flies. From east to west I have travelled 400 leagues, from Philadelphia to the mouth of the Missouri. I have, besides, made more than twenty other journeys, either along the sea coast, or in following the course of most of the great rivers of the United States. I have visited also parts of the Bahama Islands.

—ANDRÉ MICHAUX

❖ 16 ❖

Michaux's Last Days

1794–1802, Kentucky, Paris, Madagascar

While the rebellion that Michaux nearly incited may have come to a rather unceremonious, perhaps even inglorious, end, for Michaux it provided a fresh start. Not all that well-suited to the life of a spy, the botanist now returned to his research with renewed vigor. He spent the next two years doing what he had done before Edmond Genet conscripted him into service: he botanized with abandon. Intrigued by what he had seen in Kentucky during his military mission in 1793 but unable to do justice to what he knew was waiting to be discovered, Michaux focused much of his work in the next few years on the Mississippi River Valley and the American West. In two separate journeys, one in 1795 and another in 1796, he foraged for plant life along the Mississippi.

When he returned, he made sure to call on friends he had made in 1793 when visiting under very different circumstances. He took lodgings with General Thomas Barbee in Danville and dined with prominent Kentuckians, including Isaac Shelby. If anything, his earlier foray may have provided Michaux with a tantalizing glimpse into the region. As usual, he regularly traveled with Indigenous guides, and he gleaned new knowledge from them, too. His journal is replete with lists of new specimens collected. At one point, he recorded a special concoction of plants and herbs used to treat venereal diseases that he learned from Indigenous people. It was a treatment he likely intended to introduce in Europe and an example of how Europeans could incorporate Indigenous knowledge into their own practices. He also traveled to important trading villages, like Kaskaskia and Cahokia, and observed the unique blending of cultures that occurred in these posts. He encountered many Frenchmen at these two sites who were deeply engaged in the fur trade, relics of New France's control of the territory decades ago. They were, he noted, unlike other French people he had met. These traders had adopted the Native style of dress and life. "They do not wear pants," he recorded of the Frenchmen immersed in Indigenous cultures that he met in Kaskaskia, "but rather have a piece of cloth, less than half a meter long, between their thighs, which is held in front and in back, above the kidneys, with a belt."[1]

Michaux also made what he believed was a major botanical discovery in 1796: the yellowwood tree. The plant resembled an Asian tree that recently had been introduced to botanical gardens in Europe. Such a find, connecting a species in Kentucky with one from Asia, would shake up what botanists knew about the natural world. Michaux's supposition proved correct: there are similar species of the plant native to Asia. More practically, Michaux believed the yellowwood would make an excellent source for dyes. Its domestication thus promised to reap new profits for anyone able to harvest it. Excited by its commercial promise, he presented seeds of the plant to the territorial governor of the Southwest, William Blount. Its potential use as a new dye was precisely the type of symbiotic relationship between natural history research and commercial development that many of those involved in botany sought.[2]

Blount was overjoyed with the gift that, as he wrote in response to Michaux, would prove "beneficial to the community." More than that, Blount saw the seeds as an opportunity to score some partisan points. Blount was an enemy of Hamiltonians and shared the view among Jeffersonians that the French Revolution was part of a global effort to improve the human condition. He thus published a letter that was soon reprinted in several American newspapers praising Michaux's discovery and thanking the French Republic for the support that made it happen. His effusive gratitude was clearly meant as a dig to those, like Hamilton, who saw the French Revolution as a deviation from the American one. "If proofs were wanting of the disposition of the French Republic," Governor Blount proclaimed, "to promote the general happiness of the whole human family, the researches in which you are engaged under their authority could be adduced as one."[3]

It was for this generous act, and not his role with Clark, that Michaux garnered the attention of the American public. It became, his biographers noted, "Michaux's most widely reported plant discovery." Michaux also sent yellowwood seeds to friends in Europe and others in the United States. Several appear to have been planted and studied by Michaux's French colleagues. One still lives in Bartram's Garden in Philadelphia, "where it is a living link to these botanists," as the editors of Michaux's journal note. For a while, yellowwood was used as Michaux anticipated, as a dye, and its wood was integrated into various objects, such as guns. Today, though, it is primarily an ornamental tree, much like the one in Bartram's Garden.[4]

Though basking in the glow of his celebrated find, Michaux never took his eye off the regions sitting unexplored on the other side of the Mississippi. The large river, though now open to Americans, still served as a boundary between the United States and Spanish and Native American territories. Crossing it, Michaux realized, involved great risk, something he had learned through his earlier travels and noted in his journal. It required "traversing through Native American territories always at war with US inhabitants, crossing rivers by swimming, etc.," as he recorded in his notebook. Still, the West beckoned, and Michaux refused to relent, something he also explained to his mentor André Thouin in October 1795: "To fulfill the task that results from my mission and to know North America better, it remains for me to visit the western regions."[5]

While in Kentucky in 1795 and 1796, Michaux may have made some speculative probes west of the Mississippi. He certainly laid the groundwork for a future expedition by performing some important acts of botanical diplomacy. He contacted Pierre de Luzières, the Frenchman who had earlier plotted with Audrain in Pittsburgh to establish a royalist French colony under Spanish control. The royalist de Luzières was never fond of the French plan to overthrow Spanish control of Louisiana and spread republicanism across the continent. He had watched with angst from the western side of the Mississippi as Clark organized a military force on the opposite banks. He had also fingered Michaux as, in his own words, one of the chief "French renegades" who had stirred up a group of "American vagabonds."[6]

Michaux now realized that he needed to butter up de Luzières. Unlike Audrain and Tardiveau, de Luzières still had good ties to the Spanish government, and Michaux knew that he could facilitate Michaux's safe passage through Louisiana. Michaux deployed his usual tactics to win over his former rival. He sent de Luzières "a collection of very rare seeds" as a gesture of goodwill and promised to send him "the rarest objects that botany can offer . . . if I could learn the things that might please you more, I would reserve those for you." He also sent words of reassurance. "I will do all that is possible to contribute to the peace of the people of the territory in which you live," he wrote to de Luzières in December 1795, a clear renunciation of his former role.[7]

With the same objective in mind, Michaux made friendly overtures to the Spanish official Manuel Gayoso, the commandant at Nogales who had hammered out a mutual defense treaty with various Native groups and who had hurriedly reinforced his fort in expectation of an imminent Clark-led assault. Still scarred by the threat of invasion, Gayoso viewed Michaux's return to Kentucky with trepidation and carried an arrest warrant for the Frenchman, should their paths cross. Michaux once again used seeds as diplomatic tools to show a former enemy that science, unlike politics, knew no boundaries. As he had done with de Luzières, he sent Gayoso "seeds of rare trees that are likely to do well in the climate of Natchez." He also once again denounced his earlier efforts, performed only at the behest of Genet, and even provided Gayoso with a warning to be on the lookout for recidivist Americans.[8]

Michaux's lobbying paid off. On a cold December night in 1795, Michaux sat huddled on the eastern banks of the Mississippi, while Gayoso and some soldiers settled on the other side. When the Spaniards noticed the travelers, they sent a boat across the river to investigate, fearful, it seems, of an incursion into Spanish territory. When Gayoso learned that Michaux was in the group, he crossed the river to meet him. The two talked politics. Gayoso informed him that France and Spain had recently entered into a peace treaty. Michaux, for his part, made peace with Gayoso. At the end of the meeting, Gayoso "offered [Michaux] his services," likely meaning assistance in Michaux's scientific work, and revoked his arrest warrant for the botanist. They departed as friends—or, at least, on friendly terms.[9] It may have helped that Gayoso, in addition to being a military officer, was, like so many engaged in the Enlightenment project, a natural historian and astronomer.

Michaux also made a visit to his former partner, George Rogers Clark, in Louisville in February 1796. There, he met a broken man who begged the French botanist to assist him in recouping his lost investment. Clark had begun the project with hope of military glory and financial reward. If he was successful, he would have established an independent republic with him at its head and laid claim to massive amounts of fertile land. His frustrations with the United States also had spurred him to act. He felt betrayed by a nation he had served. He had expected compensation and support in return for his accomplishments on behalf of the American cause but instead found himself largely ignored by the country he helped create. He was so despairing in 1793 that he renounced his allegiance to it and threw his lot in with France, a new revolutionary nation that promised to provide him with the security and status that he sought. The man Michaux met in 1796 now felt forsaken by yet another revolutionary government. Clark sent his accounts from the failed plot to the French government for reimbursement, where they were promptly ignored. The total was in the thousands. There was little Michaux could do for him.

If Clark was left desolate by the episode, Michaux emerged largely unscathed from it. In fact, he was in an even better position to pursue his research. He managed to establish working relationships with former enemies like Gayoso, and he also strengthened his scientific network within the United States through the contacts he had made in Kentucky as well as Philadelphia. The APS connection provided a particular boon to Michaux in the years that followed. Michaux kept Nicholas Collin, someone Michaux appeared to have had no contact with before 1793, informed of his travels and discoveries, and the two exchanged seeds. Collin extended the reach of Michaux's work by sending some of Michaux's specimens to Sweden on behalf of the Frenchman. Michaux also stayed in touch with Charles Willson Peale and, though still short on cash himself, contributed money to support Peale's natural history museum. He also relied on his old friend Bartram's beneficence. The Philadelphia botanist bought important natural history books for Michaux. In short, Michaux, thanks to his involvement in the Clark expedition, now enjoyed a wider network of scientific collaborators throughout North America.[10]

Throughout these years, Michaux's home base remained in Charleston. His assistant Saunier—with whom Michaux seems to have had a tense relationship—managed the smaller New Jersey garden, though the latter made no shipments to France after 1792. Michaux, however, continued to ship specimens across the Atlantic from South Carolina. Throughout, Michaux continued to consider himself a servant of the French government, but as affairs in France evolved, Michaux's status always appeared precarious. In 1795, the Reign of Terror that marked the years 1793–95 came to a pause as a new regime, called the Directory, assumed power. The Directory operated under a new constitution approved by the French people. The

Directory itself referred to a five-person executive, but the government had a bicameral legislature and other administrative departments. The military, with Napoleon Bonaparte at the head of the army, provided additional security for the nation—and some much-needed successes on the battlefield.

With the advent of yet another new government and the reestablishment of stable state institutions, Michaux came under greater scrutiny than he had in the early years of the French Revolution. Now, Michaux received complaints that his shipments were too infrequent and unimpressive. They expected more from him and suspected he might be wasting funds. Michaux was put on the defensive, explaining that it took time to create the specialized crates needed to transport specimens safely on a rough ocean crossing. He also had avoided sending rare items during periods of active war out of fear that "English pirates" could seize them. In the spring of 1796, French officials were so concerned with Michaux's performance that they asked Ambroise Marie François Joseph Palisot de Beauvois, a fellow botanist then living in Philadelphia, to inspect Michaux's garden in South Carolina.[11]

Palisot de Beauvois's extensive report was a mixed bag for Michaux. He allayed officials' fears that Michaux was lollygagging and instead praised Michaux's dedication and work ethic. "It could not be in better hands than those of the zealous and hardworking Citizen Michaux," he concluded of the South Carolina garden. He also vouched for the importance of Michaux's mission. Botanical research on this scale was, he argued, vital to the government's interests and should be sustained. "I do not doubt that soon the territory of France will be enriched because of the care, zeal, and hard work of Citizen Michaux," he wrote. He also raved about Michaux's collection techniques, perhaps to address concerns that Michaux's methods were unnecessarily time-consuming or wasteful.[12]

While applauding Michaux as an individual, however, Palisot de Beauvois did offer some very self-serving criticisms. He argued that Michaux's plantation was poorly located. The warm and humid South, Palisot de Beauvois reported, meant that Michaux was unable to grow many plants acclimated to the colder and drier North, a climate he believed was more akin to France's. He thus told French officials that they needed to establish a new garden in more centrally located Philadelphia, where plants from both the North and South could thrive. He also proposed expanding the scope of the project to include animal life. Palisot de Beauvois then suggested the perfect person to spearhead this expansion: himself. It was a convenient move for someone who had seen the violence and uncertainty of the Revolution in France and likely wanted to avoid returning to the fray. Though Palisot de Beauvois was adamant that Michaux's operation in South Carolina continue alongside this other proposed garden, Michaux, who never read the report, sensed a rival.[13]

In fact, Michaux was growing more jealous as he saw competitors take the limelight from him. "During my absence someone steals that which I want to communicate to my country before all others," he complained. The British, in particular, bothered the patriotic Frenchman. British botanists like John Fraser continued to scoop him by publishing descriptions of plants Michaux had discovered first. "The thing that is most disagreeable," he confided to his mentor André Thouin in 1796, "is that it is this vain nation, proud and treacherous, that is able to harm me the most because of the ease of communication between Charleston and England."[14]

To add to his woes, Michaux also knew that the turbulent Atlantic crossing had often harmed his shipments. Many of the collections from his Canadian expedition, for instance, were lost. With so many specimens destroyed, the only record of "their importance" rested, as Michaux noted, in "my herbarium." In the summer of 1796, with rivals continuing to steal what he saw as his rightful acclaim, he decided to rectify the situation. He would return to France. He wanted to deposit his herbarium in an archive for safekeeping and publish his findings for the world to see—and for himself and France to get due credit for his endeavors.[15]

His desire to return to France was driven by another aspiration. He remained determined to pursue his expedition to the Pacific. But, in part prompted by his American colleagues, he concluded that he needed to go home first. As his American friends reminded him, if he left for the West, he might never return, and if that were to happen without publishing his findings, then his life's work would be lost forever. "All the educated Americans who live on the border of the wilderness and who are more aware of the dangers are surprised and reproach me for wanting to begin new travels before publishing what I have already acquired," he wrote; "After all these considerations, I propose to interrupt for some time the voyages that I planned to undertake west of the Mississippi."[16]

Michaux departed from Charleston on August 13, 1796, aboard the *Ophir*, a merchant frigate destined for Amsterdam, a neutral port that provided greater safety in the midst of a war between France and Great Britain. He carried, as the French minister in Philadelphia described, "the fruits of twelve years hard work and research." It was an enormous haul—sixteen huge cases of specimens and four trunks filled with material. Still, he left the United States feeling his work in North America was incomplete and vowed that he would race back to the field. "If I can get my collection safely to France, I could in 8 or 10 months put my collections in order for publication and be back at the Mississippi before this space of time," he wrote to a colleague.[17]

Michaux returned with more than his scientific work. He also brought an enslaved boy, about twelve years old, across the Atlantic. Little is known about the child, named Merlot, though there are hints that he had been born in West Africa before being brought to the United States and sold. One is left to speculate about the true nature of Michaux's relationship with Merlot. Michaux biographers have suggested that because slavery in France was banned, Michaux may have "adopted" the child. The child's wishes remain completely unknown, and he was probably not adopted in any formal or informal way, but Michaux certainly relied on Merlot for assistance—and would continue to do so in the future. In any case, Merlot is a reminder that Michaux was surrounded by and depended upon enslaved labor throughout his time in South Carolina and had become so reliant on this labor that he brought one of the people he enslaved back to France. There, Merlot most likely lived in a state of quasi-enslavement.[18]

The crossing was surely memorable for both Michaux and Merlot. After traveling thousands of miles through North American woods, attempting to instigate an invasion of Louisiana, and venturing as far south as the Caribbean and as far north as Hudson Bay, Michaux's return voyage turned out to be his riskiest adventure of all. At first, it was smooth sailing. After losing sight of land on August 18, little of note happened except for a gale that battered the ship for two days. Dangers, however, emerged as soon as they drew nearer to European shores in early October. A British frigate patrolling the English Channel stopped the vessel as it entered the waterway. A naval officer boarded the American ship, checked the papers, and inspected it for contraband. The captain, satisfied with what he found, reassured the passengers "that they were not capturing any ships."[19]

They continued on. As Michaux's ship approached the Dutch coast on October 9, a beautiful day quickly turned disastrous for the *Ophir*.[20]

"At 5 P.M.," Michaux recorded in his journal, "there arose a storm that became extremely severe in less than two hours; it continued throughout the night doubling its furor."

By daybreak, the craft emerged from the storm still floating but demasted. Seeing little hope, the captain decided to ground the foundering vessel, but this move only made matters worse. The storm had passed, but the sea continued to rage, and heavy waves pounded the boat. The situation turned perilous. "The sails were in shreds in less than fifteen minutes. A mast was broken, the ship was half overturned and was shaken severely for one-half hour," Michaux wrote.

Word of the vessel in distress spread along the Dutch coastline. Soon a crowd of two hundred people assembled on the beach to help the passengers and crew, while those onboard struggled to hang on. "We were completely drenched so that all the crew and I were losing our strength," Michaux recorded in his journal. After three hours, Michaux gave up on life. "I felt my strength ebbing," he recounted, "and I went down to the lower deck and waited for the end of my suffering and for death."

Michaux passed out soon thereafter. The next thing he remembered was waking up by the side of a warm hearth in a home in the village of Egmond. Michaux's first thoughts turned to his life's work. Everything that mattered to him was on that ship, and he recalled seeing cargo swept away by the waves. The townspeople assured him that some material had landed on the shore, and that a few boxes were surely his. Merlot, too, survived the dangerous episode.

In the days that followed, much to Michaux's happy amazement, he recovered most of his valuable luggage. "Almost all my collections were saved," he enthused to his mentor Thouin. The only scientific items he lost were a few notebooks, the contents of which he believed he could replicate, and a box of taxidermied animals. He did, however, lose all of his personal belongings and clothes, a minor loss to Michaux given what could have happened.

Michaux spent the next six weeks nursing himself and his specimens back to health. He worked tirelessly from four in the morning to eight at night drying and preserving his sopping-wet collections. He carefully inspected every case, undoing the damage the seawater had caused, trying to salvage every item. By the first week of November, he was confident of success. "I finished today the work on the plants," he told a friend on November 7, "and I am happy that nothing will be lost."

By the end of November, feeling that both he and his collection were fully restored, Michaux embarked on the final leg of his passage: an overland trip to Paris. A month later, on December 23, Michaux arrived in Paris, a changed man returning to a much-changed city. He had left it as the thirty-nine-year-old royal botanist with his teenage son and a French gardener, and he returned as Citizen Michaux at age fifty under a very different regime and with Merlot at his side. When he arrived in the city, he expected to see the fruits of his many years' labor blossoming in Parisian gardens. The devastation wrought by the French Revolution soon checked his ebullience. The gardens sat in disrepair, and his living collection lay in ruins. "Of the 60,000 trees which he had sent to France," his friend and first biographer recounted, "a small number only remained." Michaux nonetheless held out hope that he could revive what had been lost, for he still possessed thousands of seeds that might sprout new life. He also threw himself into publishing his findings, believing that even if the physical plants were lost, at least they could live on in print.[21]

Michaux's first days in Paris were a bustle of socializing that included reconnecting with his mentors and reuniting with friends he had made in the United States. He stayed at Satory, his boyhood home, visited prominent natural historians including Le Monnier, Thouin, Lamarck, and Jussieu. He also visited Mangourit, the former consul at Charleston who was Michaux's friend and also deeply involved in Genet's plots. Mangourit was now stationed in Paris but still in the diplomatic service as the "charge d'affaires of the French Republic for the United States," the official tasked with managing France's US relations. He also made a point to meet with Samuel Fulton, George Rogers Clark's son-in-law, who was in Paris trying to recover Clark's costs, a sign that the Clark episode was still very much alive for Michaux.[22]

Of course, Michaux remained financially strapped. He lived with his son, now twenty-six, for at least part of the time at 674, rue Hyacinthe, conveniently located just a few blocks from the gardens at the Tuileries. While there, he pleaded with government officials to reimburse him for his American expenditures. He presented receipts and accounts showing what he had done in the preceding years in service of the French Republic. He had no luck. Michaux also dreamed of a return to America, where he could complete the expedition that remained unfinished. He lobbied the government to send him back to the United States and provide him with the support needed to undertake that daring transcontinental trek. The government, its attention taken by the politics of the Revolution and its coffers depleted by war, proved unresponsive.[23]

Dispirited and disaffected, Michaux once again sought an escape from France and refuge in the field. Lacking the funds to pay for a return to the United States himself, and with a government unable to underwrite the expected costs, another opportunity arose that took his research in a completely different direction: the South Seas. In 1801, a scientific expedition was heading to Australia. The fifty-five-year-old botanist was asked to join a group of younger natural historians. Michaux, surrounded by tumult, as Napoleon had just seized power, and desperate for money, agreed to embark on this new adventure.[24]

It would prove to be his last. Perhaps finally wearying of travel, or frustrated by a martinet of a captain, Michaux abandoned the expedition in Mauritius (called Isle de France in Michaux's time) off the southeast coast of Africa. Michaux was overwhelmed by the biodiversity he saw on the island. He decided that he would rather be stuck in a lush environment in the Indian Ocean than on a crowded ship that seemed doomed. His sense was right. The expedition to Australia remained beset by problems, and many on it never made it home. Unfortunately, the same fate awaited Michaux.[25]

He spent nine months on Mauritius. His time there was very productive. He boasted of his discoveries when he wrote to his scientific colleagues in Paris. He also assured them that the prospects for a French colony on the island were promising. He surmised that several European crops would thrive in the climate and devised plans to introduce and cultivate these crops on the island.

Michaux hacked his way through the dense, tropical forests of Mauritius accompanied by Merlot. Though Merlot was technically manumitted when he arrived in France because slavery had been temporarily abolished, it is unclear how much freedom Merlot truly experienced or exercised. We also do not know if the adolescent wished to undertake the risky voyage to the Indian Ocean or if he was an unwilling companion. Merlot, nonetheless, showed great aptitude and interest in botany. Someone who met him years later, long after he and Michaux had parted ways, noted that "he has the habit of making collections." That Michaux continued to include a formerly enslaved person such as Merlot on his last expedition only adds to the supposition that one of the reasons Michaux chose South Carolina for his primary garden was the prevalence of an unfree labor system, a system that allowed him to train workers to his specifications to maintain the intensive work his garden required while he traveled.[26]

In June 1802, Michaux and Merlot undertook a six-hundred-mile sea voyage from Mauritius to Madagascar. The plant and animal life he encountered once again left him awestruck. In fact, there is some evidence that Michaux was planning to lay down his own roots on the island. He scouted the area in search of a spot to build a garden like the one he had had in South Carolina. But Michaux was waylaid by an unexpected enemy. The humid climate was home to tropical diseases alien to the Frenchman's immune system. In the fall, Michaux fell ill with a severe fever, and though he initially recuperated, a second bout sapped him of his remaining strength. He died in October 1802 at fifty-six years old.[27]

What happened to Michaux's final remains became something of a mystery. For more than a century, no one was quite sure what had happened to his body. In the mid-twentieth century, French scientists working on Madagascar decided to try to find his burial site. After talking to local residents, they learned that there was a grave purported to be of a French explorer on a high hill overlooking a river. They hiked their way to it and found a tomb that appeared to be Michaux's. Local residents had even maintained it. It was a fitting resting site. The explorer who had spent the bulk of his professional life away from his native country, working diligently, even rabidly, in the field, now rested far from France, surrounded by lush forests.[28]

Merlot, meanwhile, found himself thrown into great jeopardy by Michaux's death. His ambiguous status, made even more uncertain by local customs, left him in a legal limbo. At first, he wanted to return to Mauritius, but he lacked the funds needed for the trip. He then turned to what he knew best: botany. He established himself as a trusted gardener of the Madagascar elite, including the king. Evidence suggests that at some point Merlot was forced into slavery on the island. Meanwhile, Michaux's son, François André, who had remained in Paris and served as his father's executor, lodged ineffective objections to Merlot's enslavement, arguing that he was a free man under France's laws.[29]

Merlot's reenslavement may have been temporary. A hint that his circumstances improved emerged in a letter written several years later by a French natural historian, Theodore Leschenault. At the time, Leschenault was conducting research on Java, a small island in the Indian Ocean now part of Malaysia. The natural historian had known Michaux; in fact, he and Michaux were shipmates on that ill-fated voyage to Australia. Leschenault, like Michaux, was traveling the globe in search of new botanical discoveries. During his quest on Java, he met a free Black man with an African name, Bognam-nonen-derega, who told the Frenchman he was West African by birth but had been "attached to the service of the celebrated explorer Michaux."[30]

It seems likely that Merlot would have discarded the name chosen by those who enslaved him to reclaim his birth name or choose another he now found more suitable. Moreover, what were the odds of someone on Java knowing Michaux? It is not a tale easily invented, and there seems to have been no point in doing so. If Bognam-nonen-derega was indeed the man once known as Merlot, imagine the life he had led. Born in West Africa, or perhaps in Saint-Domingue, as others have speculated, he was either enslaved and endured the Middle Passage or was born into slavery and transported to the American mainland, to be sold in South Carolina. Then he was brought across the Atlantic to France, where presumably he served as Michaux's manservant in Paris in a state of quasi-slavery/quasi-freedom, before then traveling around Africa to Madagascar, where he was likely enslaved once again. He somehow freed himself and ended up in Malaysia. There, he shared with this European natural historian how to use certain plants to create poisoned arrows, a sign of his continued interest in natural history. It was a remarkable life. Merlot's (or Bognam-nonen-derega's?) journey, with its twists and turns, though, was not the only one redirected by André Michaux's time in North America. In fact, Michaux left numerous legacies that shaped his world and reverberate still in our own, many of which remain, much like Merlot's own life, obscured by time.

❖ 17 ❖

Hidden Legacies

The Michaux Subscription List raised three initial questions: Who was this Frenchman receiving such support from leading Americans? What did the APS actually do in this episode? And what ended up happening to the proposed expedition? The immediate answers were, on the face of it, simple. Michaux was France's royal botanist dispatched to North America to take part in the Enlightenment project to discover new plants and improve French society. The APS, the leading scientific organization in the United States at the time, used its networks to raise an enormous sum to underwrite an expedition that would serve science and American national interests. The expedition never launched, and the effort failed, in large part because Michaux, the botanist, was momentarily swept up in French revolutionary politics. An aborted plot that ended abruptly makes for a somewhat anticlimactic story, though, and perhaps these superficial conclusions are a reason why this episode has been so rarely studied in recent years. The truth, however, is that these pat answers conceal the true legacies of Michaux's time in North America. Michaux's adventures, as botanist and as conspirator, left surprising and lasting impressions on individuals, on the United States, and in science that reverberated for decades after his death and still have echoes today.

First, there is André Michaux himself. A name largely unknown today, he was, in my opinion, one of his generation's greatest scientific explorers of North America, arguably surpassed only by Lewis and Clark's successful transcontinental expedition a decade later. He traveled from Florida to Hudson Bay and throughout the trans-Appalachian region, often traveling with only a few guides and aides. More important than the ground he covered were his contributions to science. These left a visible and lasting mark on the American landscape. Michaux introduced mimosa trees, several species of rhododendrons, and other plants to American gardens. We are still surrounded by Michaux's work today. In addition, although many of the sixty thousand trees he shipped across the Atlantic were lost, the Jardin des Plantes in Paris preserved his herbarium so scholars could study and appreciate the extent of his accomplishments.

Michaux also identified an enormous number of new species during his extensive travels. According to one botanist's recent estimate, he identified more than two thousand individual plants in his journals. Many of these were new to science. This same estimate indicates that he is responsible for describing fifty-six new genera in his time, thirty-six of which are still in use, and for naming more than one thousand species of plants. Today, botanists recognize his contributions by including the designation *Michx.* after a plant's name that he is credited with describing. He was, in the words of Mangourit, the French consul from Charleston, "one of the most extraordinary men." A modern botanist agreed in a 2004 retrospective: "He made a remarkable number of important discoveries for the botanical world."[1]

In a strange twist of history, today Michaux's most tangible legacy survives in the coffers of the APS, in large part because of the bond he forged with the institution during its fundraising campaign for him. When his son, François André Michaux, died without an heir in 1855, his will left the bulk of the Michaux estate to the institution that had tried to do so much for his father. The younger Michaux had, as his father wished, followed in his paternal footsteps. François André became a noted botanist and traveled extensively throughout North America, often retracing his father's paths. The French government funded some of his travels, hoping that he might be able to liquidate the Charleston and New Jersey properties that were still, technically, French property. The Charleston garden lay neglected, while Michaux's aide Saunier still lived on the New Jersey property, though he used it primarily for his own purposes. In 1802, thanks in part to François André's work, the French government did sell the Charleston property, while Saunier managed to secure rights to the New Jersey plot.[2]

During François André's stay in the United States, the American Philosophical Society became his intellectual home. His father had introduced him to the Society when he was still a boy during his first visit to North

America, and now he met with some of his father's closest friends at the APS. He became so enmeshed with the Society that the institution elected him a member in 1809, a recognition his father never received. When he returned to France, he maintained a close correspondence with several of its most prominent members. In fact, the best likeness of François André resides today in the Society's holdings. It was drawn by Charles Willson Peale's son and APS member Rembrandt Peale, a symbol of the intergenerational connections formed through the institution. François André also returned with seeds that eventually sprouted more than 250,000 trees, something that surely fulfilled his father's wishes.[3]

François André Michaux died childless, but by bequeathing his wealth to the APS, he hoped that the family name would live on by supporting science. That is in fact what has happened in ways François André probably could not have predicted. By the time the Society received the Michaux gift in the 1870s (its disposition was held up for a variety of bureaucratic and legal reasons), scientists and reformers were calling on governments to preserve forests and other natural habitats threatened by industrialization and population growth. The Society took up this cause and used the funds to underwrite a series of lectures by one of the leading conservationists in Pennsylvania, Joseph Rothrock. Rothrock traveled throughout the state delivering talks on the need to conserve its forests. People were persuaded. Inspired by what he said, Pennsylvania's state government created a division of forestry, with Rothrock serving as its inaugural director. One of the new department's first acts was to preserve a large tract of forest in southwestern Pennsylvania, which the state aptly named Michaux State Forest. The creation of this state park, and of the state's department of forestry, can thus trace a direct lineage back to the Subscription List.[4]

The Society continued to use the Michaux endowment in creative ways, all in the same pioneering spirit of Michaux. In the early twentieth century, the Michaux fund supported an urban forest in Philadelphia's Fairmount Park, again a fitting tribute to Michaux's work. In the 1940s, the Society even considered purchasing the land in Charleston that was Michaux's home in order to reestablish a botanical garden. Today, the remnants of these funds are used to acquire books, often in natural history, for the Society's research library and to fund fieldwork for young scholars who are continuing in the spirit of André and his son, François André. It is a lasting testament to the bond forged between the French natural historian and the Society in the 1790s.[5]

The APS's involvement in drafting the Subscription List and its subsequent instructions to Michaux also left a lasting impact on both Thomas Jefferson and, subsequently, American history. Michaux had almost undertaken the transcontinental expedition that Jefferson had long dreamed of. Although Jefferson had toyed with the idea for more than a decade, even trying to recruit, of all people, George Rogers Clark in the 1780s, Michaux's attempt in 1793 was the closest Jefferson had yet come to realizing it. Unlike earlier times when the idea was simply bandied about before being dismissed, Michaux's proposal was so real that Jefferson was forced to think more deeply about what such a project would entail. By negotiating with Michaux about intellectual rights, by working with fellow APS members to identify Michaux's scientific priorities, by talking about the route, and by undertaking all the other planning that went into Michaux's expedition, Jefferson was able to more fully understand the issues surrounding such a project. He could better appreciate its promise, its priorities, and its potential problems.

Jefferson stayed true to his vision of the United States as an expanding nation and eventually realized that dream of a transcontinental voyage when president of the United States. In 1803, during Napoleon's reign in France, Jefferson, as president, was able to purchase the Louisiana Territory, a sprawling expanse that stretched from New Orleans across the Great Plains and to modern-day Montana. The purchase and control of the region west of the Mississippi River provided Jefferson with another chance to launch an exploratory expedition to the Pacific. This time, as the head of the federal government, he had access to more powerful institutions that might underwrite the project. He cajoled Congress into appropriating $2,500 to outfit a team to survey this newly acquired domain. While it was about $750 more than what the APS had raised, its inflation-adjusted value made it comparable to the prize the APS had offered Michaux. Jefferson then appointed two individuals with connections to his earlier attempts to lead the adventure. The co-commanders were Meriwether Lewis, the Virginian whom Jefferson had rejected in 1792, and, in yet another strange twist of history, William Clark, the younger brother of George Rogers Clark.

In 1803, as Lewis and Clark prepared to depart, Jefferson, as president of the United States, took the same hands-on approach to managing the instructions of the explorers. He drew up a new set for Lewis and Clark to follow, but its core elements mirrored the Society's instructions for Michaux, a clear indication of the formative impact of this failed endeavor on Jefferson's thinking. Jefferson, for example, gave Lewis and Clark the same primary charge that the APS had tried to give Michaux: to find the fastest route to the Pacific Ocean. Its priority in this federally funded endeavor showed just how much the APS's priorities had reflected those of the nation—not a problem for Lewis and Clark but a sticking point for the patriotic Frenchman Michaux. The subsidiary instructions Lewis and Clark received were also similar to Michaux's. They were to conduct reconnaissance on Native American groups and to observe natural history. Jefferson even passed on the same advice that Lewis and Clark should write on birch bark if necessary, though there is no evidence that he again suggested that they tattoo their findings onto their bodies. The two sets of instructions bore such a clear relationship to one another that the editors of *The Papers of Thomas Jefferson* spent pages documenting the similar phraseology and resonances between the two. It was clear that Michaux had provided Jefferson with a trial run for Lewis and Clark.[6]

As Jefferson prepared for Lewis and Clark's mission, he remained the American Philosophical Society's president as well as the president of the United States. Though now in Washington, DC, he stayed in touch with many of the APS's most active members and knew that the institution still had an important role to play in this new undertaking. He ordered Lewis to travel to Philadelphia before heading West so he could consult with APS members and learn from the best. The Society's members, including Benjamin Rush and Caspar Wistar, two individuals who had worked with Jefferson to draft Michaux's instructions, shared all that they knew about the geography of the interior and helped Lewis acquire the best instruments and the right medicines. Conversely, the APS members were so impressed with Lewis's knowledge of natural history that they elected him a member in 1803, just before he departed for the West. It was the realization of an initiative begun in 1793. Later, Thomas Jefferson sent the official journals of the expedition to the APS for safekeeping, where they now reside in the Society's vault alongside the Michaux journals, Subscription List, and the instructions Jefferson drafted for this earlier expedition.

There was, though, more to Jefferson's involvement with Michaux than a shared commitment to the advancement of knowledge. He was also, if only passively, involved with Michaux's clandestine mission to organize an invasion of Spanish Louisiana by US citizens. Certainly, he was aware of it and did little to stop its initiation. As with the Michaux Subscription List, then, parsing Jefferson's decision-making during the Genet affair and his long-forgotten involvement in a near-rebellion against federal authority in Kentucky also sheds light on both Jefferson in this historic moment and on inherent Jeffersonian traits that would continue in the years to come. Though historians have largely turned a blind eye to what would surely have been seen as negligent if not openly treasonous acts by Jefferson had they had been more widely known at the time—acts that could have ended his political career—there is ample documentation for his involvement, including Jefferson's own firsthand account in his *Anas,* a compilation of important events that he made to chronicle his time as US secretary of state. Even the editors of *The Papers of Thomas Jefferson* concluded of Jefferson's letter of introduction for Michaux that "there can be no doubt that he knew of Genet's plans for the expedition when he prepared the final version." Others have decided to ignore the whole episode, almost as a way to avoid the implications of what Jefferson almost helped unleash. "With the story of what Michaux did in Kentucky in the fall of 1793 and of the continuing unrest in the region," Dumas Malone, the author of a definitive multivolume biography of Jefferson, told his readers, "we are not concerned here."[7]

We should be concerned with it, though. If we place the affair within its historic moment, it becomes clear that Genet's machinations illuminated and brought to the fore three philosophical and political challenges with which Jefferson was then grappling: his own political ideology, which emphasized a limited role for government while he served in an administration that embraced a more energetic view of the federal government; his view that the American and French Revolutions were global movements that needed encouragement; and his attempt to navigate the emerging partisan environment enveloping the country. Jefferson's decisions reflected his attempt to chart a safe passage through these very turbulent waters, one in which he stayed true to his beliefs without betraying his obligations to the national interest.

As the first secretary of state in the brand-new government of a very young nation, Jefferson found himself in a bind unique to his time and foreign to us today. He was simultaneously a high-ranking official in the president's administration and an emerging leader of that administration's opposition. When Genet appeared on the scene, Jefferson embraced the ambassador because he hoped the Frenchman could help persuade the Washington administration to shift its position on foreign policy and more vigorously embrace the French cause. Jefferson's political inclinations thus sucked him into the intrigue surrounding Genet and forced him to make quick decisions in circumstances that were largely new and foreign to both him and to those operating in this new system. Eventually, he found himself in a morally dubious position. His difficulties, both with Genet but also with other policies with which he disagreed, ultimately forced Jefferson to realize the intractability of his situation. That was why he decided the only way he could maintain his own moral standing was to extricate himself from the administration and leave Philadelphia, thus his attempt to resign in August 1793 and his exit at the end of that year.

Still, Jefferson's behind-the-scenes maneuvering during the Genet affair revealed certain political instincts that would persist throughout his career. In the following years, Jefferson proved to be an effective partisan operator, often working in the shadows and through allies like Madison to manipulate the political landscape and strengthen his personal standing and advance his political agenda. Such tactics are not necessarily untoward. Sometimes leadership depends on a leader working in the background while letting others appear to drive action. Jefferson felt compelled to do so in 1793, when he saw the Washington administration taking positions that he felt betrayed the principles of the young nation. He continued to mobilize opposition forces through surrogates while in retirement at Monticello. He deployed these tactics again when he was thrown into the uncomfortable position of vice president under his ideological foe John Adams.

Jefferson's canniness certainly reflected elements of his own personality, but they were also influenced by a political situation he inherited. Jefferson's actions from the Genet affair through to his term as vice president reveal someone learning to practice modern partisan politics in a country unused to, and indeed hostile to, such behavior. These years were a struggle for Jefferson and his political allies. First, they had to confront the reigning sentiments of the day in which Americans generally viewed partisanship as an inherent ill. When they voiced their opposition to the Federalists, Jefferson's allies faced criticisms that ranged from accusations that their actions were self-serving attempts to seize power to more serious charges of sedition. The Constitution itself made their position even more difficult. Before the Twelfth Amendment in 1804, the vice president was simply whoever received the second-most electoral votes. That the framers structured the offices of president and vice president in such a way showed that partisanship was far from their minds—if they had been more aware of the possibility, then they surely would have realized the likelihood that the vice president would often be an opponent of and rival to the president. It was not until after Jefferson's election as president that the Twelfth Amendment was ratified. It made the vice-presidential nominees the choice of a presidential candidate, not simply the second-largest vote-getter. It was a tacit acknowledgment of partisanship that was meant to resolve the very problem Jefferson had been confronting since the Constitution's inception.[8]

While Jefferson was able to find a way through this very uncomfortable situation, others mixed up in the Kentucky plot were less fortunate. Indeed, many of those involved remained battered by the ill-fated quest to invade Spanish Louisiana. Edmond Genet was perhaps the most completely displaced. First, he was entirely unsuccessful in his primary objectives in 1793. Spanish Louisiana was not and would not become an independent republic allied with the United States and France. Instead, rather than forging a wedge between Spain and the United States, perhaps even forcing the two nations to take up arms against each other, the affair ultimately drew Spain and the United States closer. Worse for Genet, he became a man without a country. He faced an uncertain fate after he was ousted from his post in February 1794. Genet feared that if he returned to a Paris seized by the Jacobins, he might suffer the same cold-steel fate that befell so many during the height of the Terror. He thus pleaded for asylum from the very administration he had infuriated. In a remarkable act of generosity, Washington, who was himself shocked at the deadly turn of events in France, decided to save Genet's head. He allowed Genet to stay in the country he had done so much to disrupt.[9]

Genet's sullied reputation in Philadelphia forced him to remove to a small farm outside the city where he could wallow in anonymity. He eventually found refuge in New York, a city where he had built a network of supporters. Perhaps chastened by his time as ambassador, his temper seemed to have cooled in the new city, and his antics subsided. In fact, Genet thrived. He entered the city's elite and married Cornelia Clinton, the daughter of New York governor DeWitt Clinton. They bought a farm on Long Island, settled down, and raised a family.[10]

While he might have become more mild-mannered, Genet still fumed whenever he heard the name of Jefferson. After reviewing his time in Philadelphia, he revisited all his interactions with Jefferson and concluded that his supposed friend had manipulated him to serve Jefferson's own ends. At one point, he rather unbelievably accused Jefferson, the ardent Francophile, of manipulating Genet to strengthen Great Britain's position with the United States. In 1797, on July 4, a date that brought Jefferson to many people's minds, a still-infuriated Genet sat down to unload on his former confidante. "I have decided to address," he wrote, "the real author of my ills."[11]

He never sent the letter, but in the early twentieth century, a journalist and author, Meade Minnigerode, rediscovered it in something of an archival coup. A Genet descendant showed him a secret trunk of letters that had been passed down through the family. Generations of the family had imbibed its contents and tried to resuscitate their patriarch's reputation. Genet's son, having absorbed his father's harangues firsthand, even wrote an entire book that tried to rehabilitate Genet's damaged name by castigating his father's great nemesis, Jefferson. His heirs followed suit. Their efforts, along with Minnigerode's, have had little effect. Genet's legacy remains as tarnished today as it was in the 1790s. Historians cast him as a brash, intemperate, unruly, naïve, perhaps even delusional figure.[12]

Minnigerode's book reproduced Genet's July 4 invective in full. The text runs more than twelve typed pages that use a font smaller than that used in the rest of the book. In it, Genet recalled every episode from his time in Philadelphia. Time and again, Genet cast himself as a pawn duped by Jefferson, whose outward friendship masked his darker intentions. Though Genet never sent the letter, he kept it in his papers. It is so long and convoluted that the editors of *The Papers of Thomas Jefferson* preferred to give an extended summary rather than reproduce the entire document.

Genet was not the only one left dislocated by the affair in Kentucky. Almost everyone else who was deeply involved in the plot suffered in its aftermath, perhaps none more so than George Rogers Clark. As Clark's military mobilization unwound and his neighbors cheered the rapid turn of events, Clark sat in his frontier home with debts piling high. He had advanced an enormous sum to underwrite the project. He did so because he expected to recoup them from Genet and with the prizes from his expected conquest. With that plan shot, his unpaid bills mounted and pushed him to the brink of bankruptcy. His appeals for reimbursement to Jean Antoine Joseph Fauchet, the French ambassador in Philadelphia, went nowhere.[13]

Rebuffed at home, a desperate Clark hatched another plan. He cast his sights across the Atlantic. A direct appeal to the French government seemed like the only remaining avenue, so he sent one of his lieutenants, Colonel Samuel Fulton, to Paris to lay his accounts before the French Assembly. This Kentucky frontiersmen traveled first to Philadelphia, where Fauchet again appeared intractable, and then to France, where he lobbied the French National Assembly—to no avail. Stonewalled at every turn, he returned to Kentucky empty-handed. Clark would live until 1818 and see Jefferson ask his younger brother, William Clark, to join Meriwether Lewis in a successful transcontinental trek. George Rogers Clark, though, would never regain his former stature and died penniless and disregarded.[14]

Several of the lesser French characters involved in the plot faded into obscurity; indeed, some were more or less pushed into oblivion because of their participation. Barthélemi Tardiveau, the would-be colonizer whose brother served as translator for La Chaise, fell out of favor with the governor of Louisiana because of his sibling's actions. Audrain, the Pittsburgh-based merchant who was Barthélemi Tardiveau's partner, came under the same suspicion when spies reported that he backed Clark and had privately declared his devotion to the French Revolution. The Spanish governor of Louisiana, nervous about both men's true loyalties, rescinded his offer to support their proposed community of French refugees. The third partner, de Luzières, the French monarchist based in St. Louis, had taken out huge loans in anticipation of receiving the grant. Having lost the governor's backing, he, like Clark, was financially ruined. Pusgignoux, the Spanish spy, was sent to Cuba by Spanish officials, far from the scene of his treachery, where he vanished from the historic record. Today, no one knows who this figure really was.[15]

At least one conspirator, Charles DePauw, the merchant who sold his inventory to fund the expedition, recovered from his losses and has a last name still readily recognized by many Americans. In the years that followed, his trading houses boomed. In the nineteenth century, his heirs continued to accumulate wealth, eventually serving as the chief benefactors for DePauw University. Still, a cloud followed Charles DePauw for years after the expedition's collapse. In the early nineteenth century, with memory of the plot still alive, and some individuals trying to chase down debts owed to them by the conspirators, officials decided to further investigate what had actually happened in Kentucky. They heard of DePauw's potential involvement and deposed him and others to get to the bottom of it. DePauw gave one of the most detailed extant accounts of what had happened in Kentucky in 1793, including the support the plot received from many prominent Kentuckians. Indeed, the government investigation and interrogations that DePauw faced decades later reveal a key aspect of the Kentucky conspiracy. It may have been a brief episode but it was not forgotten. Its legacy lasted and lingered, often in subtle but important and powerful ways.[16]

If there were any winners in the conspiracy of 1793, it proved to be the Kentuckians. To be sure, they achieved their immediate aim. They had free access to the Mississippi River. More than that, though, they realized that they were a powerful political force. That confidence infused their actions in the years to come. In fact, this event helped crystalize cultural patterns and political principles that lasted for several decades.

First, the pattern of audacious frontier leaders threatening to separate from the United States persisted. Clark's, it turns out, was only one of several conspiracies in the region that threatened the American republic, and not even the first. Years earlier, another Revolutionary War veteran, James Wilkinson, had attempted a similar plot. Wilkinson had settled in Kentucky and was, like his neighbors, frustrated with the Spanish tariffs on the Mississippi. He took a different approach to solving the problem. Instead of invading, he tried to ally with the foreign power. In 1787, he renounced his American citizenship and swore allegiance to Spain, in exchange for the rights to steer the American territory back into Spain's dominion. Although his plan failed, the idea lingered in Wilkinson's mind. While there is no evidence he joined Clark's scheme, there is evidence that after its failure he approached Spanish officials to rekindle his earlier efforts. In fact, he may have been another source of information to Spanish officials during the affair. After it, he told Louisiana's governor that he had secretly worked to undermine the plot so as to be of service to Spain. In 1794, the Spanish governor sent Wilkinson $12,000 in recognition of his efforts to serve Spanish interests.[17]

In 1804, an even more formidable conspiracy emerged in the region. Aaron Burr, then the sitting vice president, secretly plotted to create an independent colony in an area of what is now modern-day Texas. When Burr's conspiracy was revealed in 1807, President Thomas Jefferson took swift action. He tried Burr for treason, and even called Wilkinson, who had at first aided Burr's shenanigans before outing him to Jefferson, to testify against Burr. Much to Jefferson's consternation, Burr was acquitted, but his reputation was tarnished beyond repair.[18]

In short, the machinations of Clark and his supporters were simply one of several serious attempts by disillusioned Americans to establish an independent country in the West. The frequency with which such schemes emerged and the seriousness with which the federal government took them reveal two key aspects of the early republic: the federal government's grasp on its frontiers was fragile, and the future boundaries of the nation we now know were continually contested and uncertain. Western Americans' rebellious behavior was also, somewhat ironically, a product of the revolutionary age, one that began with the American Revolution and continued with the French Revolution. In other words, the very ideas that gave rise to an independent United States also threatened its demise on its western frontiers, as citizens living far from the eastern seats of power attempted to establish their own independent states that they believed could better serve their interests. For the federal government, such independent mobilizations forced officials to act and, by warding off these attempts, establish federal power in regions of uncertainty. For Washington, the passage of a series of laws accomplished this end. Later, under Jefferson, the trial of Burr, though an acquittal, nonetheless sent a clear message to others about the boundaries of citizenship and Jefferson's willingness to assert federal power to rein in citizens.

In that way, the Michaux-Clark expedition was an important, perhaps even essential, part of a process to establish the federal government's authority on the frontiers of what was becoming an expanding nation that adhered to Jeffersonian notions of state power. The tension between federal power and the pursuit of individual and state sovereignty that Clark's plot exposed would define American politics in the years that followed. Indeed, this cultural pattern may have become more ingrained as a result of the events of 1793 and 1794. As the partisan environment grew more heated, Kentucky became a hotbed of Jeffersonianism and a battleground in which fundamental principles that first emerged during the Clark affair were contested. The debate about the proper role of the federal government that underlay Governor Shelby's inaction and Clark's justification remained unresolved—and still does to this day.[19]

In the years immediately following Clark's failure, the Washington and then Adams administrations advocated for a more energetic and encompassing federal government and dismissed the complaints of those who advocated for more local control, of whom the Kentuckians were among the most vociferous. The Democratic Societies in Kentucky continued to prove useful to Jefferson as he sought renewed ammunition to attack the Adams administration. They helped form the backbone of a coherent and loyal opposition to Federalist policy, one that culminated in 1798, when Kentuckians united in a convention similar to the one held in June 1794. The 1798 meeting formed to oppose the Adams administration's Alien and Sedition Acts. These laws were meant to silence a vocal opposition because the Federalists in power believed, once again, that a dangerous combination of foreign interference and partisan resistance was threatening to undermine the government.[20]

To Jeffersonians, the Alien and Sedition Acts were undemocratic and unconstitutional. Once again, Jefferson schemed behind the scenes. Working through his closest ally, James Madison, Jefferson used his and Madison's political allies to fire volleys at the Adams administration. Leaders in Kentucky, sitting safely distant from the seat of the federal government and thus unlikely to be harassed by federal officials, passed a series of resolves in 1798 that challenged the legality of the law and asserted states'-rights principles. Their pronouncements echoed the same rationales enunciated to justify the proposed actions of Clark and his men. While Madison had authored a similar set of resolutions in Virginia, Kentucky's were far more radical, asserting a much stronger right of individual states to ignore laws. The draft of this firebrand statement came from the pen of Thomas Jefferson, then the sitting vice president of the United States.[21]

The Kentucky Resolutions stood as a statement of states'-rights ideology that had a lasting influence on America's political culture. The arguments laid the foundation for John Calhoun's argument for the rights of states to nullify laws ahead of the Civil War, and the sentiments articulated within them continued to shape politics throughout the twentieth century. While the Kentucky Resolutions may have provided a concrete distillation of the firmly held belief that states possessed great authority, almost sovereignty, within the federal system, the patterns of partisan behavior that led to the Kentucky Resolutions, and the political beliefs expressed in them, were all present during Clark's earlier mobilization and the convention that followed its dissolution. The events of 1793 and 1794, then, helped establish these types of oppositional politics. By establishing acceptable means for citizens to dissent from the policies of the federal government, these forms of organizing also, and perhaps counterintuitively, counteracted the disaffection felt by those on the frontiers and muted their desire to break free from a government that seemed distant and unaware of Kentuckians' concerns. Protesting policies, and knowing that they were being heard, made those in these distant regions feel more connected to the government, even as they sometimes felt frustrated by it.

There is, finally, the memory of the proposed assault on Spanish Louisiana. It is yet another element of this story that remains as obscured as both Michaux and Jefferson's involvement in the Genet affair. The potential invasion did, however, leave a mark. In the years immediately following its demise, historians recounted the episode regularly in their works, and it was widely known and discussed. Historians often pick stories to tell that resonate with the concerns of their present, and this failed conspiracy certainly had relevance to the nineteenth century. The story of an American trying to seize Spanish land and turn it into a republic seemed like a precursor to the nineteenth-century filibustering missions Americans took into countries in South America. *Filibustering* in the nineteenth century referred to Americans who organized independent assaults on foreign territories, often in South America, with the hope of establishing an independent republic modeled on the American system. In organization and intent, then, they resembled Clark's plan. The antebellum period was rife with such episodes. It was also a time of deep political division, in which questions about the role of government and its ability to maintain the Union were paramount. In short, the issues raised by Clark's gambit were understandable and relatable to those living in the early nineteenth century and who looked to the past to understand their present.

Yet, as the union and government strengthened in the wake of the Civil War, the story faded from historical accounts. With the rise of the United States in the twentieth century as an international superpower, Americans basked in the prosperous glow of global dominance. As Americans lost touch with how fragile the government and nation were in the late eighteenth century, so too, perhaps, did historians. As the country and its government seemed more secure, perhaps Clark's scheme appeared outlandish, or at least disconnected from the modern reality. It was an event easy to dismiss or ignore outright. The survival of the nation seemed like a fait accompli, and Clark's planned attack an absurdity that had no chance of succeeding.

It is worth remembering, though, that no one at the time considered it such. There is no doubt that Clark, a veteran of the Revolutionary War, and his supporters, many of whom had fought alongside him, were prepared to launch an assault on New Orleans that, if successful, would establish a new entity separate from the United States. Their frustration with a federal government that they found unresponsive to their needs and their deep-seated sense of disenfranchisement motivated them to take radical action. The Washington administration was well aware of their tenuous hold on power and saw the Clark expedition, and other similar movements in the 1790s, as tests of the government's authority. Had things gone differently in the Clark episode, had different decisions been made by leaders in government or on the frontiers, the course of American history could have changed dramatically. For the frontiersmen on the banks of the Mississippi River preparing to fight, and for those in the halls of power in the nation's capital trying to preserve the union, the potential insurrection was very real and posed a dangerous threat to the nation's foundations. Perhaps it is an episode with lessons that echo once again.

❖ EPILOGUE ❖

Remnants and Relevance

My research journey into the past ended with a literal journey in the present. When the pandemic began in March 2020, I had no idea what to expect. But near the end of the following March, after a year of being confined to my own house, trapped inside with three children under the age of twelve, the kids' spring break loomed large for my wife and me. We dreaded the prospect of a week without any school and without anything to do with the kids. We knew we wouldn't be able to accomplish much work. We decided it was time to get away, in as socially distanced a fashion as possible. Our escape had a second purpose. After a year of living vicariously through Michaux's own travels, it was time for me to travel to him. My wife and I set our sights on Charleston.

My own expedition led me to a most unusual place: a drainage tunnel in Charleston, South Carolina. It was so narrow that I had to crouch and wade through the ankle-deep water to get through. I was there because my companion had spent years documenting Michaux's time in Charleston. My friend was sure that he had located Michaux's plantation on the other side of the tunnel. As we emerged into the bright spring afternoon, we were greeted by huge magnolias, larger than any I had seen in Philadelphia. We walked around, searching for some undiscovered evidence of Michaux, but found nothing except cement ruins from past military uses. On our way back, my partner proved braver than I. He wanted to walk back in the creek looking for the remains of a dam he had found on an earlier excursion. I chose to take the higher ground. As Michaux noted in his journals, there are alligators in Charleston, after all. Eventually he found it: a series of broken logs, clearly cut and shaped by human hands, that protruded from the banks of the creek. There was no doubt that a dam once rested here and, given the look of the logs, no reason to doubt that it had once served Michaux's purposes. My new friend wondered if he should send samples of the wood to a lab for carbon dating to prove that it was a dam from Michaux's time.

As we made our way out and back to the car, my colleague stopped once again. He looked down and found a sapling of an oak tree—a burr oak. Its distinctive leaves reminded him of an example he had seen in the Jardin des Plantes in Paris, the site to which Michaux sent many of his specimens. He took a sample with him. That night he emailed me. The burr oak was not native to South Carolina. We both had to wonder if it was a descendant of a tree Michaux had brought to his garden. Even if I found no certain remnants of Michaux, that find capped off an amazing experience. Even better, I soon discovered that my adventure did not end there. A few weeks later, a mysterious package from South Carolina arrived at my APS office. I opened it to find shards of what looked like eighteenth-century pottery. I suspected my friend had gone back and dug.

After visiting Michaux's garden, I reflected on my year with Michaux. I had an interesting relationship with him. While trapped inside because of the pandemic, I had come to rely on Michaux and his travails. Every day, I joined him on some adventure somewhere. Still, as I look back, Michaux was different from other historical figures I have studied. Many of the people I have written about were colorful characters whose correspondence and personality comes through in their writing and others' accounts of them. Michaux, on the other hand, was stiff. I never found a hint of humor in anything he wrote or said. There was a seriousness and formality to everything he did, something even his first biographer, someone who knew Michaux, noted. That certainly came through in Michaux's correspondence and journals. You could also see it in what others wrote about him. His friendships were based upon shared research interests. His social interactions were always work-related, and there was little hint of socializing in his private life. He was dogged, a workaholic always focused on his research—maybe I could relate to that.

Over the course of the year, I became obsessed with his story because I was in awe of all that he did, and I soon met a small band of other devotees who felt the same way, including and especially Charlie Williams, the keeper of the International Michaux Society and coeditor of *André Michaux in North America,* a translation of Michaux's journals and many of his letters that proved a boon for my research. They, like me, realized that Michaux's life and contributions were of great significance, both in his own time and in the years that followed his passing. Many of his individual expeditions were among the most ambitious undertaken in his era. If you combined all of his individual journeys and consider how lightly he traveled, I believe he had no peer. Yet, I was struck by how obscure he and his achievements are today. Indeed, as I learned more about him and his era, I was surprised by how relatively unknown he was even in his own time. Michaux has never received the recognition he deserved, then or now. Still, his legacy, like his garden on a US Air Force property, remains with us, hidden to all except for those fortunate few who look. Like that burr oak we found growing in the ground, there are remnants of Michaux still blooming throughout the country.

I had to wonder why his name remained and remains so unrecognized. Was it because he was a Frenchman in a foreign country? Had he been an American, would he have been more celebrated? Perhaps, but I don't think that is quite right: we know of James Cook and Charles Darwin, just as we know of Lewis and Clark. There was, I think, another reason, one that his friends predicted. Even while Michaux was alive, his friends and admirers feared that his fate was to be relegated to obscurity. They knew that his never-ending wanderlust was his greatest asset and his greatest enemy. They tried to slow him down, to force him to write, in order to preserve his name for posterity. They chided him to publish, to share his work with the rest of the world.

"Stop him," Mangourit begged of the French government, "and place at his side an editor already initiated in botany and an illustrator." Mangourit went on, demanding that he share his experiences with the world: "Here is the account I demand of Michaux: the editing of his notes, the telling of his memories; this is a treasure of which he is the depository."[1]

The French government heeded Mangourit's advice. In 1796, soon after Michaux returned from the United States, the interior minister echoed Mangourit's words and told Michaux to stop traveling and start writing.

It wasn't just his pure research that people demanded. They also wanted his memoirs. "If you continue your research, you will leave to France only the material of your discoveries," the minister of interior affairs told Michaux, "and . . . France will be deprived of a much more valuable gift, your thoughts." It was the type of work everyone knew was needed for Michaux to enshrine his reputation.[2]

Michaux followed this order and spent the first few years in Paris trying to publish. It was a struggle. His meager resources were certainly a factor, but I also get the impression that Michaux's mind was built for the field and not the writing desk. He was a doer, always on the move, trying to work with plants, and his mind likely found the work of compiling, editing, and engraving mundane. After Michaux's death, his friends realized that his failure to publish threatened his legacy. "Michaux left few works," his friend and first biographer Deleuze lamented, "for, being almost incessantly employed in traveling, he had little time to arrange his observations, and he thought it more useful to introduce new vegetable productions into Europe, than to describe them."[3]

When Michaux left for the South Seas, his first book, a study of oaks in the United States, was nearing completion, but it showed only a small sliver of his research. Another book, documenting the flora of North America, a potentially major contribution, was underway as well. His son and a colleague posthumously finished the book in Michaux's name. These two books are revered by botanists and horticulturalists today. But, surely, one of the chief reasons Michaux's reputation remains confined to a small group of specialists is because his friends' fears proved all too prescient. He never gave us that "more valuable gift," his thoughts and especially an account of his exploits.[4]

For historians, though, Michaux did leave us a valuable gift. Though he never published as widely or extensively as his peers wished, Michaux did leave behind many records—true treasures—that help us resurrect his life and legacy, many of which reside in manuscripts held by archives in the United States and France. As Mangourit noted, Michaux was the sole "depository" of his story during his life. In death, thanks to these paper depositories, pieces of Michaux live on. I hope that, to some extent, this book may help do what Mangourit hoped Michaux would do himself; by sharing his story, this book may elevate awareness of Michaux so he might receive more of the credit that his peers knew he deserved. That, in fact, is often the chief task of a historian: to uncover lost or overlooked stories in order to more fully shape our collective understanding of the past and, when possible, show their connections to our present.

I further hope that this book might also show how historical research can be its own type of expedition into the past—one that can only happen with the existence of archives that conserve the documents that tell these stories. In this case, a single document held by the APS for more than two hundred years spurred a research adventure that led me to other sources, to journals, letters, newspaper articles, and account books, all of which transported me—and I hope my readers—to another place and time to find the answers I sought. It was a journey that took unexpected turns but that, ultimately, revealed important and sometimes surprising stories about the nation's earliest years and a remarkable figure who shaped those times. This expedition, though, was only made possible because institutions had cared for these materials. These institutions and their documents preserved the thing that Michaux never gave us himself: his thoughts.

❖ AUTHOR'S NOTE ❖

Writing this book was a wonderful and unexpected journey for me that eventually involved many others who helped me find the right path. I incurred many debts as I turned what was intended as a small side project that I kept to myself into a book. When I started researching Michaux, I thought that perhaps I could deliver a lecture for the APS on the Subscription List. Soon, the project overtook me. I kept my work mostly to myself until early 2021, when I realized I had written a book manuscript.

It took me a long time to turn that first draft into the book it became, and I would like to thank those who helped me improve it. I had a wonderful group of friends and advisors read that first manuscript and provide me with much-needed encouragement—and corrections and guidance. I want to thank Maude de Schauensee, Bob Legnini, Martine Rothblatt, Mary Beth Norton, Barbara Oberg, Bruce Kuklick, Mike Selverian, Albert Oehrle, Charles Jackson Bird, Gerry O'Shea, Robert Peck, Keith Thomson, James Hill, and John and Chris Van Horne. All credit for the original title goes to Rogers Smith and to Bob Hauser for the subtitle. I thank Bob Hauser in particular for the close readings he gave to several drafts and his always enthusiastic encouragement. George Lucas provided feedback and was responsible for finding the right home for the book. Cameron Strang provided a model outside review of the manuscript; I tried to address all of his helpful suggestions and corrections. Bertrand Van Ruymbeke provided wonderful encouragement and important reminders about the French context, both in South Carolina and across the ocean. Nadine Zimmerli has been a spectacular editor who has dedicated an enormous amount of her time to shaping the book. She has in fact been a model editor: accessible, supportive, and opinionated. Kathryn Dettmer provided helpful research assistance and translations for many documents, often improving mine or correcting my overreliance on Google Translate. Many of my colleagues at the APS gave great assistance, especially Brenna Holland. Special thanks go to Linda Jacobs, whose inquiry about the Subscription List led me on this quest.

While this book project started when I was confined to my house during the pandemic, Thomas Jefferson's home at Monticello provided a wonderful and important escape for me to expand my thinking and make significant headway on the project. The director of the International Center for Jefferson Studies then, Andrew O'Shaughnessy, was a gracious host who allowed my family to stay at Tufton Farm and imbibe the spirit of Jefferson. It was there where I presented for the first time some of my earliest findings, and the library's resources proved essential for my research on Jefferson and his biographers. I am indebted to him. J. Jefferson Looney, the editor in chief of the Jefferson Papers at the Thomas Jefferson Foundation, was a source of support and information. His enthusiasm helped me persist after the pandemic wound down and I found that I had less time to focus on Michaux. Jeff was the original editor of the Michaux Subscription List, and his interest in it remained strong and his knowledge was even greater. I learned an immense amount from him while at Monticello and even more after, as he provided crucial feedback on my manuscript, correcting errors and strengthening the argument. Although he may not be entirely satisfied with how I dealt with currency comparisons in the final text, I will admit that I think he was probably right that such comparisons are too hard to make. External pressures—primarily people asking me, "Well, how much does that really mean?"—required me to stick with the comparison used in this book. I encourage curious readers to check out the footnotes for links to calculators and to explore the issue themselves.

I finished this book while serving as executive director of the George Washington Presidential Library at Mount Vernon. There, immersed in Washington's life and surrounded by scholars, I was able to further develop important elements of the book and expand my thinking on Washington's role, especially in events that involved Washington's presidential leadership. Several colleagues at Mount Vernon also helped my thinking, perhaps without even knowing it. The scholarship of Douglas Bradburn, CEO of Mount Vernon, is some of the most significant work on citizenship in the early republic to date. Aside from sharing his deep historical knowledge, Doug also provided a model for leadership himself. I hope he doesn't disagree too much with what I have written!

Megan Romney provided immeasurable support day in and day out. Working on various projects with Stephen McLeod, Julie Almacy, Allison Wickens, and other members of the Mount Vernon team strengthened my knowledge of the early republic and reminded me of the significance of history today. I'm grateful to have had them as colleagues.

This book would not have been possible without the work of generations of previous scholars. I hope to have done justice to their work in the notes, but I am sure there are several I missed. I would especially like to thank Charlie Williams, Eliane Norman, and Walter Taylor. Without their masterful book *André Michaux in North America: Journals and Letters, 1785–1797,* my book would not have been possible. Had it not been published when it was, I would not have been able to sustain this project during the pandemic. I hope that its publication will spur even more research on Michaux. I am also deeply indebted to the editors of *The Papers of Thomas Jefferson,* both past and present, and the other Founders papers' projects. Without access to their research online during the pandemic, I would not have been able to complete this book. Interested readers can consult transcriptions of both the Subscription List and Jefferson's Instructions to Michaux at https://founders.archives.gov. The Michaux Subscription List is available at https://founders.archives.gov/documents/Jefferson/01-25-02-0088, and the Instructions are at https://founders.archives.gov/documents/Jefferson/01-25-02-0569.

Special thanks, as always, go to Laura Spero, my greatest editor and collaborator, and to Anna, Clara, and Keenan, who inspired this work in so many ways—and showed genuine interest in the story.

In my earlier book, *Frontier Rebels,* I integrated dialogue based off the sources. While my earlier drafts of this book used a similar technique, after receiving feedback, I chose to eliminate that from the text. However, for this book, in most cases, I removed unnecessary capitalization from sources so as to make quotes read easier. Even though I did not create dialogue in this book, I did try to use quotations in a way that mimics dialogue, and, even though I made no material changes to the quotes, I did use clauses in the middle of quotations, such as "Michaux wrote to his superior," in a way similar to ellipses. My goal in so doing was to make the original text as readable as possible.

Finally, I have a plea for my readers who have made it this far. André Michaux led a remarkable and inspiring life, and I believe this book is just the tip of the iceberg for research. More than anything, I hope future researchers will explore his life, his science, and the conspiracy of 1793. At a minimum, the sources he left behind should be more often utilized by scholars of the era. I suspect historians of science, of culture, and of politics could find even more in those sources—and other sources that I missed. I was able to write most of this book during the pandemic and had to rely primarily on materials available online or at the APS. Once the world opened back up, my time shifted back to work, and I had to accept that my project had to come to an end. I know, though, that there is a lot more to find and learn.

❖ NOTES ❖

PROLOGUE

1. For the story of the passing of Francis Dercum, see Edward Carter, *"One Grand Pursuit": A Brief History of the American Philosophical Society's First 250 Years, 1743–1993* (Philadelphia: American Philosophical Society Press [hereafter cited as APS], 1993), 62; and for Judson Daland, see ibid., 23.
2. A full transcription of Michaux's Subscription List can be found online on Founders Online at https://founders.archives.gov/documents/Jefferson/01-25-02-0088.
3. "Michaux Subscription List," American Philosophical Society [hereafter cited as APS], 2006, https://www.amphilsoc.org/exhibits/treasures/michaux.htm.
4. I was able to independently verify this account in the American Philosophical Society's *Yearbook for 1979* (Philadelphia: APS, 1980), 158; and in a transcript of an oral history of Whitfield Bell, APS Library, 18–19.
5. Harlow Unger, *"Mr. President": George Washington and the Making of the Nation's Highest Office* (Boston: Da Capo, 2013), 174.

1. THE EDUCATION OF ANDRÉ MICHAUX

1. Details on Michaux's life here and throughout are pulled from several sources. The most useful for me have been J. P. F. Deleuze, *The Annotated Memoirs of the Life and Botanical Travels of André Michaux,* ed. with a postscript by Charlie Williams (Athens, GA: Fevertree, 2011); André Michaux, *André Michaux in North America: Journals and Letters, 1785–1797,* ed. Charlie Williams, Eliane M. Norman, and Walter Kingsley Taylor (Tuscaloosa: University of Alabama Press, 2020), esp. 1–24; and Henry Savage and Elizabeth Savage, *André and François André Michaux* (Charlottesville: University Press of Virginia, 1986). I try to refer to specific

facts in the notes below, though there is a significant overlap between these three books regarding Michaux's early life. Satory today houses a military encampment surrounded by lush forests. I have not been able to determine specifically where the Michaux farm sat within this area, but you can view the proximity by visiting the following coordinates in Google Earth: 48.779747882314126, 2.1059771326549286. I invite you to zoom out to see the forest and take a 3D fly through the area to get a sense of the terrain (Satory sat on a hill) and its close proximity to Versailles, as I did. See also Regis Pluchet, "Michaux Mysteries Clarified," *Castanea* (December 2004): 228–32, for more extensive information on the family and its genealogy.

2. Deleuze, *Annotated Memoirs,* 2.
3. Ibid.
4. Michaux's loss and depression is well documented by all of his biographers. See Deleuze, *Annotated Memoirs,* 2; Savage and Savage, *André and François André Michaux,* 6–9; and Michaux, *Michaux in North America,* 2. A Michaux descendant has uncovered important new elements of the family and its history. See Pluchet, "Michaux Mysteries Clarified," 228–32, esp. 229–30, for this early period.
5. Deleuze, *Annotated Memoirs,* 2. For more information on Le Monnier, see Michaux, *Michaux in North America,* 419–20n10; and Charles Coulston Gillispie, ed., *Complete Dictionary of Scientific Biography* (New York: Charles Scribner's Sons, 1973), 8:177–78. I have chosen to use "Le Monnier" instead of Lemonnier because it appears more often that way in the sources I have.
6. See esp. Deleuze, *Annotated Memoirs,* 2–3; and Savage and Savage, *André and François André Michaux,* 7–9.
7. On the Ethiopian grass experiments, see Deleuze, *Annotated Memoirs,* 2; and on Angiviller and the court, see Savage and Savage, *André and François André Michaux,* 7–8.
8. Deleuze, *Annotated Memoirs,* 3. These snippets come from *Encyclopedia Britannica;* see https://www.britannica.com/biography/Bernard-de-Jussieu; https://www.britannica.com/biography/Joseph-de-Jussieu; https://www.britannica.com/biography/Antoine-Laurent-de-Jussieu; and https://www.britannica.com/biography/Antoine-de-Jussieu.
9. Interestingly, the Prussian Academy claims that Le Monnier was part of an expedition to Lapland in 1735 that was led by Pierre Louis Moreau de Maupertuis, the first president of the Prussian Academy of Sciences. The expedition was attempting to gauge a meridian line. Most likely

Le Monnier's brother Charles, who was elected to the Prussian Academy the year before Louis-Guillaume, joined that expedition. Louis-Guillaume did undertake a trip to extend the meridian line farther south in 1739. You can read Le Monnier's biographical entry at the Prussian Academy here: https://www.bbaw.de/die-akademie/akademie-historische-aspekte/mitglieder-historisch/historisches-mitglied-louis-guillaume-le-monnier-1606.

10. Indeed, an antagonistic undercurrent between natural historians and natural philosophers developed as these differences were drawn, with many natural philosophers believing their work superior to that of natural historians. The terms of the Magellanic Prize, an award created in 1786 by the American Philosophical Society (today the oldest scientific prize granted by an institution in the United States), laid bare this disciplinary rivalry: "a gold medal to be awarded from time to time under prescribed terms, to the author of the best discovery or most useful invention relating to navigation, astronomy, or natural philosophy (mere natural history only excepted.)." For the Magellanic Prize, see https://www.amphilsoc.org/prizes/magellanic-premium-american-philosophical-society. See also Richard Yeo, *Defining Science: William Whewell, Natural Knowledge and Public Debate in Early Victorian Britain* (Cambridge: Cambridge University Press, 1993), chap. 2.
11. As the eighteenth century gave way to the nineteenth, universities hired more professors to train a rising generation in the transformative ideas animating these fields. It is no mistake that the learned societies formed in the late seventeenth and early eighteenth centuries formed around the vague but all-encompassing idea of natural history and philosophy, while the first professional associations, such as the Royal Astronomical Society (1820) and Royal Chemical Society (1841), formed in the first half of the nineteenth century. Indeed, a new vocabulary developed to describe those who conducted science. They were no longer natural historians but *scientists,* a new term coined in the first quarter of the nineteenth century to describe those who pursued scientific inquiry professionally. *Scientist* soon displaced both *natural historian* and *natural philosopher* to better describe the world that had come to be. Michaux, the farmer-turned-botanist working in the late eighteenth century, straddled the era of the self-taught natural historian and the specialized professional scientist of the nineteenth century. He was part of a transitional generation, and his training and approach to research reflected elements of the world before him and anticipated the one to come. On the increasing professionalization,

disciplinary divides, and creation of the term *scientist,* see Yeo, *Defining Science,* esp. chap. 2 and pp. 3, 5, and 110–11.

12. Palisot de Beauvois, "Report on the garden of the republic found two miles from Charleston under the direction of Citizen Michaux," in Michaux, *Michaux in North America,* 316. For more on Beauvois, see Charles C. Gillispie, "Palisot de Beauvois on the Americans," *Proceedings of the American Philosophical Society* (March 1992): 33–50.
13. Deleuze, *Annotated Memoirs,* 2; Savage and Savage, *André and François André Michaux,* 8.
14. "Note G," in *Memoirs, Correspondence, and Private Papers of Thomas Jefferson,* ed. Thomas Jefferson Randolph (London, 1829), 1:144; "Summary of Public Service, [after 2 September 1800]," Founders Online, National Archives.

2. A CIRCUITOUS ROUTE TO AMERICA

1. For the United States' position toward James Cook, see "From Benjamin Franklin to All Captains and Commanders of American Armed Ships, [10 March 1779]," Founders Online, National Archives, https://founders.archives.gov/documents/Franklin/01-29-02-0057. [Original source: Benjamin Franklin, *The Papers of Benjamin Franklin,* vol. 29, *March 1 through June 30, 1779,* ed. Barbara B. Oberg (New Haven, CT: Yale University Press, 1992), 86–87.] The APS owns a copy of this passport.
2. For a sense of this jealousy, see J. P. F. Deleuze, *The Annotated Memoirs of the Life and Botanical Travels of André Michaux,* ed. with a postscript by Charlie Williams (Athens, GA: Fevertree, 2011), 3.
3. Banks's biography and centrality to British and European science is well documented. For two good works, see Richard Holmes, *Age of Wonder: How the Romantic Generation Discovered the Beauty and Terror of Science* (New York: Vintage, 2009); and Adrian Tinniswood, *The Royal Society and the Invention of Modern Science* (New York: Basic, 2019). Michaux's interactions with Banks have proven somewhat elusive. Michaux, like so many other European scientists, sent material to Banks and the Royal Society. Based on internal evidence from these letters, especially the one Michaux sent Banks from the Middle East in 1784, most biographers have concluded that the two met in London during Michaux's stay in London.
4. Deleuze, *Annotated Memoirs,* 3.
5. Ibid., 4; André Michaux, *André Michaux in North America: Journals and Letters, 1785–1797,* ed. Charlie Williams, Eliane M. Norman, and Walter Kingsley Taylor (Tuscaloosa: University of Alabama Press, 2020), 4–5.

6. Deleuze, *Annotated Memoirs,* 4.
7. Ibid., 24. Deleuze's depiction conforms to my own reading from the historic record. Michaux frequently writes about not wanting to waste a moment and seemed always concerned that he work as efficiently as possible. He never seemed to take a break, and everything he did was focused, in some measure, on his work. His drive also manifested itself in the very high expectations he held for those who worked for him, a subject covered in a later chapter.
8. Ibid., 4–6; Savage and Savage, *André and François André Michaux,* 14–15 (quotations on 15).
9. See Deleuze, *Annotated Memoirs,* 4–6; and esp. Savage and Savage, *André and François André Michaux,* 14–15.
10. Regis Pluchet, "Michaux Mysteries Clarified," *Castanea* (December 2004): 228–32.
11. Deleuze, *Annotated Memoirs,* 4–6; Savage and Savage, *André and François André Michaux,* 14–15. The list of equipment is gleaned from the items Michaux later had stolen from him in the Middle East.
12. E. T. Hamy, *Voyage d'André Michaux en Syrie et en Perse (1782–1785) d'après son journal et sa correspondance* (Geneva, Société Générale D'Imprimerie, 1911), 6.
13. Ibid., 15, and "internal wars."
14. Savage and Savage, *Andre and François André Michaux,* 17; Hamy, *Voyage d'André Michaux en Syrie et en Perse,* 6–8.
15. André Michaux to François André, March 21, 1784, Michaux Papers, APS. The best accounts of Michaux's Middle Eastern expedition are Savage and Savage, *André and François André Michaux,* chaps. 2 and 3; and Deleuze, *Annotated Memoirs,* 5–7. These quotations come from Savage and Savage, *André and François André Michaux,* 19–20.
16. Savage and Savage, *André and François André Michaux,* 19–20.
17. Ibid., 26–28
18. Ibid., 28–33.
19. On Desaint's widowhood, see Pluchet, "Michaux Mysteries Clarified."
20. The American Philosophical Society holds both letters in the Michaux Papers.
21. André Michaux to François André Michaux, May 15, 1783, and March 21, 1784, Michaux Papers, APS.
22. André Michaux to François André Michaux, May 15, 1783, Michaux Papers, APS.
23. André Michaux to François André Michaux, May 15, 1783, and March 21, 1784, Michaux Papers, APS.

24. Maurizio Valsania, *First among Men: George Washington and the Myth of American Masculinity* (Baltimore, MD: Johns Hopkins University Press, 2023).
25. André Michaux to François André Michaux, March 21, 1784, Michaux Papers, APS. Deleuze mentions the dictionary, perhaps the first French-Persian dictionary compiled, in *Annotated Memoirs,* 5.
26. For the weight, see Georges Perrot and Charles Chipiez, *The History of Art in Chaldea and Assyria,* trans. Walter Armstrong (New York, 1884), 197–201. For the translation, see W. M. Hinke, *A New Boundary Stone of Nebuchadrezzar I from Nippur* (Philadelphia: University of Pennsylvania Press, 1907), 1–2 and 34.
27. Translations available in William J. Robbins and Mary Christine Howson, "André Michaux's New Jersey Garden and Pierre Paul Saunier, Journeyman Gardner," *Proceedings of the American Philosophical Society* 102, no. 4 (1958): 351; Savage and Savage, *André and François André Michaux,* 34–35; Deleuze, *Annotated Memoirs,* 7.
28. During and especially after the American Revolution, there was an incredible increase in intellectual exchange between colonists, US scientists, and French scholars. For a brief summary of Michaux's place, see Savage and Savage, *André and François André Michaux,* 34–38; and Elizabeth Hyde, "André Michaux and French Botanical Diplomacy in the Cultural Construction of Natural History in the Colonial World," in *Elephants and Roses: French Natural History, 1790–1830,* ed. Sue Ann Prince (Philadelphia: APS, 2013), esp. 90–91. Gilbert Chinard documents the exchanges that occurred prior to Michaux, noting that missionaries in Canada and the Great Lakes occasionally sent material. The eastern seaboard, however, remained largely untouched, though some natural historians in British North America shipped material to French counterparts (Chinard, "André and Francois André Michaux and Their Predecessors: An Essay on Early Botanical Exchanges between America and France," *Proceedings of the American Philosophical Society* [August 1957]: 344–61, see esp. 350–51 for the opening of scientific exchange between the United States and France during the American Revolution). See also William Robbins, "French Botanists and the Flora of the Northeastern United States: J. G. Milbert and Elias Durand," *Proceedings of the American Philosophical Society* (August 1957): 362–65.
29. André Michaux, "Abridged Memoir," in Henry Savage Papers, South Caroliniana Library, University of South Carolina; translation and copy provided by Charlie Williams.

30. Robbins and Howson, "Michaux's New Jersey Garden"
31. "Instructions to M. André Michaux Botanist to the King for the exercise or commission that his majesty is pleased to confide in him to go to different regions which will be indicated to him to make a study of and do research on the diverse forest products, trees and even beasts, game birds, etc. that can be hoped to be acclimatized and naturalized in France," August 9, 1785, Angiviller, Michaux Papers, Microfilm 330, APS, Reel 3, 33–37. Research and translation assistance by Kathryn Dettmer.
32. André Michaux, "Abridged Memoir," in Henry Savage Papers, South Caroliniana Library, University of South Carolina; translation and copy provided by Charlie Williams. See esp. Michaux, *Michaux in North America;* and Savage and Savage, *André and François André Michaux,* 33–39. André Michaux and Francis Boott, "Memorial of the Botanical Labours of André Michaux," *Edinburgh Journal of Medical Science* 1 (1826): 127.

3. MAKING AMERICA HOME

1. On Michaux's plans, see Henry Savage and Elizabeth Savage, *André and François André Michaux* (Charlottesville: University Press of Virginia, 1986), 38–41.
2. Ibid., 40–41.
3. André Michaux to Louis-Guillaume Le Monnier, New York, December 9, 1785, and André Michaux to Comte d'Angiviller, New York, December [9?], 1785, in André Michaux, *André Michaux in North America: Journals and Letters, 1785–1797,* ed. Charlie Williams, Eliane M. Norman, and Walter Kingsley Taylor (Tuscaloosa: University of Alabama Press, 2020), 27–31, 31–32; André Michaux and Francis Boott, "Memorial of the Botanical Labours of André Michaux," *Edinburgh Journal of Medical* Science 1 (1826): 127–28; André Michaux to Comte d'Angiviller, December [?], 1785, in Michaux, *Michaux in North America,* 31; André Michaux to Louis-Guillaume Le Monnier, New York, December 9, 1785, ibid., 27.
4. For a discussion of Otto's botanical interests, see Elizabeth Hyde, "André Michaux and French Botanical Diplomacy in the Cultural Construction of Natural History in the Colonial World," in *Elephants and Roses: French Natural History, 1790–1830,* ed. Sue Ann Prince (Philadelphia: American Philosophical Society, 2013), 92. On Otto's meeting with Michaux and initial reaction, see Louis-Guillaume Otto to Comte d'Angiviller, New York, November 25, 1787, in Michaux, *Michaux in North America,* 26–27; and William J. Robbins and Mary Christine Howson, "André Michaux's New

Jersey Garden and Pierre Paul Saunier, Journeyman Gardner," *Proceedings of the American Philosophical Society* 102, no. 4 (1958): 353.

5. Louis-Guillaume Otto to Comte d'Angiviller, New York, November 25, 1787, in Michaux, *Michaux in North America,* 26–27; William J. Robbins and Mary Christine Howson, "André Michaux's New Jersey Garden and Pierre Paul Saunier, Journeyman Gardner," *Proceedings of the American Philosophical Society* 102, no. 4 (1958): 353.
6. André Michaux to Louis-Guillaume Le Monnier, New York, December 9, 1785, in Michaux, *Michaux in North America,* 27–31, for his December shipment and commentary on cranberries and sweet potatoes; André Michaux to Comte d'Angiviller, December [9?], 1785, ibid., 31–32. On the January shipment, see André Michaux to Comte d'Angiviller, January 18, 1785, ibid., 32–33.
7. André Michaux to Louis-Guillaume Le Monnier, December 9, 1785, in Michaux, *Michaux in North America,* 27.
8. For its location and an incredible description of the garden and its history, see esp. Robbins and Howson, "Michaux's New Jersey Garden."
9. André Michaux to Comte d'Angiviller, January 18, 1785, in Michaux, *Michaux in North America,* 32–33.
10. For his acquisition, see André Michaux to Comte d'Angiviller, January 18, 1785, in Michaux, *Michaux in North America,* 32–33; and André Michaux to Comte d'Angiviller, New York, May 13, 1786, ibid., 33–34n. On the New Jersey laws, see Robbins and Howson, "Michaux's New Jersey Garden."
11. "An Act to Enable André Michaux to purchase lands in the State of New Jersey under certain restrictions," Francois André Michaux Collection, Box 1, APS.
12. The passage of the law was well documented in the local newspapers. See, for example, "Legislative Acts/Legal Proceedings," *Elizabethtown Political Intelligencer and New-Jersey Advertiser,* May 3, 1786, [1]. I have found references to the law in at least six newspapers from 1786. For Otto's lobbying, see Robbins and Howson, "Michaux's New Jersey Garden"; and Savage and Savage, *André and François André Michaux,* 45–46. "Elizabeth Town, April 19 Mr. Michaux, Botanist to His Most Christian Majesty Having Purchased a Lot of Ground," *Elizabethtown Political Intelligencer and New-Jersey Advertiser,* April 19, 1786, [3]; "New-York, June 16," *New York Daily Advertiser,* June 16, 1787, [2].
13. For his early days in the United States, see esp. Robbins and Howson, "Michaux's New Jersey Garden," 353; and Savage and Savage, *André and*

François André Michaux, 44. Louis-Guillame Otto to Comte d'Angiviller, November 25, 1785, in Michaux, *Michaux in North America,* 26.

14. Michaux's observations were recorded in a series of letters he wrote to his superiors in 1786; see esp. André Michaux to Cuvillier, New York, May 1786, in Michaux, *Michaux in North America,* 40–41.
15. Michaux's frustrations came to the fore very early on and continued throughout his stay in New York. Complaints appear in several letters written at the time; see esp. André Michaux to Comte d'Angiviller, New York, December [9?], 1785, in Michaux, *Michaux in North America,* 31; André Michaux to Cuvillier, New York, May 12, 1785, ibid., 40–41; and André Michaux to André Thouin, New York, August 1786, ibid., 48.
16. André Michaux to d'Angiviller, December [9], 1785, in Michaux, *Michaux in North America,* 31.
17. See esp. André Michaux to Le Monnier, January 26, 1786, in Robbins and Howson, "Michaux's New Jersey Garden," 359. For a discussion of an attempt at a New Jersey garden and the establishment of a small one in Connecticut, see Hyde, "André Michaux and French Botanical Diplomacy," 91–92; and Robbins and Howson, "André Michaux's New Jersey Garden," 355–56. See esp. André Michaux to André Thouin, New York, January 19, 1786, in Michaux, *Michaux in North America,* 35–36.
18. André Michaux to Le Monnier, January 26, 1786, in Robbins and Howson, "Michaux's New Jersey Garden," 359.
19. Michaux mentioned Williamsburg as a possible location almost as soon as he landed in New York. See André Michaux to Le Monnier, December 9, 1785, New York, in Michaux, *André Michaux in North America,* 31.
20. Comte de Vergennes to Benjamin Franklin, Philadelphia, August 9, 1785, in Michaux, *Michaux in North America,* 42; André Michaux to Comte d'Angiviller, New York, July 15, 1786, ibid., 44.
21. André Michaux to Cuvillier, New York, July 15, 1786, in Michaux, *Michaux in North America,* 44–45.
22. André Michaux to Comte d'Angiviller, Philadelphia, June 11, 1786, in Michaux, *Michaux in North America,* 41.
23. For Maryland and Virginia commentary, see André Michaux to Angiviller, July 15, 1786, in Michaux, *Michaux in North America,* 44–45. I am grateful to Kathryn Dettmer for providing a full translation of this document.
24. "To George Washington from Lafayette, 3 September 1785," n. 1, Founders Online, National Archives.
25. "[Diary entry: 19 June 1786]," Founders Online, National Archives; "To George Washington from Lafayette, 3 September 1785," ibid., https://

founders.archives.gov/documents/Washington/04-03-02-0206. [Original source: *The Papers of George Washington,* Confederation Series, vol. 3, *19 May 1785–31 March 1786,* ed. W. W. Abbot (Charlottesville: University Press of Virginia, 1994), 224–25.]

26. For Washington's attempt to get seeds for Lafayette, see the following exchange of letters: "To George Washington from Lafayette, 17 December 1784," Founders Online, National Archives, https://founders.archives.gov/documents/Washington/04-02-02-0155. [Original source: *The Papers of George Washington,* Confederation Series, vol. 2, *18 July 1784–18 May 1785,* ed. W. W. Abbot (Charlottesville: University Press of Virginia, 1992), 194.]; "From George Washington to Lafayette, 15 February 1785," Founders Online, National Archives, https://founders.archives.gov/documents/Washington/04-02-02-0249. [Original source: *The Papers of George Washington, Confederation Series,* vol. 2, *18 July 1784–18 May 1785,* ed. W. W. Abbot (Charlottesville: University Press of Virginia, 1992), 363–67.]; "From George Washington to Lafayette, 25 July 1785," Founders Online, National Archives, https://founders.archives.gov/documents/Washington/04-03-02-0143. [Original source: *The Papers of George Washington,* Confederation Series, vol. 3, *19 May 1785–31 March 1786,* ed. W. W. Abbot (Charlottesville: University Press of Virginia, 1994), 151–55.]

27. Hyde, "André Michaux and French Botanical Diplomacy," 89–100, esp. 90–91.

28. "To George Washington from André Michaux, 20 June 1786," Founders Online, National Archives, https://founders.archives.gov/documents/Washington/04-04-02-0118. [Original source: *The Papers of George Washington,* Confederation Series, vol. 4, *2 April 1786–31 January 1787,* ed. W. W. Abbot (Charlottesville: University Press of Virginia, 1995), 120.]; "[Diary entry: 29 June 1786]," ibid., https://founders.archives.gov/documents/Washington/01-04-02-0003-0006-0029. [Original source: *The Diaries of George Washington,* vol. 4, *1 September 1784–30 June 1786,* ed. Donald Jackson and Dorothy Twohig (Charlottesville: University Press of Virginia, 1978), 354–55.]; "[Diary entry: 1 July 1786]," ibid., https://founders.archives.gov/documents/Washington/01-05-02-0001-0001-0001. [Original source: *The Diaries of George Washington,* vol. 5, *1 July 1786–31 December 1789,* ed. Donald Jackson and Dorothy Twohig (Charlottesville: University Press of Virginia, 1979), 1.]; "From George Washington to Lauzun, 31 July 1786," ibid., https://founders.archives.gov/documents/Washington/04-04-02-0169. [Original source: *The Papers*

of George Washington, Confederation Series, vol. 4, *2 April 1786–31 January 1787,* ed. W. W. Abbot (Charlottesville: University Press of Virginia, 1995), 178–79.]

29. On Michaux's botanizing, see Michaux, *Michaux in North America,* 45. On the travel to South Carolina, see André Michaux to Comte d'Angiviller, Charleston, September 30, 1786, ibid., 49.
30. For Michaux's impressions of the South, see André Michaux to Comte d'Angiviller, Charleston, September 30, 1786, in Michaux, *André Michaux in North America,* 49; André Michaux to Comte d'Angiviller, November 12, 1786, Charleston, ibid., 49–52 (quote on 50); and André Michaux to Comte d'Angiviller, Charleston, December 2, 1786, ibid., 52–54.
31. André Michaux to Comte d'Angiviller, in Michaux, *Michaux in North America,* 51. For a discussion of Goose Creek men, see L. K. Spero, "'Stout, Bold, Cunning and the Greatest Travellers in America': The Colonial Shawnee Diaspora" (Ph.D. diss., University of Pennsylvania, 2010); Eugene Sirmans, *Colonial South Carolina: A Political History, 1663–1763* (Chapel Hill: University of North Carolina, 1966), esp. pt. 1; Michael Heitzler, *Goose Creek: A Definitive History, 1670–2003* (Charleston, SC: History Press, 2005), esp. chaps. 4 and 5; and esp. *South Carolina Encyclopedia,* s.v. "Goose Creek," https://www.scencyclopedia.org/sce/entries/goose-creek/. For Michaux's description of this garden, see André Michaux to Comte d'Angiviller, Charleston, November 12, 1785, in Michaux, in *Michaux in North America,* 49–52. For a map depicting its location, see Heitzler, *Goose Creek,* 167.
32. On Michaux's son, see André Michaux to Comte d'Angiviller, Charleston, November 12, 1786, in Michaux, *Michaux in North America,* 50–51; André Michaux to Comte d'Angiviller, Charleston, December 26, 1786, ibid., 54; and André Michaux to Comte d'Angiviller, Charleston, November 12, 1786, ibid., 51.
33. André Michaux to Comte d'Angiviller, Charleston, November 12, 1786, in Michaux, *Michaux in North America,* 51–52.
34. Robbins and Howson, "Michaux's New Jersey Garden," provides a detailed discussion of Saunier, his background, and work in New Jersey. André Michaux to Comte d'Angiviller, Charleston, November 12, 1786, in Michaux, *Michaux in North America,* 50.
35. Michaux's most pointed argument for his preference for the South's flora is in André Michaux to Comte d'Angiviller, Charleston, November 12, 1786, in Michaux, *Michaux in North America,* 49–52; and André Michaux to Comte d'Angiviller, Charleston, December 2, 1786, ibid., 52–54.

36. André Michaux to Comte d'Angiviller, Charleston, December 2, 1786, in Michaux, *Michaux in North America,* 53.
37. Michaux, *Michaux in North America,* 11, for Michaux's slave-owning and Census report.
38. Central Office of Accounting, "Report requested by the Minister of the Interior, July 3, 1800," Documents on his botanizing in the United States, 1785–1807, Film 330, APS Library, Reel 3, 149. I am indebted to Kathryn Dettmer for the translation of this document.
39. On Michaux's plantation and its operation, see esp. André Michaux to Comte d'Angiviller, Charleston, April 2, 1787, in Michaux, *Michaux in North America,* 56–57.
40. Quote from Savage and Savage, *André and François André Michaux,* 34–35. See also King's Appointment, Michaux Papers, APS. I am indebted to Kathryn Dettmer for the translation of the latter.

4. A BOTANIST UNLEASHED

1. André Michaux to Comte d'Angiviller, Charleston, December 2, 1786, in *André Michaux in North America: Journals and Letters, 1785–1797,* ed. Charlie Williams, Eliane M. Norman, and Walter Kingsley Taylor (Tuscaloosa: University of Alabama Press, 2020), 53; André Michaux to Count d'Angiviller, Charleston, November 12, 1786, ibid., 51.
2. "Thursday, April 19," in Michaux, *Michaux in North America,* 59.
3. Michaux, *Michaux in North America,* 58.
4. "May 29," in Michaux, *Michaux in North America,* 67.
5. "May 6," in Michaux, *Michaux in North America,* 64.
6. "May 26," in *Michaux in North America,* 66; Henry Savage and Elizabeth Savage, *André and François André Michaux* (Charlottesville: University Press of Virginia, 1986), 70.
7. For Fraser, see *American National Biography,* s.v. "John Fraser," https://doi.org/10.1093/anb/9780198606697.article.1302571; G. S. Boulger and Marcus B. Simpson, "Fraser, John (bap. 1750, d. 1811), botanist," *Oxford Dictionary of National Biography;* and esp. "A Biographical Sketch of John Fraser, the Botanical Collector," in W. J. Hooker, *A Companion to the Botanical Magazine* (London, 1836), 300–303. The most recent biographical appraisal, one that added new information on Fraser's time in the United States, is Marcus B. Simpson Jr., Stephen Moran, and Allie W. Simpson, "Biographical Notes on John Fraser (1750–1811): Plant Nurseryman, Explorer, and Royal Botanical Collector to the Czar of Russia," *Archives of Natural History* 24, no. 1 (1997): 1–18.

8. Savage and Savage, *André and François André Michaux,* 72–75; "June 9," in Michaux, *Michaux in North America,* 70.
9. "June 10," in Michaux, *Michaux in North America,* 70.
10. "June 10" and "June 11," in Michaux, *Michaux in North America,* 70–71.
11. "June 19," in Michaux, *Michaux in North America,* 74.
12. "Report requested by the Minister the 1st prarial year 8," p. 144, Michaux Papers on microfilm, APS. For medicinal recipes, see Michaux, *Michaux in North America,* 508n99. "June 19," ibid., 74. For languages, see J. P. F. Deleuze, *The Annotated Memoirs of the Life and Botanical Travels of André Michaux* (Athens, GA: Fevertree, 2011), 24.
13. "June 19," in Michaux, *Michaux in North America,* 74; André Michaux to André Thouin, Charleston, November 6, 1787, ibid., 80–83. The quote on his reevaluation is from Savage and Savage, *André and François André Michaux,* 77–78.
14. Michaux, *Michaux in North America,* 23
15. "April 18" and "April 20," in Michaux, *Andre Michaux in North America,* 96; Deleuze, *Annotated Memoirs,* 12; "Lespedeza," in A. T. Johnson, H. A. Smith, A. Stockdale, *Plant Names Simplified: Their Pronunciation, Derivation and Meaning* (Sheffield, UK: 5M, 2019), 86.
16. For Fish, see Robert L. Gold, "That Infamous Floridian, Jesse Fish," *Florida Historical Quarterly* 52, no. 1 (1973): 1–17 (François André's comments on 6–7).
17. "Wednesday, March 12," in Michaux, *Michaux in North America,* 87–88. For an account of his trip, see ibid., chap. 3; and esp. Walter Kingsley Taylor and Eliane M. Norman, *André Michaux in Florida: An Eighteenth-Century Botanical Journey* (Gainesville: University Press of Florida, 2002).
18. "Tuesday, April 1, 1788," in Michaux, *Michaux in North America,* 93; "April 27," ibid., 97; Deleuze, *Annotated Memoirs,* 12.
19. "February 16," in Michaux, *Michaux in North America,* 120. For Dunmore, see James Corbett David, *Dunmore's New World: The Extraordinary Life of a Royal Governor in Revolutionary America—with Jacobites, Counterfeiters, Land Schemes, Shipwrecks, Scalping, Indian Politics, Runaway Slaves, and Two Illegal Royal Weddings* (Charlottesville: University of Virginia Press, 2015).
20. "February 26," in Michaux, *Michaux in North America,* 120.
21. For Michaux's intellectual rivalry with Catesby, see André Michaux to Comte d'Angiviller, April 28, 1789, in Michaux, *Michaux in North America,* 123.
22. André Michaux to Comte d'Angiviller, April 28, 1789, in Michaux, *Michaux in North America,* 123. For Michaux's accounting, see "February 26–May 10," ibid., 120–22; André Michaux to Comte d'Angiviller, April 28,

1789, ibid., 123; and André Michaux to Sir Joseph Banks, May 20, 1789, ibid., 123. Deleuze provides the number of trees in *Annotated Memoirs,* 12.

23. Most biographers discuss the *Shortia,* and the phrase "holy grail" is often used. The best account of Asa Gray's search is Charles F. Jenkins, "Asa Gray and His Quest for *Shortia galacifolia,*" *Arnoldia* 51, no. 4 (1991): 4–11. Deleuze, *Annotated Memoirs,* 30–32, 39–40; Charlie Williams, Eliane M. Norman, and Gerard G. Aymonin, "The Type Locality of *Shortia galacifolia* T. & G. Visited Once Again," *Castanea* (December 2004): 169–73.
24. Jenkins, "Asa Gray and His Quest," 6.
25. Ibid., 5–6.
26. Ibid.; Charlie Williams's postscript "Two Hundred Years of Remembering André Michaux" in Deleuze, *Annotated Memoirs,* 32. As it happens, this entire decades-long search may have been unnecessary. In 1866, Charles Sargent, one of the many botanists who had joined Gray in his quest, decided to sit down and read Michaux's private journals at the American Philosophical Society. Opening those leather-bound books and thumbing through the brittle rag-paper pages, he believed he had located the secret to the botanical holy grail. On December 11, 1788, Michaux provided finely detailed directions to a site at which he claimed to have discovered a mysterious new plant. His instructions were perhaps the most specific he ever wrote. It was as if he knew he had found something special and wanted to make it easy to return to the spot. Sargent suspected Michaux was describing the *Shortia.* Sargent raced out to the spot and, sure enough, found the plant in the area the journals instructed. Scientists have, rather ironically, determined that Sargent's find was pure luck. Several botanists inspecting the evidence have concluded that Michaux's original descriptions were for another native plant that resembled the *Shortia,* so Sargent's apparent breakthrough a hundred years after Michaux's was purely a coincidence. Still, though Sargent was mistaken, if someone had visited the APS to consult the private journals at some earlier point, they too may have made the same accidental discovery ("December 11," in Michaux, *Michaux in North America,* 113–14). For discussion of the specificity of his directions, see Michaux, *Michaux in North America,* 446–47n35. Note that many scientists now contend that Michaux had first encountered *Shortia* on an earlier expedition in 1787 but left his more extended commentary for his second finding in 1788. For Sargent's find, see Jenkins, "Asa Gray and His Quest, esp. 7–9"; and Charlie Williams's concluding essay in Deleuze, *Annotated Memoirs,* 32.

27. André Michaux to André Thouin, Charleston, November 6, 1787, in Michaux, *Michaux in North America,* 83.
28. André Thouin to André Michaux, Paris, November 21, 1789, in Michaux, *Michaux in North America,* 140.
29. Ibid., 140–41.

5. REVOLUTIONARY DISRUPTIONS

1. "January 8," in André Michaux, *André Michaux in North America: Journals and Letters, 1785–1797,* ed. Charlie Williams, Eliane M. Norman, and Walter Kingsley Taylor (Tuscaloosa: University of Alabama Press, 2020), 156.
2. Michaux's list of seeds can be found in Michaux, *Michaux in North America,* 146–52. See Michaux, *Michaux in North America,* 11, for Michaux's slave-owning and census report.
3. "December 5," in Michaux, *Michaux in North America,* 111.
4. "September 20–30," in Michaux, *Michaux in North America,* 135 and 143; Henry Savage and Elizabeth Savage, *André and François André Michaux* (Charlottesville: University Press of Virginia, 1986), 107.
5. William J. Robbins and Mary Christine Howson. "André Michaux's New Jersey Garden and Pierre Paul Saunier, Journeyman Gardener," *Proceedings of the American Philosophical Society* 102, no. 4 (1958): 351–70.
6. For the attempt to recall Michaux, see his letter to Angiviller from April 15, 1791, in Michaux, *Michaux in North America,* 160–61. Quotes from André Michaux, "Report for the Minister of the Interior, February 1797," ibid., 165–66; and André Michaux and Francis Boott, "Memorial of the Botanical Labours of André Michaux," *Edinburgh Journal of Medical* Science 1 (1826): 129.
7. André Thouin to André Michaux, Paris, March 10, 1792, in *Michaux in North America,* 166–67 and 165; Savage and Savage, *André and François André Michaux,* 113–14; Michaux and Boott, "Memorial of Botanical Labours of André Michaux," 129–30.
8. Savage and Savage, *André and François André Michaux,* 113–14; Michaux and Boott, "Memorial of Botanical Labours of André Michaux," 129–30; "Abridged memoir concerning my journeys in North America," 1793, trans. Henry Savage, Henry Savage Papers, South Caroliniana Library, University of South Carolina; transcription by Charlie Williams. I thank Charlie Williams for sharing his document with me.
9. Savage and Savage, *André and François André Michaux,* 113–14; Michaux and Boott, "Memorial of Botanical Labours of André Michaux," 129–30; André Michaux to Comte d'Angiviller, April 15, 1791, in Michaux, *Michaux in North America,* 160–61.

10. For accounts of Michaux's revolutionary sympathy, see Savage and Savage, *André and François André Michaux,* 109.
11. Michaux and Boott, "Memorial of the Botanical Labours of André Michaux," 129, 130.
12. For Michaux's travels to and around New York, see Michaux, *Michaux in North America,* chap. 7, esp. 169–74. For his investment in arms, see André Michaux to Comte d'Angiviller, April 15, 1791, ibid., 161. His support of an arms trade is intriguing. I have not been able to locate any additional information on it, though the records may exist waiting to be discovered. This comparison is taken from https://www.bankofengland.co.uk/monetary-policy/inflation/inflation-calculator.
13. This quote comes from Michaux's "Abridged memoir concerning my journeys in North America," 1793, trans. Henry Savage, Henry Savage Papers, South Caroliniana Library, University of South Carolina; transcription by Charlie Williams. I thank Charlie Williams for sharing his document with me.
14. "June 4," in Michaux, *Michaux in North America,* 173–74.
15. "June 7–July 31," in Michaux, *Michaux in North America,* 174–79. The July 24 entry has the information on Nooth.
16. "August 7," in Michaux, *Michaux in North America,* 181, for information on the interpreter and other Native guides. See also Savage and Savage, *André and François André Michaux,* 118. Note that Savage referred to the interpreter as "Metis," but, as noted in the translation of Williams, Norman, and Taylor, that was more likely an adjective for his mixed-race background than his name. For more on go-betweens as important early American actors, see James Merrell, *Into the American Woods: Negotiators on the Pennsylvania Frontier* (New York: Norton 2000).
17. "August 7," in Michaux, *Michaux in North America,* 181; Michaux and Boott, "Memorial of the Botanical Labours of André Michaux," 130. Though Michaux said he had only three guides, I trust his diary entry more than an account written years later. On their possible language, see "Abridged Memoir concerning my journey," Henry Savage Papers, South Caroliniana Library, University of South Carolina. He wrote, "I traveled among the Algonquin Indians from the mouth of the Saguenay River as far as the territories of Hudson's Bay."
18. Michaux, *Michaux in North America,* 180; *Dictionary of Canadian Biography,* s.v. "Charles Albanel," http://www.biographi.ca/en/bio/albanel_charles_1E.html.
19. "August 13," in Michaux, *Michaux in North America,* 183.

20. For the sealskin wrapping, see "August 29," in Michaux, *Michaux in North America,* 189. For the quote, see André Michaux to François André Michaux, Philadelphia, December 30, 1792, ibid., 201.
21. "August 22," in Michaux, *Michaux in North America,* 185.
22. "August 31," in Michaux, *Michaux in North America,* 189.
23. "September 2," in Michaux, *Michaux in North America,* 190.
24. This account of this leg of the journey is based on Michaux's journals in *Michaux in North America,* 190–92. Michaux recounted this decision in several places. See esp. "September 6," ibid., 190–91; and Michaux and Boott, "Memorial of the Botanical Labours of André Michaux," 130.
25. Michaux and Boott, "Memorial of the Botanical Labours of André Michaux," 130.
26. "September 2," in Michaux, *Michaux in North America,* 190.
27. "September 3," in Michaux, *Michaux in North America,* 190.
28. André Michaux to François André Michaux, December 30, 1792, in Michaux, *Michaux in North America,* 200–201.
29. André Michaux to Michel-Ange Bernard Mangourit, January 15, 1793, in Michaux, *Michaux in North America,* 208–11 (quote on 210). Michaux summarized his thinking in several documents, almost all of which recount a similar rationale. See Michaux and Boott, "Memorial of the Botanical Labours of André Michaux," 131; and "Abridged Memoir," Savage Papers, South Caroliniana Library, University of South Carolina.
30. André Michaux to François André Michaux, December 30, 1792, Philadelphia, in Michaux, *Michaux in North America,* 201.

6. THE PROMISE AND PERILS OF THE WEST

1. Thomas Jefferson to Giovanni Fabbroni, June 8, 1778, Sol Feinstone Collection, David Library of the American Revolution at the American Philosophical Society.
2. "To Thomas Jefferson from the American Philosophical Society, 7 January 1797," Founders Online, National Archives; "From Thomas Jefferson to the American Philosophical Society, 28 January 1797," ibid.
3. Henry Savage and Elizabeth Savage speculate that Jefferson and Michaux met in Paris in *André and François André Michaux* (Charlottesville: University Press of Virginia, 1986), 38. I have my doubts. Once they met in Philadelphia, neither gave any indication of a previous meeting. Many biographers note the rivalry between Buffon and Jefferson; see esp. Keith Thomson, *Jefferson's Shadow: The Story of His Science* (New Haven, CT: Yale University Press, 2018), esp. chap. 9. For a recent work on Buffon

and Jefferson, see Gordon Sayre, "Jefferson Takes on Buffon: The Polemic on American Animals *in Notes on the State of Virginia*," *William and Mary Quarterly* 78, no. 1 (2021): 79–116. Buffon's magisterial *Histoire naturelle, générale et particulière* was published in thirty-six volumes beginning in 1749 and ending in 1788, the year of Buffon's death. Of particular relevance for this debate was his series on quadrupeds, or four-footed animals.

4. The American Philosophical Society owns a copy Jefferson sent to them, along with several other first editions, including the first one printed in the United States. See https://www.amphilsoc.org/exhibits/nature/jefferson.htm.
5. Michaux's estimate of time is in André Michaux to Consul Mangourit, March 5, 1793, in André Michaux, *André Michaux in North America: Journals and Letters, 1785–1797,* ed. Charlie Williams, Eliane M. Norman, and Walter Kingsley Taylor (Tuscaloosa: University of Alabama Press, 2020), 212–13. "December 10," ibid., 203; André Michaux and Francis Boott, "Memorial of the Botanical Labours of André Michaux," *Edinburgh Journal of Medical* Science 1 (1826): 131.
6. "December 10," in *André Michaux in North America,* 203; Michaux and Boott, "Memorial of the Botanical Labours of André Michaux," 131.
7. "From Thomas Jefferson to George Rogers Clark, 4 December 1783," Founders Online, National Archives.
8. Ibid.
9. See Edward Gray, *The Making of John Ledyard: Empire and Ambition in the Life of an Early American Traveler* (New Haven, CT: Yale University Press, 2008), see esp. 124–26.
10. Caspar Wistar to Moses Marshall June 20, 1792, in John Harshberger, *The Botanists of Philadelphia and Their Work* (Philadelphia, 1899), 102–6. Note that Humphry Marshall had suggested to Benjamin Franklin that the APS support such an initiative as early as 1785. On Lewis's offer and Jefferson's response, see "Thomas Jefferson to Paul Allen, 18 August 1813," Founders Online, National Archives.
11. "Thomas Jefferson to Paul Allen, 18 August 1813," Founders Online, National Archives.
12. André Michaux, "Abridged Memoir," Henry Savage Papers, South Caroliniana Library, University of South Carolina.
13. "From Thomas Jefferson to Benjamin Smith Barton, 2 December 1792," Founders Online, National Archives.
14. See David MacDonald and Raine Waters, *History of Kaskaskia: The Lost Capital of the Illinois* (Carbondale: Southern Illinois University Press,

2019), esp. 43–46, for a summary of his background; and Robert M. Owens, "Jean Baptiste Ducoigne, the Kaskaskias, and the Limits of Thomas Jefferson's Friendship," *Journal of Illinois History* (2002): 109–36, for the most exhaustive accounting of his life that informs much of my analysis. Note that MacDonald and Waters make a convincing argument for Ducoigne's earlier birth.

15. Edward Cole to George Croghan, July 3, 1767, in Collections of the Illinois State Historical Library, British Series, *The New Regime, 1765–1767,* ed. Clarence Walworth Alvord and Clarence Edwin Carter (Springfield: Illinois State Historical Library, 1916), 580–81 (quote on 581). On the population, see Raymond Hauser, "The Illinois Indian Tribe: From Autonomy and Self-Sufficiency to Dependency and Depopulation," *Journal of the Illinois State Historical Society* (May 1976): 127–38; and Owens, "Jean Baptiste Ducoigne," 111. Owens has slightly different numbers, though the range is about the same. On Ducoigne's hunt, see MacDonald and Waters, *History of Kaskaskia,* 46–47. For more on the Confederacy, see Dennis Sweatman, "Comparing the Modern Native American Presence in Illinois with Other States of the Old Northwest Territory," *Journal of the Illinois State Historical Society* 103, no. 3/4 (2010): 252–315.
16. MacDonald and Waters, *History of Kaskaskia,* 47–48; William Henry Harrison to Henry Dearborn, 1804, in *Governor's Messages and Letters: 1800–1811,* ed. Logan Esarey (Indianapolis: Indiana Historical Commission, 1922), 114–15.
17. Michael Kranish, *Flight from Monticello* (New York: Oxford University Press, 2010), 271–74. Evidence of Ducoigne's visit at Monticello comes from a letter Jefferson sent his daughter in 1792; see Thomas Jefferson to Martha Jefferson Randolph, December 31, 1792, Founders Online, National Archives; and a letter he sent to Ducoigne years later, "From Thomas Jefferson to Jean Baptiste Ducoigne, [21 June 1796]," ibid.
18. The following comes from "Speech to Jean Baptiste Ducoigne, [ca. 1] June 1781," Founders Online, National Archives.
19. In addition to the speech and its footnote, Jefferson mentions the Ducoignes' son in this letter as well: "From Thomas Jefferson to Jean Baptiste Ducoigne, [21 June 1796]," Founders Online, National Archives; "From Thomas Jefferson to Robert Scot, 30 May 1781," ibid., for the medal; and "Speech to Jean Baptiste Ducoigne, [ca. 1] June 1781," ibid., for the commission. Owens, "Jean Baptiste Ducoigne," 115; Colonel John Gibson to George Rogers Clark, August 20, 1781, in Collections of the Illinois State Historical Library, *George Rogers Clark Papers, 1771–1781,* ed. James Alton

James (Springfield: Illinois State Historical Library, 1912), 590. Arthur St. Clair to Henry Knox, May 1, 1790, in *The St. Clair Papers,* ed. William Henry Smith (Cincinnati, 1882), 2:139.

20. "From Thomas Jefferson to Martha Jefferson Randolph, 31 December 1792," Founders Online, National Archives; "Speech to Jean Baptiste Ducoigne, [ca. 1] June 1781," ibid.
21. For more on the early federal period, see David Andrew Nichols, *Red Gentlemen and White Savages: Indians, Federalists, and the Search for Order on the American Frontier* (Charlottesville: University of Virginia Press, 2008).
22. For more on the Spanish policies toward the Mississippi and New Orleans, see Alexander Deconde, *This Affair of Louisiana* (New York: Charles Scribner's Sons, 1976), esp. 38–40, 51–55, and chap. 4.
23. Owens, "Jean-Baptiste Ducoigne," 117 (quote on 119).
24. Instructions to André Michaux, Caspar Wistar Papers, APS.

7. AMERICA'S SCIENTIFIC INSTITUTION

1. For information on the silk endeavor, see Zara Anishanslin, "Producing Empire: The British Empire in Theory and Practice," in *The World of the Revolutionary American Republic: Land, Labor, and the Conflict for a Continent,* ed Andrew Shankman (Abingdon, Oxfordshire: Routledge, 2014), 27–53, esp. 42–45; and "Charles Thomson," in Whitfield J. Bell Jr. and Charles B. Greifenstein, *Patriot-Improvers: Biographical Sketches of Members of the American Philosophical Society* (Philadelphia: APS, 2010), 1:184. For a list of funders, see *Directions for the Breeding and Management of Silkworms* (Philadelphia, 1770), xi–xv. For the government's sponsorship, see *The Statutes at Large of Pennsylvania from 1682 to 1801, Volume 10* (Harrisburg, 1904), 474–75; *Directions for the Breeding and Management of Silkworms* (Philadelphia, 1770); and Anishanslin, "Producing Empire," 27–53, esp. 42–45.
2. "From Thomas Jefferson to Benjamin Smith Barton, 2 December 1792," Founders Online, National Archives. As has been pointed out by others, this letter is misdated and is likely from January. "To Thomas Jefferson from Benjamin Smith Barton, 4 January 1793," ibid.
3. Benjamin Franklin, "A Proposal for Promoting Useful Knowledge, 14 May 1743," Founders Online, National Archives.
4. Ibid.
5. Ibid.
6. For the best history of the Society, see Edwin Carter, *"One Grand Pursuit": A Brief History of the American Philosophical Society's First 250 Years,*

1743–1993 (Philadelphia: American Philosophical Society, 1993). For the orientation of colonists eastward, see Michael Zuckerman, "Identity in British America: Unease in Eden," in *Colonial Identity in the Atlantic World,* ed. Nicholas Canny and Anthony Pagden (Princeton, NJ: Princeton University Press, 1987), chap. 5.

7. For member information, see Early Minutes and the online member directory: https://search.amphilsoc.org/memhist/search.
8. James Madison to Thomas Jefferson, March 18, 1787, Sol Feinstone Collection, David Library of the American Revolution at the American Philosophical Society; James Madison Meteorological Journals (1784–1793), APS.
9. "To George Washington from William Hamilton, 17 March 1792," Founders Online, National Archives; "To George Washington from William Hamilton, 6 March 1797," ibid.
10. On Adams, the APS, and AAAS, see Carter, *"One Grand Pursuit,"* 19.
11. Ibid., 20.
12. "December 10," in André Michaux, *André Michaux in North America: Journals and Letters, 1785–1797,* ed. Charlie Williams, Eliane M. Norman, and Walter Kingsley Taylor (Tuscaloosa: University of Alabama Press, 2020), 203. See Patrick Spero, "The Other Presidency: Thomas Jefferson and the American Philosophical Society," *Proceedings of the American Philosophical Society* 162, no. 4 (2018): 321–60.
13. "To Thomas Jefferson from Benjamin Smith Barton, 4 January 1793," Founders Online, National Archives. For the press of time, see also André Michaux to Michel-Ange-Bernard Mangourit, January 15, 1793, in Michaux, *Michaux in North America,* 210, where he writes of an opportunity to leave in six weeks, a reference to Ducoigne's potential departure.
14. "To Thomas Jefferson from Benjamin Smith Barton, 4 January 1793," Founders Online, National Archives.
15. André Michaux, Notebook 7, in Michaux, *Michaux in North America,* 205–6.
16. For estimates on the value of a livre, see George Rude, "Prices, Wages and Popular Movements in Paris during the French Revolution," *Economic History Review* 6, no. 3 (1954): 248. André Michaux, Notebook 7, in Michaux, *André Michaux in North America,* 205–6.
17. "To Thomas Jefferson from Benjamin Smith Barton, 4 January 1793," Founders Online, National Archives.
18. André Michaux, Notebook 7, in *André Michaux in North America,* 205–6.

19. "American Philosophical Society's Subscription Agreement for André Michaux's Western Expedition, [ca. 22 January 1793]," Founders Online, National Archives. The following paragraphs are based on this document.
20. Ibid.
21. "To Thomas Jefferson from George Washington, 22 January 1793," Founders Online, National Archives; "From George Washington to Thomas Jefferson, 22 January 1793," ibid.
22. It is very difficult to make good comparisons between value in the 1790s and today. To see an estimate that places it at twice the average annual income, see John Bach McMaster, *A History of the People of the United States, from the Revolution to the Civil War* (New York: D. Appleton, 1915), 2:617. For this project, I have also used income as a way to compare, similar to my attempt to use daily labor in France to compare the value of the livre. Modern equivalent based on MeasuringWorth.com and comparing 1793 to 2023, https://www.measuringworth.com/calculators/uscompare/result.php?year_source=1793&amount=100&year_result=2023.
23. Modern equivalent based on MeasuringWorth.com and comparing 1793 to 2023, https://www.measuringworth.com/calculators/uscompare/result.php?year_source=1793&amount=870&year_result=2023.
24. On Page, see Spero, Patrick Spero, "The Other Presidency: Thomas Jefferson and the American Philosophical Society," *Proceedings of the American Philosophical Society* 162, no. 4 (2018): 321–60. On King, see David Gary, "Rufus King and the History of Reading: The Use of Print in the Early American Republic" (Ph.D. diss., City University of New York, 2013); *Encyclopedia of Alabama,* s.v., "Benjamin Hawkins," http://www.encyclopediaofalabama.org/article/h-1058; and Chester McArthur Destler, "The Gentleman Farmer and the New Agriculture: Jeremiah Wadsworth," *Agricultural History* 46, no. 1 (1972): 135–53.
25. André Michaux to Louis Bosc, New York, April 1, 1793, in Michaux, *Michaux in North America,* 213–14; "To Thomas Jefferson from David Rittenhouse, [10 April 1793]," Founders Online, National Archives.

8. AMERICA'S SCIENTIFIC COMMUNITY

1. "To Thomas Jefferson from David Rittenhouse, [10 April 1793]," Founders Online, National Archives.
2. "From Thomas Jefferson to David Rittenhouse, 11 April 1793," Founders Online, National Archives.

3. "April 19," American Philosophical Society Minutes, 1793–1798, American Philosophical Society, https://diglib.amphilsoc.org/islandora/object/american-philosophical-society-minutes-1787-1793.
4. "To Thomas Jefferson from David Rittenhouse, [10 April 1793]."
5. For biographical background, see "James Hutchinson Papers," APS, https://search.amphilsoc.org/collections/view?docId=ead/Mss.B.H97p-ead.xml; and the work of previous APS librarian Whitfield Bell, in Whitfield J. Bell Jr., "Hutchinson, James (1752–1793), physician and surgeon," *American National Biography,* February 1, 2000. For Fothergill's biography, see *Oxford Dictionary of Biography,* s.v. "John Fothergill." On Fothergill's aide, see the James Hutchinson Letters at the APS, esp. James Hutchinson to Katherine Rickey Hutchinson Milnor, June 24, 1776, and September 20, 1776, and John Fothergill to James Hutchinson, November 9, 1776. Fothergill also penned several letters of recommendation and introduction for Hutchinson so he could find employment on his return to the United States.
6. Thomas Horrocks, "Caspar Wistar," in *American National Biography;* and the finding aid to the Caspar Wistar Papers at the APS, https://search.amphilsoc.org/collections/view?docId=ead/Mss.B.W76-ead.xml/. On his election to the curator position, see the APS's Early Minutes, 1787–1793.
7. See Keith Thomson, *The Legacy of the Mastodon: The Golden Age of Fossils in America* (New Haven, CT: Yale University Press, 2008), 42–44.
8. See esp. Whitfield Bell, "John Vaughan," in *American National Biography,* and the finding aid, John Vaughan Papers, APS, which is based largely but not entirely off Bell's entry. A wonderful firsthand account can be found in *The Life and Writing of Jared Sparks,* ed. Herbert Baxter Adams (Boston: Houghton, Mifflin, 1893), 1:133–35.
9. On Vaughan's time in Europe and move to the United States, see the letters between John Vaughan and William Temple Franklin, esp. those dated May 6, 1776, August 1, 1778, November 1, 1779, December 23, 1780, and March 10, 1781, William Temple Franklin Papers, APS.
10. On his trip to America, see John Vaughan to William Temple Franklin, May 18, 1782, and May 29, 1782, in William Temple Franklin Papers, APS. "Headquarters" from John Vaughan to William Temple Franklin, December 13, 1781, William Temple Franklin Papers, APS.
11. See esp. John Fredriksen, "Jonathan Williams," in *Dictionary of American Biography,* and finding aid, Jonathan Williams Papers, APS. Jonathan Williams, "Memoir of Jonathan Williams, on the Use of the Thermometer in Discovering Banks, Soundings, &c," *Transactions of the American Philosophical Society* 3 (1793): 82–100.

12. On Nicholson, see Robert Arbuckle, "John Nicholson," in *American National Biography;* Robert Arbuckle, "John Nicholson and the Pennsylvania Population Company," *Western Pennsylvania Historical Magazine* 57 (October 1974): 4, Robert Arbuckle, *Pennsylvania Speculator and Patriot: The Entrepreneurial John Nicholson, 1757–1800* (University Park: Pennsylvania State University Press, 1975), esp. 165 and finding aid for the Sequestered John Nicholson Papers, Pennsylvania Archives, Pennsylvania Museum and Historical Commission (https://web.archive.org/web/20170421111931/http://phmc.state.pa.us/bah/dam/mg/mg96.htm) and Social Networks and Archival Context https://snaccooperative.org/view/25070834. Arbuckle states that he owned twelve million acres in his dictionary entry from 1999, though I suspect that might be a conflation with his debts. When he died, Arbuckle estimated he owed $12 million to creditors and had three to four million acres of land. On the impeachment, see *An Account of the Impeachment and Trial of the late Francis Hopkinson* (Philadelphia, 1794), 38.
13. For a description of this experience, see "A descriptive catalogue of Mr. Peale's exhibition of perspective views, with changeable effects; or, Nature delineated, and in motion" (Philadelphia: Printed by Francis Bailey, at Yorick's Head, in Market Street: [1786]), American Philosophical Society, https://diglib.amphilsoc.org/islandora/object/text:333. Peale's biography is well-known, especially in the APS, where his papers are held. The most recent complete biography is by Charles Coleman Sellers, *Charles Willson Peale* (New York: Charles Scribner's Sons, 1969), but the *Charles Willson Peale Papers* edited by Lillian Miler provides the most exhaustive window on the man. See *Early Minutes of the American Philosophical Society,* 221–22, for his renting of rooms. For an example of the APS apparently depositing collections with Peale, see *Early Minutes,* 214. Correspondence data is based on an analysis using Founders Online. Nicholas Collin, "Nicholas Collin's Appeal to American Scientists," ed. Whitfield Bell, *William and Mary Quarterly* 13, no. 4 (1956): 519–50 (quote on 547).
14. For the best account of Collin, an important figure in the history of the APS and early American science who is all but forgotten today, see Collin, "Nicholas Collin's Appeal to American Scientists," 519–50.
15. Ibid., "Appeal to American Scientists"; Nicholas Collin, "Introduction to Vol. the Third: An Essay on Those Inquiries in Natural Philosophy, Which at Present Are Most Beneficial to the United States of North America," *Transactions of the American Philosophical Society* (1793): iii–xxvii.
16. Collin, "Introduction," xxiv.

17. Ibid.
18. See "Accounts" in the APS Archives, "Creation of Committee to collection subscription for Michaux Expedition," "Subscription list for André Michaux for exploration in the Western World," "J[oh]n Vaughan to Sam[ue]l H. Smith," APS Archives, Record Group IIa for the items mentioned here and below.
19. "American Philosophical Society's Subscription Agreement for André Michaux's Western Expedition, [ca. 22 January 1793]," Founders Online, National Archives, has information on the April 23 request. Original in APS Archives, Record Group IIa, "Creation of Committee to collection subscription for Michaux Expedition, April 23, 1793."
20. On Rembrandt Peale, see Receipt. J[oh]n Vaughan paid to Dr. Wistar 12.50, which he paid to Mr. Rembrandt Peale, April 23, 1793, APS Archives, Record Group IIa.
21. Silvio Bedini, "David Rittenhouse," in *American National Biography;* "Sketch of David Rittenhouse," *Popular Science Monthly* 36 (1890): 835–42; William Barton, *Memoirs of the Life of David Rittenhouse* (Philadelphia, 1813), see esp. 350–59 for the APS's appointment of Rittenhouse as president; and Brooke Hindle, *David Rittenhouse* (Princeton, NJ: Princeton University Press, 1964), for the most recent complete biography. Whitfield Bell and Charles Greifenstein also offer a wonderful portrait of Rittenhouse in *Patriot-Improvers: Biographical Sketches of Members of the American Philosophical Society,* vol. 3, *1767–1768* (Philadelphia, APS, 2010), 66–83.
22. "John Ewing," in Bell and Greifenstein, *Patriot-Improvers,* 3:50–59; "John Ewing," in Penn Biographies, https://archives.upenn.edu/exhibits/penn-people/biography/john-ewing. On the border, see John Potter, "The Pennsylvania and Virginia Boundary Controversy," *Pennsylvania Magazine of History and Biography* 38, no. 4 (1914): 407–26.
23. "William Smith," in Bell and, *Patriot-Improvers,* 3:35–49; Robert Calhoon, "William Smith," *American National Biography,* https://www-anb-org.proxy.library.upenn.edu/view/10.1093/anb/9780198606697.001.0001/anb-9780198606697-e-0100844.
24. Sarah Naramore, "I Sing the Body Republic: How Benjamin Rush Created American Medicine" (Ph.D. diss., University of Notre Dame, 2018). For the most recent biography, see Stephen Fried, *Rush: Revolution, Madness, and Benjamin Rush, the Visionary Doctor Who Became a Founding Father* (New York: Crown, 2018). See also Robert Sullivan, "Benjamin Rush," in *American National Biography.* For Rush's own memoirs, see the manuscript version in the APS's vault, Benjamin Rush, "Travels through Life," APS.

9. AMERICAN INTERESTS AND SCIENTIFIC PRIORITIES

1. "To Thomas Jefferson from Benjamin Smith Barton, 4 January 1793," Founders Online, National Archives.
2. André Michaux to Mangourit, January 15, 1793, in André Michaux, *André Michaux in North America: Journals and Letters, 1785–1797,* ed. Charlie Williams, Eliane M. Norman, and Walter Kingsley Taylor (Tuscaloosa: University of Alabama Press, 2020), 210.
3. Mangourit to Lebrun, in *André Michaux in North America,* 211.
4. André Michaux to Mangourit, March 5, 1793, in Michaux, *André Michaux in North America,* 212–13; André Michaux to Louis Bosc, April 1, 1793, ibid., 212–15 (quote on 215).
5. Michaux to Mangourit, March 5, 1793, in Michaux, *André Michaux in North America,* 212–13.
6. "Memorandum Books, 1793," Founders Online, National Archives.
7. "Instructions to André Michaux," Caspar Wistar Papers, APS. Also available at "American Philosophical Society's Instructions to André Michaux, [ca. 30 April 1793]," Founders Online, National Archives, at https://founders.archives.gov/documents/Jefferson/01-25-02-0569.
8. Ibid.
9. André Michaux to Louis Bosc, Paris, April 1, 1793, in Michaux, *André Michaux in North America,* 213–15 (quote on 215).
10. Ibid.
11. Ibid.
12. "Instructions to André Michaux," Caspar Wistar Papers, APS.
13. "Instructions to André Michaux," Caspar Wistar Papers, APS.
14. Benjamin Rush, "An inquiry into the natural history of medicine among the Indians of North America, and a comparative view of their diseases and remedies with those of civilized nations read before the American Philosophical Society, February 4, 1774," in *Medical Inquiries and Observations* (Philadelphia, 1794), 58; Laura Murray, "Vocabularies of Native American Languages: A Literary and Historical Approach to an Elusive Genre," *American Quarterly* 53, no. 4 (2001): 590–623, esp. 606. See also Edward Gray, *New Babel: Languages and Nations in Early America* (Princeton, NJ: Princeton University Press, 2014); and Peter Onuf, "We Shall All Be Americans," *Indiana Magazine of History* 95, no. 2 (1999): 103–41.
15. Murray, "Vocabularies of Native American Languages," 590–623, esp. 606. See also Gray, *New Babel;* and Onuf, "We Shall All Be Americans." As noted linguist Mary Haas wrote, "They wanted to know about the raw materials of the new places and so collected plant and animal specimens,

mineral specimens and all other things which attracted their attention. In this context there developed what might be called the 'natural history' approach to languages" (quoted in Murray, "Vocabularies of Native American Languages," 606–7). See also Keith Thomson, *Jefferson's Shadow: The Story of His Science* (New Haven, CT: Yale University Press, 2018), 105–6 and 250. Jefferson outlined his project in his *Notes on the State of Virginia.* I am especially indebted to Jefferson Looney, "Thomas Jefferson: Practical Scientist," *Journal of the Pennsylvania Academy of Science* 67, no. 2 (1993): 94–99, and 97, for a specific discussion of linguistics and how it fit within Jefferson's scientific project.

16. "Instructions to Michaux," Caspar Wistar Papers, APS.
17. For the best analysis of the Buffon and Jefferson debate, see Gordon Sayre, "Jefferson Takes on Buffon: The Polemic on American Animals in the *Notes on the State of Virginia,*" *William and Mary Quarterly* 78, no. 1, 79–116. Elizabeth Kolbert, *The Sixth Extinction: An Unnatural History* (New York: Henry Holt, 2014), chap. 2; Elizabeth Kolbert, "The Lost World: The Mastodon's Molars," *New Yorker,* December 8, 2013, https://www.newyorker.com/magazine/2013/12/16/the-lost-world-2. Thomas Jefferson, *Notes on the State of Virginia* (Philadelphia, 1788), 54.
18. See Sayre, "Jefferson Takes on Buffon"; Onuf, "We Shall All Be Americans"; and Thomson, *Jefferson's Shadow.* Thomas Jefferson, *Notes on the State of Virginia* (1788), 54.
19. Benjamin Smith Barton, "Notes on Animals," 19–20, Benjamin Smith Barton Papers, APS. This conclusion is based on a keyword search of *The Papers of Thomas Jefferson* at Founders Online. The APS published an edited version of Barton's notes in 1974; see Benjamin Smith Barton, *Notes on Animals* (Philadelphia: APS, 1974), 22–24.
20. Barton, "Notes on Animals," Benjamin Smith Barton Papers, APS, 19–20; Barton, *Notes on Animals,* 22–23.
21. Mary Thompson, "Sheep," in *Digital Encyclopedia of George Washington,* Mount Vernon Ladies Association, https://www.mountvernon.org/library/digitalhistory/digital-encyclopedia/article/sheep/.
22. Thomas Bloomer Balch, "Picturesque Narratives: South West Range," *Christian World* 3 (1843): 183; Thomas Jefferson to George Washington, June 28, 1793, Founders Online, National Archives. On Jefferson's continued fascination, see *Thomas Jefferson Encyclopedia,* Monticello, s.v. "Sheep," https://www.monticello.org/site/research-and-collections/sheep.
23. Edward Gray, *The Making of John Ledyard: Empire and Ambition in the Life of an Early American Traveler* (New Haven, CT: Yale University Press,

2008), 129; Patrick Spero, "The Other Presidency: Thomas Jefferson and the American Philosophical Society," *Proceedings of the American Philosophical Society* 162, no. 4 (2018): 321–60.

24. "Instructions to André Michaux," Caspar Wistar Papers, APS.
25. "Instructions to André Michaux," Caspar Wistar Papers, APS.
26. "Instructions to André Michaux," Caspar Wistar Papers, APS.
27. Michaux to American Philosophical Society, April 29, 1793, in APS Archives. Translation in Henry Savage and Elizabeth Savage, *André and François André Michaux* (Charlottesville: University Press of Virginia 1986), 131.
28. Ibid.
29. Ibid.
30. On the departure of Ducoigne, see the War Department Papers, especially the letters from John Stagg calling for supplies for the leaders. For a report on their progress, see Samuel Hodgdon to James O'Hara, May 5, 1793, War Department Papers, https://wardepartmentpapers.org/s/home/item/44656, and May 10, https://wardepartmentpapers.org/s/home/media/126728; and Henry Knox to Isaac Craig, May 8, 1793, War Department Papers https://wardepartmentpapers.org/s/home/item/44641; André Michaux and Francis Boott, "Memorial of the Botanical Labours of André Michaux," *Edinburgh Journal of Medical Science* 1 (1826): 131.
31. André Michaux and Francis Boott, "Memorial of the Botanical Labours of André Michaux," *Edinburgh Journal of Medical Science* 1 (1826): 131.

10. ENTER EDMOND GENET

1. The following biographical sketch is based on Henry Ammon, *The Genet Mission* (New York: Norton, 1973); see page 5 for the physical description. "Genet's Instructions," Isaac Shelby Papers, University of Kentucky, https://exploreuk.uky.edu/fa/findingaid/?id=xt72ng4gmz0h. Thanks to Kathryn Dettmer for her translation.
2. Ammon, *The Genet Mission,* 8–9.
3. "Plan for a Revolution," in *Correspondence of Clark and Genet* (Washington, DC, 1897), 945–53.
4. Ibid.
5. George Rogers Clark to [French Minister], Louisville, February 5, 1793, in *Correspondence of Clark and Genet,* 970. The most focused accounts of this entire episode are Frederick Turner, "The Origin of Genet's Projected Attack on Louisiana and the Floridas," *American Historical Review* 3, no. 4 (July 1898): 650–71; and the dissertation of his student Regina Katharine Crandall, "Genet's Projected Attack on Louisiana and the Floridas,

1793–94" (University of Chicago, 1902). Wesley Campbell offers a useful corrective to Turner's work, highlighting the realpolitik that also guided their policy decisions (Campbell, "The Origin of Citizen Genet's Projected Attack on Spanish Louisiana: A Case Study in Girondin Politics," *French Historical Studies* 33, no. 4 [October 2010]: 515–44).

6. On O'Fallon, see Louise Phelps Kellogg, "Letter of Thomas Paine, 1793," *American Historical Review* 29, no. 3 (April 1924): 501–5; and on the Christmas huddle, see Crandall, "Genet's Projected Attack," 72n1.
7. The other letter is George Rogers Clark to [French Minister], Louisville, February 5, 1793, in *Correspondence of Clark and Genet,* 970.
8. "Letter of Thomas Paine," 504.
9. Two historians, Frederick Turner, in "The Origin of Genet's Projected Attack," and Louise Phelps Kellogg, in "Letter of Thomas Paine," have argued that the timelines suggest that the French government was aware of Clark's proposal before Genet left and that it informed their instructions. Regina Katharine Crandall, on the other hand, makes a fairly convincing argument that this timeline would have been hard to carry out. If O'Fallon sent his letter from Kentucky in late December 1792, it would have needed to be posted from the American frontier to Paris in six weeks' time. The discovery of Paine's February 17 letter in the early twentieth century is vague enough to leave some doubt. The most astute recent chronicler of Genet's instructions is convinced that Clark's letter did not arrive in time to influence the ministry's orders (see Crandall, "Genet's Projected Attack," 72n2; Kellogg, "Letter of Thomas Paine," 504; and "Genet's Instructions," in *Correspondence of Clark and Genet,* 961–62). See also Pickering to N. Webster, Trenton, November 1, 1797, in *Correspondence of Clark and Genet,* 1099–100, for an almost contemporaneous discussion about the timing of Clark's overtures and Ternant's role.
10. Genet to Ministers, Charleston, April 16, 1793, in *Correspondence of French Ministers,* ed. Frederick Jackson Turner (Washington, DC: American Historical Association, 1904), 212.
11. Ammon, *The Genet Mission,* 44.
12. "Genet's Instructions," in *Correspondence of Clark and Genet,* 959–60.
13. Genet's reception has been well documented. For two studies, see Ammon, *The Genet Mission;* and David Waldstreicher, *In the Midst of Perpetual Fetes.* The quote is from "Imlay's Observations," in *Correspondence of Clark and Genet,* 954.
14. Newspapers throughout the country reported on Genet's every move. Many also reported on his welcome to Philadelphia; see esp. "American;

French; Citizen; Gray's; Ambuscade; Printers," *Philadelphia General Advertiser,* May 14, 1793, for the advance plans; and *Philadelphia Federal Gazette,* May 16, 1793, [3], for a report on the greeting.

15. "Philadelphia, Friday, May 17," *Philadelphia General Advertiser,* May 17, 1793, [3]; "[Philadelphia; State-House; Charles Biddle; Robert Henry Duncan; M. Genest; Republic; France]," *Philadelphia General Advertiser,* May 17, 1793, [3], among many others.
16. "[Philadelphia; State-House; Charles Biddle; Robert Henry Duncan; M. Genest; Republic; France]," *Philadelphia General Advertiser,* May 17, 1793, [3].
17. Charles Biddle, *Autobiography of Charles Biddle* (Philadelphia, 1883), 251–52; for the address, see "Philadelphia, 18th May, 1793," *Philadelphia Federal Gazette,* May 18, 1793, [2]; and "[Mr. Genet; Rittenhouse]," *Philadelphia General Advertiser,* May 18, 1793, [3]. On three abreast, see "[Genet; Philadelphia]," *Philadelphia General Advertiser,* May 20, 1793, [3].
18. Biddle, *Autobiography,* 251–52; for the address, see "Philadelphia, 18th May, 1793," *Philadelphia Federal Gazette,* May 18, 1793, [2]; and "[Mr. Genet; Rittenhouse]," *Philadelphia General Advertiser,* May 18, 1793, [3]. On three abreast, see "[Genet; Philadelphia]," *Philadelphia General Advertiser,* May 20, 1793, [3]. For the estimates, see Ammon, *The Genet Mission,* 55.
19. See esp. the article in *Columbian Centinel* (Boston), May 29, 1793, [1]. See also "Citizen Genet, Minister Plenipotentiary," *New York Daily Advertiser,* May 22, 1793, [2]. "Citizen Genet, Minister Plenipotentiary, from the Republic of France, to the Citizens of Philadelphia," *Philadelphia General Advertiser,* May 20, 1793, [3].
20. For the German Society welcome, see "Citizen Genet, Minister Plenipotentiary from the Republic of France," *Dunlap's American Daily Advertiser* (Philadelphia), May 20, 1793, [3]; and for the French, see "Philadelphia, 18th May, 1793," *Philadelphia Federal Gazette,* May 18, 1793, [2]. On the May 19 event and toasts, see *Philadelphia Federal Gazette,* May 22, 1793; "Philadelphia, April 23," *Supplement to Dunlap's American Daily Advertiser* (Philadelphia), May 23, 1793, [4]; and Thompson Westcott, *History of Philadelphia* (Philadelphia, 1884), 1:473–74.
21. For reports of the June 1 celebration, see Biddle, *Autobiography,* 252–53; Ammon, *The Genet Mission,* 54–58; and *Dunlap's American Daily Advertiser* (Philadelphia), June 4, 1793, [2].
22. André Michaux, *Andre Michaux in North America: Journals and Letters, 1785–1797,* ed. Charlie Williams, Eliane M. Norman, and Walter Kingsley Taylor (Tuscaloosa: University of Alabama Press, 2020), 202–3.

23. Stanley Elkins and Eric McKitrick, *The Age of Federalism* (New York: Oxford University Press, 1995), 330–74, esp. 336–41. On Jefferson's views, see, among others, Ammon, *The Genet Mission,* 46–51. For a discussion of Washington's cabinet on this issue, see Alexander Deconde, *Entangling Alliance: Politics and Diplomacy under George Washington* (Durham, NC: Duke University Press, 1958), chaps. 7, 8, and 9, esp. p. 227.
24. "From Alexander Hamilton to——, [18 May 1793]," Founders Online, National Archives.
25. Ibid.
26. "On the Reception of Edmond Charles Genet in Philadelphia, [14–16 May 1793]," Founders Online, National Archives.
27. Ammon, *The Genet Mission,* 42.
28. "Neutrality Proclamation, 22 April 1793," Founders Online, National Archives.
29. "From George Washington to Thomas Jefferson, 12 April 1793," Founders Online, National Archives. [Original reference from Crandall, "Genet's Projected Attack," 39n3.] Ammon, *The Genet Mission,* 59.

11. A NEW MISSION

1. Clark to French Minister, Louisville, February 5, 1793, in *Correspondence of Clark and Genet* (Washington, DC, 1897), 968.
2. Ibid.
3. Ibid., 970.
4. Robert V. Remini, "Andrew Jackson Takes an Oath of Allegiance to Spain," *Tennessee Historical Quarterly* 54, no. 1 (1995): 2–15.
5. André Michaux to Genet, Philadelphia, May 20, 1793, in Michaux, *Andre Michaux in North America: Journals and Letters, 1785–1797,* ed. Charlie Williams, Eliane M. Norman, and Walter Kingsley Taylor (Tuscaloosa: University of Alabama Press, 2020), 219.
6. Genet to Ministers, July 25, 1793, in *Correspondence of Clark and Genet,* 987–90 (quote on 988–89); Henry Savage and Elizabeth Savage, *André and François André Michaux* (Charlottesville: University Press of Virginia 1986), 135.
7. "Authorization to Michaux," in *Correspondence of Clark and Genet,* 995–96; "Genet's Instructions," in *Correspondence of Clark and Genet,* 990–95. See also Charlie Williams, "Explorer, Botanist, Courier, or Spy? André Michaux and the Genet Affair of 1793," *Castanea* (December 2004): 101–2.
8. Genet to Ministers, July 25, 1793, in *Correspondence of Clark and Genet,* 987–90 (quote on 989). On the role of scientific exploration, science, and

spying, see Cameron Strang, *Frontiers of Science, Imperialism and Natural Knowledge in the Gulf South Borderlands, 1500–1850* (Chapel Hill: University of North Carolina Press, 2018), esp. chaps. 4 and 5.

9. On the potential imminence of war, see Frederick Turner, "The Origin of Genet's Projected Attack on Louisiana and the Floridas," *American Historical Review* 3, no. 4 (July 1898): 664–65. For the way the improving relations factored into matters, see Genet's summary of his discussion with Jefferson in Genet to the Ministers, July 25, 1793, in *Correspondence of Clark and Genet,* 982; Regina Katharine Crandall, "Genet's Projected Attack on Louisiana and the Floridas, 1793–94" (Ph.D. diss. University of Chicago, 1902), 118.
10. Compiled by sorting Founders Online, National Archives; "To James Madison from Thomas Jefferson, 19 May 1793," Founders Online, National Archives.
11. Ammon, *The Genet Mission* (New York: Norton, 1973), 83; "Editorial Note: Jefferson and André Michaux's Proposed Western Expedition," Founders Online, National Archives; and see esp. "Notes of Cabinet Meeting and Conversations with Edmond Charles Genet, 5 July 1793," ibid.
12. Genet to Ministers, July 25, 1793, in *Correspondence of Clark and Genet,* 982.
13. "Notes of Cabinet Meeting and Conversations with Edmond Charles Genet, 5 July 1793," Founders Online, National Archives.
14. Ibid.
15. Ibid.
16. "Notes of Cabinet Meeting and Conversations with Edmond Charles Genet, 5 July 1793," Founders Online, National Archives.
17. "From Thomas Jefferson to Isaac Shelby, 28 June 1793," Founders Online, National Archives. See esp. the editorial comments on the drafting and redrafting of this letter. Jefferson maintained the same date as his original letter, though he changed its contents after meeting with Genet on July 5.
18. Ibid.
19. Genet to Ministers, July 25, 1793, in *Correspondence of Clark and Genet,* 982.
20. Brown to Clark, June 24, 1793, and Brown to Shelby, June 24, 1793, in *Correspondence of Clark and Genet,* 982–83.
21. Genet's account is in Genet to Ministers, July 25, 1793, in *Correspondence of Clark and Genet,* 982. See Ammon, *The Genet Mission,* 84–85, in which he makes Jefferson and Genet's accounts appear to be markedly different, with Genet offering a rosier account of their meeting. See a deposition

John Brown gave later recounting this episode in *American State Papers, Miscellaneous,* 1:931, https://memory.loc.gov/ll/llsp/037/0900/09470931.tif. His reference to heads of departments may have implied Jefferson as secretary of state.

22. Andrew Johnston, "Citizen Genet," in *Cyclopædia of Political Science, Political Economy, and of the Political History of the United States,* ed. John Lalor (New York, 1899), 2:331; Turner, "Origins of Genet's Projected Attack," 669; Samuel Wilson, *A Review of "Isaac Shelby and the Genet Mission"* (Lexington, KY: Published by the author, 1920) has many summaries of earlier historians take on the episode. Thomas Ruys Smith, *River of Dreams: Imagining the Mississippi before Mark Twain* (Baton Rouge: Louisiana State University Press, 2007), 29; Stanley Elkins and Eric McKitrick, *The Age of Federalism* (New York: Oxford University Press, 1995), 349. Harlow Unger, *"Mr. President": George Washington and the Making of the Nation's Highest Office* (Boston: Da Capo, 2013), 174. The exception to this hesitancy is Charlie Williams in "Explorer, Botanist, Courier, or Spy?," 102–3.
23. "From Thomas Jefferson to William Stephens Smith, 13 November 1787," Founders Online, National Archives.
24. "From Thomas Jefferson to James Monroe, 28 June 1793," Founders Online, National Archives.
25. For the list of letters, see Notebook 7, June 22–July 1, in Michaux, *Michaux in North America,* 226–27.
26. Evidence of the shipment's contraband is found in Depauw's Deposition, in *Correspondence of Clark and Genet,* 1104. The receipt is found in "Payment for Transportation of Baggage to Pittsburgh," in *Papers of the War Department,* https://wardepartmentpapers.org/s/home/item/45009. For the failure, see *Early Proceedings of the American Philosophical Society held at Philadelphia for the Promotion of Useful Knowledge* (Philadelphia, 1884), 244, 278, and 298 and for afterlife of the money, see APS Archives, Record Group IIa, APS, especially John Vaughan to Samuel Smith, March 18, 1799.
27. Genet, "Michaux Instructions," in *Correspondence of Clark and Genet,* 994.
28. André Michaux, "July 15," in Michaux, *Michaux in North America,* 227.

12. MICHAUX'S DUAL AND DUELING EXPEDITIONS

1. For the trip, see André Michaux, *André Michaux in North America: Journals and Letters, 1785–1797,* ed. Charlie Williams, Eliane M. Norman, and

Walter Kingsley Taylor (Tuscaloosa: University of Alabama Press, 2020), 225–28.

2. For a profile of Brackenridge, see Patrick Spero, *Frontier Country: The Politics of War in Early Pennsylvania* (Philadelphia: University of Pennsylvania Press, 2016), conclusion. Walter Blair, *The Literature of the United States: An Anthology and History from the Colonial Period through the American Renaissance* (Chicago: Scott Foresman, 1966), 1:498; Steven Moore, *The Novel: An Alternative History, 1600–1800* (New York: Bloomsbury, 2013), 938.
3. Thomas Jefferson, "Notes on a Conversation with Hugh Henry Brackenridge, 27 March 1800," Founders Online, National Archives.
4. "For the National Gazette. Thoughts on the Present Indian War," *Philadelphia National Gazette,* February 2, 1792, [109].
5. The most recent biography of Wilkinson, a shady character whose exploits are detailed in many different books, is Andro Linklater, *An Artist in Treason: The Extraordinary Double Life of General James Wilkinson* (New York: Walker, 2009), see esp. 71–102. See esp. Wesley Campbell, "The Origin of Citizen Genet's Projected Attack on Spanish Louisiana: A Case Study in Girondin Politics," *French Historical Studies* 33, no. 4 (October 2010): 515–44. "Plans for Revolution," in *Correspondence of Clark and Genet* (Washington, DC, 1897), 951.
6. On the visit, see "July 28," in Michaux, *Michaux in North America,* 228. See Spero, *Frontier Country,* conclusion, for more on the switching of allegiances.
7. "July 29 to August 14, 1793," in Michaux, *André Michaux in North America,* 228–30.
8. See, Spero, *Frontier Country.*
9. "August 13," in Michaux, *André Michaux in North America,* 230.
10. On Vigo, see Dorothy Riker, "Francis Vigo," *Indiana Magazine of History* 26, no. 1 (1930): 12–24.
11. Audrain had lived in Bucks County, Pennsylvania, before moving to Pittsburgh; see *Pennsylvania Archives: Papers of the Governors,* 3:1032, for an account of a theft he suffered. For biographical details, see Clarence Burton, *History of Detroit, 1780–1850: Financial and Commercial* (Detroit: Report of Historiographer, Clarence M. Burton, 1917), 19–21.
12. The best account of this scheme can be found in Carl J. Ekberg, *A French Aristocrat in the American West: The Shattered Dreams of De Lassus de Luzières* (Columbia: University of Missouri Press, 2010), 26–27 and 35–72. For another excellent account of the scheme and its characters upon which I have relied, see Howard Rice, *Barthélemi Tardiveau: A French*

Trader in the West (Baltimore, MD: John Hopkins University Press, 1938), esp. 41–47. For Audrain, see Russell Magnaghi, *French in Michigan* (East Lansing: Michigan State University Press, 2016), 16. The following paragraphs rely on these sources.

13. Eckberg, *A French Aristocrat in the American West,* 23–27.
14. Quote from Eckberg, *A French Aristocrat in the American West,* 35
15. John Francis McDermott, "John B. C. Lucas in Pennsylvania," *Western Pennsylvania History* (1938): 209–30.
16. Quote and description in Michaux, André *Michaux in North America,* 229.
17. Ammon, *The Genet Mission,* 85–86.
18. "August 14–August 29," in Michaux, *André Michaux in North America,* 230–32.
19. Ibid.

13. ORGANIZING A NEW EXPEDITION

1. "August 23, 24, and 27," in André Michaux, *André Michaux in North America: Journals and Letters, 1785–1797,* ed. Charlie Williams, Eliane M. Norman, and Walter Kingsley Taylor (Tuscaloosa: University of Alabama Press, 2020), 231.
2. For this frontier political mentality, see Patrick Spero, *Frontier Country: The Politics of War in Early Pennsylvania* (Philadelphia: University of Pennsylvania Press, 2016).
3. For his arrival and visit with Orr, see "August 28 and 29," in Michaux, *Michaux in North America,* 231–32. On Limestone, see Lowell Harrison and James Klotter, *A New History of Kentucky* (Lexington: University Press of Kentucky, 1997), esp. 52, for its role. Reuben Gold Thwaites, *Early Western Travels, 1748–1846* (Cleveland: Arthur H. Clark, 1904), 3:36.
4. "September 3," in Michaux, *Michaux in North America,* 232.
5. Ibid.
6. "September 5," in Michaux, *Michaux in North America,* 232.
7. "September 6 and 7," in Michaux, *André Michaux in North America,* 232, 483n40. On where he stayed and the line of credit, see "De Pauw's Statement," in *Correspondence of Clark and Genet* (Washington, DC, 1897), 1104. For Simpson, see Richard Reid, *Historical Sketches of Montgomery County* (Lexington, KY: James M. Byrnes, 1926), 17–18. He appears to have been a builder and community leader in Mt. Sterling in the 1790s, likely based in Lexington before then. On where he stayed, see "The Testimony of Charles De Pauw," in *Correspondence of Clark and Genet,* 1104.

8. Michaux had been given the name of a Tardiveau in Philadelphia, like Barthélemi, since it noted this person's home was Kaskaskia. For his visit, see "September 9 and 10," in *André Michaux in North America,* 233. On the Political Club of Danville, see Thomas Speed, *The Political Club: Danville, Kentucky* (Louisville: J. P. Morton, 1894).
9. Arthur St. Clair to Thomas Jefferson, 1794, in *The St. Clair Papers: The Life and Public Service of Arthur St. Clair* (Cincinnati: Robert Clarke, 1882), 2:326–27.
10. "September 11," in Michaux, *Michaux in North America,* 233. On Logan, see Stephen Aron, "Benjamin Logan," in *American National Biography;* and Thwaites, *Early Western Travels,* 3:40.
11. "September 11," in Michaux, *Michaux in North America,* 233.
12. For the strongest argument that Shelby knew nothing, see Archibald Henderson, "Isaac Shelby and the Genet Mission," *Mississippi Valley Historical Review* 6, no. 4 (1920): 451–69. For a rebuttal, see Samuel Wilson, *A Review of "Isaac Shelby and the Genet Mission"* (Lexington, KY: [Published by the author], 1920). See also Charlie Williams, "Explorer, Botanist, Courier, or Spy? André Michaux and the Genet Affair of 1793," *Castanea* (December 2004): 103–4, for a sympathetic view of Shelby; and for a more critical view, see Regina Katharine Crandall, "Genet's Projected Attack on Louisiana and the Floridas, 1793–94" (Ph.D. diss., University of Chicago, 1902), 118.
13. "September 17," in Michaux, *Michaux in North America,* 234.
14. On Michaux and Clark's meeting, see "September 16–20," in Michaux, *Michaux in North America,* 234–35.
15. "September 15," in Michaux, *Michaux in North America,* 234.
16. André Michaux to George Rogers Clark, October 7, 1793, in *Correspondence of Clark and Genet* 1010; André Michaux to George Rogers Clark, October 10, 1793, ibid., 1012.
17. Clark to Genet, October 3, 1794, in *Correspondence of Clark and Genet,* 1009.
18. The deposition on uniforms can be found in Dunbar Rowland, *Encyclopedia of Mississippi History* (Madison, 1867) 1:752; and esp. J. F. H. Claiborne, *Mississippi, as a Province, Territory and State* (Jackson, 1880), 152–53. This uniform likely dealt with another Clark (this one, Elijah Clarke) who was involved in the invasion's plans. For information on him and his involvement, see Absalom Chappell, *Miscellanies of Georgia* (Columbus, 1874), 37–43. For his purchases, see "Clark's Claims," in *Correspondence of Clark and Genet,* 1071–73. The record I am referencing here is "No. 2," on page

173. He would end up spending much more, as indicated by the other records. Clark to Michaux, October 15, 1793, in *Correspondence of Clark and Genet,* 1013.

19. Clark to Michaux, October 15, 1793, in *Correspondence of Clark and Genet,* 1013; Clark to Sullivan, October 17, 1793, ibid., 1014.
20. Clark to Genet, October 3, 1793, in *Correspondence of Clark and Genet,* 1008–9.
21. Clark to Michaux, October 3, 1793, in *Correspondence of Clark and Genet,* 1009.
22. For the subscribers, see *Correspondence of Clark and Genet,* 1073–74.
23. Albert V. Goodpasture, "Colonel John Montgomery," *Tennessee Historical Magazine* 5, no. 3 (1919): 145–50, also available here: https://penelope.uchicago.edu/Thayer/E/Gazetteer/Places/America/United_States/Tennessee/_Texts/THM/5/3/John_Montgomery*.html; John Montgomery to Clark, Clarksville, October 25, 1793, in *Correspondence of Clark and Genet,* 1018–19.
24. Clark to Genet, October 3, 1793, in *Correspondence of Clark and Genet,* 1008.
25. "November 10, 1793," in Michaux, *Michaux in North America,* 237.
26. Crandall, "Genet's Projected Attack," 118.
27. Isaac Shelby to Thomas Jefferson, January 13, 1794, in *American State Papers,* 1:455–56.
28. Ibid.
29. Ibid.
30. Ibid. James Brown to Isaac Shelby, February 16, 1794, in *Correspondence of Clark and Genet,* 1040–41; "Isaac Shelby and the Genet Mission," 467.
31. "Depauw's Statement," in *Correspondence of Clark and Genet,* 1104.
32. Pis-Gignouse to Spanish Ambassador, *Correspondence of Clark and Genet,* 1002–3; Carondelet to Alcudia, No. 29, in *Correspondence of Clark and Genet,* 1046–48.
33. Ibid.
34. "De Pauw's Statement," in *Correspondence of Clark and Genet,* 1104.
35. On Tardiveau being an interpreter, see *Barthélemi Tardiveau,* 86–87n72; and Crandall, "Genet's Projected Attack," 114–15n3. Logan to Clark, December 31, 1793, in *Correspondence of Clark and Genet,* 1026.
36. For Genet's authorship, see "De Pauw's Statement," in *Correspondence of Clark and Genet,* 1104. Jefferson also noted that Genet had authored a proclamation in his note in the *Anas.*
37. *Centinel of the North-Western Territory,* January 25, 1794.

38. "Enclosure: Extract of a Letter from Kentucky, 25 January 1794," Founders Online, National Archives.
39. *Centinel of the North-Western Territory,* January 25, 1794.

14. THE RETURN

1. "December 15," in André Michaux, *André Michaux in North America: Journals and Letters, 1785–1797,* ed. Charlie Williams, Eliane M. Norman, and Walter Kingsley Taylor (Tuscaloosa: University of Alabama Press, 2020), 240–41; Henry Ammon, *The Genet Mission* (New York: Norton, 1973), see esp. quotations from Jefferson on page 88.
2. *American State Papers, Miscellaneous,* Declaration of the Democratic Society of Kentucky, 1:929–30; Lowell Harrison and James Klotter, *A New History of Kentucky* (Lexington: University Press of Kentucky, 1997), 73–74. Kenneth Owen, *Political Community in Revolutionary Pennsylvania, 1774–1800* (New York: Oxford University Press, 2018), 132–34; Matthew Schoenbachler, "Republicanism in the Age of Democratic Revolution: The Democratic-Republican Societies of the 1790s," *Journal of the Early Republic* 18, no. 2 (1998): 237–61.
3. On Genet's supposed role, see George Clinton Genet, *Washington, Jefferson, and Citizen Genet,* ([New York], 1899), 34. R. R. Palmer, *The Age of Democratic Revolution* (Princeton, NJ: Princeton University Press, 2014), esp. 18.
4. "To Thomas Jefferson from James Monroe, 17 June 1791," Founders Online, National Archives.
5. Owen, *Political Community,* 132, for articles and the Democratic Society of Pennsylvania, "Principles, Articles, and Regulations," May 30, 1793, https://explorepahistory.com/odocument.php?docId=1-4-16F; Jeffrey Davis, "Democratic-Republican Society," in *The Encyclopedia of Greater Philadelphia,* https://philadelphiaencyclopedia.org/archive/democratic-republican-societies-2/.
6. Ibid.
7. Alexander Hamilton, "Jacobin, No. 1, July 31, 1793," Founders Online, National Archives,
8. Alexander Hamilton, "Jacobin No. VIII," August 26, 1793, Founders Online, National Archives.
9. "To James Madison from Thomas Jefferson, 7 July 1793," Founders Online, National Archives.
10. "From Thomas Jefferson to James Madison, 7 July 1793," Founders Online, National Archives.

11. Ibid.
12. "IV. Thomas Jefferson to Gouverneur Morris, 16 August 1793," Founders Online, National Archives.
13. "Notes of a Conversation with George Washington, 6 August 1793," Founders Online, National Archives
14. Ibid.
15. James Albach, *Annals of the West* (Pittsburgh, PA, 1858), 671–74. See also for the testimony of Charles DePauw indicating Genet as the likely author. "Depauw's Statement," in *Correspondence of Clark and Genet,* 1104.
16. Albach, *Annals of the West,* 671–74.
17. "To Thomas Jefferson from Josef Ignacio de Viar and Josef de Jaudenes, 27 August 1793," Founders Online, National Archives.
18. "August 29," in *The Journal of the Proceedings of the President, 1793–1797,* ed. Dorothy Twohig (Charlottesville: University Press of Virginia, 1981), 234n1. This quote is recorded in the presidential journal entry for August 29, and Jefferson writes a very similarly phrased passage to the Spanish.
19. "From Thomas Jefferson to Isaac Shelby, 29 August 1793," Founders Online, National Archives.
20. Ibid.
21. "Pis-gignouse to Spanish Ambassador," in *Correspondence of Clark and Genet,* 1002–3; Carondelet to Alcudia, No. 29, ibid., 1046–48.
22. "To Thomas Jefferson from Josef de Jaudenes and Josef Ignacio de Viar, 2 October 1793," Founders Online, National Archives; "From Thomas Jefferson to Isaac Shelby, 6 November 1793," ibid.
23. Lawrence Kinnaird, *Spain in the Mississippi Valley, 1765–1794* (Washington, DC: Government Printing Office, 1949), xx; Arthur Preston Whittaker, *The Spanish-American Frontier: The Westward Movement and the Spanish Retreat in the Mississippi Valley* (Boston: Houghton Mifflin, 1927), 176–77 and 193–94.
24. "December 13 and 14," in Michaux, *Michaux in North America,* 240.
25. "December 12–January 10," in Michaux, *Michaux in North America,* 240–43.
26. Ibid.
27. "January 10," in Michaux, *Michaux in North America,* 243.
28. "January 12," in Michaux, *Michaux in North America,* 243.
29. "January 12, 14 16, and 17–18," in Michaux, *Michaux in North America,* 243; André Michaux to Clark, December 27, 1793, ibid., 244.
30. "March 9," in Michaux, *Michaux in North America,* 250–51.

31. Michaux, *Michaux in North America,* 492–93n50; "March 22," ibid., 252.
32. Harry Ammon, *The Genet Mission* (New York: Norton, 1973), 158–70.
33. Samuel Fulton to Clark, March 21, 1794, in *Correspondence of Clark and Genet,* 1051–52.

15. THE END OF AN EXPEDITION

1. For the rumor, see Carondelet to Alcudia, *Correspondence of Clark and Genet* (Washington, DC, 1897), 1048. For the purchase, and departure day, see "Extract of a letter from Lexington, Ky," *American State Papers,* 1:458. For iron works and auctions, see ibid., 1:459–60.
2. Carondelet to Alcudia, March 20, 1794, in *Correspondence of Clark and Genet,* 1046–51; *American State Papers,* 1:459–60.
3. Carondelet to Alcudia, January 1, 1794, in *Correspondence of Clark and Genet,* 1027–29.
4. Carondelet to Alcudia, January 24, 1794, in *Correspondence of Clark and Genet,* 1038–40; Gayoso to Alcudia, February 18, 1794, in *Correspondence of Clark and Genet,* 1042–45. For more on this imperial system of strategy and diplomacy, the formative book is Richard White, *The Middle Ground: Indians, Empires, and Republics in the Great Lakes Region, 1650–1815* (Cambridge: Cambridge University Press 2010).
5. See esp. Carondelet to Alcudia, January 25, 1794, *Correspondence of Clark and Genet,* 1038–40.
6. Ibid.
7. Gayoso to Alcudia, February 18, 1794, *Correspondence of Clark and Genet,* 1042–45.
8. For an example of how these issues became interwoven, see Knox's letter to Anthony Wayne on March 31, 1794, that is included as note 1 in "To George Washington from Henry Knox, 2 April 1794," Founders Online, National Archives. For a summary of the geopolitical situation, see Stanley Elkins and Eric McKitrick, *The Age of Federalism* (New York: Oxford University Press, 1985), 438–39.
9. "To George Washington from Henry Knox, 15 May 1794," n. 1, Founders Online, National Archives.
10. "Enclosure: Extract of a Letter from Kentucky, 25 January 1794," Founders Online, National Archives; "To George Washington from Edmund Randolph, 27 February 1794," ibid. On James Brown, see James Brown to Shelby, February 16, 1794, in *Correspondence of Clark and Genet,* 1040–42. For Fauchet, see Henry Ammon, *The Genet Mission,* (New York: Norton, 1973), 157–70.

11. "Cabinet Opinion on Expeditions against Spanish Territory, 10 March 1794," Founders Online, National Archives; "To George Washington from Edmund Randolph, 11 March 1794," ibid.
12. "To George Washington from Edmund Randolph, 11 March 1794," Founders Online, National Archives.
13. Ibid.
14. Ibid.
15. "To George Washington from Edmund Randolph, 19 March 1794," Founders Online, National Archives and "Proclamation on Expeditions Against Spanish Territory, 24 March 1794," ibid.
16. "Proclamation on Expeditions Against Spanish Territory, 24 March 1794," Founders Online, National Archives.
17. "Enclosure: Extract of a Letter from Kentucky, 25 January 1794," Founders Online, National Archives; "To George Washington from Edmund Randolph, 27 February 1794," ibid. On James Brown, see James Brown to Shelby, February 16, 1794, in *Correspondence of Clark and Genet,* 1040–42. See also John Brown's deposition recounting his involvement in *American State Papers, Miscellaneous,* 1:931, https://memory.loc.gov/ll/llsp/037/0900/09470931.tif.
18. Isaac Shelby to Thomas Jefferson, January 13, 1794, in *American State Papers,* 1:455–56.
19. Ibid.
20. Edmund Randolph to Isaac Shelby, March 29, 1794, in *American State Papers,* 1:456–57.
21. Henry Knox to Anthony Wayne, March 31, 1794, in *American State Papers,* 1:458–59; "To George Washington from Henry Knox, 2 April 1794," Founders Online, National Archives.
22. "To George Washington from Henry Knox, 14 May 1794," Founders Online, National Archives; Knox to Wayne, March 31, 1794, in *Anthony Wayne, A Name in Arms: Soldier, Diplomat, Defender of Expansion Westward of a Nation; The Wayne-Knox-Pickering-McHenry Correspondence,* ed Richard Knopf (Pittsburgh: University of Pittsburgh Press, 1959), 313–20; Wayne to Knox, May 26, 1794, in *Anthony Wayne: A Name in Arms,* 332–34.
23. "From George Washington to the United States Senate and House of Representatives, 20 May 1794," Founders Online, National Archives.
24. *United States Statutes at Large,* vol.1, *Public Acts of the Third Congress,* 1st Session, Chapter 50, https://www.loc.gov/law/help/statutes-at-large/3rd-congress/session-1/c3s1ch50.pdf. See also Harry Ammon, *The Genet Mission,* (New York: Norton, 1973), 169–70.

25. On the act being made perpetual, see ibid. and *Papers Relating to the Foreign Relations of the United States* (Washington, DC, 1872), part 2, 1:539.
26. "To George Washington from Edmund Randolph, 15 July 1794," Founders Online, National Archives.
27. Edmund Randolph to Isaac Shelby, March 29, 1794, in *American State Papers,* 1:456–57.
28. See David Andrew Nichols, *Red Gentlemen and White Savages: Indians, Federalists, and the Search for Order on the American Frontier* (Charlottesville: University of Virginia Press, 2008), esp. chaps. 6 and 7; and Calloway, *The Indian World of George Washington* (Oxford: Oxford University Press, 2018), 437.
29. "To George Washington from Henry Knox, 12 May 1794," Founders Online, National Archives; Wayne to Knox, June 10, 1794, in *Anthony Wayne,* 339–42. For Clark's accounts, see "Clark's Claims," in *Correspondence of Clark and Genet,* 1071–72.
30. "To George Washington from Kentucky Citizens, 24 May 1794," Founders Online, National Archives.
31. Ibid.
32. Lexington Resolutions, in *Correspondence of Clark and Genet,* 1056–58.
33. "To George Washington from Henry Knox, 14 July 1794," Founders Online, National Archive.
34. "To George Washington from Edmund Randolph, 15 July 1794," Founders Online, National Archives.
35. Ibid.
36. "To Thomas Jefferson from Edmund Randolph, 28 August 1794," Founders Online, National Archives; "To George Washington from Henry Knox, 14 July 1794," ibid.
37. "To Thomas Jefferson from Edmund Randolph, 28 August 1794," Founders Online, National Archives; Samuel Flagg Bemis, *Pinckney Treaty: A Study of America's Advantage from Europe's Distress* (Baltimore, MD: Johns Hopkins Press, 1926); Deconde, *This Affair of Louisiana* (New York: Charles Scribner's Sons, 1976), 60–62.
38. Carondelet to Alcudia, New Orleans, July 30, 1794, in *Correspondence of Clark and Genet,* 1069–70.
39. Ibid. On other discussions, see Whittaker, *Spanish-American Frontier,* 101–2, 176, 192–93.
40. On the Pinckney Treaty, see *A New History of Kentucky,* 73–74; and esp. Bemis, *Pinckney's Treaty.*

16. MICHAUX'S LAST DAYS

1. "December 11," in André Michaux, *André Michaux in North America: Journals and Letters, 1785–1797,* ed. Charlie Williams, Eliane M. Norman, and Walter Kingsley Taylor (Tuscaloosa: University of Alabama Press, 2020), 288.
2. For his work in Kentucky, see Michaux, *Michaux in North America,* 303, 517n55; and William Bryant, "Botanical Explorations of André Michaux in Kentucky: Observations of Vegetation in the 1790s," *Castanea* (December 2004): 211–16.
3. Dozens of newspapers published this report. For a representative example, see *Aurora General Advertiser* (Philadelphia), May 7, 1796, 6.
4. Michaux, *André Michaux in North America,* 516–17nn53 and 55; "Yellowwood," University of Kentucky, https://www.uky.edu/hort/?q=Yellowwood.
5. André Michaux to André Thouin, April 1, 1795, in *Correspondence of Clark and Genet* (Washington, DC, 1897), 266–68.
6. "Renegades" and "vagabonds," in Michaux, *Michaux in North America,* 289.
7. André Michaux to de Luzières, December 2, 1795, in Michaux, *Michaux in North America,* 289–90.
8. Ibid.
9. "December 16," in Michaux, *Michaux in North America,* 292, 512n7. On Gayoso, see Cameron Strang, *Frontiers of Science, Imperialism and Natural Knowledge in the Gulf South Borderlands, 1500–1850* (Chapel Hill: University of North Carolina Press, 2018), esp. 131–36 and 181–85.
10. André Michaux to Nicholas Collin, November 14, 1794, in Michaux, *Michaux in North America,* 262–63 and 487–88n98.
11. On pirates, see André Michaux to André Thouin, April 13, 1796, in Michaux, *Michaux in North America,* 313. For Palisot de Beauvois, see ibid., 315–16; "Report on the Garden," ibid., 316–19; and André Michaux to Bosc, August 22, 1798, ibid., 319–20. On the New Jersey garden and Saunier, see also William J. Robbins and Mary Christine Howson, "André Michaux's New Jersey Garden and Pierre Paul Saunier, Journeyman Gardner," *Proceedings of the American Philosophical Society* 102, no. 4 (1958): 359–70.
12. "Report on the Garden," 316.
13. Ibid., 316–19; André Michaux to Bosc, August 22, 1798, in Michaux, *Michaux in North America,* 319–20.
14. On the encouragement, see André Michaux to André Thouin, Paris, June 8, 1796, in Michaux, *Michaux in North America,* 320–21.

15. André Michaux to André Thouin, April 1, 1795, in Michaux, *Michaux in North America,* 268.
16. Ibid.
17. André Michaux to André Thouin, June 8, 1796, in Michaux, *Michaux in North America,* 321; Pierre Auguste Adet to Charles Delacroix, Philadelphia, October 28, 1796, ibid., 322–23.
18. On Merlot, see Michaux, *Michaux in North America,* 11, 340–44.
19. André Michaux, "October 5," in Michaux, *Michaux in North America,* 326.
20. The following is based on André Michaux, "October 9," in Michaux, *Michaux in North America,* 327–28; André Michaux to André Thouin, October 14, 1796, ibid., 329–30; André Michaux to Charles Louis L'Heritier de Brutelle, ibid., 330; André Michaux to Bosc, November 25, 1796, ibid., 331.
21. Deleuze, J. P. F. Deleuze, *The Annotated Memoirs of the Life and Botanical Travels of André Michaux,* ed. with a postscript by Charlie Williams (Athens, GA: Fevertree, 2011), 20. There is some hint that some of his trees—perhaps as many as half—were sent to Austria. James Reveal, "No Man Is an Island: The Life and Times of André Michaux," *Castanea* (2004): 14; Rodney True, "Francois André Michaux, The Botanist and Explorer," *Proceedings of the American Philosophical Society* 78, no. 2 (December 1937): 316.
22. Michaux, *Michaux in North America,* 333–34.
23. For his residence, see Regis Pluchet, "Michaux Mysteries Clarified," *Castanea* (December 2004): 230; and for lobbying to return, see Henry Savage and Elizabeth Savage, *André and François André Michaux* (Charlottesville: University Press of Virginia, 1986), 168–69.
24. Savage and Savage, *André and François André Michaux,* 169–71; Michaux, *André Michaux in North America,* 339–44.
25. This and the following paragraphs are based largely on Savage and Savage, *André and François André Michaux,* 173–80; and Michaux, *Michaux in North America,* 342–44.
26. Quote from *André Michaux in North America,* 344.
27. For the best account of Michaux's death, see Pluchet, "Michaux Mysteries Clarified," 228–32.
28. Michaux, *Michaux in North America,* 344.
29. For Merlot, see esp. ibid., 343–44.
30. Ibid., 344.

17. HIDDEN LEGACIES

1. James Reveal, "No Man Is an Island: The Life and Times of André Michaux," *Castanea* (2004): 14; Rodney True, "Francois André Michaux, The Botanist and Explorer," *Proceedings of the American Philosophical Society* 78, no. 2 (December 1937): 313–14. These numbers come from Reveal, "No Man Is an Island," 36, and his appendices, which list all the genera and names.
2. For what happened to the garden and Saunier, see William J. Robbins and Mary Christine Howson, "André Michaux's New Jersey Garden and Pierre Paul Saunier, Journeyman Gardner," *Proceedings of the American Philosophical Society* 102, no. 4 (1958): 360–70; and for Francois André's trip to the United States, see Rodney True, "Francois André Michaux, The Botanist and Explorer," *Proceedings of the American Philosophical Society* 78, no. 2 (December 1937): 317–18.
3. For the Michaux legacy, see Henry Savage and Elizabeth Savage, *André and François André Michaux* (Charlottesville: University Press of Virginia, 1986), 339–61; Charlie Williams, "Postscript, Two Hundred Years of Remembering André Michaux," in J. P. F. Deleuze, *The Annotated Memoirs of the Life and Botanical Travels of André Michaux*, ed. with a postscript by Charlie Williams (Athens, GA: Fevertree, 2011), 27–40; and True, "Francois André Michaux," 322.
4. For a brief discussion of Francois André's final years and will, see True, "Francois André Michaux," 325–26. For Rothrock's summary of the funds initial use, impact, and place within the conservation movement, see J. T. Rothrock, "On the Growth of the Forestry Idea," *Proceedings of the American Philosophical Society* (January 1894): 332–42; and Susan Dudley and David Goddard, "Joseph T. Rothrock and Forest Conservation," *Proceedings of the American Philosophical Society* (February 1973): 37–50.
5. For the use of the funds, see J. R. Schramm, "The Memorial to Francois André Michaux at the Morris Arboretum, University of Pennsylvania," *Proceedings of the American Philosophical Society* (April 1956): 145–49; and "Influence—Past and Present—of Francois André Michaux on Forestry and Forest Research," *Proceedings of the American Philosophical Society* (August 1957): 336–43. For the twentieth-century uses, see "C-Co" and "F Correspondence," APS Archives.
6. "IV. Instructions for Meriwether Lewis, 20 June 1803," Founders Online, National Archives.
7. "From Thomas Jefferson to Isaac Shelby, 28 June 1793," Founders Online, National Archives; Malone, *Jefferson and His Times: Jefferson and the Ordeal of Liberty* (Boston: Little, Brown, 1962), 108.

8. Barbara Oberg, "A New Republican Order, Letter by Letter," *Journal of the Early Republic* 25, no. 1 (Spring 2005): 1–20.
9. Henry Ammon, *The Genet Mission* (New York: Norton, 1973), chaps. 11–12.
10. Ibid.
11. Meade Minnigerode, *Jefferson, Friend of France, 1793: The Career of Edmond Charles Genet, Minister Plenipotentiary from the French Republic to the United States, as Revealed by His Private Papers, 1763–1834* (New York: G. P. Putnam's Sons, 1928), 413–25.
12. "Citizen Genet Asks for a New Verdict," *New York Times*, April 1, 1928. See Ammon, *The Genet Mission*, for a critical take on Michaux.
13. For Clark's affairs, see the series of desperate letters and reports in *Correspondence of Clark and Genet* (Washington, DC, 1897); and Regina Katharine Crandall, "Genet's Projected Attack on Louisiana and the Floridas, 1793–94" (Ph.D. diss., University of Chicago, 1902), 196–204. Many of those reports are also available in Crandall's notes.
14. Crandall, "Genet's Projected Attack," 196–204.
15. On the end of the colony, see Carl J. Ekberg, *A French Aristocrat in the American West: The Shattered Dreams of De Lassus de Luzières* (Columbia: University of Missouri Press, 2010); Howard Rice, *Barthélemi Tardiveau: A French Trader in the West* (Baltimore, MD: John Hopkins University Press, 1938); and *Correspondence of Clark and Genet*, 1047–51, esp. 1049 for Tardiveau and Audrain being implicated.
16. "Depauw's Statement," in *Correspondence of Clark and Genet*, 1102–7.
17. The most recent biography of Wilkinson is Howard Cox, *American Traitor: James Wilkinson's Treason and Betrayal of the Republic* (Washington, DC: Georgetown University Press, 2023), esp. 91 for his claims; see also Andro Linklater, *An Artist in Treason: The Extraordinary Double Life of General James Wilkinson* (New York: Walker, 2009).
18. R. Kent Neymayer, *The Treason Trial of Aaron Burr: Law, Politics, and the Character Wars of the New Nation* (Cambridge: Cambridge University Press, 2012).
19. Carondelet to Gayoso, July 30, 1794, and Gayoso to Alcudia, September 19, 1794, in *Correspondence of Clark and Genet*, 1069, 1079 and 1081.
20. For a good account of the Alien and Sedition Acts, see, Stanley Elkins and Eric McKitrick, *The Age of Federalism* (New York: Oxford University Press, 1995), 691–755.
21. Ibid.; "Editorial Note: The Kentucky Resolutions of 1798," Founders Online, National Archives.

EPILOGUE

1. Mangourit to Charles de la Croix, October 24, 1796, in André Michaux, *André Michaux in North America: Journals and Letters, 1785–1797,* ed. Charlie Williams, Eliane M. Norman, and Walter Kingsley Taylor (Tuscaloosa: University of Alabama Press, 2020), 334.
2. Minister of the Interior to Michaux, in Michaux, *Michaux in North America,* 336.
3. J. P. F. Deleuze, *The Annotated Memoirs of the Life and Botanical Travels of André Michaux,* ed. with a postscript by Charlie Williams (Athens, GA: Fevertree, 2011), 25.
4. For a good summary of these books and their reception, including critiques in Michaux's time, see James Reveal, "No Man Is an Island: The Life and Times of André Michaux," *Castanea* (2004): 22–68.

❖ INDEX ❖

References to figures and maps are indicated by f *and* m *following the page numbers.*

Recent books in the series
JEFFERSONIAN AMERICA

Sacred Capital: Methodism and Settler Colonialism in the Empire of Liberty
Hunter Price

Empire of Commerce: The Closing of the Mississippi and the Opening of Atlantic Trade
Susan Gaunt Stearns

Black Reason, White Feeling: The Jeffersonian Enlightenment in the African American Tradition
Hannah Spahn

Replanting a Slave Society: The Sugar and Cotton Revolutions in the Lower Mississippi Valley
Patrick Luck

The Celebrated Elizabeth Smith: Crafting Genius and Transatlantic Fame in the Romantic Era
Lucia McMahon

Rival Visions: How the Views of Jefferson and His Contemporaries Defined the Early American Republic
Dustin Gish and Andrew Bibby, editors

Revolutionary Prophecies: The Founders and America's Future
Robert M. S. McDonald and Peter S. Onuf, editors

The Founding of Thomas Jefferson's University
John A. Ragosta, Peter S. Onuf, and Andrew J. O'Shaughnessy, editors

Thomas Jefferson's Lives: Biographers and the Battle for History
Robert M. S. McDonald, editor

Jeffersonians in Power: The Rhetoric of Opposition Meets the Realities of Governing
Joanne B. Freeman and Johann N. Neem, editors

Jefferson on Display: Attire, Etiquette, and the Art of Presentation
G. S. Wilson

Jefferson's Body: A Corporeal Biography
Maurizio Valsania

Pulpit and Nation: Clergymen and the Politics of Revolutionary America
Spencer W. McBride

Blood from the Sky: Miracles and Politics in the Early American Republic
Adam Jortner

Confounding Father: Thomas Jefferson's Image in His Own Time
Robert M. S. McDonald

The Haitian Declaration of Independence: Creation, Context, and Legacy
Julia Gaffield, editor

Citizens of a Common Intellectual Homeland: The Transatlantic Origins of American Democracy and Nationhood
Armin Mattes

Between Sovereignty and Anarchy: The Politics of Violence in the American Revolutionary Era
Patrick Griffin, Robert G. Ingram, Peter S. Onuf, and Brian Schoen, editors

Patriotism and Piety: Federalist Politics and Religious Struggle in the New American Nation
Jonathan J. Den Hartog

Becoming Men of Some Consequence: Youth and Military Service in the Revolutionary War
John A. Ruddiman

Amelioration and Empire: Progress and Slavery in the Plantation Americas
Christa Dierksheide

Collegiate Republic: Cultivating an Ideal Society in Early America
Margaret Sumner

Era of Experimentation: American Political Practices in the Early Republic
Daniel Peart